Miguel A. Roig-Francolí
University of Cincinnati

Understanding
Post-Tonal Music

 **McGraw-Hill**
Higher Education

Boston   Burr Ridge, IL   Dubuque, IA   New York   San Francisco   St. Louis
Bangkok   Bogotá   Caracas   Kuala Lumpur   Lisbon   London   Madrid   Mexico City
Milan   Montreal   New Delhi   Santiago   Seoul   Singapore   Sydney   Taipei   Toronto

McGraw-Hill
Higher Education

Published by McGraw-Hill, an imprint of The McGraw-Hill Companies, Inc., 1221 Avenue
of the Americas, New York, NY 10020. Copyright © 2008. All rights reserved. No part of
this publication may be reproduced or distributed in any form or by any means, or stored in a
database or retrieval system, without the prior written consent of The McGraw-Hill Companies,
Inc., including, but not limited to, in any network or other electronic storage or transmission, or
broadcast for distance learning.

This book is printed on acid-free paper.

1 2 3 4 5 6 7 8 9 0 DOC/DOC 0 9 8 7

ISBN: 978-0-07-293624-7
MHID: 0-07-293624-X

Editor in Chief: *Emily Barrosse*
Publisher: *Lisa Moore*
Sponsoring Editor: *Christopher Freitag*
Marketing Manager: *Pamela Cooper*
Developmental Editor: *Beth Baugh*
Project Manager: *Holly Paulsen*
Manuscript Editor: *Barbara Hacha*
Design Manager: *Kim Menning*

Text Designer: *Glenda King*
Cover Designer: *VP Graphic Design*
Illustrator: *Joseph Hupchick*
Supplements Producer: *Louis Swaim*
Production Supervisor: *Rich DeVitto*
Composition: *10/12 Times by Thompson Type*
Printing: *PMS 3298, 45# New Era Matte Plus,*
R. R. Donnelley & Sons

Cover: Vicente Pascual. *In Illo Tempore IV* and *In Illo Tempore XIX*. 2003. Mixed media on
canvas. © 2007 Artists Rights Society, New York/VEGAP, Madrid.

Credits: The credits section for this book begins on page 371 and is considered an extension of the
copyright page.

Library of Congress Cataloging-in-Publication Data
Roig-Francolí, Miguel A.
    Understanding post-tonal music / Miguel A. Roig-Francolí.
        p. cm.
    Includes bibliographical references (p.   ) and index.
    ISBN-13: 978-0-07-293624-7 (alk. paper)
    ISBN-10: 0-07-293624-X (alk. paper)
    1. Music—20th century—Analysis, appreciation. 2. Music theory—History—20th century.
    3. Music—20th century—History and criticism. I. Title.
MT90.R65 2008
780.9'04—dc22   2007013180

Dedication

To Jennifer, Gabriel, and Rafael

To learn, read.
To know, write.
To master, teach.

About the Author

MIGUEL A. ROIG-FRANCOLÍ, a native of Spain, holds graduate degrees in composition from the Madrid Royal Superior Conservatory and Indiana University, and a Ph.D. in music theory from Indiana University. He is currently a Professor of Music Theory at the College-Conservatory of Music, University of Cincinnati, and has also taught at Ithaca College, Northern Illinois University, Indiana University, and the Eastman School of Music. His research interests include Renaissance compositional theory and practice, the music of Ligeti, large-scale coherence in post-tonal music, and the pedagogy of music theory. Roig-Francolí is the author of *Harmony in Context* (McGraw-Hill, 2003), and his articles and reviews have appeared in numerous journals and encyclopedias in the United States and Europe. Roig-Francolí's compositions have been widely performed in Spain (including performances by eight major symphony orchestras and by the National Ballet of Spain), England, Germany, Mexico, and the United States. He has received commissions from the National Orchestra of Spain and the Orchestra of Spanish Radio-TV. Among his many honors are first prize at the National Composition Competition of the Spanish *Jeunesses Musicales* (1981), second prize at the UNESCO International Rostrum of Composers (Paris, 1982), and the University of Cincinnati's 2007 A.B. "Dolly" Cohen Award for Excellence in Teaching.

Contents

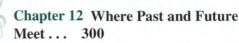

Preface

Understanding Post-Tonal Music is a textbook on the analysis, theory, and composition of twentieth-century post-tonal music. The book is primarily intended for undergraduate or general graduate courses on the analysis of twentieth-century music. Because the book also includes numerous composition exercises at the end of each chapter (in imitation of the models analyzed in the corresponding chapter), it may also be used as a composition textbook for composition students.

As its title indicates, the emphases of this book are on *understanding* and on *the music*. Moreover, the title establishes a clear limit to the scope of the repertoire studied in this book: only post-tonal music is covered. Thus, while tonal music (that is, music based on functional harmonic tonality or on its extensions) was composed in the twentieth century (and is still being composed in the twenty-first century), twentieth-century tonal music is not studied here. We will now review some of the defining characteristics of this text.

Focus on Understanding

Post-tonal music may be intimidating to some listeners and performers, and often one of the main reasons is a lack of understanding of the compositional and musical processes involved in this music. Because of the great diversity of musical idioms and compositional techniques that we find in twentieth-century post-tonal music, listeners and performers cannot take for granted that they know and understand the musical styles or languages involved, as they do with the quite familiar styles and languages involved in the music of the common-practice period. I often have experienced in class that the attitude of students toward a post-tonal piece they listen to for the first time, and which they may at first frown at, changes completely after the piece is studied and they fully understand it. That understanding has often led, on the part of the students, to enjoyment and excitement—and to such rewarding exclamations as, "This piece is cool!"

Focus on the Music: Analysis and Theory

The emphasis of this book is thus, above all, on the music. To understand the music, the music is analyzed. Theoretical issues and systems are thoroughly covered, but they usually grow out of a need to provide a system to understand the music, and not the other way around. That is, rather than presenting theory and then illustrating it with examples, the process followed in this book is that of presenting music and deriving or applying whatever theory is needed to understand the music. The analyses provide in-depth explorations of the musical structure and compositional techniques for each particular composition. Existing current scholarship has been incorporated, with the necessary pedagogical adaptations, into the analyses and the theoretical discussions. Analyses and discussions do not focus only or mainly on pitch organization, but also on issues of meter, rhythm, and temporality (both throughout the book, and in particular in Chapters 10 and 13), form, texture, relationships between text and music, and a variety of aesthetic issues that affect listeners and performers of post-tonal music.

Focus on Listening

Understanding through analysis should translate into better listening. Listening—that is, intelligent and informed listening—is constantly encouraged in this book, and the intent is that analysis and understanding will help the student become a better listener and hence a better performer, composer, or teacher of post-tonal music. The student is normally encouraged and directed to analyze what can be heard, and, conversely, to hear what can be analyzed. In other words, the results of our analyses will normally help the student hear the compositional and structural elements that are relevant and particularly interesting in a given piece or repertoire.

Composers and Repertoire

Several pieces are analyzed in each chapter, and whenever possible, complete pieces or movements have been considered. If the analyzed compositions or movements are particularly long, substantial and representative fragments are chosen for analysis. All the pieces or fragments analyzed in the text are included in the accompanying anthology. Most of the pieces assigned for homework are also included in the anthology. The coverage of composers and repertoire in this book is as broad as allowed by the constraints of in-depth analysis of complete pieces or large fragments. Quality has been given precedence over quantity. Even so, the book includes analyses of a total of thirty-one pieces by twenty-five composers, ranging chronologically from Claude Debussy and Igor Stravinsky to Kaija Saariaho, Augusta Read Thomas, and Thomas Adès.

Organization

The book is organized following a roughly chronological plan and, within that, by general topics. This modular organization following two simultaneous criteria acknowledges that twentieth-century music is best understood not only in technical terms, but also in a historical context, and that stylistic and compositional developments do not take place in a historical vacuum.

An initial general topic, pitch centricity, covers music by Debussy, early Stravinsky, and Bartók in Chapters 1 and 2. Pitch-class sets are informally introduced in these two initial chapters, in a way that should be both musical and pedagogical. The next topic, atonal music, is covered in Chapters 3 and 4. In Chapter 3, pitch-class sets are studied formally, setting the stage for the analyses of Webern and Schoenberg atonal pieces in Chapter 4. Chapters 5 and 6 discuss two seemingly contradictory, yet highly complementary, stylistic trends: neoclassicism, as found in the music of Stravinsky and Hindemith, and ultramodernism, as found in Ives and Crawford. Chapters 7 and 8 are devoted to the study of "classical" twelve-tone music, with reference to works by Dallapiccola, Schoenberg, Berg, and Webern, and Chapter 9 deals with serial practices after World War II, as illustrated by Stravinsky, Boulez, and Babbitt.

Chapter 9 thus provides a link between music before and after World War II. Post–World War II music, which is covered in the last six chapters (9 through 14), receives thorough attention in this text. The general topics in these chapters, and following serialism, are issues of temporality (Chapter 10, including analyses of music by Messiaen,

Carter, and Stockhausen), aleatory composition, sound mass, and other post-serial techniques (Chapter 11, with reference to Cage, Lutosławski, and Ligeti), quotation and collage (Chapter 12, with focus on Rochberg and Berio), minimalism (Chapter 13, which includes analyses of music by Reich, Andriessen, and Pärt), and finally a review of some of the most recent compositional trends as found in pieces by Thomas, Adès, and Saariaho (Chapter 14). Despite their important role as compositional styles throughout the twentieth century, and particularly in the last fifty or sixty years, the study of electronic, computer, and spectral music has not been possible given the scope and size of this book, which is proportionate to the limited length of the course it is written for.

Assignments

Numerous exercises are provided at the end of each chapter. Exercises are of three types: (1) theoretical, in which particular theoretical concepts or methods are practiced; (2) analytical, in which pieces or fragments of pieces are analyzed; and (3) compositional, in which suggestions and models for brief compositions are provided. Analytical exercises are of two types. Some exercises include a "directed analysis" of pieces, with very specific and focused questions on particular aspects of the composition. Other exercises are more open and require a freer analysis of a piece, which the student will then articulate in the form of an essay or a brief paper. Instructors may choose to use mostly the directed analysis, and only occasionally to require an essay or paper, or they may choose to use both types of analytical exercises.

Similarly, it will be up to the instructor whether to assign the compositional exercises in each chapter. Through the systematic use of the composition exercises, however, *Understanding Post-Tonal Music* may also double as a composition textbook. By studying characteristic compositions by major twentieth-century composers, and then imitating them through the composition of original pieces modeled after them, a composition student can acquire invaluable craft and knowledge of the main compositional techniques in the past century.

Other Pedagogical Features

Besides exercises and assignments, chapters include the following features: (1) suggested topics for class discussion (in a section titled "Application and Class Discussion"), (2) a list of compositions related to the chapter's topic that the student is recommended to listen to ("Further Listening"), and (3) a list of new musical/technical terms introduced in the chapter ("Terms for Review").

Use of the Book

The contents of *Understanding Post-Tonal Music* are intended for a semester-long course (or, in schools in the quarter system, for a two-quarter course). In principle, it is possible to teach the complete book in such a course, but the book contents also offer substantial flexibility to adapt to different pedagogical situations. Although all chapters should be considered important, the modular organization of the book allows instructors to skip some of the chapters with no detriment to the general progress of the course should a slower pedagogical pace be desired to ensure better assimilation by the students. Some chapters should be considered essential; that is, skipping them would severely harm the student's ability to understand subsequent chapters. In this category are Chapters 1–4 and 7–8. The study of Chapters 5, 6, and 9, on the other hand, does not directly affect the understanding of any other chapters, and hence some of their material could be skipped if necessary. Similarly, Chapters 10–14 are self-contained, independent chapters, and instructors may choose not to cover them fully if time is an issue, or to cover only some, but not all, of the composers and pieces included in them.

Finally, the book also allows for flexibility in instructional and learning styles. Analyses and theoretical explanations are fully articulated. Logical organization and clarity of exposition have been primary considerations. Instructors may thus choose to lecture on the chapter materials. They may instead choose to assign chapters for reading previous to class meetings, and then use a discussion format or other cooperative learning techniques in class. Or they may also assign student presentations, based on assigned readings of particular chapters or chapter sections. This textbook will provide appropriate and effective support for any of these instructional styles, used either in isolation or in combination.

Miguel A. Roig-Francolí
College-Conservatory of Music
University of Cincinnati

Acknowledgments

A project of this text's scope does not result from the work of a single author. Dozens of scholars have contributed to post-tonal theory and analytical methodologies in recent decades, and this book unquestionably incorporates and builds upon their work. It is only fair that I should begin my acknowledgments by thanking all these scholars of post-tonal music without whom this book would not have been possible. Every single author cited in this text's bibliography (which is not, however, exclusive) is a member of this scholarly community to which I am grateful. I wish to mention, in particular, two subgroups within this bibliography. First, there is a small group of scholars to whom anyone interested in post-tonal theory has a debt of gratitude, and whose work is widely represented in this book. These are the master scholars who, over several decades, have laid the foundations for several closely related branches of post-tonal theory that have become mainstream methodologies broadly used both in research and in pedagogy. A minimal, but not exclusive, list of such scholars must include Milton Babbitt, Allen Forte, David Lewin, Robert Morris, George Perle, and John Rahn.

The second group to which I am very directly indebted is made up of experts on particular composers or techniques, whose work has been the point of departure for my own presentations on those composers or techniques in this book. I have always acknowledged these authors directly in the text, but I want to express once again my gratitude to them. This book is built on their (that is, our) collective knowledge and could not have been written from scratch without their previous research and publications. In particular, I am indebted (again without any intention of being exclusive) to Elliott Antokoletz, Jonathan Bernard, J. Peter Burkholder, Richard Cohn, Michael Hicks, Paul Hillier, Julian Hook, Roy Howat, David Hush, Marianne Kielian-Gilbert, Philip Lambert, György Ligeti, Charles Lord, Catherine Losada, Andrew Mead, David Neumeyer, David Osmond-Smith, James Pritchett, Claudio Spies, Joseph Straus, Steven Stucky, and Peter Westergaard.

My students represent another group without which this book would not have been written. The text's contents are a result of twenty years of teaching at a variety of institutions (including Indiana University, Ithaca College, Northern Illinois University, the Eastman School of Music, and the University of Cincinnati). The book is, of course, addressed to my students, as well as to any other students of post-tonal music elsewhere in the English-speaking world and beyond. I am indebted to a particular group of students who helped me by giving the book's first manuscript a close critical reading. These were the following graduate students, registered in the course Readings in Music Theory at CCM in Winter 2005: Jessica Barnett, Breighan Brown, Dallas Bluth, Javier Clavere, Brett Clement, Matt Denniston, Christa Emerson, Brian Hoffman, Michael Kelly, Brian Moseley, Matthew Planchak, Jessica Powell, Eric Simpson, Pierre van der Westhuizen, and Joseph Williams.

My colleagues in the music theory area at CCM have always been very supportive of my project and at various times have contributed specific suggestions on a variety of issues: David Carson Berry, Steven Cahn, Catherine Losada, and Robert Zierolf. The musical examples were copied on Finale by Joseph Hupchick (with some assistance from Brian Moseley). The Dean of CCM, Douglas Lowry, has been consistently supportive, both morally and financially (by providing generous funding for the copying of the musical examples). To all of them goes my most sincere gratitude.

Many good ideas and suggestions from the reviewers of earlier drafts were incorporated into, and contributed to the improvement of, the final version of the text. These reviewers include

Meredith Brammeier, *California Polytechnic State University, San Luis Obispo*

Roger Briggs, *Western Washington University*

Stacey Davis, *University of Texas at San Antonio*

Blaise Ferrandino, *Texas Christian University*

Richard Hermann, *University of New Mexico*

Eric Isaacson, *Indiana University*

Daniel McCarthy, *University of Akron*

Bruce Quaglia, *University of Utah*

Andrew Rindfleisch, *Cleveland State University*

Peter Winkler, *Stony Brook University*

I am grateful to my McGraw-Hill editors Chris Freitag and Melody Marcus, and to Beth Baugh, the developmental editor from Carlisle Publishing Services, as well as to the book's production editor (Holly Paulsen), copy editor (Barbara Hacha), and permissions specialist (Anne Wallingford) for their encouragement and support and for their numerous ideas and suggestions.

Last, but certainly not least, I have received an endless supply of support, encouragement, and patience from those closest to me: my wife, Jennifer, and my two sons, Gabriel and Rafael. This book is dedicated to the three of them.

Introduction

An Overview of Twentieth-Century Compositional Styles

THE CENTURY OF PLURALITY: TONAL, POST-TONAL, ATONAL, AND OTHER STYLES

The term *tonality* has been used in a variety of ways in twentieth-century music theory. To clarify our usage of this term, we will define **tonality** as a system in which pitches are organized hierarchically around a tonal center, or tonic. The tonal system prevalent in what we know as the common-practice period is usually known as major-minor, or **functional tonality**. In functional tonality, chords have a harmonic or tonal function, which we can define as the relationship of a chord with the other chords in the key, and especially its relationship with the tonic. We usually label the specific functions of chords with Roman numerals. The basic harmonic functions are tonic, dominant, and predominant, although chords can also have a prolongational function (most often by providing an extension of another chord by means of passing or neighbor linear motion). In the music of some late-Romantic or post-Romantic composers such as Richard Wagner, Hugo Wolf, Anton Bruckner, Gustav Mahler, Richard Strauss, Alexander Skryabin, and others, we find a variety of harmonic and linear procedures that have the effect of weakening functional tonality. These procedures may produce a suspension of tonality or may create a sense of tonal ambiguity, even to the point that at times the sense of tonality is completely lost.

Functional tonality (albeit extended in various ways) has continued to be an important harmonic system in the twentieth century. Much of the music by composers such as Giacomo Puccini, Maurice Ravel, Manuel de Falla, Jean Sibelius, Sergei Rachmaninoff, George Gershwin, Aaron Copland, Samuel Barber, Ralph Vaughan Williams, Benjamin Britten, or even Sergei Prokofiev or Dmitri Shostakovich, represents the continuation of the tonal traditions inherited from the two previous centuries. Tonality, moreover, has also been kept alive by other twentieth-century idioms such as musical comedy, film music, jazz, pop, and rock.

The progressive weakening (and eventual breakdown) of the tonal system in the late-nineteenth century, however, led some early twentieth-century composers to look for alternative methods of pitch organization. We will use the term **post-tonal** to refer to all the techniques and styles of pitch organization that resulted from this search for alternatives to functional tonality.

Many twentieth-century works that do not feature any kind of traditional tonality are nevertheless based on some principles of **pitch centricity,** the organization of pitches around one or more pitch centers, although not necessarily including a system of pitch hierarchies around a tonic. Although functional tonality most certainly features pitch centricity, in this book we will not discuss twentieth-century music based on functional tonality or its various extensions. We will study, however, post-tonal pitch centricity as found in the music of Claude Debussy, Igor Stravinsky, Béla Bartók, and others.

Other composers embraced radically new approaches to pitch organization. In the early twentieth-century music of Arnold Schoenberg, Alban Berg, and Anton Webern (a group usually referred to as the **Second Viennese School**), we find that intervallic and motivic cells (that is, collections of intervals or pitches used as compositional building blocks), as well as nontriadic sonorities and nonfunctional linear relationships, replace the familiar triadic, functional structures. Because this music normally does not feature any kind of tonal center or pitch centricity, we can refer to it as **atonal.** We should clarify, however, that this term should in no way be understood as defining the absence of pitch organization. Quite to the contrary, what we call atonal music often features sophisticated pitch relationships, as we will learn in Chapters 3 and 4. Intervallic and motivic cells also play a significant role in much of the music by Debussy, Stravinsky, and Bartók.

In the early 1920s, Schoenberg (followed by Berg, Webern, and others) began to use a new method of pitch organization that we know as the **twelve-tone method**, or **twelve-tone serialism.** In general (and there are exceptions to this statement), serial music, like the pre-serial atonal music of the Viennese School, tends to explicitly avoid pitch centricity. Such new compositional approaches require new theoretical formulations and analytical means. In this book we will explore and learn appropriate methods to understand atonal and serial music.

Elements other than pitch have also been used in innovative ways by numerous twentieth-century composers. Melody, rhythm, meter, timbre, texture, dynamics, and orchestration are some of the elements that composers such as Debussy, Stravinsky, Bartók, Prokofiev, and Webern, as well as Charles Ives, Edgard Varèse, and Olivier Messiaen used in strikingly new ways in the first half of the twentieth century. The second half of the century, moreover, features a fascinating diversity of serial and **post-serial** compositional and stylistic trends, which often place great emphasis on musical elements other than pitch, as we will study in the later chapters of this book. Some major post-World War II European composers are Pierre Boulez, Karlheinz Stockhausen, Luciano Berio, Witold Lutosławski, György Ligeti, Krzysztof Penderecki, and Sofia Gubaidulina. Prominent European members of the younger generation of composers include Magnus Lindberg, Kaija Saariaho, Oliver Knussen, George Benjamin, and Thomas Adès. In the United States, composers such as Roger Sessions, Milton Babbitt, George Perle, Donald Martino, or Charles Wuorinen have expanded the technical and theoretical scope of serialism, while other composers, such as John Cage, Elliott Carter,

George Crumb, Morton Feldman, Pauline Oliveros, Joseph Schwantner, or Augusta Read Thomas, have explored a variety of techniques and styles in their compositions.

In the final decades of the twentieth century we find numerous composers who base their music on extensions of the concept of tonality or pitch centricity, in styles that have often been called **neotonal** or **neo-Romantic,** in some cases featuring a clear revitalization of traditional tonality. This rediscovery of tonality and its expressive power in the late years of the century is patent in works by composers such as David Del Tredici, George Rochberg, Joan Tower, Wolfgang Rihm, Christopher Rouse, Aaron Jay Kernis, and Jennifer Higdon, or in recent works by Penderecki and Hans Werner Henze. Another powerful stylistic trend in recent decades, which we usually label as **minimalism,** has featured the adoption of much simpler compositional means than most previous music in the twentieth century. Composers who have practiced the aesthetic of simplicity in one way or another include John Cage, Arvo Pärt, Louis Andriessen, Philip Glass, Steve Reich, John Adams, and Michael Torke.

THE STYLISTIC MOSAIC

We can think of the twentieth century, from the perspective of the history of musical styles and techniques, as a complex mosaic made up of many stylistic tiles. The tiles have coexisted in the historical mosaic, often with a large degree of independence among them, but also with numerous interconnections. We can identify some of the tiles of the first decades of the century as tonal music, post-tonal pitch-centered music, atonal music, serialism, and neoclassical music. In the second half of the century, some of the tiles are serialism, aleatory composition, sound mass, collage and quotation, minimalism, electronic and computer music, besides the still existing tiles from the first half of the century (tonality, pitch centricity, atonality, neoclassicism, and so on). Composers, however, have been free to switch between tiles, or even to stand on more than one tile at a time. That is, the tiles of the mosaic are not exclusive; neither are they necessarily contradictory. Stravinsky, for instance, touched on quite a few of them (such as pitch centricity, neoclassicism, serialism) either successively or simultaneously. And so did Schoenberg (tonality, atonality, serialism, neoclassicism) as well as many other composers (such as Lutosławski, Penderecki, Stockhausen, Rochberg, Pärt, or Andriessen, to name just a few).

In this book we will think of all the tiles as equally valid options, and we will avoid the concept of a mainstream, dominant line (usually considered "progressive") that implies other secondary or subordinate lines (often viewed as "conservative," or also as marginal). From the perspective we have at the beginning of the twenty-first century, moreover, the idea of "progressive" and "conservative" trends in twentieth-century composition seems quite outdated, especially because what was once considered "conservative" by some (that is, writing tonal or pitch-centered music) is one of the preferred options among many of the major present-day composers of various age groups (from emerging composers to well-established masters), and some of the trends traditionally referred to as "progressive" are of no interest at all to many of the leading younger composers.

The twentieth century may thus be one of the most complex, rich, and fragmented periods in music history (similar in many ways, from this point of view, to the Renaissance, a period we can also think of as a mosaic of independent but interchangeable and intersecting styles). The "common-practice period" was replaced, in the twentieth century, by a "diverse-practices period." An in-depth study of all the styles and compositional techniques found in this period would require much more space than afforded by a book that aims to cover the contents of a one-semester college course. We will thus focus on the most significant aspects of twentieth-century composition, and we will study representative pieces by representative and outstanding composers within each of the stylistic and technical categories. Our main areas of study will be post-tonal pitch centricity and composition with motivic and intervallic cells, neoclassicism, the theory and analysis of atonal music, serialism, aspects of time, rhythm, and meter, and some of the major developments in post-World War II composition, including aleatory music, sound masses, borrowing from the past, neotonality, and minimalism.

Terms for Review

tonality
functional tonality
post-tonal music
pitch centricity
Second Viennese School
atonal music

twelve-tone method, or twelve-tone
  serialism
post-serial music
neotonal or neo-Romantic music
minimalism

Chapter 1

Pitch Centricity and Composition with Motivic Cells

As a result of the progressive weakening and dissolution of functional tonality in late-nineteenth-century music, some composers in the early twentieth century started investigating new methods of pitch organization. The experimentation with pitch organization often came paired with new approaches to rhythm, texture, form and formal growth, and orchestration. In Chapters 1 and 2 we will focus on composers such as Claude Debussy (1862–1918), Igor Stravinsky (1882–1971), and Béla Bartók (1881–1945), who did not necessarily seek to give up the concept of tonal center, but in whose music we normally find a systematic avoidance of functional tonality and of the traditional methods of tonal centricity associated with functional tonality. We will also use this initial chapter of the book to review some general concepts and procedures in the areas of form, formal processes, rhythm, and meter.

In the Introduction we defined **pitch centricity** as the organization of pitch structures around one or more pitch centers, although not necessarily through a system of pitch hierarchies around a tonic. Nonfunctional pitch centricity may be achieved through a variety of means. These means are *contextual,* rather than systematic. That is, there are no such things as "systems" of nonfunctional pitch centricity, and to determine a center achieved by nonfunctional means we need to examine and interpret specific musical contexts. A sense of pitch centricity, for instance, may result from the use of pedals or ostinatos, two musical elements often found in the music we will study in this chapter. We hear the passage from "La soirée dans Grenade" (1903) by Debussy, reproduced in Example 1.1, as centered on F♯ because of the F♯ bass pedal, despite the very chromatic and nonfunctional pitch content of the right hand, organized as chromatic triads moving in parallel motion.

Nonfunctional pitch centricity may also result from the use of scalar collections that are built on (or can be referred to) a pitch center, such as modal, pentatonic, whole-tone, or octatonic scales and collections (we will study modal and pentatonic scales in this chapter, and whole-tone and octatonic scales in Chapter 2). Consider the phrase by Bartók in Example 1.2. Because the two voices move in octaves, no harmony or counterpoint is involved in this phrase. Yet we have a clear sense of pitch centricity on G because the passage is built on a diatonic collection centered on G (the passage begins and

♪♪♪ Example 1.1   Claude Debussy, "La soirée dans Grenade," from *Estampes,* II, mm. 33–36

♪♪♪ Example 1.2   Béla Bartók, "Little Study," no. 77 from *Mikrokosmos,* III, mm. 1–4

ends on G, the melody keeps returning to a lowest pitch G, and there is frequent motion between G and D, scale degrees $\hat{1}$ and $\hat{5}$ in a G scale). From the pitches present in this phrase, we can imply a minor scale on G with an E natural (a raised $\hat{6}$). This is, then, a melody in the Dorian mode transposed to G.

Besides exploring alternative methods of creating pitch-centered compositions, composers in the early twentieth century were also concerned with providing unity to their compositions through motivic means. This could take the form of literal motivic relationships at the surface level, or of more abstract motivic relationships provided by some basic intervallic cells. In the absence of the unifying force of functional tonality, motivic relationships, coupled with nonfunctional methods of pitch centricity, provided strong and sufficient elements of long-range cohesion for these composers' music. In these two chapters we will examine in some detail some of their music. Our analytical focus will not only be on pitch centricity and motivic relationships, but also on any other musical elements that may be representative of either a particular composer's style or of a more general approach to composition in the early twentieth century. Our general questions as we face the analysis of twentieth-century music will thus be, How can we best understand this music? What do we need to know to understand this music, and what specific analytical methods do we need to apply? How can the knowledge of the particular stylistic and compositional idiosyncracies of this music help us to better listen to it and, if we can perform it, to better perform it?

DIATONIC COLLECTIONS

A collection of pitches that contains seven basic, unaltered pitches that are adjacent to one another on the circle of fifths (as represented by the white keys of the piano) is known as a **diatonic collection** (or a diatonic scale, when ordered in ascending or descending order). The major and natural minor scales constitute the two most familiar diatonic collections. Because major and minor scales, however, are usually found in functional contexts, we will not consider them in our present discussion. Twentieth-century post-tonal composers have been more interested in nonfunctional diatonic collections such as the modes. The basic historical modes are **Ionian, Dorian, Phrygian, Lydian, Mixolydian,** and **Aeolian,** to which we can add the modern mode **Locrian.** If we think of the white keys of the piano and of the octave C–C, each of the seven modes begins on one of the pitches of the octave in such a way that the seven modes result from a complete rotation of the diatonic collections, as illustrated in Example 1.3. Thus, Ionian is represented by the octave C–C, Dorian by the octave D–D, Phrygian by E–E, Lydian by F–F, Mixolydian by G–G, Aeolian by A–A, and Locrian by B–B. Note that although the pitch collection in each of these scales is the same (the diatonic white-key collection), the intervallic structure is not. The diatonic collection is made up of five tones and two semitones. The placement of the two semitones within the octave varies in each of the seven modes and contributes to each mode's characteristic sound. The sound of Ionian (the major scale), for instance, is characteristic because of the semitones between scale degrees $\hat{3}$–$\hat{4}$ and $\hat{7}$–$\hat{1}$, whereas Phrygian is easily recognizable because of the semitones between degrees $\hat{1}$–$\hat{2}$ and $\hat{5}$–$\hat{6}$.

It is particularly useful to think of the modes in relation to the familiar major and natural minor scales, and remember which scale degree is different in each of the modes with respect to the major and minor scales, as shown in the following list:

1. Ionian (C–C) is the same as major
2. Dorian (scale D–D) is a natural minor scale with a raised $\hat{6}$ (♯$\hat{6}$, or B♮)
3. Phrygian (E–E) is a natural minor scale with a lowered $\hat{2}$ (♭$\hat{2}$, or F♮)
4. Lydian (F–F) is a major scale with a raised $\hat{4}$ (♯$\hat{4}$, or B♮)
5. Mixolydian (G–G) is a major scale with a lowered $\hat{7}$ (♭$\hat{7}$, or F♮)
6. Aeolian (A–A) is the same as natural minor
7. Locrian (B–B) is a natural minor scale with a lowered $\hat{2}$ (♭$\hat{2}$, or C♮) and a lowered $\hat{5}$ (♭$\hat{5}$, or F♮)

♪♪ Example 1.3   The modal scales

Ionian

Dorian

Phrygian

Lydian

Mixolydian

Aeolian

Locrian

Transposing the Modes

Each of the modes can be transposed to begin on any note. A transposition will usually be reflected in the key signature, although the composer may also write some of the accidentals in the music. Every flat added to a key signature signifies a transposition up a perfect fourth (or down a perfect fifth). Thus, we can, for instance, transpose Dorian to

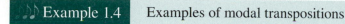

♩♪ Example 1.4   Examples of modal transpositions

G with one flat, to C with two flats, to F with three flats, and so on. Similarly, Mixolydian on C will carry one flat in the signature, Mixolydian on F will carry two flats, and so on.

Every sharp added to the signature, on the other hand, will transpose a mode down a fourth (or up a fifth). Dorian can be transposed to A with one sharp, to E with two sharps, for example, and Mixolydian can be transposed to D with one sharp, to A with two sharps, and so on. Some of these transpositions are shown in Example 1.4.

Identifying the Modes

To identify the mode of a passage in a transposed mode, we should examine the key signature and, if possible, determine the tonal center established by the particular musical context of the passage. In Example 1.2, we have no difficulty identifying G as the tonal center (the melody begins and ends on G), and we already know that a key signature of one flat in a melody in G is a clear indication of G Dorian. Or we can go through the trouble of figuring out the scale; then we realize that the intervallic pattern we identify in this scale is the pattern for the Dorian mode (a minor scale, in this case incomplete, with a raised $\hat{6}$).

Two melodies by Debussy will illustrate transposed modes in which the accidentals are written into the music rather than in the signature. The melody in Example 1.5 is clearly centered on C. We perceive it as such because both the first phrase and the whole melody begin and end on C, and because it spells out a C major scale with one accidental, B♭. In Example 1.4 we already encountered a C-major scale with a flat in the signature, and we know that it represents a transposed Mixolydian mode. Moreover, we also know that B♭ in a C scale is a lowered $\hat{7}$, the degree that defines the Mixolydian mode.

Finally, examine the violin part for the opening measures of his String Quartet no. 1 (1893), shown in Example 1.6. The key signature seems to indicate the key of Gm. The central role of G is confirmed by the opening pitch G and by the stress on G (by repetition and by accent) in mm. 1–5. As we play the melody, however, we notice the absence of F♯s and the flattening of all As (which effectively adds one flat to the signature). What is the G mode with three flats and no F♯?

Example 1.5   Debussy, "La cathédrale engloutie," from *Preludes,* book I , mm. 28–41 (melody only)

Example 1.6   Debussy, String Quartet no. 1, I, mm. 1–12 (first violin part)

PENTATONIC COLLECTIONS

A **pentatonic collection** contains only five different pitches. The most common pentatonic collection in Western music is shown in Example 1.7a. You can easily think of it as being made up of scale degrees $\hat{1}$–$\hat{2}$–$\hat{3}$–$\hat{5}$–$\hat{6}$ of a CM scale, and we call it an **anhemitonic scale** because it contains no semitones. Because there are no half-step tendencies in this scale, however, it is tonally ambiguous: any of its pitches can function as a tonal center. Example 1.7 illustrates that by rotating what was originally presented as white-key C-pentatonic, we come up with four other forms of the same pitch collection, which we can hear as centered on D, E, G, and A, respectively. To determine which of the five

 Example 1.7 The rotations of C pentatonic

Example 1.8 Debussy, "Pagodes," from *Estampes,* mm. 1–4

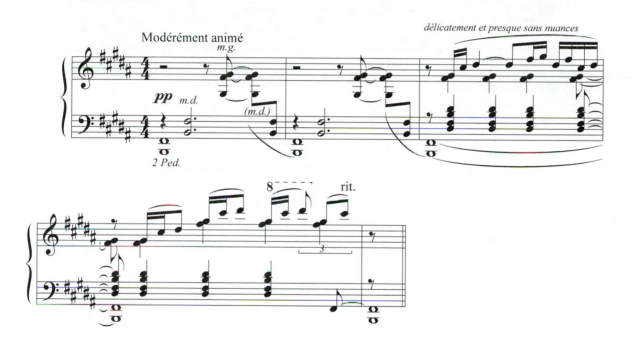

pitches of this collection functions as a center in a particular passage, we will need to examine the particular musical context in which the collection appears.

A pentatonic fragment by Debussy appears in Example 1.8. What is the complete pentatonic collection on which this passage is based? Notice that both melody and harmony are generated by the same pentatonic collection. What is its tonal center? What elements in this particular passage lead you to decide on a particular pitch as a center?

The unaccompanied melody by Ravel shown in Example 1.9, on the other hand, illustrates the ambiguous character of the pentatonic scale with respect to centricity. Notice that the melody begins on C♯ and ends on F♯. Moreover, both C♯ and F♯ are emphasized throughout the melody's contour. This emphasis is registral (both pitches function as the low point of arrival in particular melodic fragments) and rhythmic (both

♪♪♪ Example 1.9   Maurice Ravel, Trio in A Minor, III, "Passacaille," mm. 1–9

♪♪♪ Example 1.10   Four South Indian pentatonic collections

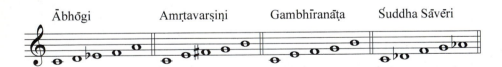

Ābhōgi   Amṛtavarṣiṇi   Gambhīranāṭa   Śuddha Sāvēri

pitches appear as dotted quarters in mm. 1–4, the longest notes in this melodic segment). Would you say that the pitch center is C♯ or F♯? Or perhaps that the melody goes back and forth between the two without clearly settling on either?

We should also mention that many other pentatonic collections are possible and used in non-Western musical traditions. Four of these, found in South Indian music, are shown in Example 1.10. Notice that, unlike the collection in Example 1.7, all of the collections in example 1.10 contain semitones.

As we have discussed and illustrated so far in this chapter, nonfunctional pitch centricity is contextual rather than systematic. To determine whether a piece or a fragment is pitch-centered, and how it is so, we need to examine (and listen to) the music closely, and we need to interpret what we see and hear in order to make decisions on pitch centricity. The following are some of the various factors that may have a bearing on pitch centricity, and hence that we should examine to help us interpret pitch centricity in a particular musical context.

1. Pedals, ostinatos, or note repetition. Stress on a note or a group of notes by pedal, ostinato, or repetition usually creates a sense of pitch centricity.
2. Use of a pitch-centered scalar collection. Pitch-centered collections are scalar collections built on a pitch (the pitch center) following some intervallic patterns. The diatonic collection can be rotated to form seven different modes. Other pitch-centered collections are the pentatonic, whole-tone, octatonic, and hexatonic scales (the latter two will be studied in Chapter 2).
3. In music built on a pitch-centered scalar collection, we need to determine both the pitch center and the scale built on it. Some of the factors that will help us determine the pitch center are beginning and ending pitches for the phrase or section we are examining; important cadential pitches within the section; pitches that are emphasized by means of melodic motion, particularly if scale degrees $\hat{1}$ and $\hat{5}$ are emphasized; and, possibly, pitches that have an important registral role (for instance, scale degrees $\hat{1}$ or $\hat{5}$ may often appear as the lowest or highest pitches in the melodic contour).

In Chapter 2 we will discuss other factors that may create pitch centricity, in particular symmetry around an axis and other types of symmetrical structures. We will now focus on a more detailed study of two compositions by Debussy and Stravinsky, respectively.

ANALYSIS 1.1: DEBUSSY, "LA CATHÉDRALE ENGLOUTIE," FROM *PRELUDES*, BOOK I (ANTHOLOGY NO. 1)

The style of Debussy's music has often been called **impressionist,** a term that we usually associate with visual arts, and particularly with the paintings of such French late-nineteenth century painters as Monet, Manet, Renoir, or Degas. Although it is perfectly appropriate to draw a parallel between the "impressionist" style of painting and Debussy's style (think of the preference for color over defined forms and shapes, or of the blurred contours created by mist, light, and reflection), we should not overlook the influence of literary **symbolism** on Debussy's style. In symbolist poetry, as represented in the work of poets such as Verlaine and Mallarmé, objects are evoked and suggested rather than named; naming an object takes away its poetic quality. As you listen to Debussy's "The Sunken Cathedral" (1910), try to identify its symbolist qualities of suggestion and evocation (what is evoked here is the image, and particularly the sounds, of an ancient cathedral submerged under the sea).

From a musical point of view, this well-known and often-analyzed piano prelude by Debussy illustrates several of the compositional issues relevant to an early twentieth-century composer. As you listen to the piece, focus on the following issues: (1) Thematic material, form, and formal processes. (2) Motives and motivic relationships, especially in mm. 1–40. (3) Scales and harmonic pitch collections. (4) Tonality or pitch

A Review of Basic Formal Concepts

Before we begin our discussion of form in this piece, however, it might be useful to review briefly some formal concepts that you already have studied in the context of tonal music, and to adapt their definitions to the new context of post-tonal music.

1. *A cadence* is a musical point of arrival that articulates or punctuates the end of a musical group (a phrase, a section, or a complete movement or piece). In tonal music, cadences are normally produced by melodic and harmonic means. The cadential harmonic conventions and progressions from tonal music are not to be found in post-tonal music. Composers of post-tonal music have used various means to achieve the cadential effects of musical punctuation, only they have done it without the support of functional harmony. The usual means of achieving a cadential effect in post-tonal music are through melody (for instance, melodic arrival on a nonfunctional pitch center), rhythm (use of longer values at the point of arrival), use of rests, or counterpoint (for instance, by creating a linear convergence of two or more voices on a pitch).

    Cadences in post-tonal music are *contextual*. That is, we have to examine the music and determine where and by what means cadences are achieved. Possible cadential procedures in different pieces or composers may vary widely. At times we will not speak of cadences, but rather of cadential gestures, that is, of musical gestures which, in the context of a piece, take on a cadential function. We will find music that features clear nonfunctional cadences (such as Stravinsky's *Agnus Dei* from Mass, Anthology no. 13; or Hindemith's Interlude in G from *Ludus Tonalis,* Anthology no. 14); or music in which we don't hear cadences as such, but the musical context provides clear enough punctuation markers (cadential gestures) for us to determine phrases

and sections (such as Debussy's "The Sunken Cathedral," Anthology no. 1, which we will analyze later in this chapter); or music in which cadences and cadential gestures are avoided altogether (such as Stravinsky's Introduction to *The Rite of Spring,* Anthology no. 4, which we will also study in this chapter).

2. *A motive* is a short, recurring musical figure consisting of a characteristic rhythmic or pitch pattern (or both), identifiable throughout a composition or a musical section. A pitch motive is associated with a particular ordering of pitches and to a particular contour. Typical motivic operations such as transposition, retrograde (reading the motive backward), inversion (reading the same intervals with their contour reversed—in such a way that a descending interval becomes ascending, and vice versa), and retrograde inversion (reading the inversion backward) preserve the character of the motive, and so do rhythmic augmentation and diminution, among many other possible motivic transformations.

3. *A phrase* is a directed motion in time from a starting point to a cadential gesture. In tonal music, a phrase implies harmonic direction toward a cadence. In post-tonal music, a phrase is a self-contained musical idea with a clear shape leading from a beginning to a point of arrival (a cadential gesture), although harmonic direction toward a cadence will normally not be a decisive factor. Post-tonal phrases are normally rhythmic, melodic, or contrapuntal, rather than harmonic.

4. *A section* is a self-sufficient musical unit, normally closing with some kind of cadential gesture. As in the case of a phrase, post-tonal sections are not usually generated by harmonic means. Besides cadential gestures, important factors that may help delineate sections are thematic content, texture and instrumentation, and use of rests to provide a sectional framework.

centricity. Do you find ambiguity in any of these areas (for instance, formally or tonally)? We will now discuss each of these points, and we will also discuss issues of tempo and proportions.

Thematic Material, Form, and Formal Processes

Form in "The Sunken Cathedral" is not a cut-and-dried matter. You may have come up with a variety of plausible interpretations, and all may be acceptable. We can first identify sections based on thematic material and tonal motion (as represented by bass motion). An initial theme is presented in mm. 1–6; new thematic material appears in mm. 7–13, over an E pedal, and the initial theme returns in mm. 14–15. The bass motion so far has taken us from the initial G down by steps to C. The next section, mm. 16–27, contains reiterations of the initial theme over three tonal areas determined by the bass line B–E♭–G, and leading to the climactic, expansive *ff* theme in C in mm. 28–46. The theme from mm. 7–13 appears again, followed by a brief development, in mm. 47–71, at the same original tonal level, but now over a G♯ pedal instead of an E pedal. The theme in C from mm. 28–46 returns in mm. 72–83, now in *pp.* The piece closes with a final statement of the opening theme in mm. 84–89.

The sections we have identified could easily be grouped in a variety of acceptable ways, and you may try some of the possibilities. We will now consider the grouping proposed by Roy Howat, the author of a book on form and proportions in Debussy.[1] Howat argues that mm. 1–27 constitute a large opening section, which he labels as A. The climactic theme in mm. 28–46 constitutes the B section, and C is the section over the G♯ pedal (mm. 47–71). The B section returns in mm. 72–83, and the piece closes with a final statement of the A material in mm. 84–89. Howat identifies this scheme as an arch form, A–B–C–B–A. The opening A section is itself divided into sections A–C–A, at mm. 1–7–14, respectively.

Our discussion of form in this piece underscores the ambiguity of its formal scheme. How about processes of formal growth? Can we speak of developments (thematic, harmonic, and tonal developments) as we know the term from our studies of eighteenth- and nineteenth-century music? Or does music grow more by repetition and reiteration?

Motives and Motivic Relationships

What motives have you identified in the piece, especially in mm. 1–40? The first one is obviously the opening D–E–B, a motive that we find repeated numerous times in this passage. It would be useful at this point to have a system to label motives in a way that would allow us to compare them to other motives or to other forms of the same motive (such as transpositions or inversions). We will formally study such a system (pitch-class set theory) in some detail in Chapter 3. However, we can still introduce and use somewhat informally the basic labeling principles of pitch-class set theory.

First, we need to understand the difference between pitch and pitch class. A **pitch** is the specific sound frequency we associate with a specific letter name. For instance, the pitch A4 sounds in a particular octave (the middle octave) with the frequency 440 Hz.[2] **Pitch class,** on the other hand, refers to all the pitches with the same name (including all enharmonically equivalent notations), in any octave. That is, pitch class A includes all As in all octaves. The type of labeling method we will now apply is used to label pitch-class collections. That is, we reduce groups of pitches (such as motives or chords) to collections of pitch classes, and we order these collections in a way that will allow us to compare them.

Some basic steps for labeling a collection of pitch classes (a **pitch-class set**) follow:

1. Place the pitch class in its most compact form within a single octave, that is, with *the shortest possible ascending span* between first and last pitch classes. In Example 1.11a, the shortest span in ascending order of our D–E–B motive is B–D–E.

[1] Roy Howat, *Debussy in Proportion* (Cambridge: Cambridge University Press, 1983), p. 159.

[2] Throughout this book we will use the system of pitch designation of the Acoustic Society of America, whereby middle C is C4, an octave above is C5, an octave below is C3, and so forth.

NOTE

*This step shows the two most important differences between an ordered collection of pitches (a motive or a particular chordal sonority) and a pitch-class set. First, because of octave equivalence, all the members of a pitch-class set will be in the same octave (we are dealing with pitch classes) rather than the possible different octaves we find in a motive or chord (made up of pitches). Second, a pitch-class set is an unordered collection: we hear a motive as pitches in a particular order (a motive functions in the realm of pitches, or **pitch space**), but to label it as a pitch-class set, we need to re-order the pitch classes in an arrangement covering the shortest possible span. We thus reduce the particular motive to an unordered collection (a pitch-class set functions in the realm of pitch classes, or **pitch-class space**). The pitch classes of the unordered collection can thus appear as a variety of musical motives or sonorities (with particular shapes) on the musical surface. In other words, the pitch-class set functions as a **motivic cell,** a basic unit or collection from which various motives can be derived.*

2. Assign the *integer 0 to the first pitch class on the left.* To label the remaining pitch classes, *count half steps from the first pitch class.* D is 3 semitones away from B, and E is 5 semitones away. We come up with the set (035).

NOTE

This labeling system is equivalent to the "moveable do" system because we assign integer 0 to the first pitch class of a set, no matter what the pitch class is (the same as in "moveable do," in which we assign the syllable "do" to scale degree Î in a particular key, no matter what the pitch class is).

3. In our final form, however, we want the set label to include *the smallest intervals to the left;* if we want the smallest interval of set (035) to appear to the left, all we have to do is read the set backward. That is, we assign 0 to the first pitch on the right, E, and we count half steps down from E. We come up with the label (025) for this set. This type of set label, which begins with integer 0 and has the smallest intervals to the left, is called **prime form.**

The opening of the second theme in mm. 7–8 includes two overlapping motivic gestures: E–C♯–D♯ and C♯–D♯–G♯. The prime forms for these sets are (013) and (027), respectively, as shown in Example 1.11b. Then the same (025) we saw in m. 1 returns in m. 14. The next section, however, illustrates the close connection between the two cells, which we represent as (025) and (027) as two related forms of the same motivic idea. In mm. 16–18, the right-hand melody repeats the (025) motive. In 19–21, on the other hand, the motive first appears as (027), B♭–C–F, and then as (025), B♭–C–G, as shown in Example 1.11c. This section leads to the statement of (027) in mm. 22–23 (G–A–D).

As it turns out, all of these motives and sets come together in the *ff* climactic theme in mm. 28–32. Example 1.11d shows that we can break up the theme into three-note

Example 1.11   Debussy's motives as pitch-class sets

a. m. 1

0 3 5   5 2 0

= (0 2 5)

b. mm. 7-8

3 1 0   (0   2   7)

= (0 1 3)

c. mm. 16-18

(025)

mm. 19-21

(027)   (025)

d. mm. 28-32

(027)   (013)   (027)   (013)

(025)

motives and that the resulting prime forms are (027), (013), (027), (013), and (025). This analysis thus demonstrates the strong motivic unity and coherence of this piece.

Scales and Harmonic Collections

We will now examine the harmonic means used by Debussy in "The Sunken Cathedral." As you listened to the piece, you must have noticed that its tonal organization somehow sounds "pitch centered," but that no functional harmonic progressions are obvious or present in any way. Let us determine how pitch centricity and nonfunctional harmonic coherence are achieved in this piece.

The Opening Theme

How is the sound of bells ascending from the depths of the sea suggested in the opening measures? In m. 1 we note that there are no chords, but only parallel, open $\frac{8}{5}$ sonorities (Example 1.12a). That in itself suggests both the sound of bells and a sense of archaic antiquity. These are precisely some of the symbolist qualities we suggested at the beginning of our discussion: the sunken cathedral is evoked by the archaic sound of bells slowly rising up from the depths. What pitch class collection is used in mm. 1–2? If we organize all of the pitch classes as a scale, such as G–A–B–D–E, we recognize the familiar anhemitonic pentatonic scale. In this particular context, we hear G as the tonal center because of the bass pedal.

Now examine mm. 14–15, where we see a complete phrase based on our pentatonic theme. What are the chords here? These are indeed chords, and they are not made up of thirds, but rather of stacked fifths. These are **quintal chords,** chords composed of fifths (Example 1.12b). Moreover, note that the prime form that results from two superposed fifths, as, in our case, G–D–A, is (027), which is one of our motivic sets for this piece. This phrase thus features (025) melodically and (027) harmonically. Refer to the phrase that closes the Prelude (mm. 84–85). What chords are used here to harmonize our theme? Notice that the intervals stacked up here are fourths. These are **quartal chords,** chords composed of fourths (Example 1.12c), and their prime form is also (027).

♪♪ **Example 1.12**   Harmonic collections in "The Sunken Cathedral"

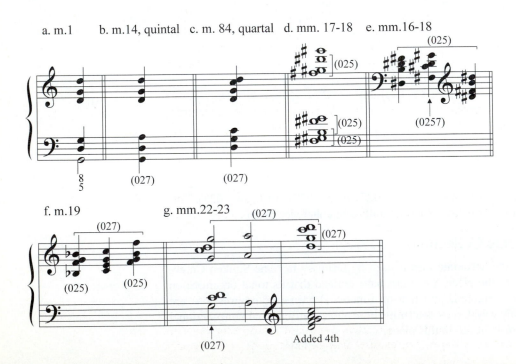

a. m.1   b. m.14, quintal   c. m. 84, quartal   d. mm. 17-18   e. mm.16-18

f. m.19   g. mm.22-23

Further Harmonizations of the Opening Theme

The section in mm. 16–27 contains various statements and reiterations of the opening theme. Mm. 17 and 18 open with an interesting chordal sonority (Example 1.12d). If you examine it carefully, you will see that it is totally made up of overlapping (025) sets. Example 1.12e shows the harmonization of the (025) melodic motive as it appears in mm. 16–18. The first and third chords are triads, but the second chord is again a nontriadic dissonant sonority. The prime form for this set is (0257). What is interesting about (0257)? What two familiar smaller sets does it contain? Example 1.12f illustrates the harmonization of (027) in mm. 19–20. Here we see that chord two is a triad, whereas chords one and three are (025) sonorities. Finally, Example 1.12g shows the statement of the (027) motive in mm. 22–23, and we see that here again the melodic (027) is harmonized by harmonic (027) sonorities.

In other words, we are discovering that some chords are built on the same pitch-class collections we identified as melodic motives. Moreover, melodic motives made up of sets (025) and (027) are harmonized with the same two sets. Chords are thus generated from motives, and nontriadic, nonfunctional sonorities result from this process.

We can also point at the chord in the left hand in m. 23 (Example 1.12g), best interpreted as a minor seventh chord on D with an added G. This is an **added-note chord,** in this case a minor seventh chord with an added fourth. Added-note chords are frequently found in the music of composers (particularly French composers) in the early decades of the twentieth century. In the most common chords of this type, a sixth, a fourth, or a second are added to either a triad or a seventh chord.

The Second Theme

Now play through the second theme, mm. 6–13. You will see that you can construct a diatonic scale with the pitches in these measures, with only one pitch missing, F♯. Here also we run into some tonal ambiguity. If you play the melody without the E pedal, you are likely to hear it centered around C♯. What mode is a C♯ minor scale with a raised $\hat{6}$ (A♯)? The fact, however, is that the E pedal is there, in three octaves. It's powerful enough that we are likely to hear it as the tonal center. Then, we have an E major scale with a raised $\hat{4}$. What is the mode? Do you hear this passage as centered on C♯ or E? Similarly, do you hear the equivalent mm. 47–53 centered around C♯ (if we consider only the melody, the scale is C♯ Dorian) or around G♯ (if we hear the pedal as the tonal center, the scale is G♯ Aeolian)?

The Climactic Theme

We find no ambiguity, however, in the tonal content of the climactic theme "in C" (mm. 27–40). Not only is it built on a C pedal, but we can easily construct a diatonic scale using the pitches from this passage. We come up with a major scale on C with a B♭, a lowered $\hat{7}$. What mode is this?

Voice Leading

What is unusual in the voice leading in mm. 1–5, 14–15, and 28–40? Whether the sonorities are open 5ths (mm. 1–5), quintal chords (mm. 14–15), or triads (mm. 28–40), the only voice leading in these passages is by parallel motion. This type of parallel voice leading, characteristic of Debussy and other French composers of this period, is called **planing.** Observe that in planing, parallel 5ths are not a problem in the least. Quite to the contrary, they become very much part of the sound sought by the composer.

In mm. 28–32 the planing follows the diatonic scale: we begin with a triad, and we move in parallel voice leading following the content of the diatonic scale. This creates triads of different qualities (M, m, or even diminished). We call this type of voice leading **diatonic planing.** Now examine mm. 62–64. We begin with a Mm7 sonority and we move in parallel voice leading in such a way that all subsequent sonorities are still Mm7 chords. Accidentals foreign to the diatonic scale are immediately introduced. This is **chromatic planing.** In diatonic planing, the diatonic scale is preserved, but the exact quality of the sonorities is not. In chromatic planing, the sonorities are preserved, whereas the diatonic scale is not.

Tonality

Let us now address the issue of the large-scale tonal plan in "The Sunken Cathedral." There is no question that this music features pitch centricity (that is, it has a tonal center). It's also quite clear that we hear the piece as a whole "in C." But we should not think in terms of CM or Cm, because we have not seen any instances of major-minor tonality and scales, let alone of functional harmonic progressions. How would you say tonality is established?

In the first place, pedal tones seem to be an essential element to create a sense of tonal center. Although we saw, for instance, that the passage in mm. 7–13 (the second theme), is tonally ambiguous (it could be interpreted as being in C♯ Dorian, if we consider only the scale, or in E Lydian, if we hear the pedal E as the tonal center), we do tend to hear it as being "in E" because of the ever-present sound of the E pedal in three octaves. If we interpret tonal areas as determined by pedals, we come up with the large-scale plan shown in Example 1.13. In the opening section, a linear bass leads from G (m. 1) to C (m. 14) through F (m. 3), E (m. 5), and D (m. 13). The three areas in mm. 16–27 are B, E♭, and G, and the latter again leads to the climactic theme, on a C pedal. A passing B♭ in mm. 42–43 connects C to A♭/G♯, the pedal for the following section (mm. 47–67). The closing sections (mm. 72–89) are again centered around C.

How can we interpret these tonal relationships? There is one prominent 5th relationship, between the opening G and the C in m. 14, connected by descending linear

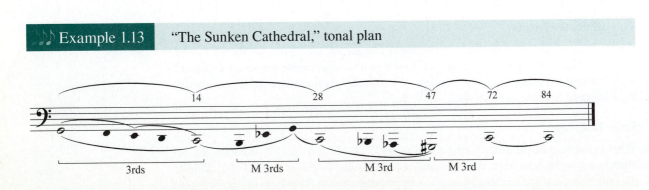

"The Sunken Cathedral," tonal plan

motion. Although we may hear the beginning as being "in G," in hindsight we hear this G as $\hat{5}$ of C (although not as a "dominant" of C, because there are no harmonic elements to define a V–I relationship). The same 5th from G to C appears again in mm. 22–28. Other than this important 5th relationship (which provides echoes of a tonal tradition otherwise not present in the piece), we notice that 3rd relationships are much more prominent than 5th relationships. The motion from G to C can also be interpreted as covering a G–E–C motion in 3rds. The tonal areas in mm. 16–27 are also related by chromatic 3rds. And, finally, the centers of the three large areas from m. 28 to the end (C–G#–C) are also related by chromatic 3rds.

NOTE

We can make a particularly interesting observation at this point. The tonal space from the initial G to the C in m. 14 is divided by E in mm. 6–7. Now examine the high-pitch motive that corresponds to the G–E–C motion. In m. 1, the high pitch is D. In mm. 6–7 it is E, and in m. 14 it is B. The resulting long-range motive is thus D–E–B. What pitch-class set is this, and how is it related to the motive in m. 1?

Formal Proportions

This prelude presents an interesting performance problem that affects its formal proportions. You may have noticed the unusual meter signature: $\frac{6}{4} = \frac{3}{2}$. For decades, this has been interpreted as meaning that a measure of $\frac{6}{4}$ (the measures with quarter notes, such as mm. 1–6 or 14–21) was of equal duration as a measure of $\frac{3}{2}$ (the measures with mostly half notes, such as mm. 7–13 or 22–83). As a result, the tempo of the $\frac{3}{2}$ measures has usually been exceedingly slow, with deadly consequences for the flow of the music. This musical problem was solved upon the discovery of a piano roll of "The Sunken Cathedral" recorded by Debussy himself in 1913. In the roll, he plays the $\frac{3}{2}$ measures at exactly double the speed of the $\frac{6}{4}$ measures. In other words, the meter signature really means that the quarter note in the $\frac{6}{4}$ measures equals a half note in the $\frac{3}{2}$ measures.[3]

From a performance point of view, this discovery has great consequences. The $\frac{3}{2}$ measures, which had often been played at an excruciatingly slow tempo, come to life when performed at a tempo twice as fast. From an analytical point of view, this tempo equivalence also has dramatic consequences that affect the proportions of the piece, as it has been elucidated by Howat.[4] This author has proposed a renumbering of the measures, following the prelude's "real time," as opposed to the "notated time." That is, in the renumbering, two measures in $\frac{6}{4}$ equal (in duration) one measure in $\frac{3}{2}$, and hence should count as only one measure. If we go back to the Howat form scheme we saw previously (ABCBA), in the notated score the measure numbers for these sections are

---

[3]See Charles Burkhart, "Debussy Plays *La cathédrale engloutie* and Solves Metrical Mystery," in *The Piano Quarterly* (Fall 1968), pp. 14–16.

[4]Howat, pp. 159–61.

♪♪ Example 1.14   The Golden Section

$$\frac{b}{a} = \frac{a}{a+b} = .618$$

a   b

.618

1–28–47–72–84, respectively, and the total number of measures is 89. After renumbering as explained above, these measures become 1–21–30–42–49, and the total is 55.

But before we can understand the significance of these numbers, we need to introduce a concept of great significance to many twentieth-century composers: the **Golden Section** (or Golden Mean). The Golden Section (GS) is a division of a given length in two in such a way that the ratio of the shorter segment to the longer segment is the same as the ratio of the longer segment to the whole. This is expressed by the formula $\frac{b}{a} = \frac{a}{a+b}$ (Example 1.14). The value of this ratio is 0.618034 (a little under two-thirds of the complete length; in general, we can simplify this value to 0.618). A numerical series directly related to the Golden Section is the Fibonacci series. In this summation series, each number is the sum of the previous two: 0, 1, 1, 2, 3, 5, 8, 13, 21, 34, 55, 89, 144, and so on. The ratio between two consecutive numbers of the Fibonacci series approximates the Golden Section, with the approximation getting closer to the GS as the numbers get higher. Thus, $\frac{34}{55} = 0.61818$, and $\frac{89}{144} = 0.618055$.

The GS is a ratio widely found in nature. For instance, it regulates the growth ratios of some plants and flowers, pine cones, and some types of snail shells. Because it has been traditionally considered as a "perfect" proportion, it has also been widely used in art and architecture throughout history. GS formal relationships can be found in buildings of ancient Greece as well as in modern architectural designs by le Corbusier. In music, GS proportions are featured in the music of various twentieth-century composers, including Debussy, Bartók and Ligeti.

We can now return to the renumbered measures for the main sections in "The Sunken Cathedral" according to Howat, 1–21–30–42–49–55. Example 1.15 shows multiple proportional relationships of interest to our discussion. Of the total of 55 measures, 34 are at the faster tempo, and 21 are at the slower tempo (21 and 34 are related by the GS). The climactic section, formerly beginning in m. 28, now arrives in m. 21 (the GS from the end of the piece). The final A section now returns in m. 49, and the beginning of the C section, in m. 30, approximates the GS of 49. And the length of the two B sections (19 and 12 measures long, as notated, or 9½ and 6 in renumbered measures) also approximates a GS proportion.

Summary

What have we learned from this fairly detailed analysis of "The Sunken Cathedral"? How much of what we have learned applies to other early twentieth-century composers? We can summarize our main points as follows:

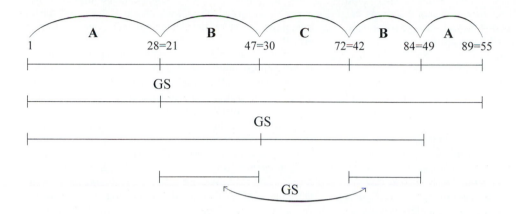

♪♪ Example 1.15 "The Sunken Cathedral," formal proportions

1. Motives are an essential component both in delineation of form and as elements of compositional cohesion.

2. Form is generated by a succession of sections (in an additive process) rather than by harmonic development or motivic transformations. Motives are repeated rather than developed. The exact formal plan is ambiguous and allows for a variety of interpretations.

3. Pitch collections include nonfunctional scales such as the modes or a pentatonic scale. Chords include not only tertian sonorities, but also quintal and quartal. Other chords are generated by a vertical presentation of the same motives that can be found in a melodic form.

4. Tonality and pitch centricity are provided by either nonfunctional, centered pitch collections (such as the modal scales) or by pedals, or both. In all cases, tonality is nonfunctional (although some echoes of functional tonality can be heard in the use of veiled, long-range V–I relationships), and it is often ambiguous. Pedals play an essential role in delineating a large-scale tonal plan.

5. In this and other pieces, Debussy seems to be interested in formal proportions, and analysis of his music has unveiled a broad use of the GS as a means to determine these proportions.

It is fair to say that every one of the points in the preceding summary can be read as general statements that apply, to one extent or another, to a lot of the music by Debussy and by other composers in the first decades of the century. "The Sunken Cathedral" thus introduces us to several of the issues relevant to early post-tonal composition, and to some of the analytical techniques that we will continue applying throughout the book, as is the case with pitch-class sets.

Musical form is a dynamic concept, inasmuch as form unfolds aurally in time, and we always hear the musical present of a composition in relation to what we already heard and what we will still hear. The unfolding of form in time, the motion from one point in the composition to a later point, is what we know as formal growth. There are many approaches to formal growth, and they all involve some basic principles. Thus, themes and ideas are first exposed, then they may be manipulated in some ways, and then they may be restated literally or in a varied form. Formal processes involve the concepts of exposition, repetition in a literal or a varied way, possible contrast, and possible return. Formal types such as binary, ternary, variation, and rondo are to a great extent built on such processes.

Some formal types include developmental processes. Developments in tonal music are usually both thematic and harmonic. Thematic development is a process by which melodic material is derived from a previously presented theme or melody, in such a way that new extended sections may be generated. Usual techniques of thematic development include repetition, transposition, variation, sequence, fragmentation, intervallic expansion or contraction, inversion, retrograde, augmentation, diminution, and so on. These types of melodic processes, in tonal compositions of the common-practice period, are invariably paired with harmonic developmental processes. Such processes include changes of mode, modulation, harmonic sequences (often using the descending or ascending circles of fifths, among other possible harmonic patterns), and a variety of possible chromatic linear processes. Classical and Romantic developmental formal types, such as sonata form and sonata rondo, are based on developmental techniques of formal growth.

Large-scale tonal motion was essential to formal design in the common-practice period. In the absence of functional tonality, large-scale formal design loses one of its traditional supports, and, in the absence of functional harmonic processes (modulation, harmonic sequences, and so on), developmental techniques of formal growth also lose one of their essential components. In our discussions of form and formal processes in post-tonal music, then, we will have to examine how composers have dealt with these issues of formal generation. Are their forms developmental or nondevelopmental? If they are developmental, by what means do they create developmental processes? Are these composers using preexisting formal types (such as binary, ternary, rondo, sonata form), or are they inventing their own formal designs? In the latter case, what are these designs, and what techniques of formal growth are used to realize them?

ANALYSIS 1.2: STRAVINSKY, INTRODUCTION TO PART I, FROM *THE RITE OF SPRING* (ANTHOLOGY NO. 4)

Although the aesthetic world of Stravinsky's Russian period, which comprises such works as *The Firebird* (1910), *Petrushka* (1911), *The Rite of Spring* (1913), *Les noces* (1917), and *Histoire du soldat* (1918), presents a strong contrast with that of Debussy's "The Sunken Cathedral," many of the technical and compositional issues faced by both composers are the same, and many of the solutions provided by both are also of a similar type. Listen to the Introduction to Part I from *The Rite,* and as you listen, focus on form and formal growth, texture, melodic and motivic relationships, tonality, and issues of rhythm and meter.

Form and Formal Growth

The formal processes in this piece are nondevelopmental. Thematic ideas are presented in succession, and then they are repeated, alternated, and combined, but never quite developed. Moreover, repetitions are usually at the same tonal level rather than transposed. Some of the most prominent thematic elements in this introduction (as shown in Example 1.16, all notated at concert pitch) are the opening bassoon theme (which we can label as the A theme); the more chromatic theme in overlapping 3rds (theme B_1),

♪♪♪ Example 1.16   *The Rite of Spring,* themes in Introduction

one measure after rehearsal 1 (the term "rehearsal" will henceforth be abbreviated as "reh.") and the accompanying descending chromatic line (theme B[2]); the theme in overlapping 4ths at reh. 3 (theme C; the overlapping 4ths are C♯–F♯ and D♯–G♯); the disjunct theme in the flute two measures after reh. 8, featuring octave displacement (theme D); the oboe theme at reh. 9 (theme E[1]), and its accompanying theme in the small clarinet (theme E[2], three measures after reh. 9).[5]

Some particular formal functions are useful to understand Stravinsky's formal processes: stratification (or layering), juxtaposition, interruption/continuation, and

---

[5]These thematic elements and their intervallic relationships are discussed in Marianne Kielian-Gilbert, "Relationships of Symmetrical Pitch-Class Sets and Stravinsky's Metaphor of Polarity," *Perspectives of New Music* 21 (1982–83): 209–240.

synthesis.[6] Stravinsky's music is often composed in layers. Different lines or textural elements are presented as clearly audible, simultaneous, but separate elements. We will refer to this process as **stratification** (or also as **layering**). Identify, for instance, all the layers you hear (and see) in reh. 7–9 in the Introduction to *The Rite*. Another common formal technique in Stravinsky's music is the abrupt interruption of a texture or idea, its replacement with a different texture or idea, followed by the eventual (or immediate) abrupt return of the previous idea. We will refer to this abrupt process of **interruption and continuation** as **juxtaposition.** Whereas in stratification, ideas are presented simultaneously, in juxtaposition they are presented side by side. Examine the passage in reh. 7, and you will see a few clear instances of abrupt interruption and continuation, that is, of juxtaposition of ideas. Finally, different ideas previously presented often come back together, in an interrelated way, toward the end of a piece or section. The function of such a passage is of unification, in a process that we will call **synthesis.** We find a section with such a function in reh. 10–11 of *The Rite*'s Introduction, where we can identify three of the previous themes (theme C in the English horn, theme E_2 in the small clarinet, and theme B_2 in the clarinet in A) now presented simultaneously in a layered counterpoint and integrated into the complex texture of the passage.

Examine now the form of the complete Introduction in terms of stratification, juxtaposition, and synthesis as formal processes. Discuss also how dynamic and textural increase or decrease play a role in formal growth. Textural increase in Stravinsky is often generated by addition of ostinato layers. Can you illustrate this with reference to the Introduction?

Melodic and Motivic Relationships

Previously, we identified the main thematic elements in the Introduction. Let us now examine how the themes are used, extended, and combined throughout the Introduction.

As you listened to the Introduction, you may have noticed a sense of pitch stasis (both harmonically and melodically). Several factors contribute to this sense. In the first place, notice that when themes are repeated (as they often are), they often appear at the same tonal level as before. For instance, compare the appearances of theme A in m. 1, 4 mm. after reh. 1, and at reh. 3, or the appearances of theme C at reh. 2 and reh. 3. Moreover, motivic repetition often takes the form of an ostinato. Motives derived from theme B_1 (based on thirds and half steps) are used as ostinatos beginning in reh. 6 through reh. 11.

Motives and ostinato cells in this piece are usually short and move within a narrow range (as is the case with both themes B_1 and C), and make substantial use of grace notes and embellishments. Their intervallic content is quite limited (mostly minor 3rds and half steps in theme B_1, two overlapping perfect 4ths in theme C). You may also have noticed the technique of lengthening or shortening themes by adding or subtracting pitches (and, correspondingly, beats). Example 1.17 illustrates this process or exten-

---

[6]These terms were first introduced by Edward Cone in his article "Stravinsky: the Progress of a Method," in *Perspectives on Schoenberg and Stravinsky,* ed. Benjamin Boretz and Edward Cone (New York: Norton, 1972), pp. 155–64. Our use of the term "stratification," however, will differ from Cone's (who uses it to mean side-by-side juxtaposition, instead of our meaning as simultaneous layering).

♪♪♪ Example 1.17   *The Rite of Spring,* thematic extension/truncation of theme A

sion/truncation as applied to theme A. In Example 1.17a we can see that the second statement of theme A (3 mm. after reh. 2) is truncated by two beats with respect to the opening statement. In Example 1.17b, moreover, we can see that theme A itself, as presented in the opening statement, is essentially made up of a single cell (bracketed under the staff) that is repeated three times (with a brief interpolation after the second cell), each with different rhythm and metric placement (at least with respect to notated meter, because we don't really perceive a clear meter in this passage). Study now the first and second statements of theme C (reh. 2 and reh. 3), and determine how they are related. What effect does this shortening and lengthening of themes have on the relative length of sections and on section balance?

Several of the thematic characteristics we have just discussed have their origin in Russian folk music. The themes from *The Rite* (and theme A in particular) have been proven to be derived from, or inspired by, Russian folk melodies.[7] This accounts, at least in part, for their short range and simple pitch and rhythmic patterns, and for the extensive use of grace notes. Moreover, the technique of building themes by an additive process of cell repetition, and of extending and truncating themes by adding or taking off cell units (and beats) is characteristic of a type of Russian instrumental ostinato found in folk dance tunes called *naígrïsh,* based on exactly this same type of improvisational technique.

---

[7]Richard Taruskin, *Stravinsky and the Russian Traditions,* 2 vols (Berkeley: University of California Press, 1996). See vol. 1, pp. 898–99.

Finally, let us examine motivic coherence in this example. At a glance, the motives listed in Example 1.16 seem to be quite contrasting. If we examine their pitch-class content carefully, however, we will discover surprising underlying relationships. Try to identify on your own the pitch-class sets for these themes, beginning with theme C, then themes D and E_1–E_2, and finally themes B_1 and A.

The prime form for theme C is (0257). As it turns out, the prime forms for theme D and for both themes E_1 and E_2 are also (0257). The set for theme B_1 is (023457). This set can also be understood as a (0257) set in which the "inner gap" has been filled in chromatically: 02(34)57. Finally, the set for theme A, larger than the rest, is (024579). This set actually contains three overlapping (0257) sets. Can you find them? One is represented by the actual integers (0257) in (024579). The other two are represented by the integers (2479) and (7902), respectively. If you renumber set (2479) beginning with 0, you indeed come up with (0257). To understand that (7902) can also be turned into (0257), think of the four pitch classes of (7902) as hours on a clock face (where 0 is the same as 12), and count hours (of half steps) clockwise from 7 (that is, assigning 0 to the first pitch class, 7). The result will be (0257). The cell (0257) thus permeates and unifies the motivic content of this Introduction.

Tonality and Pitch Centricity

It is immediately apparent, as we listen to the Introduction to *The Rite,* that functional tonal relationships are totally absent from this music. And yet we can also perceive some kind of pitch centricity or, in some cases, conflicting pitch centricities. The factors that contribute to a sense of centricity in this music are the themes themselves (and their repetition) and the ostinatos and pedals. Otherwise, there does not seem to be a long-range tonal plan in this Introduction; neither is there a single way of looking at its tonal relationships, which at best are ambiguous and multiple. In the same way that we have spoken of thematic layering, we can also speak of tonal layers and of simultaneous multiple tonal centers (for which we can use the term **polycentricity** or **polytonality,** although in no way implying major-minor tonalities).

Let's look for instance at the opening section (m. 1 to reh. 4). Theme A is totally diatonic. What would you say its tonal center is? We first need to listen to the theme carefully. In the absence of a complete diatonic scale, or of any type of tonal accompaniment, the tonality of this theme is ambiguous. The opening C seems to announce a C "tonality." As we listen to the complete theme, however, we are more likely to hear A as the tonal center because of the function of pitch A as a point of melodic arrival (and the scale is then Aeolian). All of it is, of course, obscured by the C♯–D in the horn in F, and by theme B_1 in the small clarinet in D, which seems to have a B tonal center (its melodic motion spells out a B triad). Theme C (English horn, to be read in F), on the other hand, presents new difficulties. First, we hear only four notes, which seem to rest on a D♯ "center" (because we keep hearing the D♯ as a point of melodic arrival). When one more note (E) is added in m. 5 after reh. 3, we have the collection C♯–D♯–E–F♯–G♯, with D♯ perceived as a center. This is part of a D♯ Phrygian scale. The chromatic lines in the bassoons at reh. 3 seem to confirm D♯ as a center in this passage. This interpretation, based on a possible way of hearing themes A and C, points at two pitch centers for this initial passage, a tritone apart from each other (A Aeolian and D♯ Phrygian).[8]

Beginning at reh. 7, we see a succession of pedals that should be taken into account as possible pitch centers. Thus, a C pedal begins at reh. 7 (supported by the ostinato figure in the bass clarinet), a B♭ pedal follows (supported by the ostinato figures in the bassoons), and finally a B pedal is featured beginning at reh. 10 (also supported by the ostinato figures in the bassoons). If we accept the hypothesis that pitch centricity in these areas is determined by pedals and ostinato figures, the tonal centers are C–B♭–B. We can interpret this as a cluster of tonal centers symmetrical around B (B♭→B←C). Interestingly enough, the return of theme A at reh. 12 begins on C♭ (= B) rather than the original C (and can be interpreted as A♭ Aeolian, or as featuring ambiguous C♭/A♭ centricity). This return of theme A at a different tonal level from the original stresses both the lack of closure of the Introduction and the fact that the music at reh. 12 functions not so much as a closing section, but as a transition to the next large section of *The Rite,* the "Danses des adolescentes."

Rhythm and Meter

As it becomes obvious when we listen to the piece, rhythm and meter are essential components in *The Rite.* Moreover, Stravinsky's use of rhythm and meter in this composition includes numerous innovations that in many ways represent a point of departure for later twentieth-century compositional techniques. We will now examine some of the most salient characteristics of rhythm and meter in the Introduction to *The Rite.*[9] But first, let us review some basic concepts in the area of rhythm and meter.

We will now proceed to our discussion of rhythm and meter in the Introduction to *The Rite.*

1. In the first place, we observe the frequent **meter changes** (or **mixed meters**). What is the effect, from a listener's point of view, of metric changes such as the ones we find in the initial sections of the Introduction? We should note that Stravinsky's metric changes in this piece are often directly related to the technique of thematic extension and truncation we discussed earlier. For instance, the fluctuating length of thematic cells in the opening phrase accounts for the succession of $\frac{4}{4}$, $\frac{3}{4}$, $\frac{4}{4}$, and $\frac{2}{4}$ meters. In Example 1.17a, we saw that in the second statement of theme A a two-beat-long melodic cell was left out. This is solved metrically by turning the original

[8]For an octatonic interpretation of *The Rite,* including the Introduction to Part I, see Pieter van den Toorn, *The Music of Igor Stravinsky,* (New Haven: Yale University Press, 1983) and *Stravinsky and the Rite of Spring: The Beginnings of a Musical Language* (Berkeley: University of California Press, 1987). In his article "Stravinsky and the Octatonic: A Reconsideration" (*Music Theory Spectrum* 24/1 [2002]: 68–102), Dmitri Tymoczko takes issue with van den Toorn's octatonic views and proposes instead readings of Stravinsky's music based on modal and non-diatonic scales, and on the superimposition or simultaneous use of different scales that create polyscalarity and polytonality. The polemic between the two authors continues in a "Colloquy" published in *Music Theory Spectrum* 25/1 (2003), 167–202.

[9]For an interesting analysis of rhythm, meter, and issues of form in *The Rite,* see Pierre Boulez, "Stravinsky Remains," in *Stocktakings from an Apprenticeship,* trans. Stephen Walsh (Oxford: Clarendon Press, 1991), pp. 55–110.

In order to unify our vocabulary on the temporal aspects of music, we will now review the definitions of some basic concepts in the areas of rhythm and meter.[10] These are all concepts that apply generally to music (not just to post-tonal music) and that should be familiar to you from your studies of tonal music.

1. Rhythm. The term **rhythm** refers to the grouping, patterning, and partitioning of musical events. The "musical events" we most often apply this term to are "notes," but we can also speak, for instance, of harmonic rhythm, orchestral rhythm, or large-scale formal rhythm.

2. Meter. **Meter** refers to the measurement of the number of pulses between regularly recurring accents. It is usually acknowledged that meter, at least at the surface level, requires a pattern of accents that recurs regularly.

3. We will refer to regularly recurring, undifferentiated time points as **pulses.** By superimposing a pattern of regularly recurring accents on a stream of pulses, we create a metric context for those pulses. Pulses in a metric context are called **beats.**

4. **Metric accents** result from metric organization. In a metric context, some beats are more accented than others (some beats are strong, some are weak). The first beat of a measure is called a **downbeat,** and the last beat is an **upbeat.** A note or group of notes placed on an upbeat are called an **anacrusis.**

5. Meters are **symmetrical or divisive** when we think of them in terms of their divisions, and the divisions form symmetrical patterns, as in the case of $\frac{2}{4}$, $\frac{4}{4}$, $\frac{3}{4}$, $\frac{6}{8}$, $\frac{9}{8}$, and so on. **Asymmetrical or additive meters,** on the other hand, result from combining (adding) metric units that form an asymmetrical metric structure. Thus, we think of $\frac{5}{8}$ as a meter that combines two unequal metric units (3 + 2 or 2 + 3), and the same with $\frac{7}{8}$ (4 + 3 or 3 + 4), $\frac{11}{8}$, and so on.

---

[10]Further elaborations of these definitions, as well as examples illustrating them, can be found in Miguel Roig-Francolí, *Harmony in Context* (New York: McGraw-Hill, 2003), Chapter B.

6. Besides metric accents, numerous other nonmetrical factors can create musical accents. Nonmetrical accents are **rhythmic accents.** Rhythmic accents can result from such varied causes as grouping of notes, note length (we hear longer notes as accented, and we call an accent produced by duration an **agogic accent**), a sense of harmonic or tonal arrival, or a **dynamic accent** (any dynamic mark or articulation symbol that is interpreted as an accent, such as sforzando, an accent mark, and the like).

7. Rhythmic accents may create a conflict with metric accents in a particular passage. Some of the most standard rhythmic/metric conflicts are syncopation and hemiola. **Syncopation** is the rhythmic contradiction of a metrical pattern of strong and weak beats by placing rhythmic emphasis on one or more weak beats. **Hemiola** is the juxtaposition of, or interplay between, three and two beats at the metric level. Hemiola is created when we alternate measures in $\frac{6}{8}$ and $\frac{3}{4}$ (as in Leonard Bernstein's song "America") or when a sense of three $\frac{2}{4}$ measures instead of two $\frac{3}{4}$ measures is created by rhythmic accents within a notated $\frac{3}{4}$ meter (as in the opening of Schumann's Symphony no. 3).

8. There are various ways of creating **rhythmic and metric irregularities,** and in the remaining discussion in this chapter, as well as in future chapters (particularly Chapter 10) we will study several of them. We can now mention, however, that beats can be divided irregularly. In simple meters (such as $\frac{2}{4}$, $\frac{4}{4}$, or $\frac{3}{4}$), the regular division of the beat is into two or four parts. These beats can also be divided irregularly into three parts (triplets), five parts (quintuplets), six parts (sextuplets), and so on. The regular division of the beat in compound meters ($\frac{6}{8}$, $\frac{9}{8}$, $\frac{12}{8}$), on the other hand, is into three or six parts. These beats can also be divided irregularly into two parts (duplets), four parts (quadruplets), and so on.

9. Other common metric irregularities, particularly in twentieth-century music, are meter changes (or mixed meters), rhythmic/metric displacements, polyrhythm, and polymeter. We will see examples of these in the following discussion of *The Rite.*

$\frac{4}{4}$ measure into a $\frac{2}{4}$ measure. In other words, melodic and thematic extension and truncation go hand in hand with metric extension and truncation.

2. As melodic cells are repeated, they may be associated with different rhythms. This is evident in the opening phrase. In Example 1.17b you can verify that every time the initial motive appears (the bracketed motive), its rhythm is different.

♪♪♪ Example 1.18   *The Rite of Spring,* metric displacement of theme A

3. As melodic cells are repeated, not only may their rhythm vary, but also their metric placement. Looking again at the initial motive, in m. 1 it begins on beat 1 of a $\frac{4}{4}$ measure and immediately on the second note of a triplet in beat 3. The same motive begins on an upbeat three measures after reh. 1 and on beat two of a $\frac{3}{4}$ measure at reh. 3. These different metric beginnings (**metric displacement**) are indicated by arrows in Example 1.18.

4. If we consider the simultaneous presentation of different layers of thematic material, we will see that repeated rhythmic cells in various voices create different simultaneities (that is, vertical pitch relationships among different lines). Refer, for instance, to reh. 11 and verify the simultaneities that result from the piccolo, flute, oboe, English horn, and small clarinet lines. You will see that contrapuntal simultaneities fluctuate constantly. This contributes to our hearing lines as independent layers, rather than as part of a contrapuntally related whole.

    We can also note that different layers often feature different simultaneous subdivisions of the beat, a type of rhythmic irregularity we call **polyrhythm.** You can see various examples of polyrhythm in the measures after reh. 11, where the beat is simultaneously divided into eighth notes (small clarinet), triplets (bassoons), sextuplets (oboe), thirty-second notes (clarinet), and so on.

5. Although all layers are notated in the same meter or meters, the actual result is often **polymeter,** that is, the simultaneous presentation of more than one meter. Study the two measures after reh. 11, notated in $\frac{3}{4}$. If we consider the length of the repeated thematic unit in the small clarinet, for instance (three beats), this line is indeed in $\frac{3}{4}$ meter. The bassoon triplet ostinatos, however, feature a grouping in two beats, and if they were notated alone they would most certainly be notated in $\frac{6}{8}$. The double-bass pizzicato, on the other hand, can be heard as being in $\frac{3}{4}$, with the eighth note of this $\frac{3}{4}$ being equal to the eighth note of the bassoon's $\frac{6}{8}$. You can see

🎵🎵 Example 1.19   *The Rite of Spring,* renotation of polymetric passage

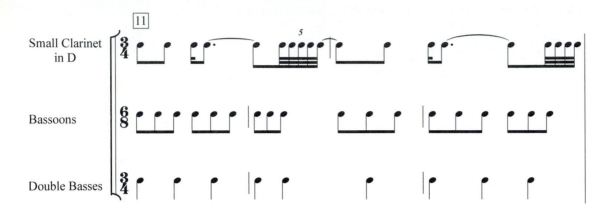

these three meters renotated in Example 1.19. What we are actually hearing here is a polymetric passage, despite the single meter Stravinsky used for his notation.

In summary, we have seen that meters change, that thematic cells are lengthened or shortened, that they are displaced metrically, that simultaneities in different layers fluctuate, and that at times we hear several meters at the same time. What effect do these rhythmic/metric techniques have on you as a listener? Is this music "metric," that is, does it feature a regularity of metric accents that would allow you to perceive meter?

APPLICATION AND CLASS DISCUSSION

In this chapter we have opened the doors to many of the issues that will pervade our study of twentieth-century music. Both of the compositions we have studied in some detail address similar compositional problems. In some cases they offer similar solutions to the problems; in other cases, the solutions are contrasting. In any case, they are both excellent representatives of early twentieth-century composition, and they both approach musical processes in ways that would have a deep impact on many twentieth-century composers.

As a class discussion, try to summarize the issues opened by these compositions and the solutions offered by these composers. Focus on the areas of form and formal growth, pitch organization and pitch-class collections, melodic and motivic elements and their role in providing coherence to the piece as a whole, harmony, texture, rhythm and meter, and finally, tonality and pitch centricity (and various means of achieving it).

Is there any piece in the repertoire that you perform to which some of the criteria and analytical approaches we have practiced in this chapter would apply? If so, bring it to class and explain how this chapter has contributed to your understanding of the piece.

Further Listening

The following list provides suggestions for further listening to music by composers studied in this chapter or related to the styles and techniques we have studied (if possible, listen while following the score):

1. Debussy, *Preludes,* book I (complete)
2. Debussy, *La mer*
3. Ravel, *Rapsodie espagnole*
4. Stravinsky, *The Rite of Spring* (complete)
5. Stravinsky, *Les noces*

Terms for Review

pitch centricity
diatonic collection
Dorian, Phrygian, Lydian, Mixolydian, Aeolian, Ionian, and Locrian
pentatonic collection
anhemitonic scale
impressionism, symbolism
pitch, pitch class, pitch-class set
pitch space, pitch-class space
motivic cell
prime form
quintal chords, quartal chords
added-note chord
planing, diatonic planing, chromatic planing
Golden Section

stratification, layering, interruption and continuation, juxtaposition, synthesis
polycentricity, polytonality
rhythm, meter
pulses, beats
metric accents, downbeat, upbeat, anacrusis
symmetrical or divisive meters
asymmetrical or additive meters
rhythmic accents, agogic accent, dynamic accent
syncopation, hemiola
rhythmic and metric irregularities
meter changes (mixed meters), metric displacement, polyrhythm, polymeter

 CHAPTER 1 ASSIGNMENTS

I. Theory

1. Write the scales for the following transposed modes, with the correct key signature:

    Dorian on C and E

    Phrygian on A and B

    Lydian on A♭ and G

Mixolydian on F and E

Aeolian on F♯ and C

Ionian on A and E♭

2. Write standard anhemitonic pentatonic scales on D, E, and A♭, and show all possible rotations for each.

3. Write two different melodic motives (pitch, rhythm and meter) on each of the following sets: (014), (015), (025), (027), and (0257).

4. Write a quartal and a quintal chord on each of the following pitches: A, F, E♭, and G♯.

II. Analysis

1. Debussy, "Sarabande," from *Pour le piano* (Anthology no. 3). Listen to this piece and study the score. Then provide answers to the following questions:

   a. What is the key of the piece, how and where is it first established, and is it a major or minor key or one of the modes (consider the scale of mm. 1–8)?

   b. Mm. 1–2: What is the harmonic/voice-leading technique? Comment about root relationships.

   c. M. 7: Describe the harmonic/voice-leading technique: What is the contrapuntal motion that generates the harmony?

   d. Mm. 11–12: What is the harmonic/voice-leading technique? (Be specific: how are sonorities related?)

   e. Mm. 23–28: What type of chord is used in this passage?

   f. Mm. 35–41: Name the harmonic technique. Describe how the sonorities change in this passage. Compare, for instance, the sonorities in mm. 35, 38–39, and 40–41.

   g. Mm. 46–49: What is the key of this phrase? What scale degree (Roman numeral) does it end on harmonically, and what is unusual about it from a *tonal* point of view?

   h. Mm. 63–65: What is the prevalent sonority in this passage?

   i. Discuss the form of the complete piece.

2. Listen to and study Stravinsky's "Danses des Adolescentes" (*Rite of Spring,* part I, reh. 13–37; score available in Mary Wennerstrom, *Anthology of Musical Structure and Style,* pp. 445–61).[11] Answer the following questions briefly, but clearly and accurately.

   a. Formal procedures. How is form generated? Refer specifically to techniques of stratification, juxtaposition, and synthesis.

   b. Is there an overall dynamic/textural/formal design? Represent it graphically.

   c. Pitch Centricity. Are there any pitch centers? How are they established? Provide specific examples.

   d. Rhythm and meter. What are the most salient aspects of this section?

   e. Harmony. Explain the following sonorities (thinking in terms of polychords—sonorities made up of two or more other simpler chords—will help in some cases):

---

[11]Wennerstrom, Mary. *Anthology of Musical Structure and Style* (Englewood Cliffs, NJ: Prentice Hall, 1983).

- Strings, reh. 13
- Bassoon and cello, mm. 1–4 after reh. 14
- Cellos and double basses, reh 16 (provide the pitch-class set for the combined sonority)

f. Comment briefly on thematic material in this section. Provide a general commentary and also specific information (range, type of intervals, type of melody) for each of the following passages:

- English horn, reh. 14 (provide pitch-class set)
- Trumpet, reh. 15
- Bassoon, reh. 19
- French horn, reh. 25 (provide pitch-class set)
- Trumpets, 5 mm. after 28

g. Explain the texture in the following passages:

- Reh. 13
- Reh. 14 (mm. 1–4)
- Reh. 28
- Reh. 32

3. Write a brief analytical paper on Debussy, "La fille aux cheveux de lin," no. 8 from *Preludes,* Book I. This piece includes numerous pentatonic passages. Identify the pentatonic structures, the scales they are based on, their pitch center, and justify your decisions. Discuss matters of pitch centricity throughout the piece, and for the piece as a whole. Discuss also thematic and motivic content, relationships between different motives, and formal design.

4. Write a brief analytical paper on Bartók, *Eight Hungarian Folksongs,* no. 1. Discuss pentatonicism in this song. What is pentatonic, and what is not? Discuss pitch centricity. How does the composer define and create centricity?

5. The following are possible pieces on which you may write brief analytical papers in application of the concepts and techniques you have learned in this chapter. You may model your papers on the discussions of "La cathédrale engloutie" and the Introduction to Part I of *The Rite* in this chapter. Your discussions should cover form, motivic and thematic relationships, harmonic techniques, pitch organization, tonality or pitch centricity, and salient aspects of meter, rhythm, and texture.

a. Debussy, "La puerta del vino," no. 3 from *Preludes,* book II

b. Stravinsky, "Ritual of the Rival Tribes," from *The Rite of Spring*

c. Stravinsky, "Soldier's March," from *L'histoire du soldat*

d. Stravinsky, "Music to Scene 1," from *L'histoire du soldat*

III. Composition

1. Compose a short piece for piano in the style of Debussy's "La cathédrale engloutie." Use a variety of the materials and techniques we have studied in that piece, including pentatonic and modal scales, planing, motivic coherence, pedal-defined centricity, quartal and quintal chords, and so on. Design your formal plan, your

long-range tonal scheme, and your formal proportions (including the use of the Golden Section) following the model provided by Debussy's prelude.

2. Compose a short piece for four instruments of your choice in the style of Stravinsky's "Introduction to Part I" of *The Rite of Spring*. Use a variety of the materials and techniques we have studied in that piece, including (0257)-derived motives; stratification, juxtaposition, and synthesis; ostinatos and motivic extension/truncation of cell-derived themes; changing meters and metric displacement of motivic cells; pedal-defined centricity and polytonality.

Chapter 2

Pitch Centricity and Symmetry

Various types of symmetrical pitch structures (as well as other types of musical symmetry) have been used by composers of post-tonal music throughout the twentieth century. We begin this chapter by examining several types of post-tonal symmetrical structures, including equal divisions of the octave, symmetrical motivic cells, and spatial symmetry around an axis. In Chapter 1 we discussed pitch centricity that resulted from the use of diatonic and pentatonic scales. In the second part of this chapter we will continue our study of pitch centricity generated by scales, in particular by three types of symmetrical collections: the whole-tone, the octatonic, and the hexatonic scales. Because the works of Béla Bartók (1881–1945) display frequent examples of symmetrical structures, including the use of whole-tone, octatonic, and hexatonic scales, we will draw upon Bartók's music for our examples and analyses throughout this chapter.

INTERVAL CYCLES AND EQUAL DIVISIONS OF THE OCTAVE

An **interval cycle** is a succession of repeated, equal intervals. In Figure 2.1 the complete chromatic space is represented as a clock face, with the twelve "hours" now representing the twelve pitch classes. In Chapter 1 we used a system to label pitch classes with integers that we compared to "moveable do": 0 was assigned to whatever pitch class was listed first in a particular set. We will also use another system of notating pitch classes with integers, comparable to "fixed do." By convention, in the "fixed do" system we will always assign integer 0 to pitch-class C, and go up the chromatic set of pitch classes, counting half steps up from C. Thus, integer and pitch-class equivalences are as follows (enharmonically equivalent pitch classes, such as F♯ and G♭, are represented by the same integer):

C–0, C♯–1, D–2, D♯–3, E–4, F–5, F♯–6, G–7, G♯–8, A–9, A♯–10, B–11

NOTE

Pitches are sounds. In order to communicate about them, we need to represent them with some symbols. Any symbols we choose to use for that purpose will be conventional: we can refer to sounds with letters (such as C, D, E), or with arbitrary syllables (such as do, re, mi), or with numbers (such as 0, 1, 2), among many other symbols. Numbers are no more conventional than letters to refer to pitches, and in some ways they are more practical. When we use numbers to refer to pitches or pitch classes, keep in mind that the number is just a way of naming a pitch class and that what we are naming with a number, the same as with a letter, is still a musical sound (a note).

Following this convention, you can think of the hours in the clock face as pitch classes, with C placed at the twelve o'clock spot. If we label intervals with an integer representing the number of semitones contained in the interval, then we refer to the semitone as interval 1 (or i1), the whole tone as interval 2 (i2), the minor 3rd as i3, the major 3rd as i4, the perfect 4th as i5, and the tritone as i6. Six interval cycles are represented in Figure 2.1. Each interval cycle is identical to the interval cycle generated by the interval's complement or intervallic inversion (the complement or intervallic inversion of the semitone i1 is the major 7th, i11; the complement of the whole tone i2 is the minor 7th, i10; and the same for i3/i9, i4/i8, and i5/i7; the complement of the tritone, i6, is also i6). For instance, interval cycle 3 (Figure 2.1c), generated by the minor 3rd, is the same as interval cycle 9, generated by the minor 3rd's inversion, the major 6th. If you read Figure 2.1c clockwise, you are reading interval cycle 3, whereas if you read it counterclockwise, you are reading interval cycle 9. Thus, we can label the six interval cycles as 1/11, 2/10, 3/9, 4/8, 5/7, and 6, respectively.[1]

NOTE

Because of octave equivalence, complementary intervals are equivalent in pitch-class space. That is, a minor second (i1, for instance E–F) and the complementary major seventh (i11, or F–E in our example) are made up of the same pitch classes, hence they form one single intervallic category in pitch-class space. This explains why, in pitch-class space, complementary interval cycles are identical.

The six interval cycles represented in Figure 2.1 in pitch-class space are as follows:

1. A *cycle of semitones* (the 1/11 cycle) divides the octave into twelve equal segments (the *chromatic scale*). There is only one chromatic scale (Example 2.1a).

---

[1]Extensive theoretical developments and analytical applications of interval cycles can be found in George Perle, *Twelve-Tone Tonality* (Berkeley: University of California Press, 1977) and *The Listening Composer* (Berkeley: University of California Press, 1990); and Dave Headlam, *The Music of Alban Berg* (New Haven: Yale University Press, 1996).

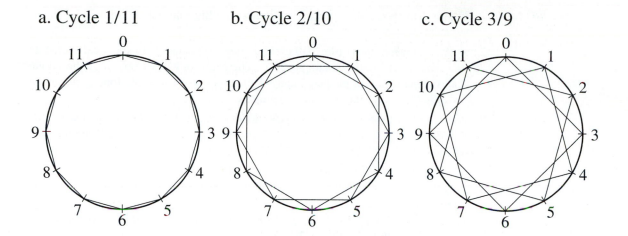

a. Cycle 1/11

b. Cycle 2/10

c. Cycle 3/9

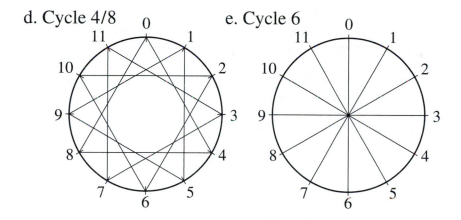

d. Cycle 4/8

e. Cycle 6

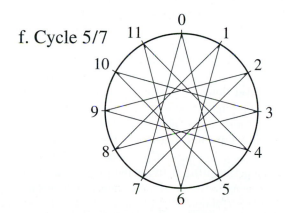

f. Cycle 5/7

Figure 2.1 The interval cycles

Figure 2.1a shows the cycle of semitones dividing the octave into twelve equal segments.

2. A *cycle of whole tones* (the 2/10 cycle) divides the octave into six equal segments (the *whole-tone scale,* Example 2.1b). There are only two possible whole-tone scales using different pitches. Figure 2.1b shows the two whole-tone cycles, each dividing the octave into six equal segments.

3. A *cycle of minor thirds* (the 3/9 cycle) divides the octave into four equal segments (the *fully diminished seventh chord,* Example 2.1c). There are only three possible different °7 chords. The three cycles of minor thirds dividing the octave into equal segments are shown in Figure 2.1c.

4. A *cycle of major thirds* (the 4/8 cycle) divides the octave into three equal segments (the *augmented triad,* Example 2.1d). There are only four possible different augmented-triad chords. The four cycles of major thirds dividing the octave into equal segments are shown in Figure 2.1d.

5. A *cycle of tritones* (the 6 cycle) divides the octave into two equal segments (Example 2.1e). There are six possible different tritones, as shown in Figure 2.1e.

6. A *cycle of perfect fourths* (the 5/7 cycle) divides the octave into twelve equal segments. There is only one 5/7 cycle (this is the familiar "circle of fifths"), because, as is the case with the 1/11 cycle, we need to go though all twelve pitch classes before we get back to the initial pitch class. Both the diatonic scale and the pentatonic scale are segments of the 5/7 cycle.

The diatonic scale, on which functional tonality is based, divides the octave unequally into some combination of tones and semitones. In pitch-class space, all six interval cycles divide the octave equally, as we can see in Figure 2.1. In pitch space, however, one cycle, the 5/7 cycle (the circle of fifths), does not divide the octave equally. Each of the five remaining interval cycles divides the octave into equal segments both in pitch and in pitch-class spaces. All of these equal divisions are non-diatonic and symmetrical (that is, we can read the pitch-class collections that result from these divisions forward or backward, and in both cases we will end up with the same intervals). The five equal divisions are illustrated as pitch collections in Example 2.1.

In Bartók's music we can find numerous instances of pitch collections that result from an equal division of the octave, both at the local level (themes and motives) and at the structural level (long-range tonal planning). Later in the chapter we will study examples that use the whole-tone scale and the octatonic scale (a symmetrical scale that contains equal divisions of the octave).

Many of Bartók's themes unfold in a chromatic space. *Music for String Instruments, Percussion, and Celesta* (1936) opens with a fugal subject that chromatically fills the space of a perfect fifth. Between the subject and the answer the total chromatic space is covered, using only the minor second, major second, and augmented second/minor third intervals (Example 2.2a). The same description (a total chromatic space covered only by means of minor, major, and augmented seconds) applies to the theme from the Concerto for Orchestra (1943) reproduced in Example 2.2b.

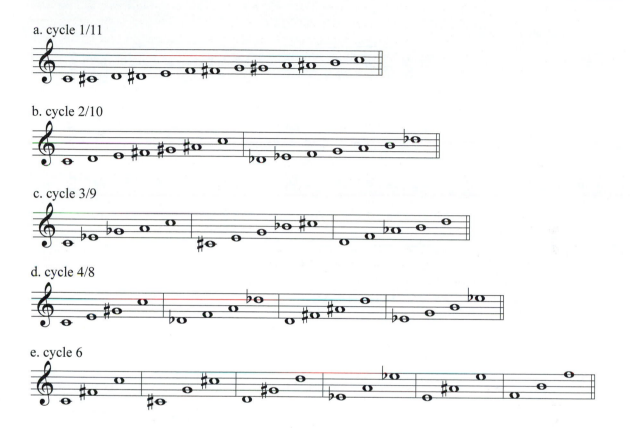

♪♪♪ Example 2.1   Equal divisions of the octave

a. cycle 1/11

b. cycle 2/10

c. cycle 3/9

d. cycle 4/8

e. cycle 6

The tritone is in many ways essential to Bartók's language. At the local level, many of his themes are based on melodic tritone relationships. This is the case with the themes from *Music for String Instruments, Percussion, and Celesta* shown in Example 2.3a–c, and the theme from the Concerto for Orchestra shown in Example 2.3d. At a more structural level, the first movement from the *Music for String Instruments, Percussion, and Celesta* begins with the fugal subject we have seen in Example 2.2a, centered around A. The climax of the movement is reached in m. 56 (the Golden Section), where all high strings sound an E♭ (a tritone away from the initial A) in octaves and *fff*. The movement ends again on a unison A.

SYMMETRICAL MOTIVIC CELLS

Symmetrical motivic cells (which we will identify as pitch-class sets) are some of the basic building blocks in Bartók's music. Three of Bartók's characteristic cells, usually

Example 2.2a   Bartók, *Music for String Instruments, Percussion, and Celesta,* I, mm. 1–8

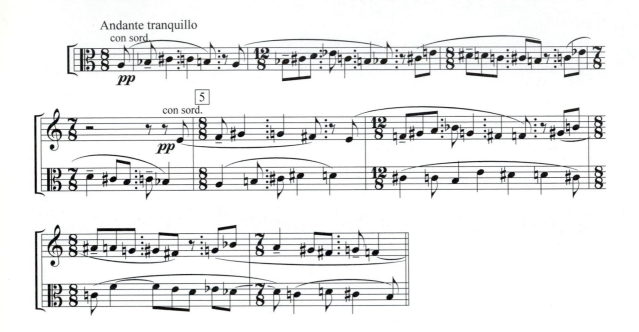

Example 2.2b   Bartók, Concerto for Orchestra, I, mm. 51–58

Example 2.3a   Bartók, *Music for String Instruments, Percussion, and Celesta,* II, mm. 5–8

a.

Example 2.3b   Bartók, *Music for String Instruments, Percussion, and Celesta,* II, mm. 19–23

b.

Example 2.3c   Bartók, *Music for String Instruments, Percussion, and Celesta,* II, mm. 176–77

c.

Example 2.3d   Bartók, Concerto for Orchestra, I, mm. 58–60

d.

♫♪ Example 2.4   Bartók's cells x, y, and z

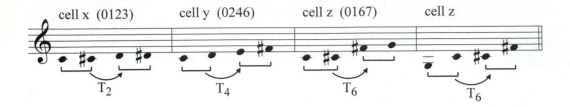

cell x (0123)   cell y (0246)   cell z (0167)   cell z

T_2 T_4 T_6 T_6

known as **cells x, y, and z,** are shown in Example 2.4.[2] Cell x, represented by prime form (0123), is a segment of a chromatic scale. Cell y, represented by prime form (0246), is a segment of a whole-tone scale. And cell z, represented by prime form (0167), can be understood as two overlapping tritones (in our example, C–F♯ and C♯–G, respectively), or as two half-step cells a tritone away from each other (C–C♯ and F♯–G). It often appears, as an actual motive, as two perfect fourths a tritone away from each other, G–C–C♯–F♯ (the two overlapping tritones are now G–C♯ and C–F♯), as also shown in Example 2.4. All three sets are of the type that we call inversionally symmetrical. We will study inversionally symmetrical sets in more detail in Chapter 3. For the time being, it will be sufficient to understand that this type of set is symmetrical around an axis of symmetry, or, in other words, that the same intervals (and the same prime form) will result whether we read these sets forward or backward (verify this property with cells x, y, and z).

Bartók's symmetrical cells, moreover, display a property common to most (though not all) symmetrical sets. We call this property **transpositional combination,** and it results when a set can be divided into two or more segments related among themselves by transposition. This is shown by the brackets and arrows in Example 2.4. Cell x, for instance, can be divided into two segments, and the second segment is a transposition of the first one up a major second. We can express this transposition by the symbol T_2, where T stands for "transposition" and 2 represents the major second, an interval that consists of two semitones. Similarly, cell y results from the transpositional combination of a whole-step cell transposed at T_4; and both arrangements of cell z feature transpositional combination at T_6.[3]

---

[2]The labels x, y, and z for these cells were first used by George Perle in "Symmetrical Formations in the String Quartets of Béla Bartók," *Music Review* 16 (1955): 300–312, and Leo Treitler in "Harmonic Procedure in the *Fourth Quartet* of Béla Bartók," *Journal of Music Theory* 3 (1959): 292–98. For a detailed study of these and other symmetrical cells in the music of Bartók, see Chapters 4 and 5 of Elliott Antokoletz's *The Music of Béla Bartók: A Study of Tonality and Progression in Twentieth-Century Music* (Berkeley: University of California Press, 1984). See also Ernö Lendvai, *Béla Bartók: An Analysis of His Music* (London: Kahn and Averill, 1971), and *The Workshop of Bartók and Kodaly* (Budapest: Edition Musica Budapest, 1983).

[3]On transpositional combination, see Richard Cohn, "Inversional Symmetry and Transpositional Combination in Bartók," *Music Theory Spectrum* 10 (1988): 19–42.

Example 2.5a   Bartók, Fourth String Quartet, I, mm. 1–2

Cells x, y, and z may appear melodically or harmonically in Bartók's music, and they may appear individually or in combinations. In the latter case, they often occur in the form of progressions from x to y and from y to z. In both cases we can think of a process of expansion, from chromatic to whole tone (x to y), or from whole tone to tritonal (y to z). Examples of x, y, and z cells used in a variety of ways appear in the Fourth String Quartet (1928). In mm. 1–2, shown in Example 2.5a, cell x is first introduced both melodically and in a two-voice texture. Mm. 5–7 show two cases of expansions from cell x to cell y. In mm. 8–11 a series of staggered entrances of cell x lead to a harmonic cell y, followed by the progressions x–y and y–x–y, as shown in Example 2.5b. A similar passage in mm. 49–52 shows a further expansion, this time from x to y and from y to z (Example 2.5c).

The z cell is a common occurrence in Bartók's music. An example of a z cell presented melodically, and furthermore harmonized with a y cell, appears in the Fourth String Quartet, m. 22 (Example 2.6a, page 48). Example 2.6b on page 48 shows a reduction of a passage from *Music for String Instruments, Percussion, and Celesta,* where cell z is presented in ever closer imitation with inverted forms of itself (stretto in inversion).

A NOTE ON IMITATION

Imitation of various types is very common in the music of Bartók. **Imitation** *is the successive statement of the same thematic material in two or more voices. Imitation may be at the same pitch level (unison or octave) or at a transposed pitch level (such as the fifth, the fourth, or any other interval). Imitation may be literal (such as real imitation in fugues) or slightly varied (such as tonal imitation in fugues). Various transformations may be applied to imitation (as compared to the original presentation of the*

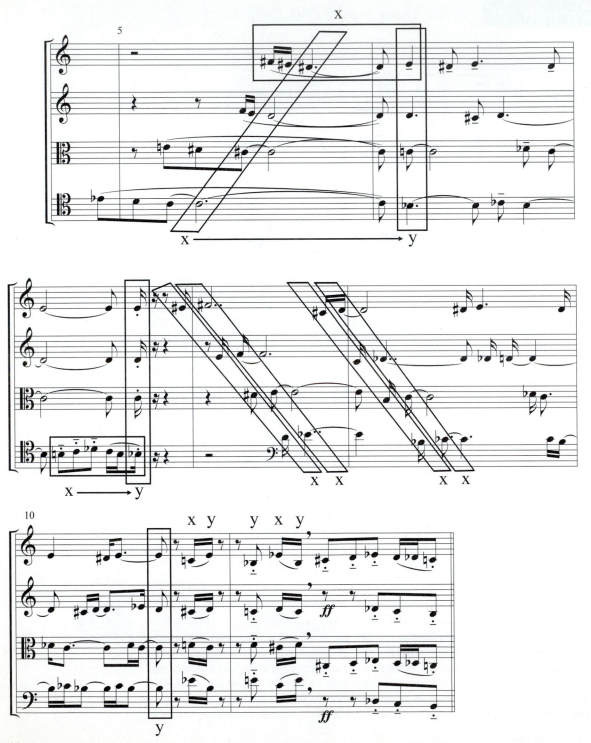

Example 2.5c   Bartók, Fourth String Quartet, I, mm. 49–52

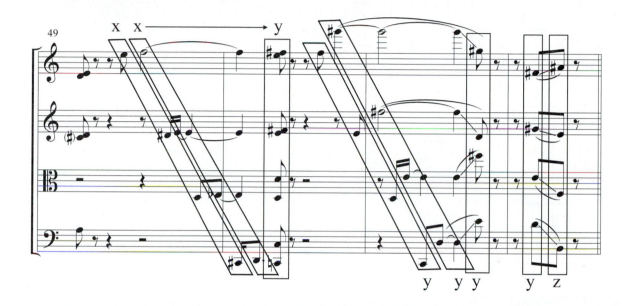

material). For instance, imitation may be by contrary motion or inversion (the up or down contour or the theme is reversed), or it may be in augmentation or diminution (note values are proportionally increased or decreased, or it may be in retrograde (the theme is read backward). Example 2.2a shows a case of literal imitation at the fifth, and Example 2.6b features imitation by contrary motion. If you look ahead to Example 6.13, you will also see imitation by contrary motion in mm. 1–2, and slightly varied imitation in mm. 12–13. See also Example 2.16, as well as numerous instances of imitation in Anthology nos. 5 and 6.

SYMMETRY AROUND AN AXIS

We will now discuss the type of symmetrical structure that results from textural, spatial **symmetry around an axis.** In this type of musical structure, the axis is a pitch or pitch class at midpoint between all the notes in the texture, and all intervals above and below this axis are the same, as if reflected in the mirror represented by the axis. In music arranged in a spatially symmetrical structure, we can say that the axis of symmetry functions as a pitch center (a literal, spatial pitch center around which all the notes are balanced). Examine the fragment from Bartók's "Whole-Tone Scale," from *Mikrokosmos* (1932–39), reproduced in Example 2.7. How is this phrase composed from a

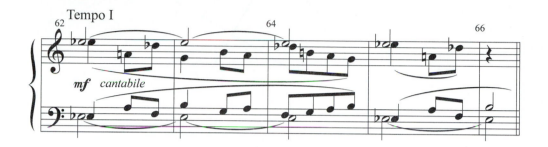

♪♪♪ Example 2.7   Bartók, "Whole-Tone Scale," from *Mikrokosmos,* vol. 5, mm. 62–66

♪♪♪ Example 2.8   Symmetrical lines around E♭/A

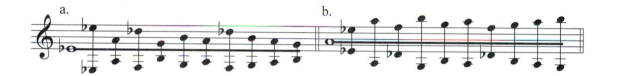

textural point of view? It is visually apparent that right and left hands feature perfect mirror symmetry, and if you look carefully, you will see that the actual intervals are indeed the same. What is the pitch that functions as an axis of symmetry? You can figure this out easily at the piano or by dividing the intervals among both voices into two equal parts. The result will be E♭ (specifically E♭4, an imaginary axis of symmetry, because this exact pitch does not appear in this phrase).

Any two pitches are symmetrical around an axis of symmetry. The axis may itself be a pitch (if you think of the sixth B–G, pitch E♭ is the axis of symmetry) or it may be an imaginary axis placed between two pitches (for instance, the fourth C–F is symmetrical around an axis that is placed between D and E♭). In pitch-class space, the sixth B–G can be inverted into the third G–B, and then the axis of symmetry becomes A, the pitch class a tritone away from our previous axis of symmetry, E♭. In other words, any two pitch classes are symmetrical around a double axis of symmetry, and the two pitch classes that make up the axis are related by tritone. Pitch classes B–G are then symmetrical around the axis A–E♭. Example 2.8 illustrates this property graphically. In Example 2.8a you can see the symmetrical lines from Bartók's "Whole-Tone Scale," showing that the axis of symmetry is E♭. In Example 2.8b, on the other hand, the order of the lines has been inverted (with the consequent inversion of the harmonic intervals between the lines), and now the axis of symmetry is A.

a.

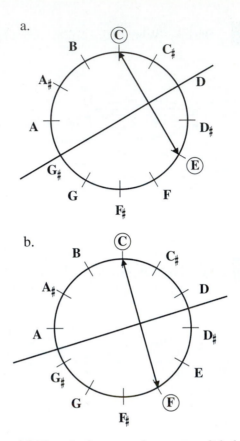

Figure 2.2 The axis of symmetry between two pitch classes

The double axis of symmetry can be easily figured out numerically. Given two pitch classes a and b (for example, C–E, or 0–4 in integer notation), their axes of symmetry are determined by the formulas $\frac{a+b}{2}$ and $\frac{a+b}{2} + 6$. In the case of C–E, the first formula gives us pitch class 2, or D, and the second formula gives us pitch class 8 (that is, 2 + 6), or G♯. If the sum of the two pitch-class numbers is an odd number, then the two axes of symmetry are two half-step dyads a tritone apart. Take pitch classes C and F, or 0–5. (0 + 5)/2 is 2.5, so the axis dyads are 2–3 (D–D♯) and 8–9 (G♯–A). We can also represent the axis of symmetry between two pitch classes on a clockface, as shown in Figure 2.2. In Figure 2.2a we see that the axis of symmetry between C and E is a line that connects the two pitch classes a tritone apart that we just figured out numerically, G♯ and D. In 2.2b we see that the axis of symmetry between C and F is a line drawn between pitch classes D–D♯ and between pitch classes G♯–A (two half-step dyads a tritone apart).

At times, symmetrical structures are not quite as apparent as in the "Whole-Tone Scale" phrase. Examine the fragment from Bartók's *Bagatelle* no. 2 (1908) reproduced in Example 2.9. You will observe that the right hand expands symmetrically around an imaginary axis of symmetry, E♭. Moreover, the major second D–E in the left hand also

 **Example 2.9**   Bartók, *Bagatelle* no. 2, mm. 19–26

is symmetrical around the same pitch class, E♭. Applying the formulas we just learned to determine the double axis of symmetry between pitch classes D and E gives us the dyad 3–9, pitch classes E♭–A. E♭ is indeed the axis in mm. 19–20. In mm. 21–23, the left hand preserves the D–E dyad centered around E♭, while the right hand introduces the A♭–B♭ dyad, centered around A. In mm. 24–26, however, both the right and left hands feature symmetrical structures centered around the A axis. In other words, in this passage Bartók is explicitly taking advantage of symmetrical pitch-class structures and of their double axis of symmetry: in mm. 19–20 the axis is E♭; in mm. 24–26 the axis switches to A, a tritone away from E♭, while in the intervening measures, 21–23, the double axis E♭–A is present if we consider each of the hands separately. We can thus say that pitch-class centricity in this passage is provided by the double axis of symmetry E♭–A.

SYMMETRICAL SCALES

We will now study two symmetrical scales that were widely used by twentieth-century composers, in particular composers in the first half of the century: the whole-tone scale and the octatonic scale. We will also discuss a third scale in the same category of symmetrical collections, the hexatonic scale.[4] The labels we will use to identify these scales

---

[4]A study of these three scale types in the context of chromatic organizations of tonal spaces can be found in Chapter 6 of Fred Lerdahl's *Tonal Pitch Space* (Oxford: Oxford University Press, 2001).

♪♪ Example 2.10   Whole-tone scales

are based on the fixed-do system of integer notation that we have discussed earlier in this chapter (and whereby integer 0 is assigned to pitch-class C).

The Whole-Tone Scale

The **whole-tone scale** divides the octave into six whole tones. There are only two possible whole tone scales using different pitch classes, as shown in Example 2.10. The first one (the "even scale") contains pitch classes (0, 2, 4, 6, 8, 10), and we will refer to it as WT_0 (because it includes pitch-class C, or 0). The second scale (the "odd scale") contains pitch classes (1, 3, 5, 7, 9, 11), and we will label it as WT_1 (because it contains pitch class C♯, or 1). The whole-tone scale contains two symmetrical halves of three notes each, and the two halves are at the distance of a tritone C–D–E//F♯–G♯–A♯). In other words, the two halves are related by transposition at the tritone, and hence the whole-tone scale features transpositional combination at T_6.

Because of the symmetrical nature of the whole-tone scale and because of its intervallic uniformity, any pitch class can function as a "center," depending on the contextual stress on one or another pitch class, although the scale immediately takes us away from any references to functional harmony or to the major-minor system. In Analysis 2.1 we will study in some detail a whole-tone piece by Bartók.

The Octatonic Scale

The **octatonic scale** is an eight-note scale in which semitones (S) and tones (T) alternate. Because of its interesting symmetrical properties and because of its various possible symmetrical partitions, this scale has been particularly favored by numerous twentieth-century composers. Study the scale in Example 2.11a. If you begin on C and play a succession of alternating semitones and tones, you will construct the first scale in the example, which we have labeled as OCT (0,1) because it includes pitch classes C and C♯. If you transpose this scale a half step up, you will have the scale we have labeled OCT (1,2), which contains pitch classes C♯ and D. Another ascending half-step transposition will give you a third scale, OCT (2,3). But if you transpose it once more up a half step (beginning on E♭), the scale will now contain exactly the same pitch classes as OCT (0,1), our original scale. In other words, only three different transpositions of this form of the octatonic scale are possible.

There is, however, another form of the scale, also shown in Example 2.11a. Instead of alternating a semitone–tone (S–T) pattern, we can also alternate a tone–semitone

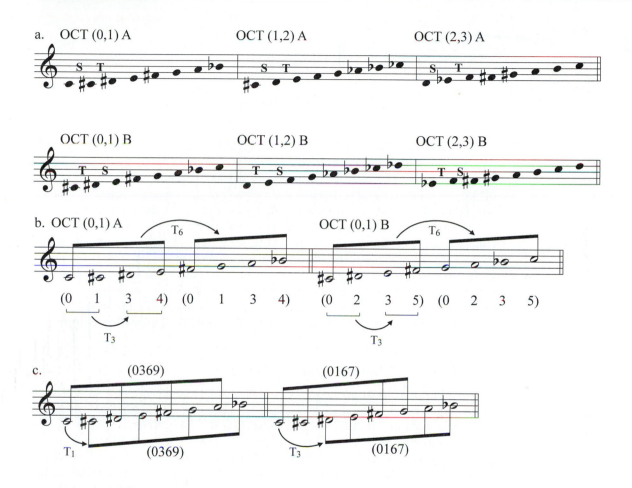

Example 2.11   Octatonic scales

(T–S) pattern. This form of the octatonic scale also allows only three possible different transpositions. The pitch-class content of these three scales, however, is the same as the content of the original three scales. So we still have only three octatonic collections, although presented in two possible orderings each. We will refer to the scale that results from alternating a S–T pattern as "model A," and to the scale that alternates a T–S pattern as "model B." Thus, the labels OCT (0,1)A and OCT (0,1)B identify an octatonic scale by both its specific pitch content and its model (the ordering of semitones and tones).[5]

---

[5]This system of labeling octatonic scales combines the systems used by Joseph Straus in *Introduction to Post-Tonal Theory,* 3rd ed. (Upper Saddle River, NJ: Pearson/Prentice Hall, 2005) and by Pieter van den Toorn in *The Music of Igor Stravinsky.*

Example 2.12   Pitch centricity in the octatonic scale

Example 2.11b shows the two halves of each scale model as pitch-class sets. The S–T pattern results in two (0134) sets related by T_6 (that is, by tritone transposition), whereas the T–S pattern results in two (0235) sets also related by T_6. Both (0134) and (0235) are symmetrical sets. Both of them feature transpositional combination at T_3, and, in turn, both models of octatonic scale feature transpositional combination at T_6.

Example 2.11c shows two of the most interesting symmetrical partitions of the octatonic scale. In the first place, we see that the scale can be formed by overlapping two diminished-seventh chords [prime form (0369)], in other words, two interval-3 cycles. From this perspective, the octatonic scale (in this case the A model) results from two (0369) sets related by transpositional combination at T_1. In the second partition, we overlap two (0167) sets (Bartók's familiar cell Z), which generate the scale by transpositional combination at T_3. Note that both (0369) and (0167) are highly symmetrical collections.

Pitch Centricity in the Octatonic Scale

The highly symmetrical nature of the octatonic scale complicates the issue of pitch centricity in octatonic music. In principle, we can assume that the pitch class on which we build a particular octatonic scale functions as the pitch center, although we will need to examine a particular musical fragment to confirm the contextual primacy of such a pitch center. Example 2.12 shows an OCT (0,1)A built on pitch class C, so we can think of C as the pitch center. A pitch center in octatonic space, however, can readily be replaced by the pitch class at the distance of a tritone, because the scale is divided symmetrically by these two pitch classes. These are indeed the two pitch classes on which we can build the symmetrical (0134) sets of OCT (0,1)A. We can thus think of a "double pitch-class center," made up of the pitch class that generates the scale and its tritone transposition, C and F♯ in Example 2.12.

The same OCT (0,1)A scale, however, can also be built beginning on D♯, a pitch class on which we can also find the (0134) of OCT (0,1)A. If D♯ is the center, then pitch class A becomes the other member of the double pitch-class center for this particular ordering of OCT (0,1)A. In general, then, in any octatonic scale we can think of four pitch classes that have the potential to become pitch centers. This "pitch-class complex" is made up of the members of the (0369) set built on the pitch class that generates a particular scale. In OCT (0,1)A, for instance, the pitch-class complex that can function as a pitch center is formed by pitch classes C–D♯–F♯–A. In Example 2.12 you can see the

♪♪♪ Example 2.13   Bartók, "Diminished Fifth," from *Mikrokosmos,* vol. IV, mm. 1–22

four members of the (0369) complex organized by tritone-related pairs. Slurs indicate the (0134) collection built on each of the four members of the complex.

Which of the four pitch classes of a (0369) complex becomes the actual pitch center, or which of the two possible tritone-related pairs becomes the double pitch-class center, depends on contextual factors that must be determined by examining a particular piece or musical passage. Let us examine the fragment by Bartók shown in Example 2.13. Various factors contribute to our hearing four distinct phrases in this passage. These factors are register, thematic material, and use of rests. Thus, we hear mm. 1–5 as the first phrase (ending on rests). Mm. 6–11 form the second phrase, also ending on rests, and related to the first one by common thematic material, but now presented at a higher register. Phrase 3 (mm. 12–19) can be heard as containing two phrase segments (mm. 12–15 and 16–19, respectively), and it is based on new, contrasting material, also treated imitatively.

Now let's identify the pitch collections in this passage. The right hand begins with a four-note ascending motive, A–B–C–D, which is imitated in the left hand by contrary motion, A♭–G♭–F–E♭. If we build an ascending scale with these pitches, starting with the lowest pitch, E♭, we come up with E♭–F–G♭–A♭//A–B–C–D (with the bars showing the motivic division of this scale in the music). This is OCT (2,3)B, with each of its two (0235) tetrachords presented separately by the motives in the two hands (and creating an imitative pattern at the tritone, hence the title, "Diminished Fifth"). In this context, we can identify pitch classes E♭–A as the double pitch-class center for this passage because each of the scale segments (the motives in each hand) are generated by upward motion from E♭ or A. The varied restatement of the first phrase, in mm. 6–11, uses the same tetrachordal collections as before, and the same OCT (2,3)B scale, but now the hands have switched motivic and pitch material: the left hand segment is generated up from A, and the right hand up from E♭. The double pitch-class center is the same, but in inverted order: A–E♭.

If we examine the pitch content of mm. 12–15, we will identify a different octatonic scale, OCT (0,1)B, minus two pitch classes, E and B♭. In the second segment of this phrase, mm. 16–19, we identify the same scale, OCT (0,1)B, now minus G and D♭. Notice that the complete OCT (0,1) B can be constructed if we consider the complete phrase in mm. 12–19. Following the same criteria as before, we choose pitch classes G–D♭ as the double center for mm. 12–15 because they are the lowest pitches in each hand, and we generate the trichordal scale fragments in each hand from these pitches. In mm.16–19, however, we hear E–B♭ as the double center because of the same reasons we just stated (note that the double center in mm. 12–15 consists of the pitches missing from mm. 16–19, and the double center in mm. 16–19 is made up of the pitches missing from mm. 12–15!).

Example 2.14   The scales and pitch-class centers in mm. 1–19 of Bartók's "Diminished Fifth"

a.   OCT(2,3)B

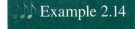

b.   OCT(0,1)B

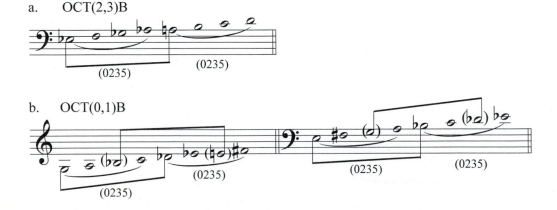

We can see this complex of double centers in Example 2.14. In Example 2.14a we see the scale for mm. 1–11, OCT (2,3)B, and the double center for this passage, E♭–A. In 2.14b, on the other hand, we see the scale for mm. 12–19, OCT (0,1)B, showing both of the possible double centers for this scale [forming the complete (0369) pitch-class complex we described previously]: G–D♭, and B♭–E. These are the two double centers that we have identified in mm. 12–19, G–D♭ for mm. 12–15, and B♭–E in mm. 16–19 (actually found as E–B♭ on the music because of the registral arrangement of the scale in these measures). We can also see, at the end of Example 2.13, that the original motive, as well as the original scale, OCT (2,3)B, and the original double pitch-class center, E♭–A, all return in the phrase that begins in m. 20.

The Hexatonic Scale

The **hexatonic scale** is a six-note scale in which semitones (S) and minor thirds (m3) alternate. The hexatonic scale can be transposed only four times by a half step before it turns into itself with the fifth transposition. Example 2.15a shows the four possible hexatonic scales, which we will label as HEX (0,1), HEX (1,2), HEX (2,3), or HEX (3,4), following the same criteria we defined previously for the octatonic scales. As with the octatonic scale, we can begin a hexatonic scale with a semitone followed by a m3, or by a m3 followed by a semitone. We will refer to the first type, which features a S–m3 pattern, as "model A," and to the second type, which features a m3–S pattern,

♪♪♪ Example 2.15   Hexatonic scales

a.

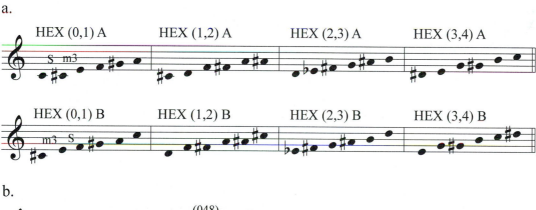

b.

as "model B." Thus, the pitch class content of HEX (0,1)A and HEX (0,1)B is the same, and the only difference between these two scales is the order of their intervals. In Example 2.15a, we can see that both models are generated by a chain of two transpositional combinations at T_4. Example 2.15b shows that the two halves of the hexatonic scale form the same set, (014), and also that the scale can be generated by overlapping two (048) sets, that is, two interval-4 cycles, or augmented triads.

Although the hexatonic scale is a very interesting symmetrical collection, it has been used by composers less often than its close cousin, the octatonic scale. Example 2.16 shows a hexatonic fragment by Bartók. What hexatonic scales are used in this passage?

ANALYSIS 2.1: BARTÓK, "SONG OF THE HARVEST," FROM *FORTY-FOUR VIOLIN DUETS* (ANTHOLOGY NO. 5)

Play through or listen to Bartók's "Song of the Harvest." Identify and label phrases or sections and thematic content, and try to determine pitch content for each section. After you identify the scales involved in this piece, try to determine possible pitch centers for each of the sections.[6]

Form: Thematic and Pitch Contents

We can speak of five phrases or sections in this duet: mm. 1–5, 6–15, 16–20, 21–29, and 30–33. Based on thematic content, we have alternation of two contrasting phrases, which we can label as a and b. (What other musical elements contribute to this characterization of phrases a and b as contrasting?) The form of the piece will thus be a_1–b_1–a_2–b_2–a_3. In other words, this is a short five-part form in which a refrain, a, is alternated with a couplet, b. Considering the relationship between the two voices, what is the basic contrapuntal principle in each of the five sections? If you examine the pitch content, you will find that the piece is completely octatonic up to the last phrase, mm. 30–33. Each of the first four phrases presents the same type of symmetrical pitch content between both voices: an (0235) octatonic tetrachord (a tetrachord is a collection of four pitches or pitch classes) is stated by each voice, with imitation at the tritone. Phrase 5, however, is not octatonic, although it is still symmetrical. Each voice states an (0235) tetrachord, but the resulting complete scale is not octatonic (notice that the interval of imitation is now a perfect fifth, not a tritone). Instead, we hear the (0235) tetrachord as a Dorian tetrachord rather than as an octatonic tetrachord (like the octatonic collection, the Dorian collection is also symmetrical).

Pitch-Class Collections and Centricity

To be more exact about the pitch content of each phrase, we can state that phrase 1 is built on OCT(2,3)B, phrase 2 on OCT(1,2)B, phrase 3 on OCT(1,2)B, phrase 4 on

---

[6]This piece is discussed by George Perle in *The Listening Composer*, pp. 86–89.

♪♪ Example 2.16   Bartók, Concerto for Orchestra, III, mm. 22–29

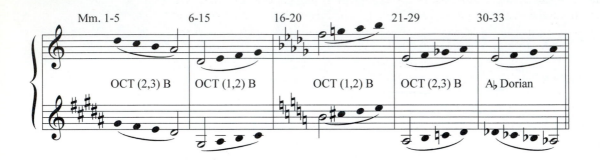

Example 2.17a   Bartók, "Song of the Harvest," pitch-class collections

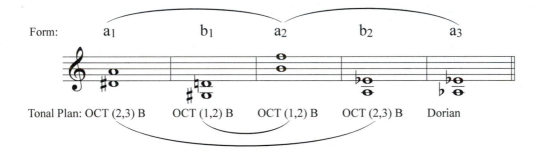

Example 2.17b   Bartók, "Song of the Harvest," form and pitch centricity

OCT(2,3)B, and phrase 5 on A♭ Dorian. These collections are shown in Example 2.17a. We should now decide how we are going to determine pitch centricity within these specific collections. It would seem logical to assign a central function to the lowest pitch class in the octatonic scale as presented in each section. And, as we know, that will also assign a central function to the pitch class a tritone away (except for the Dorian section). The double centers for each section are thus as follows: section a_1, D♯–A; section b_1, G♯–D; section a_2, B–F; section b_2, A–E♭; and section a_3, A♭–E♭ (in the Dorian section, the two symmetrical tetrachords are built on pitches a perfect fifth apart, not a tritone apart). Double-center pairs are shown as half notes in Example 2.17a.

Large-Scale Design

To put all this analysis together, let us examine Example 2.17b. Thematically, sections 1, 3, and 5 correspond as the "a" sections, creating a symmetrical formal design, as shown by the arches above the diagram. Tonally, however, we are surprised by a different symmetrical design, and different section correspondences. Section 1 and 4 (a_1 and b_2) share not only the same scale, OCT(2,3)B, but also the same double center, D#–A (or what is the same, A–E♭). In between them, sections 2 and 3 (b_1 and a_2) also share the same scale, OCT(1,2)B, but now their combined double centers (G#–D and B–F) constitute the complete pitch-center complex for this scale, G#–B–D–F. Tonal symmetry thus involves only sections 1 through 4, as shown by the arches under the diagram in Example 2.17b. What then is the function of the final Dorian section? The double pitch center for section 5 is A♭–E♭, precisely the two pitch classes on which the octatonic scales in section a_1 and b_1 are built! In other words, the final section functions as a tonal synthesis by bringing together the contrasting pitch centers of the two previous octatonic scales.

In summary, a particular feature of this piece is the conflicting symmetrical (or arch) designs between form and tonal content. Why is such a conflict interesting from a compositional, performance, or listening point of view? How does it depart from what we could expect if we think of similar formal designs in the classical repertoire, such as the five-part rondo form?

ANALYSIS 2.2: BARTÓK, "WHOLE-TONE SCALE," FROM *MIKROKOSMOS*, VOL. 5 (ANTHOLOGY NO. 6)

Play through or listen to Bartók's "Whole-Tone Scale." Identify and label phrases or sections and thematic content, and try to determine pitch content for each section. Then try to determine possible pitch centers for each of the sections.

Form and Thematic Content

Formal divisions in this piece seem to be clearly determined by texture and thematic content. The opening theme (theme a) is presented in mm. 1–6 and restated in parallel minor 3rds in mm. 7–12. We can think of these two phrases as the a_1 section. A contrasting theme (theme b) appears in mm. 13–19 (section b_1). How is this theme different from theme a, and how is the texture in this section different from the texture in section a_1? The piece continues with an alternation of sections a and b: a_2 in mm. 20–27, b_2 in mm. 28–34, and a_3 in mm. 35–40. Discuss textural differences in all these sections.

The section in mm. 41–61 can be considered a new contrasting section (section c_1). Not only does it contain a new theme (theme c), but it is also rhythmically and metrically contrasting. Can you explain how Bartók achieves this contrast? In mm. 62–67 we see another statement of the a material (section a_4). How does this section function texturally? Finally, in m. 68 we see a return of the opening material (section a_1 again), at the same tonal level as it was originally presented, and leading to the closing gesture in mm. 74–81.

In summary, the sections can then be labeled as a_1–b_1–a_2–b_2–a_3–c_1–a_4–a_1. The a material clearly functions as a ritornello or refrain, with contrasting sections (verses, episodes, or couplets) presented in between the appearances of the refrain. Example 2.18a shows the main motivic elements in each of the three themes and labels them

Example 2.18a   Bartók, "Whole-Tone Scale," motives

Theme a   Theme b   Theme c

(0268)   (0246)   (0246)   (0248)

Example 2.18b   Bartók, "Whole-Tone Scale," pitch-class collections

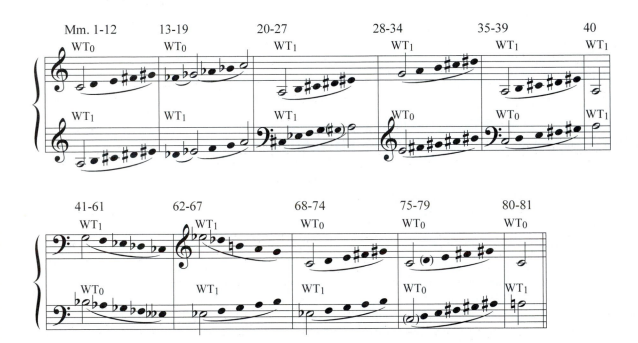

Example 2.18c   Bartók, "Whole-Tone Scale," form and pitch centricity

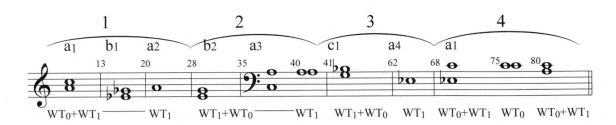

as pitch-class sets. The prime form for motive a is (0268), whereas the prime form for motive b is (0246). Two distinctive motives in theme c relate this third theme to both themes a and b: (0246) is also the prime form for motive b, and (0248) can be related to both motives a and b.

Pitch-Class Collections

It is immediately apparent, as the title indicates, that the complete piece is based on whole-tone collections. As we play through the piece, we can also see that in some sections two different collections are used, whereas other sections are based on a single collection. Example 2.18b presents the complete collection content for each of the sections we have identified previously. In essence, we see that the a_1–b_1 sections are based on $WT_0 + WT_1$; a_2 contains only WT_1; b_2–a_3 are again based on two collections, $WT_1 + WT_0$, until the cadential arrival on pitch A in m. 40, which belongs only to WT_1. The c_1 section is also based on collections $WT_1 + WT_0$, whereas a_4 contains a single collection, WT_1. The return of a_1 is again based on $WT_0 + WT_1$, whereas the closing phrase (mm. 75–79) is based only on WT_0. The final cadential interval (the m3 A–C in mm. 80–81) again brings together the two collections, $WT_0 + WT_1$.

Centricity

Deciding upon centricity in each of these sections requires some interpretation of the musical context. How have you decided what pitches function as centers? In the following discussion you can follow Example 2.18b, where central pitches in each collection have been indicated as open notes (half notes). In mm. 1–6, it seems quite clear that C is the center: not only is it the lowest pitch in the collection as presented in the music, but it is sustained as a pedal. In mm. 7–12, on the other hand, we have two different collections, one per hand. While the center in the right hand is still C, the center in the left hand is A. We have already made some reasonable decisions: 1) We have chosen as a center the lowest pitch in the collection as presented in the music, 2) the central role of a pitch may be reinforced through its use as a pedal, and 3) if two different collections are used, we will have a double center, such as the double center A–C in mm. 1–12.

Our premises are first tested in mm. 13–19, and in this section they hardly pass the test. What pitches would you say function as centers in these measures? The pitches in the E♭–G♭ pair seem to be the most logical candidates, although in this case they are not the lowest pitches in the collection (the D♭ and F♭ in m. 18 are clearly lower neighbor notes to E♭ and G♭, respectively). Moreover, in mm. 15–19, two other pitches, A and C, appear as sustained pedals and seem to anchor the collection as centers. These are the highest pitches in the two respective collections as they are presented in the music. So, it seems fair to say that in this passage, each of the two whole-tone collections has its own double center (two pitches a tritone apart): WT_0 is centered around the G♭–C pair, and WT_1 is centered around the E♭–A pair.

The next section also presents its own challenge. It includes a single collection, WT_1, and the right hand, by analogy with mm. 7–12, is centered around A. In the left hand we could think of C♯ as the center, but it does not seem necessary to have two centers when the music is based on a single WT collection. Moreover, the unexpected

G–G♯ motion in m. 23 (the G♯ is foreign to WT_1) leads clearly toward A. So it is better to decide that A is the single center in this section, and also that, in this piece, a section that uses a single collection will also feature a single center. Our premises apply neatly in the ensuing sections: the double center in mm. 28–34 is the pair E–G; in mm. 35–40, the pair C–A; and m. 40 features a single center (and a single pitch), A. Mm. 41–61 again challenge our premises because pitches B♭ and G enjoy a prominent position by virtue of their role as sustained pedals. It seems logical to designate this pair as central, despite the fact that these are not the lowest, but the highest, pitches in their respective collections. Finally, examine the remaining sections in Example 2.18b and explain why the specific pitch centers have been chosen.

Large-Scale Design

Now we can try to make sense of all this information as it defines the piece as a whole, and to do so we can refer to Example 2.18c. If we put together sections, collections, and pitch centers, as presented in this example, we can see that they can be grouped into four large units: a_1–b_1–a_2 // b_2–a_3 // c_1–a_4 // a_1. All these sections end with a return of the refrain, and all but the last one contain some combination of verse and refrain. From a tonal point of view, all four units begin with a double collection ($WT_0 + WT_1$) and a double pitch center, and end with a single collection (WT_1 in units 1, 2, and 3, and WT_0 in unit 4) and a single pitch center. In the case of unit 4, the closing phrase on WT_0 eventually leads to a final cadential gesture for the whole piece, in mm. 80–81, which again brings WT_0 and WT_1 together on the pitches A–C, the same double pitch center which was featured in the opening section of the piece. Tonal closure is thus achieved by a return of the original double center from the beginning of the piece.

How does this analysis of "Whole-Tone Scale" change your vision of this piece? Do you think you know the piece better now? Can you hear it better? How? If you perform it or were to perform it, how would this knowledge and your new way of hearing this piece affect you as a performer?

APPLICATION AND CLASS DISCUSSION

In this chapter we have continued our study of pitch centricity in twentieth-century music. What are the common elements between pitch centricity in common-practice tonal music and pitch centricity as you now understand it in post-tonal music? What are their main differences?

Has symmetry played an important role in music before the twentieth century? Why does it become such a prominent constructive principle in post-tonal music?

Is there any piece in the repertoire that you perform to which some of the criteria and analytical approaches we have practiced in this chapter would apply? If so, bring it to class for discussion, and explain how this chapter has contributed to your understanding of the piece. What other compositions can you think of that feature some type of pitch centricity and/or symmetry?

Further Listening

The following list provides suggestions for further listening to music by Bartók (if possible, listen while following the score):

1. Bartók, *Music for String Instruments, Percussion, and Celesta* (complete)
2. Bartók, Fourth String Quarter (complete)
3. Bartók, Concerto for Orchestra
4. Bartók, Concertos for piano and orchestra nos. 1 and 3

Terms for Review

interval cycle
Bartók's x, y, and z cells
transpositional combination
imitation

symmetry around an axis
whole-tone scale
octatonic scale
hexatonic scale

CHAPTER 2 ASSIGNMENTS

I. Theory

1. Write two different motives (pitch, rhythm and meter) on each of the following symmetrical sets: (0123), (0246), (0167), (0134), and (0235).

2. Write whole-tone scales on the following pitches: F, A♭, D♭, and E. Provide the correct label (WT_0 or WT_1) for each of these scales.

3. Write four different whole-tone themes.

4. Write octatonic scales beginning with the following pairs of pitches: E–F, F♯–G♯, B–C, and G–A. Provide the correct label for each of these scales, such as OCT(0,1)A or OCT(2,3)B.

5. Write four octatonic themes using different octatonic scales.

6. Write hexatonic scales beginning with the following pairs of pitches: E–F, F♯–A, B–C, and G–A♯. Provide the correct label for each of these scales, such as HEX(0,1)A or HEX(2,3)B.

7. Write four hexatonic themes using different hexatonic scales.

8. Write a phrase in two voices for piano or two flutes featuring symmetry around an axis. Your phrase may or may not be based on a whole-tone or an octatonic scale.

II. Analysis

1. Listen to and study Bartók's "From the Island of Bali," no. 109 from *Mikrokosmos* (Anthology no. 8).
    Answer the following questions briefly, but clearly and accurately.

    a. What is the scale basis for mm. 1–2?

    b. What is the prevalent motivic pitch-class set in the whole piece? Explain how and why this set is charac-
        teristic of Bartók from an intervallic point of view.

    c. The opening measures and the last four establish pitch centricity by symmetry. Around what pitch class
        (or pitch classes) are these measures symmetrical? Beware: the actual pitch classes are not present in
        either passage!

    d. The pitch centers that you should have found in question c are also established in other passages. Two of
        them are mm. 19–22 (in a similar way as the passages from question c) and, in a more "traditional" way,
        in mm. 30–38 (notice the lower staff: how is that pitch related to one of the axes of symmetry you identi-
        fied earlier? Does it help you decide for one or the other of the two axes of symmetry?). Comment briefly
        on pitch centricity and its means in these two passages.

    e. Comment on the exact type of imitation found in the following spots:

        *   mm. 1–2

        *   mm. 16–18

        *   mm. 18–20

        *   mm. 21–22 (explain and name the metric/rhythmic event found in these measures)

    f. What is the form of the composition (use letters to label the sections)? What is the role of texture in
        defining form in this piece?

2. Listen to and study Debussy's "Canope," no. 10 from *Preludes,* book II (Anthology no. 2). This piece con-
    tains elements that we have studied in Chapters 1 and 2. Answer the following questions briefly, but clearly
    and accurately.

    a. What is the form of the piece? Is tempo a factor in delineating form?

    b. What is the pitch center for mm. 1–5? How is this pitch center established? What is surprising, given
        this pitch center, about the cadence in mm. 4–5? How are the roots of the two cadential chords related
        (G♭–D)?

    c. What voice-leading technique is used in mm. 1–5? What is the scale basis for the melody (the top voice)
        in mm. 1–3?

    d. How does the melody in mm. 7–10 establish the same pitch center we saw in the opening measures?
        What scale degrees contribute to pitch centricity, and how? Answer the same questions with respect to
        the melody in mm. 11–13 and then 14–16.

    e. What is the supporting harmony for mm. 7–9? And for mm. 11–12?

    f. What pitch center is established, by fairly conventional harmonic means, in mm. 14–16? How is this
        pitch center related to the opening pitch center? Is this a fairly "traditional" relationship?

    g. What root interval determines the harmonic motion in mm. 11 to 14?

    h. What is the formal role of mm. 17–25?

i. Explain the role of melody and motives in articulating pitch centricity in mm. 17–23. If you think in terms of the main pitch center that was established in the opening measures, what degrees are emphasized in these measures?

j. Now focus on mm. 24–25. Explain how symmetry plays a role in articulating pitch centricity in these two measures.

k. Comment on the return of the opening material in mm. 26 and following. To what extent is the return literal, and how does it depart from the original?

l. What is surprising and unexpected in the cadence in mm. 29–30?

m. Although the prelude's ending seems to contradict the opening pitch center from a harmonic point of view, we have seen that, throughout the piece, the melody in the upper voice has been an essential element in establishing pitch centricity. Is this still the case in the four closing measures? How does the melody contribute to the prevalent pitch center for the whole piece?

n. Now look at the chord in mm. 30–33. Could it be that it is really generated from the top rather than the bottom? Explain.

o. The title of the prelude refers to a city in ancient Egypt. What elements (in the texture and metric/rhythmic structure of the piece, as well as in its pitch organization) evoke a remote, ancient world?

p. Write some conclusions about your analysis of this piece. What innovations can you identify in it? What elements, on the other hand, provide a link to traditional formal and tonal organization?

3. Write a brief analytical paper on Bartók's "Diminished Fifth," no. 101 from *Mikrokosmos* (Anthology no. 7). You may use the discussion of the opening measures included in this chapter (see commentary on Examples 2.13 and 2.14) as your point of departure. This piece is almost exclusively octatonic. Discuss the form of the piece (label sections with letters) and its motivic content. Identify the octatonic areas (that is, the passages based on a single octatonic scale), and identify and label the exact octatonic scale used in each. Is there any passage in which a single octatonic scale does not define the pitch content? Discuss the large-scale tonal plan for this piece (including pitch centers for each phrase or section) and how it corresponds with the formal plan.

4. The following are possible pieces on which you may write brief analytical papers in application of the concepts and techniques you have learned in Chapters 1 and 2. Your discussions should cover form, motivic and thematic relationships, pitch organization and pitch collections, tonality or pitch centricity, and salient aspects of meter, rhythm, and texture.

a. Debussy, "Voiles," no. 2 from *Preludes,* book I

b. Bartók, "Crossed Hands," no. 99 from *Mikrokosmos*

c. Bartók, "Bulgarian Rhythm," no. 115 from *Mikrokosmos*

III. Composition

1. Compose a short piece for piano using whole-tone scales, in the style of Bartók's *Mikrokosmos* pieces. Plan the form and tonal plan of your piece, as well as its motivic coherence.

2. Compose a short piece for two melodic instruments of your choice, using octatonic scales and symmetrical motivic cells derived from the octatonic scale. You may use Bartók's "Song of the Harvest" or "Diminished

Fifth" as models. Make sure to plan the form and tonal plan of the piece, as well as its motivic coherence, and be careful to write good and interesting imitative counterpoint between the two voices.

3. Compose a short piece for piano or two melodic instruments of your choice, featuring some type of symmetry around an axis. You may use Bartók's "From the Island of Bali" as your model. The piece may or may not use whole-tone or octatonic materials. You may take advantage of the double axis of symmetry by inverting your voices, as in Example 2.8, or by transposing the same music from one axis to the other, as in Example 2.9.

Chapter 3

Introduction to Pitch-Class Set Theory

In Chapters 1 and 2 we have introduced and used the concept of pitch-class set. We have seen that this concept is particularly useful to label small pitch-class collections and to compare and relate such collections among themselves. We have not only demonstrated how the system can be used analytically to uncover relationships that have immediate musical interest, but also that it would be much more difficult to discover some of these relationships without recourse to pitch-class set theory. In the following chapters we will study music in which pitch centricity is normally avoided, and which is often based on collections of pitch classes, used both motivically or as harmonic building blocks. A general term to refer to such music is "atonal." To deal with this type of music analytically, however, we will need to have a better grasp of pitch-class set theory. Although set theory has been used in recent years as a compositional method, it was originally formulated (by Milton Babbitt and Allen Forte) in the 1960s and 70s, as a theoretical and analytical system particularly applicable to the study of atonal music. We will devote the present chapter to a more systematic and formal presentation of set theory, after which we will be better prepared to succeed in our studies of atonal music.[1]

---

[1]Two pioneering articles in set theory are Milton Babbitt, "Set Structure as a Compositional Determinant," *Journal of Music Theory* 5 (1961): 72–94; reprinted in *The Collected Essays of Milton Babbitt,* ed. Stephen Peles, Stephen Dembski, Andrew Mead, and Joseph Straus (Princeton: Princeton University Press, 2003), pp. 86–108; and Allen Forte, "A Theory of Set-Complexes for Music," *Journal of Music Theory* 8 (1964): 136–83. Extensive presentations of set theory, to which this chapter is indebted, can be found in Allen Forte, *The Structure of Atonal Music* (New Haven: Yale University Press, 1973); John Rahn, *Basic Atonal Theory* (New York: Schirmer, 1980); and Robert Morris, *Composition with Pitch-Classes: A Theory of Compositional Design* (New Haven: Yale University Press, 1987), and *Class Notes For Atonal Music Theory* (Hanover, NH: Frog Peak Music, 1991). See also Joseph Straus, *Introduction to Post-Tonal Theory.* A very important book that provides a different and compelling perspective on the matters and materials studied in our Chapters 3 and 4 is David Lewin's *Generalized Musical Intervals and Transformations* (New Haven: Yale University Press, 1987).

PRELIMINARY CONCEPTS

We are already familiar with some of the basic principles of pitch-class set theory. As we know, a **pitch class** (pc) is a group of pitches with the same name, in any octave. The concept of pitch class implies the property of **octave equivalence**: in set theory we do not distinguish between octave-related pitches with the same name. For instance, any C♯ in any octave is equivalent to any other C♯ in any other octave, and they are all members of the same pitch class. Moreover, the property of **enharmonic equivalence** also applies to pitch-class set theory. Although in functional tonality a C♯ and a D♭ have different functions and cannot be used interchangeably, enharmonically spelled pitches in set theory are members of the same pitch class. That is, C♯ and D♭ are equivalent for our purposes.

We have also introduced the concept of **integer notation.** By notating pitch classes as integers we will be able to realize pitch-class set operations much more efficiently. Always think, however, that you are still dealing with pitches and pitch classes. That is, whether you represent a pitch class with a letter (F, for example) or a number (in the case of F, 5), we are still talking of ways to represent or label an essential musical element (a pitch class). We have also learned that there are two systems of using integers to denote pitch classes. In the "fixed do" system, we assign integer 0, by convention, to pitch-class C (or its enharmonic equivalents, B♯ and D♭♭) and go up the chromatic set of pitch classes, counting half steps up from C. In the "moveable do" system, integer 0 will be assigned to the first pitch class of the set, no matter what that may be. In this chapter we will use each of these systems for different purposes. For the time being, we will begin with the fixed do system. Figure 3.1 shows the integer and pitch-class equivalences that we are already familiar with (as a reminder, let's note again that enharmonically equivalent pitch classes, such as F♯ and G♭, are represented by the same integer).

Because of octave equivalence we have only twelve different pitch classes, although pitch takes place in many different octaves. We will solve the discrepancy by doing all of our pitch-class set operations in ***mod 12* arithmetic** (abbreviation for *modulo 12*). This means that we will use only twelve integers (from 0 to 11), and any integer larger than 11 (or smaller than 0) will be reduced to its equivalent integer within these twelve. To put this in musical terms, we will operate in a single octave, and any pitch outside this octave will be reduced to its equivalent within our octave. Thinking of a clock face (see Figure 3.2) will help you understand *mod 12*. If you think of midnight as being 0 hours, after 12 hours you begin the cycle again: 12 is equivalent to 0, 13 is equivalent to 1, 14 to 2, 15 to 3, and so on. You can reduce any integer to its *mod 12* equivalent by subtracting 12 (or a multiple of 12) from the given integer. For instance, 16 − 12 = 4 (so 16 is 4 in *mod 12*), 19 − 12 = 7 (so 19 is 7 in *mod 12*), and 27 − 24 = 3 (27 is 3 in *mod 12*).

C–0   C♯–1   D–2   D♯–3   E–4   F–5   F♯–6   G–7   G♯–8   A–9   A♯–10   B–11

Figure 3.1 Integer notation for the twelve pitch classes

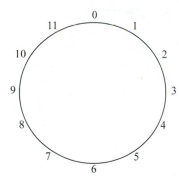

Figure 3.2 The twelve pitch classes on a clock face

U=0   m2=1   M2=2   m3=3   M3=4   P4=5   +4=6

P5=7   m6=8   M6=9   m7=10   M7=11   P8=12

Figure 3.3 Integer representation of intervals (by semitone content)

Interval and Interval Class

Similar to the way we represent pitch classes by integers, intervals can also be represented by integers. An integer representing an interval refers to the number of semitones
in that interval. Enharmonically equivalent intervals (such as an augmented fourth or
a diminished fifth) will be represented by the same integer. You can easily determine
the number of semitones for each interval by looking at the clock face in Figure 3.2 and
thinking of all intervals ascending from C. Figure 3.3 shows the number of semitones
for each interval (without listing all enharmonic equivalences). You should memorize
the integer representation of intervals.

Intervals in the realm of pitch classes (which we will refer to as **pitch-class space**)
are of a different nature than intervals in the realm of pitches (or **pitch space**). In pitch
space, intervals are directional (ascending or descending), and an interval and its inversion are not the same. We will represent ascending motion with a + sign before the
interval integer, and descending motion by means of a − sign. Thus, we can speak of
an ascending P4 from C (+5) or a descending P4 from C (−5). Moreover, an ascending
P4 from C, (C–F, +5), is not the same as a descending P5 from C, (C–F, −7). We will
use pitch space and directional intervals to describe actual pitch motion on the musical
surface. For instance, we know that Debussy's "The Sunken Cathedral" begins with the
ascending motive D–E–B, or (+2, +7). Moreover, intervals in pitch space can be simple
or compound. Thus, an ascending major tenth (+16) is not the same as an ascending
major third (+4).

In pitch-class space, on the other hand, intervals may still be ordered (if we take
into account the distance between two pitch classes considered in a particular order) or

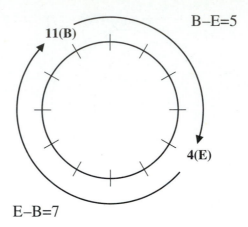

Figure 3.4 Ordered pitch-class intervals

unordered (if we take into account the shortest distance between two pitch classes), but in all cases they will be *mod 12*; that is, we will reduce all intervals to their "simple" equivalents. An **ordered pitch-class interval** is the distance between two pitch classes considered in a particular order (and, by convention, always in an ascending direction). To determine the ordered pc interval between two pcs, subtract the first pc from the second in *mod 12*. In the Debussy motive, the ordered pc interval between E and B (4 and 11) is 11 − 4 = 7. In a different context, the same two pcs could be presented in the order B–E, and then the ordered pc interval would be 4 − 11 = 5 (that is, 16 − 11 = 5 in *mod 12*). To determine an ordered pc interval on a clock face, always measure the distance between pcs clockwise (that is, ascending), as shown in Figure 3.4.

More relevant in pitch-class set theory is the concept of **unordered pitch-class interval** (also called interval class). In a space in which octave equivalence applies, interval E–B is equivalent to interval B–E, and we can represent both by means of a single integer. What matters to us here is not the direction or order of pitch classes, but the shortest span between the two pitch classes. The distance between pitch classes E and B in *mod 12* can be 11 − 4 = 7 or 4 − 11 = 5. We will choose the smallest of these, 5, to represent the unordered pitch-class interval between E and B. To determine an unordered pitch-class interval on a clock face, we measure the distance between two pitch classes following the shortest possible path, be it clockwise or counterclockwise, as shown in Figure 3.5.

In other words, inverted intervals are equivalent in unordered pitch-class space. Because of octave equivalence, the major 3rd C–E is equivalent to its inversion, the minor 6th E–C. We can then group an interval and its inversion in one single category, which we call **interval class** (abbreviated as ic). There are seven interval classes, and their intervallic content is presented in Figure 3.6. Thus, ic 0 is made up of intervals 0 and 12 (unison and octave), ic 1 is made up of intervals 1 and 11 (m2 and M7), and so on. Because two intervals in an interval class are complementary (that is, they add up to an octave), the two integers that represent each ic add up to 12. The only ic that contains

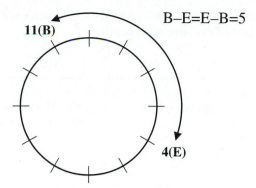

$$B-E=E-B=5$$

Figure 3.5 Unordered pitch-class interval

Interval class	Intervals
0	0, 12
1	1, 11
2	2, 10
3	3, 9
4	4, 8
5	5, 7
6	6

Figure 3.6 The interval classes

a single interval is ic 6, because the tritone inverts into itself. We can now also see that the intervals from the preceding examples are grouped as ic 5 (intervals 5 and 7, P4 and P5) and ic 4 (intervals 4 and 8, M3 and m6).

PITCH-CLASS SETS: ORDERINGS AND BASIC RELATIONSHIPS

A **pitch-class set** (pc set) is an unordered collection of pitch classes. Although the pitch-class members of a pitch-class set may appear in any order on the actual musical surface (and this is what we mean by "unordered collection"), we will have to find a system of organizing them in a way that will allow us to compare different sets. We have already seen this principle applied in Chapters 1 and 2, as when we realized that various motives from Stravinsky's *Rite,* in which pitch classes were ordered in different ways, all were members of the same set class, (0257).

NOTE

To help us understand the concepts introduced in this section, we can think for instance of pitch classes G–E–C. Whether we present them as C–E–G, E–G–C, G–C–E, or as a variety of other possible orderings, we immediately recognize this collection as "the C major triad" (in other words, we mentally order all these collections as root position C major triads). In this process, we have taken for granted that the order of pitch classes does not matter, and we have easily identified all these different groupings with a single term, "the C major triad." Moreover, we can also think of the pitch-class collections C–E–G, B–D–G, and C–F–A and easily recognize that they all belong to the same category, "major triads." We can go one step farther and recognize the collections C–E–G, G–B–E, and E–A–C as "triads," although these collections include both major and minor triads. We can do all of this because we have a well-established system to identify and label triads and tertian sonorities. Thanks to this system, we can identify and compare tertian sonorities and group them into similar categories. In most atonal music, however, we deal with nontertian, nontriadic collections. We need to define a similar system that will allow us to label any collection and to compare collections for similarity or dissimilarity. This is exactly what pitch-class set theory does, as we will learn in the following pages.

The number of elements in a set is known as its **cardinal number.** A set with a cardinal number 3 has three elements, and it is called a **trichord.** A set with a cardinal number 4 is a **tetrachord.** A set with a cardinal number 5 is a **pentachord,** one with a cardinal number 6 is a **hexachord,** and so on with cardinal numbers 7 (**septachord**), 8 (**octachord**), and 9 (**nonachord**). Sets may also have cardinal numbers 1 and 2 (**monad** and **dyad,** respectively) and cardinal numbers 10, 11, and 12, but these five cardinalities have less musical significance as unordered sets.

Normal Order

The first thing we need to do to compare collections of pitch classes is to arrange them in the same, standard ordering. We will call such an ordering the **normal order** (N.O.). *A normal order is an arranging of pitch classes in ascending numerical succession, and in such a way that they cover the shortest possible span.* Take, for instance, pitch classes B♭, F, D, and D♭. The numerical form of this collection is 10, 5, 2, 1. Example 3.1 illustrates the complete process to find the shortest possible span with both musical and numerical notations. We first arrange the pitch classes in ascending order all within the same octave, beginning with any of the pitch classes, as in, for example, 1, 2, 5, 10. Then we need to rotate this arrangement to achieve all the possible circular permutations of this ascending ordering (for a set of n elements, there are n such circular permutations or orderings, so for our tetrachord there will be four orderings). To rotate a set (an operation we call **rotation**), place the first element last, and leave the remaining

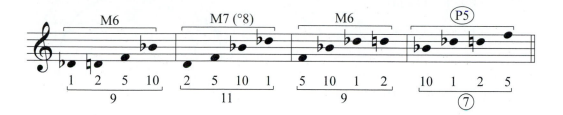

Example 3.1   Rotation of a set

elements as they are. Keep repeating the same process until you end up with the original ordering again. As shown in Example 3.1, the four orderings of our set are (1, 2, 5, 10), (2, 5, 10, 1), (5, 10, 1, 2), and (10, 1, 2, 5). One more permutation would produce our original arrangement, (1, 2, 5, 10). After we have all the possible orderings, we can determine which one covers the shortest possible span. We can do so by looking at the intervals between outer pitches (in our example, M6, M7, M6, and P5), or by subtracting the first pc integer from the last (intervals 9, 11, 9, and 5). We see that the shortest span between outer pitches in our example is provided by the fourth ordering, so this arrangement will be our normal order, which we represent in brackets: [10, 1, 2, 5].

It is not necessary, however, to go though all the orderings one by one as we have done for this example (a very cumbersome process when we are dealing with large sets). A more efficient procedure to determine the normal order of a pc set is as follows:

1. Arrange the pitch classes in ascending order, with the octave on top.

2. Look for the largest interval (computed as an ordered pitch-class interval) between two adjacent pitch classes and relist the set starting with the upper pitch class of the largest interval.

3. If more than one possible ordering results from the two previous steps, you should choose the ordering that is most closely packed to the left. To do so, first check the interval between the first and the next-to-last pcs, and choose the ordering with the smallest such interval. If that still results in a tie, check the interval between the first and third-to-last pcs, and so on.

4. If it is not possible to determine a normal order from step 3 because all steps produce ties, choose the ordering that begins with the smallest pc number.

Let's go back to our collection from Example 3.1: B♭, F, D, D♭ or 10, 5, 2, 1. We first list it in ascending order with the octave on top: 1, 2, 5, 10, 1. We check ordered pitch-class intervals between each of the adjacent pitch classes (by subtracting each pc from the pc to the right of it), and we see that the largest interval is 5 between pcs 5 and 10. We relist the set starting with the upper pc of the largest interval, that is, starting with 10, and the resulting ordering is our normal order, [10, 1, 2, 5]. This process is shown in Figure 3.7a. You can also visualize the procedure on a clock face, following the same

a.   b.

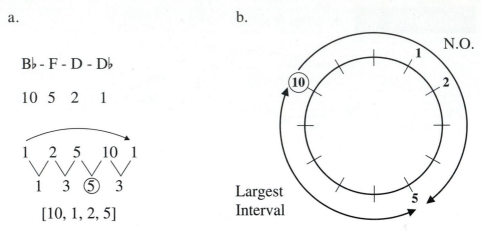

Figure 3.7 Normal order

steps, and as shown in Figure 3.7b. First, list the pcs on the clock face. Then, find the largest interval (in our example, the interval between 5 and 10), and read the set clockwise beginning on the upper pc of the largest interval, [10, 1, 2, 5], which is the N.O. for this set.

Now try the process with sets 8, 3, 2, 6 (the normal order should be [2, 3, 6, 8]) and 10, 7, 2, 9, 1 (normal order [7, 9, 10, 1, 2]). If you try with set 0, 4, 8, 9, 11, however, you will discover that steps 1 and 2 result in two possible normal orders, 4, 8, 9, 11, 0, or 8, 9, 11, 0, 4, because there are two cases of largest interval between two pcs, interval 4 between both 0–4 and 4–8, as shown in Figure 3.8. We thus need to determine which of these two orderings is most closely packed to the left. To do so, we check the interval between the first and the next-to-last pcs. For the first of the two orderings, this interval is $11 - 4 = 7$. For the second ordering, it is $0 - 8 = 12 - 8 = 4$. The second ordering, [8, 9, 11, 0, 4], is thus the normal order because it has the smallest interval between the first and the next-to-last pcs.

Try the process with set 1, 4, 7, 10. You will find that all four orderings feature the same outer interval, and moreover that step 3 does not break the tie (all orderings are equally packed to the left). We then need to apply step 4 and choose the ordering that begins with the smallest pc number, which in this case is [1, 4, 7, 10].

Transpositional Equivalence

Now that we know how to arrange sets into a standard ordering, we can start comparing different sets for equivalence relationships. First we will consider transposition. To compare sets for **transpositional equivalence** (T_n), the sets must first be arranged in normal order. *Two pitch-class sets with the same number of pitch classes are transpositionally equivalent if they can be mapped onto one another (that is, they can be transformed into one another) by adding the same number (or **transpositional operator**) to each pitch class in the set.* Take, for instance, sets [2,3,7,8,9] and [0,1,5,6,7], both

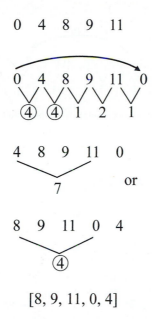

$$[8, 9, 11, 0, 4]$$

Figure 3.8 Normal order for a set with multiple shortest-span orderings

already in normal order. Is there any number we can add to each pc in the first set to map the first set onto the second set? Notice that, by convention, we will transpose the first set into the second (and not the other way around), and we will use a positive transpositional operator (and not a negative one). By adding 10 to each pc in the first set, we come up exactly with the second set. The second set is thus a transposition of the first set, and the transpositional operator is 10 (t = 10). We can say that the second set is T_{10} of the first set. Note that, by convention, we say that t = 10 (a positive value) and not −2 (a negative value). Try now determining whether the following pair of sets (all of which are already in normal order) are T equivalent, and what the transpositional operator is in each case: [0,1,3,4,6] and [2,3,5,6,8]; and [2,3,6,8] and [0,1,4,6].

To transpose a set, add the transpositional operator to each pc. For instance, to transpose [2,3,6,8] by T_2 you will add 2 to each pc of the set to produce [4,5,8,10]. You can also compare two sets for transpositional equivalence by comparing their **adjacency interval series,** that is, the set of ordered pitch-class intervals between adjacent pitch classes. In transpositionally equivalent sets, the adjacency interval series will be the same, as shown in Figure 3.9. We will represent the adjacency interval series (AIS) as a series of integers inside angles, as <1,4,1,1> for the set in Figure 3.9.[2]

The musical significance of transpositional equivalence is illustrated by the opening measures of Webern's Five Movements for String Quartet, op. 5, III (1909), a piece

---

[2]For an article that discusses the properties and implications of intervallic successions such as the AIS, see Richard Chrisman, "Describing Structural Aspects of Pitch-Sets Using Successive-Interval Arrays," *Journal of Music Theory* 21/1 (1977): 1–28.

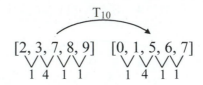

Figure 3.9 Adjacency interval series in transpositionally equivalent sets

♪♪♪ Example 3.2   Anton Webern, Five Movements for String Quartet, op. 5, III, mm. 1–6

that we will study in some detail in Chapter 4. The fragment of this piece shown in Example 3.2 includes twelve sets boxed and numbered. Normal orders for all these sets are provided on the example, and so are the transpositional equivalences among adjacent sets. We see that sets are grouped in pairs or in groups of three transpositionally equivalent sets. Thus, sets 1 and 2 are related by T_8, sets 3 and 4 by T_7, sets 5 and 6 by T_{11}. The example concludes with two chains of three trichords each, related respectively by T_9–T_{10} (sets 7–8–9) and T_9–T_4 (sets 10–11–12). Considering nonadjacent trichords, sets 1, 2, 5, 6, 10, 11, and 12 are all transpositionally equivalent.

Inversional Equivalence

As we have just seen, an important perceptual (and hence musical) property of transposition is that it preserves intervals. The same property applies also to inversional

♪♪♪ **Example 3.3**   Transposition and inversion

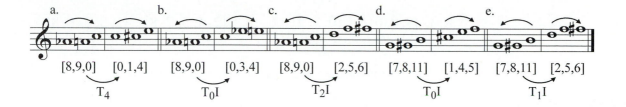

equivalence. Example 3.3 will help you understand the concept of set inversion. In 3.3a, a trichord is transposed by T_4. Both forms of the trichord present the same intervals following the same contours (that is, up or down direction): minor second up, minor third up. In 3.3b, however, we still have the same intervals, but now the second trichord features them with their contour (up or down) reversed with respect to the first trichord. Thus, we can say that the first trichord is made up of a minor third followed by a minor second down from C, and the second trichord is made up of a minor third followed by a minor second up from C. We have inverted the first trichord around the note C, and thus the two sets are mirror reflections of each other around C. By convention, our basic inversion will be around C, or pitch class 0. In our example, because the inversion is around C, no transposition is involved (or, rather, there is a transposition at the unison, or at the 0 level). Hence the T_0I label. If you take the already inverted trichord, C–E♭–E♮, and you transpose it up a major second as in Example 3.3c, you end up with the trichord D–F–F♯, which is a transposed inversion of our original trichord, and thus has the label T_2I. Similarly, the sets in Example 3.3d invert around C or pc 0 (think of C as the axis of symmetry between the two sets), and thus the inversion is T_0I. In 3.3e, we transpose the second set, [1,4,5], up a minor second to [2,5,6], so the inversion is now T_1I.

We can then define a new type of set equivalence, **inversional equivalence** (T_nI). *Two pitch-class sets are inversionally equivalent if they can be mapped onto one another by inversion followed by transposition.* We know that in Example 3.3b, set 2 is an inversion of set 1. We can verify this inversion by means of a simple procedure. In inversionally equivalent sets, the adjacency interval series will be mutually retrogradable in some of the set's ordering (usually the N.O., but not necessarily). Figure 3.10a shows that if we put the two sets from Example 3.3b in normal order, the respective adjacency interval series for these two sets are <1,3> and <3,1>. These two AIS are mutually retrogradable (they are the retrograde of each other), so these two sets are inversionally equivalent. Now let us compare the two larger sets in Figure 3.10b, already given in N.O., [2,4,5,7,8] and [2,3,5,6,8]. The adjacency interval series for these sets are <2,1,2,1> and <1,2,1,2> respectively; that is, they are the retrograde of each other, hence the two sets are inversionally equivalent. Now show that sets [11,0,3,5] and [4,6,9,10] are also inversionally equivalent.

a.   b.

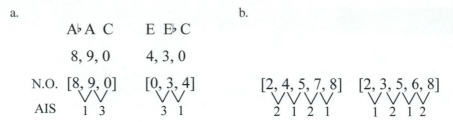

Figure 3.10 Adjacency interval series in inversionally equivalent sets

N.O.   [4, 5, 8, 0]   [9, 0, 1, 5]
             ∨ ∨ ∨   ∨ ∨ ∨
AIS   1   3   4   3   1   4

Rotate   5, 8, 0, 4   1, 5, 9, 0
             ∨ ∨ ∨   ∨ ∨ ∨
AIS   3   4   4   4   4   3

Figure 3.11 AIS in inversionally related sets that require rotation

This procedure to compare sets for inversional equivalence works for most sets in normal order. There are some exceptions, however: in some sets the form that shows the inversion is not the N.O., but one of the other rotational arrangements. These exceptional sets are some inversionally symmetrical sets (which we will study later in this chapter), or also some sets that feature a tie for the largest interval. For an example of two inversionally related normal orders that do not feature mutually retrogradable adjacency interval series, consider the normal orders [4,5,8,0] and [9,0,1,5], shown in Figure 3.11. Their respective AIS are <1,3,4> and <3,1,4>. If we rotate the normal orders, however, into 5,8,0,4 and 1,5,9,0, we see that the respective AIS are now <3,4,4> and <4,4,3>, mutually retrogradable, proving that these two sets are inversionally equivalent. Note that these sets are of the type that features a tie for the largest interval, in this case between pitch classes 8,0 and 0,4.

Any inversion will also involve a transposition, even if it's only the transposition at the 0 level (around pitch class C, or 0), or T_0I. Thus, after we know that two sets are inversionally equivalent, we need to determine the transposition that is involved in the inversion. We will refer to the transpositional operator applied to an inversion (the n in T_nI) as the **index number.** If two sets in N.O. are inversionally equivalent, the first element in one set corresponds with the last in the other set, the second element with the second-to-last, and so on (that is, the first pitch class inverts into the last, the second into the second-to-last, and so on), in such a way that the addition of each of these pairs of elements equals the index number, as illustrated by Figure 3.12. (We should note, however, that here again sometimes this property does not work with normal orders, and then the set needs to be rotated to some other form for the property to work.) In

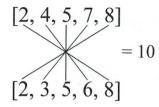

Figure 3.12 Determining the index number for an inversion

$$
\begin{array}{cccccc}
 & 10 & 10 & 10 & 10 & 10 \\
 & [\,2, & 4, & 5, & 7, & 8\,] \\
\text{subtract from 10} & 8 & 6 & 5 & 3 & 2 \\
\text{reverse} & [\,2, & 3, & 5, & 6, & 8\,] = T_{10}\,I
\end{array}
$$

Figure 3.13 Inverting a set

Figure 3.12 we see that the index number for the $T_n I$ operation between [2,4,5,7,8] and [2,3,5,6,8] is 10 (the operation is thus $T_{10}I$). In other words, in $T_0 I$ (inversion around C or 0), 0 inverts into 0, 1 inverts into 11, 2 into 10, 3 into 9, and so on. The sum of any of these pairs is 12. But in $T_{10}I$, 0 inverts into 10, 1 into 9, 2 into 8, and so on, and the sum of any of these pairs is now 10. Can you determine in this same way the index number for the equivalence between sets [11,0,3,5] and [4,6,9,10]? And for sets [5,9,10,0] and [4,9,5,2]?

To invert a set by $T_n I$, simply subtract each pc from n and reverse the order of the resulting set (the inversion of a set in N.O. will normally be the retrograde of the N.O. of the inversion, and that is why we need to reverse the order after performing the operation). In Figure 3.13 we see that we derive $T_{10}I$ of [2,4,5,7,8] by subtracting each pc from 10 and then reversing the result. Now determine $T_9 I$ of [11,0,3,5] in this same way.

NOTE

Unlike transposition, inversion undoes itself when repeated. That is, every $T_n I$ is its own inverse, so the operation goes both ways. The inversion of set [2,4,5,7,8] by $T_{10}I$ is [2,3,5,6,8], and the inversion of [2,3,5,6,8] again by $T_{10}I$ takes us back to [2,4,5,7,8].

Here again, the initial measures from Webern's Five Movements for String Quartet, op. 5, III, will help us understand the significance of inversional equivalence among pc sets. In Example 3.2, some musical events in m. 3 were left out of our commentary on transpositional equivalence because the sets formed by these events are not related by transposition, but rather by inversion. Example 3.4 shows four pc collections, boxed

and numbered. The normal orders of sets 1 and 2 show us that these two sets are related by T_9I, and, similarly, sets 3 and 4 are related by T_0I (as a matter of fact, these two sets are identical to two trichords we studied previously in Example 3.3 and Figure 3.10, the trichords [8,9,0] and [0,3,4]). In other words, all groups of two or three adjacent sets shown in both Examples 3.2 and 3.4 are related by transpositional or inversional equivalence.

Set Class and Prime Form

The normal order of a set allows us to compare sets to determine the existence (or nonexistence) of equivalence relations among them. The normal order, however, still represents specific pitch classes. That is, the normal order is equivalent to reducing all inversions of a C major triad to its root position. This allows us to compare the C major triad with all other major triads and realize that they are all transpositionally equivalent, and to compare the C major triad with all minor triads and realize that they are inversionally equivalent (the major and minor triads are mutual inversions). Now we should be able to find a label that allows us to include all these equivalent triads under one single category. In other words, a set can be transposed twelve times and inverted/transposed another twelve times, and all these forms of the set are equivalent. The collection of equivalent forms of a same set is called the **set class,** and it is represented by a numerical arrangement we call **prime form.**

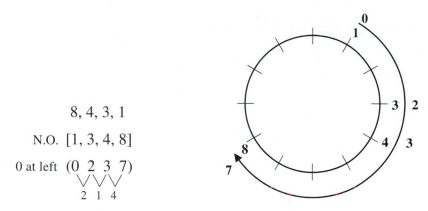

8, 4, 3, 1

N.O. [1, 3, 4, 8]

0 at left (0 2 3 7)
⌄ ⌄ ⌄
2   1   4

Figure 3.14 A shortcut to determine the prime form of a set

In Chapter 1 we learned a simple and quick procedure to determine the prime form of a set. That procedure works for most sets, but not for all. We will review it here as a quick shortcut to figure out prime forms, but we will also learn the more systematic procedure that works for any set. First, let's review the shortcut:

1. Begin from the normal order.

2. Assign integer 0 to the first pitch class and renumber the rest of the pitch classes accordingly. You can do so by transposing the normal order to begin on 0, or simply by producing the same adjacency interval series found in the normal order, but now beginning from 0.

3. The smallest possible intervals must be to the left. If they are to the right, read from the right beginning with 0 (you will have to read the set's AIS backward and beginning from 0), and then reverse the order. You will obtain the same result by subtracting all the members of the set from the last number in the set and then reversing the order (in other words, in this step we are actually inverting the set to bring the smallest intervals to the left).

Let us apply these steps to some examples. First, we will determine the prime form for set 8,4,3,1 (see Figure 3.14, where the process is shown both numerically and on a clock face). The N.O. is [1,3,4,8]. We assign 0 to the first pc and then produce the same adjacency interval series found in the N.O. (that is, <2,1,4>). Alternatively, we transpose the N.O. to begin with 0. In either case, the result is [0,2,3,7]. The first interval is 2, the last one is 4, so the smallest interval is to the left (there is a smaller interval in the center, 1, but rotating the set to place it to the left or to the right would undo our N.O. because then the set would not be arranged in the shortest possible span, and that would go against our step 1). So this is already this set's prime form, which we will notate in parentheses without commas: (0237).

We can also follow the same steps using a clock face. First, we list the N.O. on the circle, and then we assign 0 to the first pc of the N.O. and count half steps clockwise. If the smallest intervals are to the left of the resulting transposition, as is the case with our example in Figure 3.14, that will be the prime form.

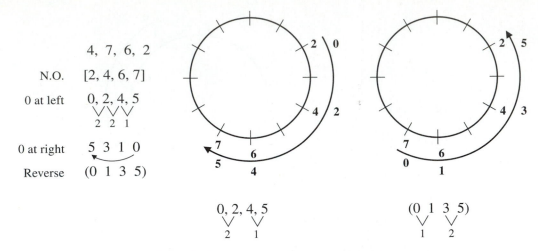

4, 7, 6, 2

N.O.   [2, 4, 6, 7]

0 at left   0, 2, 4, 5
             ⌄ ⌄ ⌄
             2 2 1

0 at right   5 3 1 0

Reverse   (0 1 3 5)

0, 2, 4, 5
  ⌄   ⌄
  2   1

(0 1 3 5)
  ⌄   ⌄
  1   2

Figure 3.15 A shortcut to determine the prime form of a set

We will now try with set 4,7,6,2. The N.O. is [2,4,6,7], which transposed to begin on 0 becomes [0,2,4,5]. The interval to the left is 2, the one to the right is 1, so this is not a valid prime form. We need to invert this set. You can read [0,2,4,5] backward from 0 (that is, you assign 0 to the rightmost pc and read the set's AIS backward from 0), and you come up with 5,3,1,0. Reverse this set to 0,1,3,5, and this is your prime form, (0135). This procedure is shown in Figure 3.15. Note that if we subtract all the members of [0,2,4,5] from the last number in this set, 5, and then we reverse the order, we obtain the same result, (0135). On a clock face, we first list the N.O. on the circle and then transpose it to begin on 0 as we did in Figure 3.14. If the smallest intervals are to the right of the resulting transposition, we will assign 0 to the last pc of the N.O. and count half steps counterclockwise, as shown in Figure 3.15.

NOTE

You can now try some on your own. What are the prime forms of [5,9,10,0], [11,0,2,4], and [9,0,3,5]? Can you demonstrate that the three trichords from Figure 3.8, [8,9,0], [0,3,4], and [2,5,6], are all members of the same set class? What is the prime form for the major triad? For the minor triad? Are they members of the same set class?

A longer procedure that works for all sets is as follows:

1. Begin from the N.O., and transpose the N.O. to begin on 0 as you did in the previous set of instructions.

2. Invert the set (by subtracting all members of the set from 12), and repeat the operations from step 1. That is, put the inversion in N.O., and then transpose it to begin on 0.

3. From steps 1 and 2, choose the result that is more packed to the left. That is, choose the form that has the smallest interval between the first and the next-to-last pcs. If

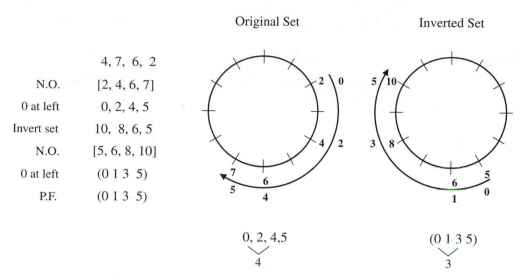

	4, 7, 6, 2	
N.O.	[2, 4, 6, 7]	
0 at left	0, 2, 4, 5	
Invert set	10, 8, 6, 5	
N.O.	[5, 6, 8, 10]	
0 at left	(0 1 3 5)	
P.F.	(0 1 3 5)	

Figure 3.16 The complete procedure to determine the prime form of a set

that still results in a tie, check the interval between the first and third-to-last pcs, and so on.

Figure 3.16 shows the application of these steps to set 4,7,6,2. After we figure out the N.O. and transpose it to begin on 0, we invert the N.O. Subtracting [2,4,6,7] from 12 gives us 10,8,6,5, which, in N.O., is [5,6,8,10]. Transposing this N.O. to begin on 0 gives us [0,1,3,5]. We compare the previous [0,2,4,5] to [0,1,3,5], and we see that the latter is more packed to the left; hence it is the correct prime form, (0135). To follow this procedure on a clock face, we first need to list both the N.O. of the original set and the N.O. of the inverted set on circles, read both clockwise, and choose the one most packed to the left.

From Figures 3.15 and 3.16, we might think that we can always achieve the same result with both methods to determine the prime form. Figure 3.17, however, shows a case of a longer set where we need to perform the second list of steps to arrive at the correct prime form. In Five Movements for String Quartet, op. 5, IV, Webern uses an ascending figure on three occasions. The first of them is shown in Figure 3.17, where we see that the N.O. for this set is [10,11,0,1,4,6,7]. Transposing this N.O. to begin on 0, we come up with [0,1,2,3,6,8,9]. Because the intervals from the left, <1,1,1>, are smaller than the intervals from the right (reading backward from the right, <1,2,3>), we might be tempted to settle on this arrangement as a prime form. As it turns out, this is not the correct prime form. If we invert the set, put the inversion in N.O., and transpose it to begin on 0, we discover that the form [0,1,2,3,6,7,9] is more packed to the left than [0,1,2,3,6,8,9], so the prime form is indeed (0123679). The process is illustrated both numerically and on a clock face in Figure 3.17.

We can now go back to Example 3.2 and verify that, among all the sets related by transpositional equivalence, the sets numbered as 1, 2, 5, 6, 10, 11, and 12 belong to the same set class. Sets 7, 8, and 9, on the other hand, are also members of the same set

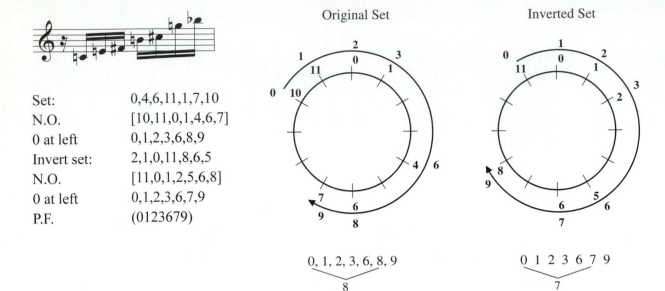

Set: 0,4,6,11,1,7,10
N.O.   [10,11,0,1,4,6,7]
0 at left   0,1,2,3,6,8,9
Invert set: 2,1,0,11,8,6,5
N.O.   [11,0,1,2,5,6,8]
0 at left   0,1,2,3,6,7,9
P.F.   (0123679)

Figure 3.17 The complete procedure to determine the prime form of a set

class, and similarly with sets 3 and 4. Identify each of the three set classes present in this example. If you refer now to Example 3.4, you can verify that each of the two pairs of inversionally related sets also represents one of the set classes you just identified in Example 3.2. Which are these two set classes?

NOTE

The normal order represents an ordering of actual, specific pitch classes. We will use it when we need to compare particular collections of literal pitch classes for operations such as transposition, inversion, and some other literal operations we will study in this chapter (for instance, literal complementarity and literal subset structure). The prime form, on the other hand, is an abstract label that represents a set class. That is, it represents all the different sets (all the transpositionally and inversionally equivalent normal orders) that make up a set class. We will use the prime form when we want to refer to the set class as a whole, to a set as a representative of a set class, or for some operations that deal with abstract, as opposed to literal, representations of sets (such as abstract complementarity and abstract subset structure, to be discussed later in this chapter).

Interval-Class Vector

It is particularly useful, both for the composer and for the analyst, to know the complete interval content of a pitch-class set. That is, to know the list of all possible intervals that can result from combining all pitch classes in a set in pairs. Because we are dealing with pitch classes, what really matters is not so much the exact intervals but the interval

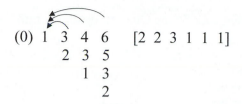

(0) 1 3 4 6   [2 2 3 1 1 1]
       2 3 5
          1 3
             2

Figure 3.18 Calculating the interval-class vector of a set

classes. The **interval-class vector** (ICV) is precisely this, a list of the complete interval-class content of a pc set. An interval-class vector contains six integers (which we will represent in brackets and without commas), and each integer indicates the number of occurrences of each ic. For instance, the ICV for set (01346) is [223111]. This means that in set (01346) there are two cases of ic 1 (intervals 1–11), two of ic 2 (intervals 2–10), three of ic 3 (intervals 3–9), and one each of interval classes 4 (intervals 4–8), 5 (intervals 5–7), and 6 (interval 6).

To determine the ICV of a set, you can build a "triangle of differences," as shown in Figure 3.18. With the set in prime form, disregard the opening zero, subtract the first integer after the zero from each of the remaining integers, and write the results on a line under the set. Then follow the same process with each subsequent line: subtract the first integer from each of the remaining integers until you get to a line with a single integer. When you have the complete triangle, count the occurrences of integers 1 or 11. This will give you the entry for ic 1 in your vector. Occurrences of integers 2 or 10 will give you the entry for ic 2; occurrences of integers 3 or 9 provide the entry for ic 3; occurrences of 4 or 8 provide the entry for ic 4; occurrences of 5 or 7 provide the entry for ic 5; and occurrences of 6 provide the entry for ic 6. These entries account for the vector [223111] in our example. Now determine the ICV for set (0148) using a triangle of differences.

One of the most immediate applications of the ICV is that it allows us to compare the interval-class content of sets. Webern's Five Movements for String Quartet, op. 5, IV, opens with two tremolo figures in the violins, as shown in Example 3.5. The respective prime forms for these figures are (0156) and (0167). The ICVs for each of these sets are [200121] and [200022]. We can see from this information that each of these sets contains two instances of ic 2, two more of ic 5, and one or two of ic 6. On the other hand, both sets display zero cases of ic 2 and ic 3, and only one case in one set of ic 4. We thus learn from the ICVs that the interval-class content of these two sets is substantially similar, a property that is interesting from both the compositional and analytical perspectives. Note also that the example closes with a pizzicato chord in the upper register. The set class for this chord is also (0156).[3]

---

[3]There is a voluminous literature on various ways of measuring similarity relations among sets. See, for instance, Robert Morris, "A Similarity Index for Pitch-Class Sets," *Perspectives of New Music* 18 (1979–80); 445–60; Eric Isaacson, "Similarity of Interval-Class Content Between Pitch-Class Sets: The IcVSIM Relation," *Journal of Music Theory* 34 (1990): 1–28; and Michael Buchler, "Broken and Unbroken Interval Cycles and Their Use in Determining Pitch-Class Set Resemblance," *Perspectives of New Music* 38/2 (2000): 52–87.

Example 3.5   Webern, Five Movements for String Quartet, op. 5, IV, mm. 1–2

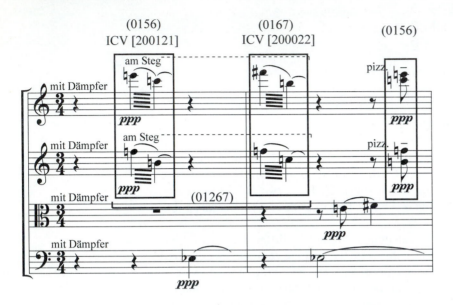

The List of Set Classes

A **list of set classes** (or prime forms) containing between three and nine pitch classes (trichords to nonachords) can be found in Appendix 1.[4] Complementary set classes are listed across from each other (we will explain set complementarity below; for the time being, simply notice that trichords are listed across from nonachords, tetrachords across from octachords, pentachords across from septachords, and so on, and that in all cases complementary cardinal numbers add up to 12, as in 3 + 9 = 12). Note that in prime forms, we will use T and E for ten and eleven, respectively. (Some sources in the literature use A for ten and B for eleven.)

In *The Structure of Atonal Music,* Forte assigned a double number to each set class, which we will call the set's **Forte name.** Forte names appear in the leftmost and rightmost columns in our list of set classes. The first integer in a Forte name (as, for instance, in 3–6) refers to the cardinal number of the set class (that is, 3–6 has three pitch

---

[4]Early forms of this list appeared in Howard Hanson's *The Harmonic Materials of Twentieth-Century Music* (New York: Appleton-Century-Crofts, 1960) and Donald Martino's "The Source Set and Its Aggregate Formations," *Journal of Music Theory* 5/2 (1961): 224–73. The most commonly used lists appear in Forte's *The Structure of Atonal Music* and Rahn's *Basic Atonal Theory.* The list in Appendix 1 is modeled after the list of set classes in Straus's *Introduction to Post-Tonal Theory,* 3rd ed., pp. 261–64, itself modeled after Rahn's. Because of slightly different methods of computing normal orders and prime forms, our list (as well as Rahn's and Straus's) differs from Forte's in six prime forms (for set classes 5–20, 6–Z29, 6–31, 7–Z18, 7–20, and 8–26).

classes). The second integer is an order number that indicates where the set appears in Forte's list (3–6 appears in the sixth place in the list of trichords). The second and second-to-last columns are a list of set classes, including all the possible prime forms with a cardinal number of 3 to 9. The third and third-to-last columns show the interval-class vectors for all set classes. Finally, the central column indicates the degrees of transpositional and inversional symmetry, two concepts explained below.

NOTE

Although the list was somewhat reordered by Rahn, the original Forte names were preserved, but now out of order in some cases. Our list follows Rahn's reordering, including the original Forte names in their reordered state.

As you can probably realize at a glance, the list of set classes is a highly useful source. In the first place, we can quickly verify whether what we think is a prime form does or does not exist. For instance, you might try to figure out mentally the prime form for set E–F–B, and come up with (017). A look at the list will tell you, however, that (017) is not a possible prime form (it does not exist on the list). Why not? What is the real prime form for this set? Moreover, the list provides you with a set's interval-class vector and other useful information that we will discuss in the following sections.

Z-Related Sets

Z-related sets are nonequivalent sets with identical interval-class vectors.[5] For each Z set in the list of set classes you will find another Z set with the same cardinal number that has the same ICV. Find, for instance, set 5–Z36, (01247), with ICV [222121]. Further down in the pentachords you will find set 5–Z12, (01356), with the same ICV. These two sets are Z related. What set is Z-related to 7–Z38?

PITCH-CLASS SETS: FURTHER PROPERTIES AND RELATIONSHIPS

Invariant Tones under Transposition

Common tones (or **invariant tones**) among various pitch or pitch class collections have been used for a variety of musical purposes in different musical periods and styles. In tonal voice leading, for instance, it is usual to leave common tones between adjacent chords in the same voice, thus minimizing the motion from one chord to the next. Some post-tonal composers (particularly Anton Webern) have also favored the use of common tones or common pitch classes between adjacent collections in their compositions, whereas other composers have favored the avoidance of common tones. Refer,

---

[5]Although the Z relation was named by Forte, its earliest formulations are found in David Lewin's "The Intervallic Content of a Collection of Notes," *Journal of Music Theory* 4 (1960): 98–101, and Hanson's *The Harmonic Materials of Twentieth-Century Music.*

♪♪ Example 3.6   Reduction of chords in mm. 1–6 of Webern's op. 5, III

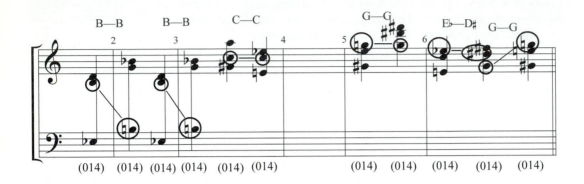

for instance, to Example 3.6. This is a reduction of all the vertical trichords heard in the upper three instruments of Webern's Five Movements for String Quartet, op. 5, III, mm. 1–6, the passage shown in Example 3.4. The trichords are grouped into four pairs and a group of three, and all belong to the (014) set class. Thus, they are all related by T_n or T_nI equivalences. Now notice the pitches marked with circles and connected with lines in Example 3.6. We see that in each of the groups of two or three chords, adjacent chords share a common pitch class (these are the marked pitches, also identified with letter names above the chords).

It is thus musically and compositionally significant to know how many invariant pitch classes are produced by particular transformations of a set (that is transpositions and inversions). We will now learn that it is quite simple to investigate the number of invariant pitch classes under transposition and under inversion.

The number of invariants (common pitch classes) produced by transposition by interval-class n (with the only exception of ic 6) will be equal to the number of times interval-class n occurs in the set. All we need to do, then, is to examine the set's interval-class vector. Take set (02357). The ICV is [132130]. Entry 1 for ic 1 means that one pitch class of the set remains invariant under T_1. Entry 3 for ic 2 means that three pitch classes of this set remain invariant under T_2. Entry 2 for ic 3 means that two pitch classes of this set remain invariant under T_3, and so on. Inverse-related values of n yield the same number of invariants. For instance, T_2 and T_{10} will each produce three invariants (entry 3 for ic 2). We can verify this statement very easily. Transposing N.O. [0,2,3,5,7] by T_2 gives us set [2,4,5,7,9], which has pitch classes 2, 5, and 7 in common with the original set. Transposing it by T_{10} results in [10,0,1,3,5], which has pitch classes 0, 3, and 5 in common with the original set. Now verify all this at the piano. How many invariants will both T_5 and T_7 of this same set produce? What are the exact invariant pitch classes in each case, if we apply these transpositions to N.O. [0,2,3,5,7]?

Interval class 6, on the other hand, requires special treatment. Each occurrence of ic 6 in a set's vector will produce *two* invariants under T_6. The vector for set (01267) is

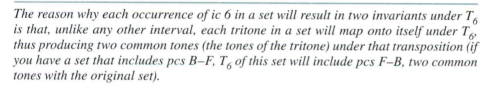

	0	1	4	8
0	0	1	4	8
1	1	2	5	9
4	4	5	8	0
8	8	9	0	4

Figure 3.19 The summation square for set [0,1,4,8]

[310132]. Entry 2 for ic 6 means that four pitch classes of this set remain invariant under T_6. Verify this both numerically and at the piano: take for example N.O. [0,1,2,6,7], transpose it by T_6, and verify how many invariants result from this transposition. Now figure out the number of invariant pitch classes under T_6 for set 6–7. What does this result mean (considering that set 6–7 is a hexachord)? Verify your result numerically and at the piano.

NOTE

The reason why each occurrence of ic 6 in a set will result in two invariants under T_6 is that, unlike any other interval, each tritone in a set will map onto itself under T_6, thus producing two common tones (the tones of the tritone) under that transposition (if you have a set that includes pcs B–F, T_6 of this set will include pcs F–B, two common tones with the original set).

Invariant Tones under Inversion

To find out the number of invariant pitch classes under inversion, we need to build what is known as a summation square.[6] Take, for instance, set [0,1,4,8]. Write the set horizontally and vertically, and then add the corresponding elements and write each addition at the intersection between two elements. The resulting square is shown in Figure 3.19.

The integers in the summation square represent index numbers for T_nI operations. Count how many times each integer occurs within the lines of the square, and that will give you the number of invariants under that index number. For instance, integer 0 appears three times, so the operation T_0I will produce three invariants. Integer 1 appears twice, so the operation T_1I will produce two invariants. Figure 3.20 lists the number of invariants for each index number.

---

[6]This type of matrix, also called invariance matrix, was originally invented by Bo Alphonce ("The Invariance Matrix," Ph.D. diss., Yale University, 1974). For an extensive discussion of the properties and applications of invariance matrices, see Morris, *Class Notes*, Chapter 14.

$$T_0I - 3 \qquad T_6I - 0$$
$$T_1I - 2 \qquad T_7I - 0$$
$$T_2I - 1 \qquad T_8I - 3$$
$$T_3I - 0 \qquad T_9I - 2$$
$$T_4I - 3 \qquad T_{10}I - 0$$
$$T_5I - 2 \qquad T_{11}I - 0$$

Figure 3.20 Invariant tones under inversion for set [0,1,4,8]

Value of n in T_nI: 0 1 2 3 4 5 6 7 8 9 10 11

Index vector for (0148):   <3, 2, 1, 0, 3, 2, 0, 0, 3, 2, 0, 0>

Figure 3.21 The index vector for set [0,1,4,8]

This list of invariants can be presented as what we call an **index vector,** where each of the twelve integers represents the number of invariant tones under inversion by the corresponding index number (the n of T_nI), ordered from 0 to 11. Thus, the index vector for set [0,1,4,8] is <3,2,1,0,3,2,0,0,3,2,0,0>, as shown in Figure 3.21. It is important to note that index vectors are different for different members of a set class (that is, transpositions and inversions of a given set). In other words, we must derive index vectors from *particular normal orders,* not from a prime form representing a set class.

To verify this list, invert N.O. [0,1,4,8] by any of the index numbers, for instance T_4I. Subtracting each pc from 4 gives us [4,3,0,8]. We get three invariant pitch classes: 4, 0, and 8. In fact, we could have figured out which three pitch classes are invariant in T_4I just by examining the summation square. Index number 4 occurs, in the square, at the intersections of 8 with 8, 0 with 4, and 4 with 0. So 0, 4, and 8 are the invariant pcs under T_4I. Similarly, index number 5 occurs at the intersection of 4 with 1, so 4 and 1 are the two invariants under T_5I. What are the two invariant pitch classes under T_9I?

Set Complementarity

The **complement** of a given set is the set formed by all pitch classes not included in the original set. The union of a set and its complement constitutes the collection of all twelve pitch classes, which we call the **aggregate.** Take, for instance, set [0,2,4,6,8,10], which is the whole-tone scale we have labeled as WT_0. This set's complement is the set formed by all the pitch classes not included in WT_0, that is, [1,3,5,7,9,11], or WT_1. From this perspective, we are dealing with the **literal complement,** that is, the set that contains the actual pitch classes not included in the original set.

0, 1, 2, (3, 4), 5, 6, (7), 8, 9, (10, 11)

0 1 2   5 6   8 9
           0   1   4   7 8

Figure 3.22 Set complementarity

We can also think, however, of abstract complementarity. An **abstract comple-ment** of a set is any member of the set class that includes its literal complement (that is, any member of the set class represented by the prime form of the literal complement). To determine the abstract complement of a set, first find its literal complement, and then put this literal complement in prime form. Any member of the set class represented by this prime form (other than the literal complement) will be an abstract complement of the original set. Take, for instance, set (0125689). The literal complement (made up of the pitch classes missing in the given set) is [3,4,7,10,11], which, in prime form, is (01478). The abstract complement of (0125689) is thus (01478) or any transposition or inversion of this set other than the literal complement itself. In Figure 3.22 you can see that these two prime forms complement each other (fit into each other) to build a com-plete sequence of the twelve pitch classes (the aggregate).

In the list of set classes, complementary set classes are listed across from each other and labeled with identical order numbers. Thus, 5–1 and 7–1 are complementary, and so are 5–2 and 7–2, 5–3 and 7–3, and so on. Notice also an interesting interval-lic property of complementary sets: The difference in the number of occurrences of each interval between two complementary sets equals the difference between cardinal numbers of the sets (except for ic6, where the difference of cardinal numbers must be divided by 2). Take sets 5–13 and 7–13. The difference between their cardinal numbers is $7 - 5 = 2$. Now compare their ICVs, [221311] and [443532], and you will see that the difference in the number of occurrences of each interval class (each member of the vec-tor) is also 2, except for ic6, in which the difference is 1 (that is, 2 divided by 2).

A variety of interesting musical applications of set complementarity appear in Webern's Five Movements for String Quartet, op. 5, IV. In Example 3.5 we became familiar with the opening two measures and with the tremolo figures represented by prime forms (0156) and (0167). The set that combines both of these tremolo figures is set 5–7 (01267). Example 3.7 shows mm. 3–6 for the same piece. In mm. 3–4 we hear a descending four-note motive presented in imitation (by violin 1, violin 2, and cello), again a member of set class (0167). For purposes of complementarity relations, how-ever, let us focus on the pentachord formed by combining the four-note motive in m. 3 with the viola figure, E–F♯, in the same measure. This is set 5–7 (01267) again. The vertical chord that opens m. 4 (the five pitch classes on the first eighth-note of the mea-sure) is also set 5–7. If we now combine the two overlapping statements of 5–7 we have just identified in mm. 3–4, the resulting set is 7–7 (0123678), the complement of set 5–7.

This complement relation becomes even more significant when we examine the next musical gesture, in mm. 4–6. We now hear a polyphonic texture in three voices

♪♪♪ Example 3.7   Webern, Five Movements for String Quartet, op. 5, IV, mm. 3–6

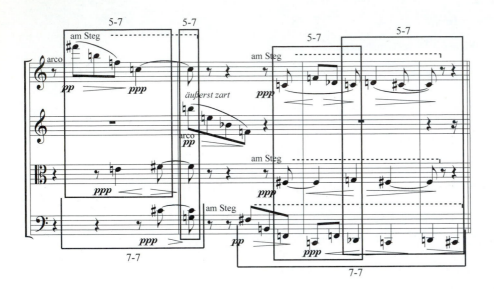

(violin 1, viola, and cello). The set that includes all the pitch classes in this fragment is again set class 7–7 (0123678). But we can also break the fragment into two overlapping pentachords, each of them beginning on the only eighth notes where all three instruments have simultaneous attacks (last eighth-note in m. 4, third eighth-note in m. 5). Both of these pentachords are members of set class 5–7, again the complement of set class 7–7. In other words, twice in a row in these measures we hear the same type of complementarity relation: two overlapping statements of set class 5–5 combine to form the complement of this set, set class 7–7.[7]

Hexachordal complementarity also features some interesting properties. If you refer to the list of set classes, you will see that there are 50 different hexachordal sets. Twenty of them are self-complementary, that is, the complement of one of these set classes is the same set class. Self-complementary hexachords do not show any set listed across from them in the list of set classes. Look, for instance, at set 6–35, (02468T), the whole-tone set (as we noted before, in prime forms we will use T and E for ten and eleven, respectively). We know that the complement of a whole-tone scale is another whole-tone scale, also a member of set class (02468T), so set class 6–35 is self-complementary and hence shows no set class listed across from it.

A further look at the list of set classes tells us that all hexachords that are not self-complementary are of the Z type, and that in all cases the complement of a

[7]These and other complementarity relations in this piece are pointed out in David Beach, "Pitch Structure and the Analytic Process in Atonal Music: An Interpretation of the Theory of Sets," *Music Theory Spectrum* 1 (1979): 7–22.

		Literal subset	Abstract subset
exclude pc 9:	2 3 5 6 9	[2, 3, 5, 6]	(0 1 3 4)
exclude pc 6:	2 3 5 6 9	[2, 3, 5, 9]	(0 1 3 7)
exclude pc 5:	2 3 5 6 9	[2, 3, 6, 9]	(0 1 4 7)
exclude pc 3:	2 3 5 6 9	[2, 5, 6, 9]	(0 3 4 7)
exclude pc 2:	2 3 5 6 9	[3, 5, 6, 9]	(0 2 3 6)

Figure 3.23 The tetrachordal subsets of pentachord [2,3,5,6,9]

Z-hexachord is its Z-related hexachord (note that all Z-hexachords listed across from each other share one common interval-class vector). In other words, all hexachords are either self-complementary or complementary with their Z-related hexachords. In both cases, a hexachord and its complement have the same interval-class vector. This interesting property means that a hexachord always has the same interval-class content as its complement.

Inclusion: Supersets and Subsets

A set can be broken up into a number of sets that are contained in it. All the sets contained in a set will be smaller than the original set; the only exception is the original set itself (which is contained in itself). Sets contained in a given set are called **subsets,** and the set that contains them is a **superset. a literal subset** is a set made up of actual pitch classes included in a given set. For instance, given pentachord [2,3,5,6,9], sets [2,3,5,6] and [2,3,6,9] are possible examples of literal tetrachordal subsets (the exact pitch classes in these tetrachords are included in the given pentachord). Can you provide a few examples of literal trichords? We can derive subsets from a given set in a systematic way. If we want to figure out all the tetrachordal subsets of a pentachord, for instance, we can go through a process of excluding each possible single pitch class from the pentachord. This process is shown in Figure 3.23, where we exclude each possible pitch-class set from pentachord [2,3,5,6,9] to generate the five possible tetrachordal subsets of this set. To figure out all the possible trichordal subsets of this pentachord (there are ten of them), we would have to exclude systematically all the possible dyads and list the resulting trichords.

More interesting than literal subsets, however, are **abstract subsets.** An abstract subset is any member of the set class that includes a literal subset (that is, any member of the set class represented by the prime form of a literal subset). The last column of Figure 3.23 shows the prime form for each of the literal subsets listed in the next-to-last column. Any members of the set classes represented by each of these prime forms are abstract tetrachordal subsets of [2,3,5,6,9]. Can you now prove that [2,3,5,6,9] contains three different (014) subsets? To find the prime forms for all the abstract trichordal subsets of a pentachord, we would systematically exclude all possible dyads and list the prime forms of the resulting trichords. There are ten resulting trichords, three of which in this case will have an (014) prime form. Because what we are looking for is abstract subsets (represented by prime forms), we can also work from the prime form of the original [2,3,5,6,9] set, (01347), from which we can visualize abstract subsets more easily. One of the (014) subsets we are looking for is the literal [0,1,4]. The other two are [0,3,4] and [3,4,7]. The prime form for all three trichords is (014). Can you demonstrate that set (0156) contains two (016) and two (015) subsets? Can you demonstrate, moreover, that set (0167) contains four (016) subsets?

Example 3.8 shows us some inclusion relationships in a musical context. In the opening three measures of Schoenberg's *Drei Klavierstücke,* op. 11, no. 1 (1909), we hear a texture made up of a melody in the upper voice and two harmonic trichords. If we consider first the complete melodic gesture as a whole, the resulting set class is (013457). Similarly, the set class that contains both chords is (014568). Both of these hexachords are shown in Example 3.8a. In Example 3.8b, on the other hand, we break up the texture into four trichords: two for the melody and one for each of the chords. The melody breaks up into set classes (014) and (015), and the two harmonic trichords are (016) and (014). All three set classes involved, (014), (015), and (016), are subsets of both hexachords, as shown in the diagram at the end of Example 3.8b. In Example 3.8c, finally, we show that the melody begins with two overlapping and inversionally equivalent members of set class (0124). This tetrachord is also a subset of both hexachords from Example 3.8a. Inclusion relationships thus connect all the main set classes involved in these measures, including two hexachords, one tetrachord, and three trichords.

Symmetry

A symmetrical set is a set that can map onto itself under transposition or inversion. A **transpositionally symmetrical set** can map onto itself under transposition. Take, for instance, set [0,4,8], the familiar augmented triad. It can map onto itself under T_0, T_4, and T_8. You may easily verify this: transpose [0,4,8] by T_0, T_4, and T_8, and see what are the resulting sets. An **inversionally symmetrical set** can map onto itself under inversion. Take [0,1,6,7] and invert it by T_1I and T_7I. You will see that the result of both operations is also [0,1,6,7]. We have already seen numerous uses of symmetrical sets by various composers. In Chapter 1 we discussed both Debussy's and Stravinsky's use of motives or harmonies generated by set class (0257); in Chapter 2 we saw examples of Bartók's motives based on set classes (0167), (0134), (0235), (0268), and (0246). And in this chapter we have seen examples of (0156) and (0167) in a piece by Webern. These are all symmetrical sets.

If you refer to the list of set classes, you will see that the middle column contains two integers. The first integer indicates the **degree of transpositional symmetry,** that

Example 3.8   Arnold Schoenberg: *Drei Klavierstücke,* op. 11, no. 1, mm. 1–3

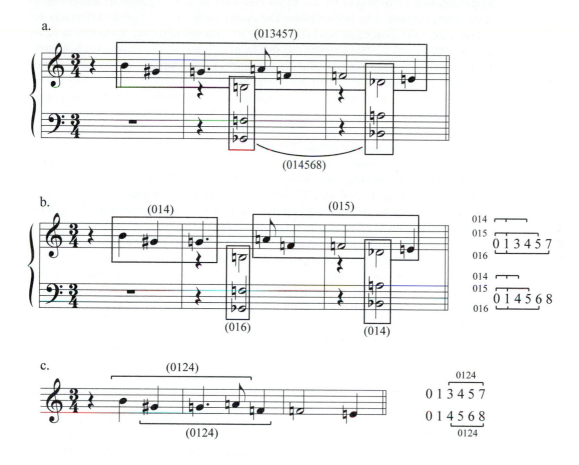

is, the number of transpositional levels at which the set maps onto itself. In all cases, the degree of transpositional symmetry is at least 1 because all sets are transpositionally symmetrical at T_0. The second integer indicates the **degree of inversional symmetry,** that is, the number of inversional levels at which the sets maps onto itself. Examine, for instance, a few particular sets, and try to understand what these degrees of transpositional and inversional symmetry mean in practice. Set 3–12 can map onto itself three times under transposition and three under inversion. Why? Can you explain why set 4–28 can map onto itself four times under each operation? And how about set 6–35? Why can it map onto itself six times under each operation?

To determine at what transpositional level a symmetrical set maps onto itself, we can examine the set's interval-class vector. A set is transpositionally equivalent if the vector contains an entry equal to the number of pitch classes in the set (or half that number in the case of ic 6). Take, for instance, set (0369), whose degree of transpositional symmetry is 4 according to the list of set classes. The ICV is [004002] and the set (a tetrachord) contains four pitch classes. The vector entry for ic 3 is 4, and the entry for ic 6 is 2 (half the number of pcs in the set). Hence, the set will map onto itself at T_0 (as all sets do), T_3 and T_9 (the two intervals that form ic 3) and at T_6 (the interval that forms ic 6). Now try to determine at what transpositional levels set (014589) will map onto itself, and do the same for sets (013679) and (02468T).

We can easily tell whether a set is inversionally symmetrical because such a set always has at least one ordering of its elements whose interval series is its own retrograde (that is, the AIS is self-retrogradable). The AIS for [0,1,6,7], for instance, is <1,5,1>, which is its own retrograde. For each such ordering, the set will map onto itself under T_nI, where n equals the sum of the first and last members of that ordering. Take, for instance, [0,2,6,8]. The four orderings of this set are [0,2,6,8], [2,6,8,0], [6,8,0,2], and [8,0,2,6]. All four result in AIS that are their own retrogrades: <2,4,2>, <4,2,4>, <2,4,2>, and <4,2,4>, respectively. Adding the first and last members for each of the four orderings, however, results in only two different numbers, 8 and 2. This means that set [0,2,6,8] is inversionally symmetrical under T_8I and T_2I. We already know that [0,1,6,7] is inversionally symmetrical under T_1I and T_7I. Can you verify that?

The ordering whose AIS is its own retrograde is often the normal order, and then the prime form itself will be symmetrical (that is, it will be the same whether we read it forward or backward). Read (0167) backward, and you will also come up with (0167). The same can be shown with (048), (0235), (0246), (0268), and many other sets. For other inversionally symmetrical sets, however, we need to rotate the prime form before we can find a self-retrogradable interval series. Take for instance set (027), which the list of set classes shows as being inversionally symmetrical. Its symmetry becomes apparent when we rotate it to become [2,7,0], a form of the set that we can equally read forward or backward. Now try with (0158).

For yet another type of symmetrical set, however, rotation is not sufficient to show symmetry intervallically. We cannot rotate (0248) in any way to achieve a self-retrogradable interval series. (The four orderings are [0,2,4,8], [2,4,8,0], [4,8,0,2], and [8,0,2,4].) Taking the last pitch class in the prime form and duplicating it at the beginning, however, gives us [8,0,2,4,8]. The adjacency interval series is now <4,2,2,4>, self-retrogradable, showing the symmetrical nature of this set. If you do the same with (027) you will also see that [7,0,2,7] is symmetrical. Now try with (0127). Does rotation demonstrate that it is inversionally symmetrical? If not, how can you prove it?

We can readily verify the symmetry of a set by representing it on a clock face. If the set's degree of inversional symmetry is 1, the set will be divided symmetrically by one axis, as shown in Figure 3.24a for sets (027), (0127), and (0248). If the degree of symmetry is 2, there will be two axes of symmetry, as in Figure 3.24b for sets (0167) and (0248). Sets with degrees of symmetry 3, 4, and 6 will feature 3, 4, and 6 axes of symmetry, respectively, as shown in Figure 3.24c for sets (048), (0369), and (02468T). In each of these cases, we can determine between what pitch classes we can draw axes of symmetry through the following procedure: If a set is inversionally symmetrical at

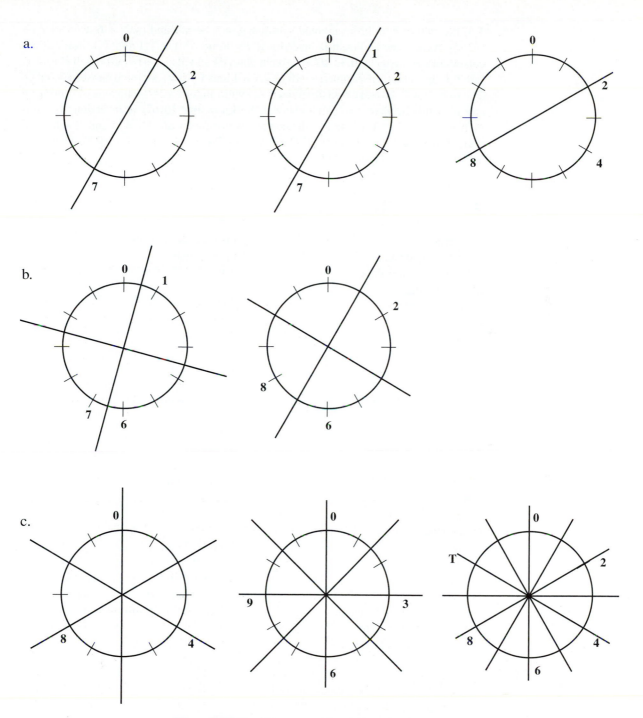

Figure 3.24 Graphic representations of inversional symmetry

T_nI, the two centers of inversional symmetry will be n/2 and (n/2) + 6. Consider set (0268). As we saw earlier, it is inversionally symmetrical at T_8I and T_2I. For T_8I, the centers of symmetry will be 8/2 = 4 (pitch class E) and also 4 + 6 = 10 (pitch class B♭). For T_2I, the centers of symmetry will be 2/2 = 1 and 1 + 6 = 7, or pitch classes C♯ and G. The two axes E–B♭ and C♯–G are indeed shown in Figure 3.24b. The axis of symmetry can also fall between two pitch classes. We know that (0167) is inversionally symmetrical at T_1I and T_7I. For T_1I, the centers of symmetry are 1/2 = .5 and .5 + 6 = 6.5 (axis .5-6.5), and for T_7I they are 7/2 = 3.5 and 3.5 + 6 = 9.5 (axis 3.5 = 9.5). These two axes are shown in Figure 3.24b.

Terms for Review

pitch class
octave equivalence
enharmonic equivalence
integer notation
mod 12 arithmetic
pitch-class space
pitch space
ordered pitch-class interval
unordered pitch-class interval
interval class
pitch-class set
cardinal number
trichord
tetrachord
pentachord
hexachord
septachord
octachord
nonachord
monad
dyad
normal order
rotation
transpositional equivalence
transpositional operator
adjacency interval series

inversional equivalence
index number
set class
prime form
interval-class vector
list of set classes
Forte name
Z-related sets
invariant tones
invariant tones under transposition
invariant tones under inversion
index vector
complement
aggregate
literal complement
abstract complement
hexachordal complementarity
subset
superset
literal subset
abstract subsets
transpositionally symmetrical set
inversionally symmetrical set
degree of transpositional symmetry
degree of inversional symmetry

CHAPTER 3 ASSIGNMENTS

Preliminary Concepts

1. *Integer notation.* Write the corresponding integer under each of the following pitch classes.

E   G♭   D♭   A♯   G   D♯   E♭   B♭   D   F♯   B   G♯
4   6   1   10   7   3   3   10   2   6   11   8

2. *Mod 12 notation.* Write the equivalent integer in *mod 12* for each of the following numbers.

19 = 7   22 = 10   14 = 2   18 = 6   13 = 1   24 = 0   30 = 6   15 = 3   23 = 11   28 = 4

3. Realize the following additions and subtractions in *mod 12* arithmetic (that is, provide the results in *mod 12*).

8 + 9 = 5   11 + 10 = 9   9 + 5 = 2   7 + 6 = 1   8 + 4 = 0
2 − 9 = 5   8 − 11 = 9   6 − 10 = 8   10 − 11 = 11   1 − 8 = 5

4. *Ordered pitch-class intervals.* Determine the ordered pitch-class interval between the following dyads and write it next to each dyad.

   a.   C–G   b.   A–C   c.   D–B   d.   F♯–B   e.   E–B♭
   f.   D–F   g.   C♯–G♯   h.   G–C   i.   C–A♭   j.   D–G♯

5. *Interval class.* Determine what interval class (or unordered pc interval) is represented by each of the following dyads.

   a. D♯–B   b. F–B   c. E–A   d. E–B   e. C♯–A   f. D–E♭   g. B–B♭   h. F♯–E   i. F–A♭   j. C♯–G

Pitch-Class Sets: Orderings and Basic Relationships

6. *Set rotation.* Convert the following sets into integer notation, place them in ascending order, and show all their possible orderings.

   a.   F–C–D–F♯

   b.   F–E♭–G–C–D♭

7. *Normal order.* Put the following sets in normal order, using integers

   a.   D♯–D–G   d.   6, 7, 1   g.   5, 8, 3, 7   j.   7,5,6,1,4
   b.   D–G♯–E   e.   D–C–A♭–E♭   h.   A♭–G–A–D
   c.   G♯–C♯–D   f.   3, 10, 11, 1   i.   D–E♭–A–F–F♯

8. *Transpositionally equivalent sets.* The following pairs of sets are given in normal order (N.O.). Determine whether each pair is made up of transpositionally equivalent sets. If yes, provide the transpositional operator.

   a.   [2,4,6]   [8,10,0]   d.   [0,3,4,7]   [3,5,6,10]
   b.   [1,2,3,8]   [11,0,1,6]   e.   [10,11,0,2,5]   [1,2,3,5,8]
   c.   [8,10,11,1]   [2,4,5,7]

9. *Transposition.* Operate the required transposition in the following sets, given in N.O.

   a. T_5 [3,5,8]
   b. T_8 [8,9,11,0]
   c. T_4 [1,3,4,8]

   d. T_{10} [0,2,4,5,8]
   e. T_2 [5,7,8,9,0]

10. *Inversionally equivalent sets.* Determine whether each of the following pairs of sets is made up of inversionally equivalent sets. If yes, provide the index number. The sets are given in N.O.

    a. [0,1,6]   [7,0,1]
    b. [8,0,3]   [1,4,8]
    c. [10,0,1,2]   [0,1,3,6]

    d. [1,2,3,7]   [10,2,3,4]
    e. [0,1,4,5,8]   [6,9,10,1,2]

11. *Inversion.* Operate the required inversion/transposition on each of the following sets given in N.O.

    a. T_5I [2,3,8]
    b. T_0I [9,10,0,3]
    c. $T_{11}I$ [1,3,6,9]

    d. T_8I [0,1,2,4,8]
    e. T_4I [3,4,6,7,10]

12. *Prime form.* Provide the prime form for each of the following sets, given in N.O.

    a. [1,4,6]
    b. [10,11,1]
    c. [2,4,5]
    d. [11,2,6]
    e. [3,5,6]

    f. [1,2,6,7]
    g. [7,9,1,2]
    h. [5,7,8,0]
    i. [1,3,4,5]
    j. [3,7,8,9]

    k. [1,2,3,5,7]
    l. [8,10,1,2,4]
    m. [9,10,2,3,4]
    n. [9,10,2,3,5]
    o. [2,5,6,7,10]

13. *Forte names.* Using the list of set classes, provide Forte names for each of the sets listed in Exercise 12.

14. *Prime form verification.* The following sets may or may not be in prime form. Using the list of set classes, verify whether they are in prime form. If they are not, provide the correct prime form.

    a. (056)
    b. (036)
    c. (034)
    d. (046)

    e. (0156)
    f. (0236)
    g. (0245)
    h. (0267)

    i. (01356)
    j. (01345)

15. *Interval-class vector.* Without looking at the list of set classes, figure out the interval-class vector for each of the following sets. Include your triangles of differences with your answers.

    a. (0247)
    b. (0146)

    c. (02468)
    d. (01257)

    e. (01457) this not this one!

16. *The list of set classes.* Answer the following questions with the help of the list of set classes.

    1. What is the complement of each of the following set classes?

       a. 4–10 (0235)
       b. 5–14 (01257)
       c. 7–11 (0134568)

       d. 6–Z11 (012457)
       e. 8–5 (01234678)

2. What tetrachords contain two tritones each?

3. What pentachords contain no ic 3 members?

4. What is the Z-related set class for set class 7–Z17? And for set class 6–Z49?

5. What is the interval-class vector for set class 7–11?

6. The following set classes have curious interval-class vectors. Why? Provide the "common" name for each of these set classes.

   a. 3–12   c. 6–1

   b. 4–28   d. 6–35

Further Properties and Relationships

17. *Invariant tones under transposition.*

    1. Set (0258). How many pcs remain invariant under T_1?

       And under T_3?   And under T_8?   And under T_6?

    2. What transpositions produce the maximum number of invariant pcs for set 7–35?

    3. What transpositions produce the minimum number of invariant pcs for set 5–7?

18. *Invariant tones under inversion.* Realize a summation square for each of the following two sets and list the respective index vectors. Then answer the questions for each set class.

    1. Set (0247). Index vector:

       a. What inversions produce the maximum number of invariants?

       b. What inversions produce no invariants?

       c. How many invariants does T_9I produce?

       d. How many invariants does T_6I produce?

    2. Set (012678). Index vector:

       a. There are only two inversions that produce no invariant for this set. What are they?

       b. On the other hand, two inversions result in the set mapping onto itself (that is, the set is inversionally symmetrical at two inversion levels). What are they?

       c. How many invariants do T_1I, T_3I, T_7I, and T_9I produce?

       d. How many invariants do T_0I, T_4I, T_6I, and $T_{10}I$ produce?

19. *Complementarity.*

    1. Without looking at the list of set classes, determine the abstract complement for the following two sets.

       a. (0123478)   b. (012368)

    2. Looking at the list of set classes, determine the complement of the following hexachords:

       a. (012367)   b. (023457)

20. *Inclusion.*

    1. How many times is the abstract subset (026) included in (0268)?

    2. Is (015) an abstract subset of (01267)? If yes, how many different (015) abstract subsets does (01267) contain?

    3. The set (016) is included eight times in (012678). List all the three-integer sets that are (016) subsets of this hexachord.

21. *Symmetry.*

    1. The following list contains all the inversionally symmetrical pentachords. Some of them feature a clearly apparent symmetry in their prime form; others don't. For those that do, prove the symmetry by listing their interval series. For those that don't immediately look symmetrical, show what kind of transformation will make it apparent (rotation, or duplicating the last pc at the beginning of the prime form).

       a. (01234)

       b. (01268)

       c. (01348)

       d. (01356)

       e. (01478)

       f. (02346)

       g. (02468)

       h. (02469)

       i. (02479)

       j. (03458)

    2. With the help of the list of set classes, provide a list of all inversionally symmetrical tetrachords.

Chapter 4

Analyzing Atonal Music

We now have sufficient knowledge and understanding of pitch-class set theory to apply it to the analysis of what is often called "free atonal music." The qualifier "free" does in no way imply that this music or its pitch structures are free from organizational principles. Rather, this music is free in that, in the first place, it does not follow in any systematic way the tenets of either tonality or pitch centricity. Free atonal music follows whatever compositional criteria the composer may have established for a particular piece, and these criteria may or may not involve, in a particular piece, the organization of pitch. Atonal music is often based on motivic and intervallic cells that are manipulated by the composer in a variety of ways. Because we can interpret these motivic collections as pitch-class sets, pitch-class set theory is particularly suitable to help us understand many of the pitch structures and motivic relationships of this music, as we will discover in this chapter. It is important to keep in mind, however, that pitch-class set theory was formulated decades after the music we are going to study in this chapter was composed. This means, of course, that we should not think of set theory as a *compositional tool* that was available to the composers that we will now study, but rather as an *analytical tool* that is available to us to understand and interpret some of the pitch structures we find in their music.

Early twentieth-century atonal music is best represented by the three composers of the Second Viennese School: Arnold Schoenberg (1874–1951), Anton Webern (1883–1945), and Alban Berg (1885–1935). We will focus our study on two pieces from the same year (1909) by two of these composers: a movement for string quartet by Webern (Five Movements for String Quartet, op. 5, III) and a song by Schoenberg ("Angst und Hoffen," no. 7 from *Book of the Hanging Gardens,* op. 15). Although the Webern piece is perhaps the most complex of the two, we will begin with it because its very complexity allows us to touch on many issues pertinent to atonal music in general. First, however, we will examine some of the basic issues involved in the analysis of atonal music by means of pitch-class set theory, and we will do so with some brief examples by Webern, Berg, and Schoenberg.

ANALYZING ATONAL MUSIC

The main difficulty in analyzing atonal music is precisely that there is not a general organizational system to guide our analysis (unlike, for instance, the analysis of tonal music, which is based on our knowledge of functional tonality and the various ways it can be manifested in musical structures). This lack of a universal system means that there is no such thing as a single correct analysis of a piece. Various skillful analysts may, and often do, come up with various interesting and convincing, but remarkably different, analyses. We will thus have to learn to be imaginative in the way we approach an atonal composition and to use the analytical tools we have in a logical and musical way. This will allow us to come up with convincing (and defensible) analyses, even if they are different from what other analysts come up with. And we should also keep in mind that what we are trying to do is not to find out what the composer had in mind or how the piece was composed (we would not be able to figure that out in any case), but rather to interpret what the composer did, on the basis of our observation and study of the score.

Interpreting the Musical Surface

The first step in the analysis of an atonal piece, the same as with any other piece, is *to listen to it, or play or sing through it, several times.* As we listen, we will identify musical, textural, and formal units, aurally and visually on the score, using our traditional musical knowledge. Thus, we will hear and mark motives, phrases, sections, repetitions of material, imitations, chords, arpeggios, melodies, melodic fragmentations, melodic variations, and so on. We should also hear rhythmic patterns, rhythmic motives and groupings, and timbral or registral units (for instance, a chord in the brass section, or a tremolo by several string instruments in the high register). This process is essential for us to understand, and talk about, the music. Let us try it with the opening six measures of Webern's Five Movements for String Quartet, op. 5, IV, reproduced in Example 4.1. (To begin with, and if possible, listen to this passage ignoring the analytical annotations on this example, that is, focusing only on the "original" score, while you identify and mark as many musical elements as you can.) We already discussed some aspects of this fragment in Chapter 3, but let us now approach it afresh, as if we knew nothing about it.[1]

We have heard two opening measures that feature two tremolos in the violins, a repeated pedallike E♭ in the cello, a two-note motive in the viola, and a pizzicato chord in the violins. Mm. 3–6 feature contrapuntal, polyphonic textures. We hear a descending four-note motive in the first violin, imitated in canon by the second violin in m. 4, and by the cello also in m. 4 (while the viola repeats the same two-note motive we heard in m. 2, with a slight rhythmic variation). Then in mm. 5–6, we hear a three-voice poly-

---

[1]There are numerous published analyses of this piece. See, for instance, Gary Wittlich, "Sets and Ordering Procedures in Twentieth-Century Music," in *Aspects of Twentieth-Century Music,* ed. Gary Wittlich (Englewood Cliffs: Prentice Hall, 1975), pp. 388–476; David Beach, "Pitch Structure and the Analytic Process in Atonal Music: An Interpretation of the Theory of Sets"; Charles Burkhart, "The Symmetrical Source of Webern's Opus 5, No. 4," *Music Forum* 5 (1980): 317–34; and Straus, *Introduction to Post-Tonal Theory,* pp. 119–25.

♪♪ Example 4.1	Webern, Five Movements for String Quartet, op. 5, IV, mm. 1–6

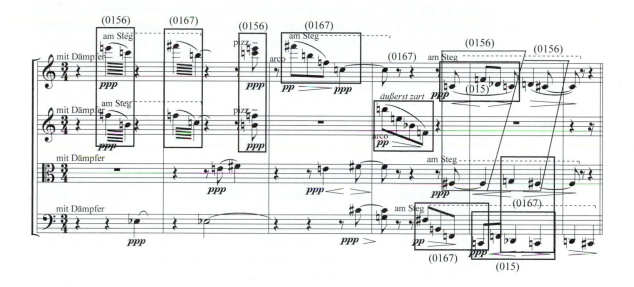

phonic texture in the first violin, viola, and cello. This texture consists of a brief canon between the violin and the cello (beginning on the pick up to m. 5), while the viola has its own free line. Finally, we hear an ascending arpeggiated figure that closes the passage.

Identifying and Analyzing Pitch-Class Sets: Segmentation

After we understand and describe the musical elements in a passage such as this, we can start *identifying segments that we may analyze as pitch-class sets,* that is, as possibly significant structural collections. After identifying segments and the sets that make up these segments, we will *examine possible relationships among these sets.* The type of relationships that will be significant to us are set equivalence (transposition or inversion, that is, membership in the same set class), inclusion (subsets of larger sets), complementarity, intervallic similarity (which we may identify by comparing interval-class vectors), and so on.

Identifying segments for analysis brings up the complex problem of **segmentation** in atonal music (that is, the division of a musical surface into fragments that we can analyze as pitch-class sets).[2] It makes sense to begin with the segments that we have

[2]The problem of segmentation in pc-set analysis has been discussed, among others, by David Beach, "Pitch Structure and the Analytic Process in Atonal Music: An Interpretation of the Theory of Sets"; Christopher Hasty, "Segmentation and Process in Post-Tonal Music," *Music Theory Spectrum* 3 (1981): 54–73, and Dora Hanninen, "Orientations, Criteria, Segments: A General Theory of Segmentation for Music Analysis," *Journal of Music Theory* 45/2 (2001): 345–434.

identified on the musical surface. Following this criterion, we identify the sets that make up the two tremolo figures in mm. 1–2 as members of the (0156) and (0167) set classes, respectively (to do so we would go through the steps we learned in Chapter 3 to identify the prime form of a set), while the pizzicato chord at the end of m. 2 is also a (0156) set. The four-note motive in mm. 3–4 is also a good immediate candidate for identification as a pitch class set, and we find out that its prime form is (0167).

NOTE

Generally, small sets (trichords and tetrachords) tend to be more significant than larger sets, although at times identifying hexachords or septachords is perfectly acceptable if the surface of the music is based on such larger pitch-class segments.

If segmentation is not so clear on the musical surface, we will need to try out various possibilities to investigate what may work and what may not. In any case, we should always try to pick segments made up of contiguous elements (that is, elements that are next to each other), rather than picking notes from here and there in a random way. Moreover, you should not necessarily try to account for all pitches in the music, but rather try to focus on segments and pitch collections that make musical sense to you. The polyphonic section in m. 5 of our example allows for various possible segmentations. First, it seems to make sense to figure out the set for the head motive of the violin-cello canon C–F–D♭–C, and it is (015). Then we can explore various possibilities that would include two of the voices, and that would account for the viola notes. Because we have been identifying mostly tetrachords, we can focus on tetrachordal segments. Example 4.1 identifies three that make particular sense: the violin motive together with the simultaneous F♯ in the viola, forming set class (0156); the last two notes of the violin theme together with the simultaneous two notes of the viola, also forming set class (0156); and the same last two notes in the viola together with the simultaneous two notes in the cello, forming (0167).

NOTE

Different segmentations would also be possible, and would perhaps show other interesting set relationships. For instance, the segmentation of mm. 3–6 we discussed in Chapter 3 (see Example 3.7), different from the one we are discussing here, demonstrated complementarity relations that are essential in the structure of this piece.

We could continue our analysis, but this should suffice to illustrate some issues and criteria involving segmentation. We have chosen segments that are clearly delineated in the music, and, when various possibilities arise, as in m. 5, we have picked groups of notes that are simultaneous or contiguous in some way. What we have found seems to make a lot of sense. We have identified only two set classes among the tetrachords in this whole passage, (0156) and (0167), and we see they are used in a variety of musical and textural contexts. We also identified one trichordal segment, (015), a subset

> **♪♪♪ Example 4.2**   Webern, Five Movements for String Quartet, op. 5, IV, mm. 8–9 (first violin only)

of (0156). In other words, we discover a remarkable consistency in the pitch-class collections that make up this passage. Note also that if we compare the ICVs for both tetrachords, we see that their intervallic structures are indeed very similar: [200121] for (0156), and [200022] for (0167).

Analyzing Melodies and Harmonies

There are various ways of analyzing a melody, and here again we may have to consider multiple possibilities of segmentation before we find one that is convincing. Breaking the melody into equal segments may make sense at times (trichords or tetrachords). It is possible for segments to overlap with each other, and it is also possible to choose segments that span over rests. Example 4.2 shows an analysis of the first violin melody in Webern's op. 5, IV. By choosing a segmentation that includes only trichords, spans over a rest, and allows the last two trichords to overlap, we discover a nice, consistent trichordal structure in which all three trichords are members of set class (014).

When *analyzing chordal structures* (harmonies), at times we will consider only the actual chord. But at other times it will make sense to include, along with the chord, other pitch classes that may be presented simultaneously to the chord in one or more melodic lines. In other words, we can analyze melody and harmony separately, but we may also want to examine their interaction. This is illustrated by the fragment in Example 4.3, from a 1908 song by Berg. The texture is clearly made up of a vocal line and a harmonic accompaniment in the piano, in block chords (numbered 1–7 on the example). If we analyze each chord as a pc set, we see that all chords except numbers 2, 5, and 7 form (0268) set classes. The three exceptions are all (026) sets. In the case of these three trichords, however, we may try to check the note in the melody that sounds simultaneously with the chord. In each of the three cases, we find that the pitch class in the vocal line does indeed complete the (0268) set, thus providing total consistency to the harmonic succession in this phrase, all made up of (0268) chords.

Segments That Involve Nonadjacent Pitch Classes

So far we have examined only sets made up of pitch classes that were immediately contiguous in the music. It is also possible to consider groups of noncontiguous pitch classes if they are associated by register, duration, timbre, and so on. This is most

♪♪♪ Example 4.3   Alban Berg, "Schlafend trägt man mich," no. 2 from *Four Songs*, op. 2, mm. 1–4

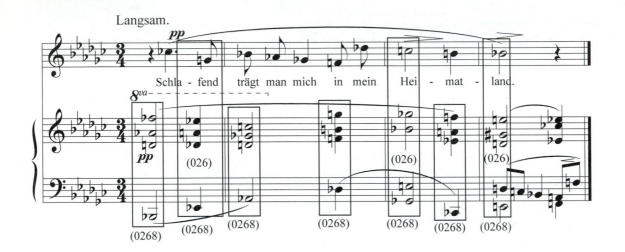

♪♪♪ Example 4.4   Schoenberg, "Angst und Hoffen," vocal part, mm. 1–2

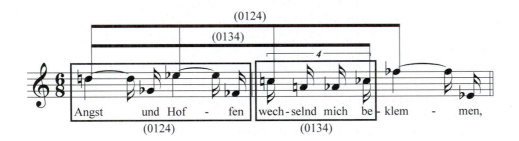

evident when we analyze a compound melody, that is, a melody made up of two or more lines in different registers. An example from a piece by Schoenberg that we will analyze in more detail later in this chapter will clarify this concept. In Example 4.4 we can see the opening two measures for the 1909 song "Angst und Hoffen" (you can see the complete context for this phrase in Anthology no. 11). We observe that, here again, we have a texture made up of a vocal melody and a piano accompaniment. We will study the piano part and the interaction between the voice part and the piano in our analysis later in this chapter. But for now, we can remark that the first eight notes in the voice outline the upper and lower voices of the piano part. We can first consider the tetrachordal segments that make up this opening melodic fragment, that is, notes 1–4 and 5–8 in the voice. The first tetrachord is (0124), and the second tetrachord is (0134). Both of these sets are significant, as we will see later, both in the piano part and throughout the song.

But, as we have discussed already, we hear this melody as a compound melody functioning in two different registers and actually doubling the notes of the piano's upper and lower voices. Let us then consider the upper line of this compound melody. The beams over the melody show two possible tetrachords that result from reading the upper line in the compound melody as an independent line. We see that, in either case, we pick pitches that are not adjacent, but that are associated linearly and by register. This is thus a perfectly acceptable segmentation. If we consider the line D–E♭–C–C♭, the set class is (0134). If, instead, we consider D–E♭–C–F♭, the set class is (0124). Both of these sets are relevant to our analysis because they are the same sets that we just identified by grouping adjacent pitches in the melody into trichords.

ANALYSIS 4.1: WEBERN, FIVE MOVEMENTS FOR STRING QUARTET, OP. 5, III (ANTHOLOGY NO. 10)

We are now ready to move on to the analysis of a complete atonal piece. As we just saw in our introductory discussion, we will approach the analysis of an atonal piece following the same process we would follow to analyze any other type of piece. First, we should listen to the piece several times and try to understand as much of its formal structure as possible as we listen. We should then focus on general musical elements that will allow us to identify sections and formal aspects of the piece. After we understand the basic compositional material, we can start focusing in more detail on pitch structure and pitch organization. Let us thus begin with general musical considerations.[3]

Texture, Sections, and Form

What are the textural, motivic and thematic, rhythmic, and instrumental elements that distinguish phrases and sections? Are sections clearly delimited, and how? You will hear that this movement features unquestionable drive and musical power; a good performance of it can easily keep you on the edge of your seat!

Let us first focus on the elements that seem to determine sections, and let us describe them in simple, standard musical terms. You may have noticed that a logical break up of the movement would be into three large sections, consisting of mm. 1–8, 9–14, and 15–23. Can you provide musical reasons for such a division into three sections?

We will thus think of mm. 1–8 as section 1. In mm. 1–6 we hear a C♯ pedal in the bass in quarter notes. The upper strings perform a series of chordal motives (we hear them vertically as trichords and horizontally as large leaps) in mm. 1–3, followed by a six-note canonic gesture in two voices in m. 4, and further trichordal gestures (either as vertical trichords or as imitative melodic motives) in mm. 5–6. The trichordal texture

---

[3]For an analysis of this piece, to which our present discussion in indebted, see Charles Lord, "An Explication of Some Recent Mathematical Approaches to Music Analysis" (Ph.D. dissertation, Indiana University, 1978), pp. 108–123.

is again interrupted by a two-voice imitative passage, this time by contrary motion and using seven notes, in m. 7, and a final statement of the two-chord motivic element from mm. 1–3 in m. 8. Note that the section closes with an ascending, leaping figure in the cello alone, which we can hear as a cadential gesture.

Section 2 (mm. 9–14) features contrasting characteristics with respect to section 1. Mm. 9–10 display a new texture in this piece, a melodic line in the first violin, accompanied by pizzicato lines in second violin and viola. The next section, mm. 11–14, is based on a more complex contrapuntal texture, presenting pizzicato motivic groups of varied length in close imitation. See, for instance, the brief canons between cello and second violin beginning in the last quarter note of m. 10 (on the same theme that we already heard in the first violin and viola in m. 4) and partially replicated by the first violin (mm. 11–12) and the second violin and cello (mm. 12–13). In mm. 12–14, moreover, a long melodic line is presented by the first violin in the high register, creating a contrasting element with the contrapuntal texture in pizzicato under it. The section closes in m. 14 with a cadential gesture in the second violin, parallel to the cello gesture with the same function in m. 8: both are trichordal, both feature large leaps, and, in fact, the gesture in m. 14 is a textural inversion of the same intervals found in the cadential gesture in m. 8 (a m6 and a M7).

Before you continue reading, examine section 3, determine the main compositional elements, and think whether they are related to elements we have previously seen in the piece or whether they represent new and contrasting material. In the first place, we see that the cello features a three-note ostinato throughout the section. The viola and second violin begin the section with pizzicato figures reminiscent of their material in mm. 9–10, and then continue with their own three-note ostinato, presented in canon, beginning in m. 18. This three-note ostinato is the same motive that was presented in imitation beginning in the last quarter note of m. 10 (m3 up–m9 down). Above the ostinato figures in the three lower instruments, we hear a long melody in the first violin. This melody is clearly an extension of a melody we have encountered previously. Which melody, and where? Mm. 22–23 close the movement with a forceful melodic statement in octaves, borrowing also a line that we have heard before. Where? Similarly, the very closing gesture brings back a pitch class that was significant earlier in the piece. Where, and how?

After this discussion you can listen to the piece again, and you should find that it is now easier to follow and understand what is going on musically and to make sense of various formal and thematic/motivic relationships. How could we summarize all these relationships and the way they come together formally? It is not easy to label a piece such as this one formally. We should make clear that there is not one single exclusive way to understand the form of this and similar pieces, and we can easily come up with (and find in the literature) conflicting formal interpretations of this movement. Even our assumption that the piece consists of three main sections can be questioned. According to some analysts, this movement can be read as a type of binary (with two main sections, mm. 1–15 and 16–23).[4] Would you argue for a binary or a ternary interpretation?

---

[4]See, for instance, Kent Williams, *Theories and Analyses of Twentieth-Century Music* (Fort Worth: Harcourt Brace, 1997), pp. 263–272.

If you decide for ternary, how would you define the relationship between the three parts, and how would you label them with letters? We can return to these considerations as a conclusion, after we study pitch organization in more detail.

Pitch Organization

We can now examine the pitch content of the motives and chords we have just identified. We will apply the same procedures and criteria we previously studied for segmentation, labeling of sets, and determining set relationships.

Section 1

Look, for instance, at section 1 in our example. (We already discussed some characteristics of the opening measures of this section in Chapter 3; see Examples 3.2 and 3.4). If we disregard the C♯ pedal for now, we see that all the chords in the upper strings are trichords. The canonic theme in m. 4 is a hexachord, which can in turn break up into various trichordal subsets. In m. 5 we have again two vertical trichordal statements, followed by a brief canon on a trichordal melodic motive, and again three chordal statements in m. 6 that create both vertical and horizontal trichords. Before you continue reading, identify all the trichords in mm. 1–8, as well as the hexachords in m. 4 and the septachords in m. 7.

Example 4.5 shows a possible analysis of pc sets in mm. 1–8. This analysis immediately tells us that the piece features a strong coherence in pitch collections and in motivic relationships. As we already know from Chapter 3, all the vertical trichords in mm. 1–3 are of the (014) type, and so are the vertical trichords in mm. 5, 6, and 8. Harmonic coherence is thus provided in this section by the (014) trichord. If we look at horizontal trichords, we see that the first three pcs in each of the upper voices in mm. 1–3 form the trichords (015), (015), and (037). We will get back to (037) later, but the significance of (015) is immediately noticeable as we continue our analysis. The melodic trichord used canonically in mm. 5–6 is also of the (015) type, and so is the cadential gesture in the cello in m. 8. Otherwise, the three chords in m. 6, which we saw were of the (014) type as vertical chords, also spell out three (014) melodic trichords. It seems fair to state, then, that section 1 is permeated by two trichords, (014) and (015), which give it a very tight coherence. It is also interesting to notice the use of adjacent transpositions or inversions of (014) that allow for one invariant pitch class, that is, for a common pitch class between adjacent chords. The trichords numbered 1 and 2 in Example 4.5, for instance, related by T_8, have an invariant B♮; sets 6 and 7, related by T_0I, have an invariant C♯; sets 10 and 11, related by T_{11}, have an invariant G♮, and so on. Example 4.6 shows the three pairs of (014) trichords in mm. 1–5 (trichords 1–2, 6–7, and 10–11, following the numbering of sets from Example 4.5), with indication of both the T or TI operation that relates each pair and the invariant pitch class between the members of each pair. What are the invariant pitch classes between sets 15–16, 16–17, and 20–21? What about the larger sets in mm. 4 and 7? Determine what they are and how they are related.

The two sets in m. 4 are of the same type, (012468), related by T_7. The two sets in m. 7 are also of the same type, (0123578), related by T_1I. Sets 8 and 9 are arranged

♪♪♪ Example 4.5   Webern, Five Movements for String Quartet, op. 5, III,
                    mm. 1–8, pc-set analysis

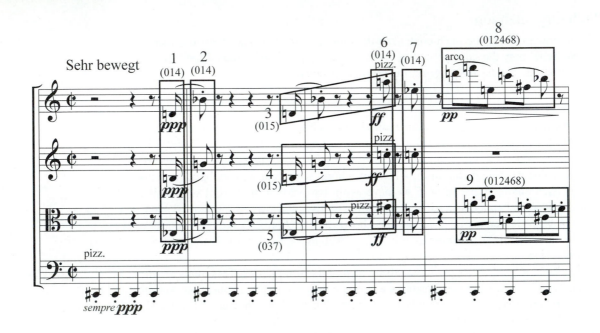

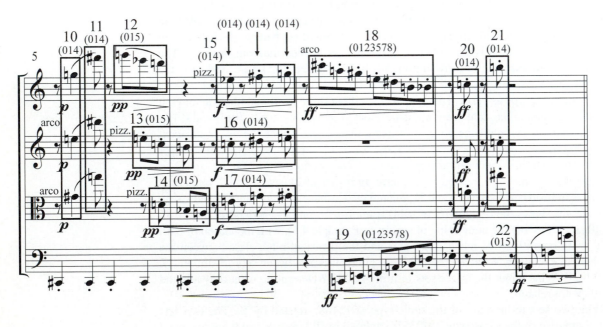

♪♪♪ **Example 4.6**   Webern, op. 5, III, the pairs of (014) trichords in mm. 1–5

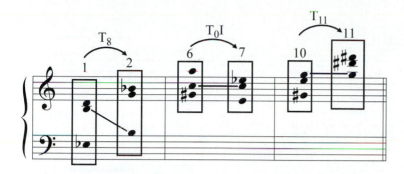

♪♪♪ **Example 4.7**   Webern, op. 5, III, the figures in mm. 4 and 7

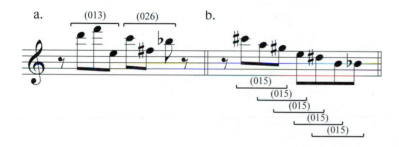

as two adjacent trichords, (013) and (026), two trichords that have not yet appeared in the piece (Example 4.7a). Both (014) and (015), however, are also subsets of (012468). Can you find the (014) and (015) subsets in this hexachord? (You should find one of the former and two of the latter.) Sets 18 and 19, on the other hand, are presented as a series of overlapping (015) trichords: every three adjacent notes in these sets is a (015) set (Example 4.7b). If you look at set (0123578), moreover, you should be able to find (014) once as a subset, and (015) five times!

Section 2

The beginning of section 2 (mm. 9–10, see Example 4.8) allows us to continue our trichordal analysis, and we discover that some of the trichords are already familiar to us, whereas others are less familiar or new. Thus, the melody in the first violin breaks up into three trichords, (014), (012), and (015). (014) and (015) function as a connection

🎵🎵🎵 Example 4.8   Webern, Five Movements for String Quartet, op. 5, III,
                         mm. 9–14, pc-set analysis

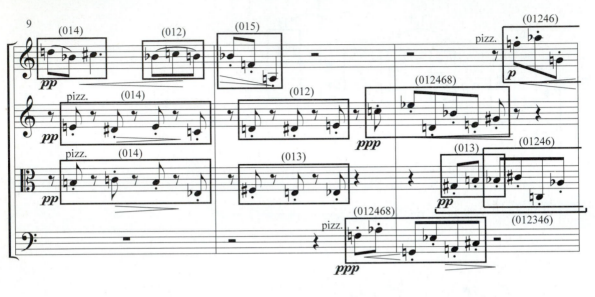

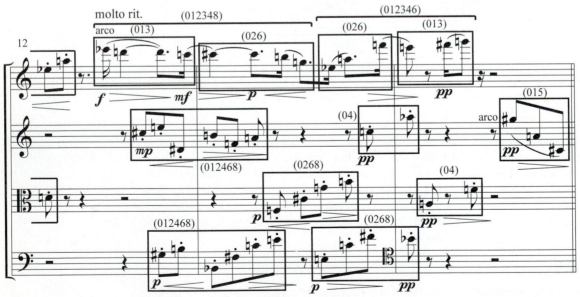

with section 1, and (012) is new in the piece. In the accompanying voices, we see (014) again, along with (013) and (012). From here on, in mm. 11–15, the texture requires segmentation into larger sets. We are already familiar with the theme used canonically by the cello and the second violin in mm. 10–11, the same theme from m. 4, thus also the same set class, (012468). The viola figure in m. 11 can be understood as forming either a single hexachord, (012346), a set we will come back to soon, or two overlapping sets: a (013) trichord and a (01246) pentachord. The latter, a shortened version of the theme from m. 4, is immediately imitated by the first violin with the same gesture and the same (01246) set. The complete (012468) is featured in mm. 12–13 by the cello and the second violin, whereas shorter subsets of this hexachord follow in the viola, cello, second violin, and viola, respectively: (0268) and (04), twice each. In other words, the function of this contrapuntal passage in section 2 is to provide a brief development on the theme from m. 4. To do so, the theme is varied and broken up into shorter statements, while the hexachord on which it is built is also broken up into various subsets, including a pentachord, a tetrachord, a trichord, and a dyad, all subsets of (012468).

Two more elements are worth mentioning in the middle section. First is the long first-violin melody in mm. 12–14. If we break it up into trichordal segments, we come up with the following set of trichords: (013), (026), (026), (013). These are the same adjacent trichords into which the set in m. 4 is divided in the music (see Example 4.7a)! Note, however, that if we consider the melody in mm. 12–14 as two hexachords, each made up of a (013) plus a (026), we end up with two hexachords that are different among themselves and different from the hexachord in m. 4: (012348) and (012346). (You will observe that the latter is the same hexachord that we already identified in the viola figure in m. 11.) In other words, the melody in the first violin provides both a connection and an element of contrast with section 1. The second element we should mention is the cadential gesture, again of the (015) type, that closes the section in m. 14, as in m. 8.

Section 3

Before we begin discussing section 3, study it for a while and try to identify what elements you think we have already discussed in the previous sections and what elements, if any, seem to be new to section 3. How would you approach the study of pc sets in section 3?

First, let us look at the trichordal content of mm. 15–17, as shown in Example 4.9. The cello ostinato outlines (014) throughout the section. The pizzicato figures in the viola and second violin, on the other hand, feature three trichords: (013), (014), and (015). We see immediately that the two prominent trichords from section 1, (014) and (015), which were hardly present in section 2, are now back. Next we can look at the three ostinato voices in mm. 18–21 (the three lower voices). In mm. 18–19, the second violin/viola canon is based on (013) motives, which change to (026) in mm. 20–21. These are the two trichords that we already found associated in m. 4, and again in the violin melody of mm. 12–14.

It is also interesting to identify the harmonic trichords formed by the three lower voices in mm. 18–21. In mm. 18–19, the three trichords resulting from the ostinatos are (026) and (037). (026) is quite familiar to us, and (037) appears for the first time

♪♪ Example 4.9   Webern, Five Movements for String Quartet, op. 5, III,
                        mm. 15–23, pc-set analysis

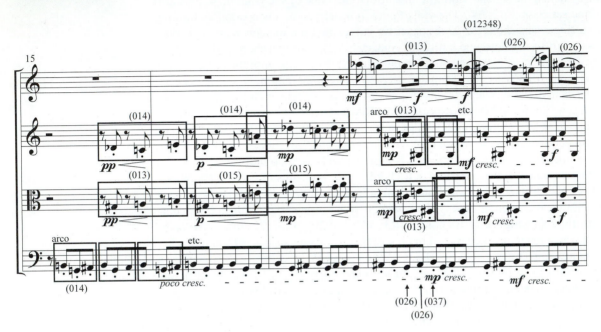

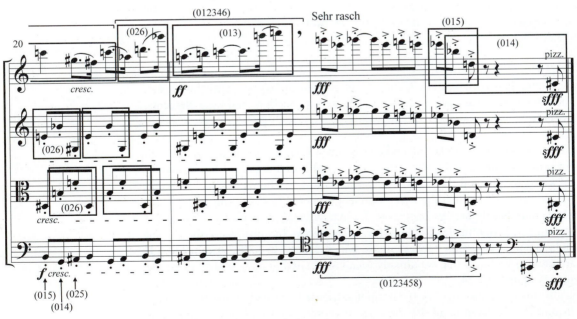

since its presence as a horizontal trichord in the viola in mm. 1–3. The harmonic trichords in mm. 20–21 are (015), (014), and (025). Of these, (025) is the only totally new trichord we have identified in section 3, and it can be seen as closely related to both (015) and (026).

The first-violin melody in mm. 18–21 is an extension of the melody from mm. 12–14, and, broken into adjacent trichords, turns out to be based on the same sets that we already saw in mm. 12–14: (013), (026), (026), (026), (013). The complete melody divided into two hexachords also results, as in mm. 12–14, into (012348) and (012346). The closing statement in octaves in mm. 22–23 is a transposition of the first-violin phrase from mm. 9–10, and the set class for this phrase is (0123458), a set that contains the hexachord (012348) from the violin melody. The last three pitch classes in this phrase, E♭–B♭–D, constitute a final appearance of (015), the "cadential gesture" trichord. Finally, the last three pitch classes in the piece, B♭–D–C♯, form a closing (014) set class.

Conclusions

We should now try to bring together all the preceding observations into some conclusions that should mostly address two issues: How is pitch coherence achieved in this atonal composition? And how does pitch structure contribute to our understanding of the seemingly ambiguous formal design of this piece? Before you continue reading, try to provide answers to these questions.

Coherence in this movement is achieved by the consistent use of a very limited number of pitch-class collections. Motivic and harmonic unity in section 1 is determined by two trichords, (014) and (015). Section 2 introduces a prominent new trichord, (012), and is otherwise based on two musical elements: a contrapuntal development on the thematic gesture introduced in m. 4 and a melodic line in the first violin. The contrapuntal development uses the original thematic element, which is represented by set class (012468), and breaks it up into various smaller segments or subsets. The violin melody contains only two trichords, (013) and (026), the same two trichords into which the theme from m. 4 is divided. Section 3 can be interpreted as a synthesis of the two previous sections. (014) and (015) become prominent again in this closing section, and the first-violin melody from section 2 is again presented and extended in section 3. Several of the trichords that have been previously presented, (014), (015), (026), and (037), along with the new (025), are now heard as harmonic sonorities resulting from the triple ostinato in the lower voices.

There is thus little doubt about the coherence provided by motives and pc collections in this movement, and our analysis demonstrates the value of pitch-class set theory in illuminating pitch coherence in a piece such as the one we have just studied. What would you say is the role of pitch-class C♯ in this composition? In this otherwise atonal piece, Webern seems to be playing with a semblance of pitch centricity by building the first section on a C♯ pedal, and by returning to the same C♯ to close the piece in a powerful *sfff* pizzicato. Although the C♯ is unrelated to the pc set structure of the movement, it contributes to its overall pitch coherence by providing a beginning and ending point of reference.

Having considered all of this, how would you label the form of the piece? Assuming that we decide to stick with the ternary division we have used throughout our analysis, there are at least two interpretations that would incorporate our conclusions regarding thematic and pitch relationships. We could label the first interpretation as A–B–B¹, taking into account that section 2 is contrasting (although it grows from the theme in m. 4) and that section 3 can be seen as a varied presentation of the same material used in section 2. Another interpretation, perhaps even more appropriate, would be A–B–(A + B), by which we mean that section 3 is really a synthesis or a combination of both of the previous sections. In any case, it is evident that here form is not a clear-cut matter, and that various different interpretations are possible and not necessarily mutually exclusive.

ANALYSIS 4.2: SCHOENBERG "ANGST UND HOFFEN," NO. 7 FROM *BOOK OF THE HANGING GARDENS*, OP. 15 (ANTHOLOGY NO. 11)

Schoenberg's song "Angst und Hoffen" is a good example of the turn-of-the-twentieth-century cultural movement known as **expressionism.** In sharp contrast with the stylistic trend we know as neoclassicism, which we will discuss in the next chapter, expressionism represents a gesture of the dying Romantic period. It is a movement centered in Vienna, in the same cultural environment where we find Sigmund Freud and philosopher Ludwig Wittgenstein, with some of its most prominent exponents being Stefan George and Richard Dehmel in poetry, Wassili Kandinsky and Oskar Kokoschka in painting, and Schoenberg and Berg in music. Expressionism in general favors violent emotions and intense depictions of inner life, which are often presented in a distorted and fragmented way. Expressionist art often delves into the world of the subconscious and of psychic conflicts, and it displays a taste for the strange, the macabre, or even the grotesque at times. A familiar and typically expressionist image is provided by Edvard Munch's famous painting, *The Scream* (1895). In Schoenberg and Berg, musical expressionism is often paired with expressionist texts and is characterized by dissonant and usually nontriadic harmony, avoidance of tonal centers, use of intervallic-motivic cells often connected by means of nontonal linear relationships, musical expression of intensely dramatic texts, wide melodic leaps, and extreme registers. Schoenberg often talked in his teaching about what he called the ***Grundgestalt*** or "basic shape," a single idea or motive from which a complete composition may be generated. Schoenberg called the process of motivic manipulation and continuous development through which a piece is generated from a single idea "**developing variation.**"[5] We will now study "Angst und Hoffen" against this backdrop of stylistic expressionism.

---

[5]On Schoenberg's *Grundgestalt,* see Patricia Carpenter, "*Grundgestalt* as Tonal Function," *Music Theory Spectrum* 5 (1983): 15–38; and David Epstein, *Beyond Orpheus* (Oxford: Oxford University Press, 1987), Chapter 2. On the topic of Schoenberg's use of motive and developing variation, see Jack Boss, "Schoenberg's Op. 22 Radio Talk and Developing Variation in Atonal Music," *Music Theory Spectrum* 14/2 (1992): 125–49.

The Poem

Schoenberg's *Book of the Hanging Gardens* is a collection of fifteen songs on poems by Stefan George. The text for "Angst und Hoffen" follows, both in the original German version and in an English translation. Read the poem several times, and listen to the song several times following the text.

Angst un hoffen wechselnd mich beklemmen,	Anguish and hope in turn seize me.
Meine worte sich in seufzer dehnen,	My words trail off in sighing.
Mich bedrängt so ungestümes sehnen,	Such tempestuous longing assails me
Daß ich mich an rast und schlaf mich kehre,	That I do not turn to rest or sleep
Daß mein lager tränen schwemmen,	That tears flood my couch,
Daß ich jede freude von mir wehre,	That I ward off every pleasure,
Daß ich keines freundes trost begehre.	That I seek no friend's consolation.

As befits an expressionist text, this poem (which David Lewin has described as "an exploration of an affective disorder") describes intense emotions and their overpowering effects on the poet.[6] Line 1 presents the contrasting emotions that torment ("seize") the poet: anguish and hope. Line 2 describes a consequence of those emotions, sighing that interferes with the poet's speech. Line 3 again presents an intense emotion that "assails" the poet: tempestuous longing. Finally, lines 4–7 are a list of further consequences (or, to use Lewin's word, "symptoms") that result from those strong emotions; our unhappy poet can't sleep or rest, the poet weeps, the poet does not enjoy any pleasure, and, finally and perhaps most importantly, the poet is miserably lonely and does not even try to find a remedy to it. We could thus think of two major divisions for this poem: lines 1–3 and lines 4–7, which, as Lewin points out, is a somewhat unbalanced design, "befitting the subject matter." Now listen to the song again, and determine how its phrases and divisions correspond with the text.

Formal Organization

The basic formal divisions of the song follow the text lines quite closely. Each of the seven lines is assigned its own music, and musical lines are set apart by various factors, such as changes of meter, tempo changes, and rests. The boundaries between lines 1 and 2 (mm. 1–2 and 3–4 respectively) are a change of meter and an eighth-note rest, and the same can be said of lines 2 and 3 (boundary in bar 5). There is no rest between lines 3 and 4 (bar 7), but there is a change of meter and a change of tempo. Line 5 is introduced by a sixteenth-note rest (bar 9), line 6 by an eighth-note rest, and finally line 7

---

[6]A compelling analysis of this song and how it is shaped by the poem can be found in David Lewin, "A Way into Schoenberg's Opus 15, Number 7," *In Theory Only* 6/1 (1981): 3–24. The present discussion of the song's text and its relationship to formal design is largely based on Lewin's observations. For a general study of the op. 15 cycle, see Allen Forte, "Concepts of Linearity in Schoenberg's Atonal Music: A Study of the Opus 15 Song Cycle," *Journal of Music Theory* 36/2 (1992): 285–382.

by a change of meter, a quarter-note rest, and a change of tempo. On the surface and at a glance, the melody for all seven lines does not seem to have any prominent recurring motivic or thematic relationships, although we will immediately see that there are indeed multiple motivic relationships of a less obvious nature. Motivic relationships, however, are immediately observable at the surface level in the piano accompaniment. It is interesting to note that phrasing in the piano part is not synchronic with phrasing in the voice part. That is, phrases in voice and piano overlap, and this helps create a sense of continuity and forward drive in the song.

The three tempo changes divide the song into three large sections. The first section, *Nicht zu rasch,* is the fastest. The second section slows down to a *Langsamer,* whereas the third section slows down even more to a *Sehr langsam.* The music itself in mm. 15–19 further slows down the pacing by means of longer values. This division groups the lines into 1–3 (the emotions) and 4–6 (the list of symptoms). Line 7, the final symptom, is given its own section and its own tempo, thus putting the emphasis of the song on the poet's voluntary and narcissistic state of loneliness. This also explains the unusual piano setting for this song: the right hand is set alone, and seems not to seek or need the help or consolation of the left hand. The whole song can be seen as a progressive loss of energy leading to the final state of total exhaustion. After all the activity and the progressive loss of energy in sections 1 and 2, section 3 not only slows down in tempo, but by the last measures of the song we have the feeling that the music, along with the poet's sighs, drags and crawls and barely makes it to the end. Even the progression of rests introducing phrases 4–7 seems to point to this exhaustion of energy. Rests get longer, from no rest to introduce line 4 (notice that the text in line 4, "that I do not turn to rest," refers to the absence of rest!), to a sixteenth-note rest, then an eighth-note rest, then a quarter note, and finally the long rests of the last three measures, left to the lonely right hand of the pianist.

The Musical Material: Motives and Collections

Although motivic associations in the voice part may not be so obvious, first focus on the piano part for motivic relationships. What motives and collections can you identify in the piano part? What are the intervallic characteristics of these collections? Do some of them recur throughout the piece in one form or another?

The first three beats of the piano part introduce us to the three most significant pitch collections in the piece. In m. 1 we hear two trichordal sonorities (the "Angst und Hoffen" chords): an augmented triad, and a quartal chord consisting of an augmented fourth and a perfect fourth. The latter is a characteristic chord in Schoenberg, Berg, and Webern, one that we find repeatedly in the music of these composers in various compositional contexts (including both atonal and serial music), and is often referred to as the **Viennese trichord.** We can also observe the voice leading that connects both chords: the upper voice moves up by half step, the lower voice down by step, and the middle voice retains the common tone between the two chords. Following these chords, a third element appears in m. 2, beat 1, two parallel minor thirds related by half-step motion. If you look now at the vocal line in these three beats, you will discover that it is really a compound melody (that is, a melody made up of two lines). The upper line, D–E♭–C–C♭, unfolds the voice leading of the upper voice in the piano part. The lower line in the voice's compound melody, G♭–F♭–A–A♭, outlines the voice leading in the piano's lower voice. With the only exception of the whole tone in the G♭–F♭ dyad, all other voice leading dyads are half steps. You may remember, from your studies of Renaissance and Baroque music, that the half step (particularly the descending half step) has been associated to a particular affect (grief, sadness, sorrow) since at least the sixteenth century. We know this basic text-painting device as a "sigh." Musical sighs are indeed an appropriate gesture in a song where the poet's sighs are so prevalent!

Now examine and listen to the complete song, focusing on the piano accompaniment, and determine the relevance of the elements we have just identified (the augmented triad, the Viennese trichord, the parallel descending thirds, and the half-step voice leading) in the composition of the whole song. First, how are the three elements present in mm. 2–4, after the first statement in beats 1–3? What variations are introduced in these elements in these measures? How are the musical sighs particularly present in the accompaniment to line 2, "My words trail off in sighing"? (Notice both the vocal line and piano part at the word "Seufzer"—"sighs.") What sections are based almost entirely on the connection between the augmented triad and the Viennese trichord, or on either one of the two collections (note that these collections may also be presented in arpeggiated form)? Beware that Schoenberg does not always spell the augmented triad chord as in measure one (in root position). Some of the augmented sonorities are spelled as though inverted (as in C–E–A♭), rather than as two major thirds. The Viennese trichord also allows for two different arrangements: you may have the tritone below and the perfect fourth above, or you may have the perfect fourth below and the tritone above.

Pitch-Class Set Analysis

Now that we know the piece a little better, we can go more in depth to understand its pitch structure. The diagrams in Example 4.10 will help you follow this discussion. All the essential pitch-class material in this song is presented in mm. 1–2, reduced in Example 4.10a. The "Angst und Hoffen" chords are (048)—the augmented triad—and (016)—the Viennese trichord. The set that contains both initial chords is (01248). The parallel-third motives form tetrachord (0134). If we look at the two initial tetrachords in the voice part, we see that the initial motive in m. 1 forms a (0124) set class—a subset of (01248), whereas the second motive, in m. 2, forms the same tetrachord as the piano accompaniment, (0134). Stems and beams in Example 4.10 indicate prominent linear (that is, horizontal) motives. The four "high pitches" in the vocal part (D–E♭–C–F♭) outline again set class (0124), the same as the initial voice motive in m. 1. And the piano's upper voice in the opening three beats, D–E♭–C–C♭, forms the tetrachord (0134). A new tetrachord, the chromatic set (0123), is first presented as the upper piano voice in m. 2 (the "sighs" in parallel thirds), C–C♭–B♭–A, and again in an overlapping statement repeated in mm. 2–3: B♭–A–A♭–G.

Example 4.10b shows a similar diagram for mm. 5–6. First, we notice the presence of some sets familiar from mm. 1–2: (0124) again used as a melodic set and (0134) used in the form of the motive in parallel thirds. The upper voice in the ascending scalar

♪♪ Example 4.10   Schoenberg, "Angst und Hoffen," pc set analysis

a. Mm. 1–2

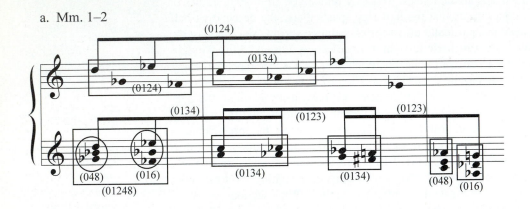

b. Mm. 5–6

c. Mm. 12–19

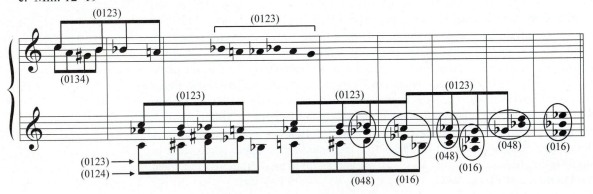

Given that pitch-class set theory was formulated only a few decades ago and was not available to Schoenberg, Webern, Berg, and others, a frequent and logical question from students at this point is whether those composers knew about (and whether their intention was to do) the things we find through pitch-class set analysis. This excellent question opens a polemical matter, the issue of intentionality. As an example, it might be very tempting, when we find a passage organized around a particular group of pitch-class sets in, for example, a piece by Schoenberg, to assume, even to state, that Schoenberg indeed organized the passage by means of the group of sets that we have discovered. The fact, however, is that there is no evidence that Schoenberg used anything similar to pitch-class sets. Schoenberg used motivic relationships and motivic manipulations or variations (he wrote and spoke about this issue quite extensively), and he certainly used intervals (the raw material of any pitch organization by any composer). But it would be far fetched to state that he used pitch-class sets or that he used pitch-class collections in a way similar to our pitch-class sets. We simply don't know, and there is nothing to document that he did.

According to an important school of thought in literary criticism, we can never know exactly what an author thought he or she was doing, and in any case, knowing it is irrelevant. What matters is what we find, whether or not the composer knew about it. This way of thinking about an author's intentions was originally articulated in a famous and highly influential article by William Wimsatt and Monroe Beardsley, titled "The Intentional Fallacy." This position, however, has also been strongly contested. Other scholars believe that it is legitimate to take into account an author's intentions when those intentions are known to us in some way (for instance, through the author's sketches or through his or her writings, lectures, and analyses of his or her own work).[7]

The position we will adopt in this book is a compromise between both positions regarding a composer's intentions. When a composer's intentions and methods are not clearly known, we will refrain (the best we can) from attributing what we find through analysis to the composer, and we will avoid statements such as, for instance, "in mm 15–16 Schoenberg uses set classes (014) and (015) to achieve a sense of continuity with the previous section." In these cases, we will just do our analysis, and state what we find in the music as "being there," regardless of whether the composer knew about it. Although we should not underestimate the craft and knowledge of a good composer, composers often do things (precisely thanks to their craft) in intuitive ways, and we should feel free to take credit for finding them through our analyses.

At other times, however, composers may have written extensively on their own work and compositional methods. This is the case, for instance, of Paul Hindemith, Olivier Messiaen, and Milton Babbitt. In cases such as this, we will look at the information provided by the composer and use it if it is pertinent to this composer's piece that we are analyzing. In other words, we shall willingly invoke a composer's intentions when they have been clearly articulated by the composer himself or herself, and in that case there is no reason for not giving the composer credit for what we positively know he or she did!

This position accounts for two different types of analyses that you will find in this book. Some of our analyses are *interpretive*. That is, we look at a score, and we interpret what we see in the music, the best we can and through whatever means are available to us. The analysis is thus an interpretation (with, perhaps, a good dose of subjectivity involved) by an "outsider," so to speak. Examples of interpretive analyses are all the analyses we have done so far in Chapters 1, 2, and 3.

A different type of analysis will take place occasionally. When we do know some of the composer's intentions, and the methods and techniques he or she used, we will apply them to try to understand the compositional process involved in a piece by that composer. Rather than interpretive, this type of analysis is *generative*. That is, we try to understand how the piece was put together (how it was generated) and what the composer knew and applied when he or she put it together. Examples of generative analysis in this book, at least to some extent, are our discussions of music by Hindemith, Messiaen, Boulez, Babbitt, Carter, among others, and also of the serial music of Schoenberg and Webern. Even when we know a composer's intentions to some extent, however, interpretive analysis can be very valuable: it can provide a different analysis of the piece to balance the composer's own, it can uncover aspects not discussed nor revealed by the composer, or it can also uncover things that not even the composer is aware of!

---

[7]"The Intentional Fallacy" was first published in *Sewanee Review* 54 (1946):468–88. It has been reprinted in various sources, including William Wimsatt, *The Verbal Icon: Studies in the Meaning of Poetry* (Lexington: University of Kentucky Press, 1954), pp. 3–18. For a good selection of articles that articulate the opposite view, see *On Literary Intention*, ed. David Newton-de Molina (Edinburgh: University Press, 1976). For an interesting article that discusses these issues as applied to music analysis, and in particular to pitch-class set theory and the analysis of Schoenberg's atonal music, see Ethan Haimo, "Atonality, Analysis, and the Intentional Fallacy," *Music Theory Spectrum* 18/2 (1996): 167–99.

figure in m. 6 combines and overlaps both (0134) and (0124). An apparently new set, (0248), appears in the form of the leaping motive in the piano in the first halves of both mm. 5 and 6. This set, however, is also a subset of (01248), the combined set for the "Angst und Hoffen" chords.

Mm. 7–11 are permeated by the "Angst und Hoffen" trichords in the piano part. Mm. 12–19 (see Example 4.10c), on the other hand, represent a synthesis of the pitch-class material for the whole song, as well as a return to all the significant sets introduced in mm. 1–2. In the voice, we first find the tetrachord (0134) embedded into the "sighing" tetrachord (0123), to the words "Daß ich jede freude von mir wehre," ("that I ward off every pleasure"). The same "sighing set" appears again at the beginning of phrase 7, in m. 14. The piano part in mm. 13–19 is rich in references to the sets we have identified in mm. 1–2. First, we see three statements of the (0123) "sighing tetrachord" in the top voice of the piano's chordal texture. The first two of these sets are actually the top part of a wedge figure made up of two converging (0123) lines: C–B–B♭–A in the top voice and C–C♯–D–E♭ in the bottom voice. If we think, however, of the bottom voice as moving to the low B♭ in m. 14, we end up with a C–C♯–D–B♭ motive, which is the familiar (0124) set class. The piano part finally closes with three statements of the "Angst und Hoffen" trichords, first presented twice in their "sighing" type of voice leading (with the upper voice descending by a half step), and finally presented at the same pitch level and with the same voice leading as in m. 1, but now, after having exhausted all the musical and emotional energy, in a much slower tempo and in values twice as long as the original values.

APPLICATION AND CLASS DISCUSSION

To conclude this chapter, listen to the Schoenberg song again and summarize, in the form of a class discussion, what you have learned through our analysis. How does the analysis change the way you listen to the song? How would this knowledge affect your performance and rendition of the song if you were to perform it? Would you rather perform this song knowing all these things we have discussed, or not knowing them? Why?

Do the same with reference to Webern's op. 5, III. How does our analysis affect the way you listen to the piece? What effect would the analysis have on your performance of the piece if you were to perform it?

How do you find pitch-class set theory useful after having analyzed these two pieces? Could you understand these pieces in the way you do now without the support of what you learned in Chapter 3?

Further Listening

The following list provides suggestions for further listening to music by composers studied in this chapter or related to the styles and techniques we have studied (if possible, listen while following the score):

1. Schoenberg, *Drei Klavierstücke,* op. 11
2. Schoenberg, *Book of the Hanging Gardens,* op. 15 (complete)
3. Schoenberg, *Fünf Orchesterstücke,* op. 16
4. Schoenberg, *Pierrot Lunaire,* op. 21
5. Webern, Five Movements for String Quartet, op. 5 (complete)
6. Webern, Four Pieces for Violin and Piano, op. 7
7. Berg, Five Orchestral Songs, op. 4
8. Berg, Four Pieces for Clarinet and Piano, op. 5

Terms for Review

segmentation	developing variation
expressionism	Viennese trichord
Grundgestalt	

 CHAPTER 4 ASSIGNMENTS

I. Analysis

1. Analyze mm. 1–5 (up to the indication "tempo" in m. 5) of Webern's "Wie bin ich froh!" (Anthology no. 21). Apply the principles of segmentation we discussed at the beginning of this chapter to come up with musical units that can be analyzed as pc sets. Then identify the set classes for your segments and provide a brief discussion of how they are related.

2. Listen to and study Webern's *Five Movements for String Quartet,* op. 5, II (Anthology no. 9). Write a brief analytical paper on this piece, using analytical diagrams as needed to clarify your presentation.

   a. Identify the sections of the piece. Discuss the texture and musical material in each section. Then address form and formal relationships in this movement.

   b. Provide a pitch-class set analysis of the piece (or, minimally, of mm. 1–6). First, analyze the chordal collections and provide prime forms for all of them. Discuss possible relationships among them, particularly inclusion relationships (subsets and supersets). Then do the same with the melodic lines. Break the lines into small sets (from three to five elements in most cases) and try to find relationships among them and also between them and the chordal sets.

3. Listen to and study Berg's song "Schlafend trägt man mich," from *Four Songs,* op. 2 (Anthology no. 12). Write a brief analytical paper on this song, using analytical diagrams as needed to clarify your presentation.

   a. Read the poem, and identify the lines on the music and how they correspond with musical phrases. Look at the first line of text and the music it is set to. How does the music, especially the bass line, convey the sense of return to the homeland? Does the initial vocal phrase return anywhere later in the song?

b. Focus now on the piano part in mm. 1–4. This piano accompaniment is highly homogeneous from the point of view of set classes, as we learned in our discussion of Example 4.3. As you will remember, most chords are tetrachords. For those that are only trichords, we were able to complete the tetrachord as needed by taking into account the pitch class from the voice part sounding simultaneously with the particular chord. Determine whether all these tetrachords are subsets of a larger and familiar pitch class collection. As a matter of fact, these chords alternate between two forms of that collection. Explain.

c. You will find similar homogeneity in the piano material in mm. 4–8. Identify the collections (set classes) in this section. In some cases you will need to consider one beat at a time, in some cases two beats, but in all cases you should consider the set made up of pitch classes from both hands.

d. Is there any prominent trichordal melodic motive in the piano part, mm. 4–8? Is the same motive present somewhere in the vocal part in mm. 1–4? Is it present in the vocal part anywhere later in the song?

e. Look at the descending line in the voice part in mm. 9–10 (five pitches). What is the set class? Is this thematic element present anywhere else in either the voice or the piano? For instance, look at the first five pitches in upper voice of the piano part (mm. 1–3). How about later in the song?

f. The initial trichordal motive in the voice part and the first three pitches in the upper line of the piano part (both in mm. 1–2) are members of the same set class. What is it? How many times is this trichordal set class a subset of the pentachord you have identified in question e?

II. Composition

1. Compose a short piece for string trio or quartet, in a "free atonal" idiom. Your piece should have both formal and pitch-class coherence, but it should avoid all types of tonal and functional references. Be spare with your pitch materials and careful with the textures you compose. Try to achieve pitch coherence by means of motivic relationships, and by using a limited number of pitch-class sets in your composition, following the models we have studied in this chapter.

2. Compose an atonal song for voice and piano on a short English poem of your choice. The compositional guidelines stated for composition assignment 1 also apply to this composition assignment. Use a limited number of pitch-class collections and motives in your song, write sparingly, and establish some relationships (motivic, textural, and in set classes) between the voice and the piano part.

Chapter 5

Drawing on (and Reinterpreting) the Past . . .

In the Introduction to this text we referred to the history of music in the twentieth century as "a complex mosaic made up of many stylistic tiles." We also mentioned that different stylistic "tiles" of trends have coexisted, and that composers have often switched between tiles in the mosaic, or even stood on different tiles at the same time. A particularly important stylistic trend throughout the twentieth century is what we know as **neoclassicism.** This is a very broad term that we use to refer to the deliberate incorporation into music of stylistic and technical elements proper of music from the past, which are imitated and used as models (as "classics") to generate textures, forms, genres, and so on. Neoclassicism establishes a dialogue with the past by incorporating and reinterpreting it as an active element in the music of the present. In general, neoclassical styles contributed to the move away from Romantic and post-Romantic idioms that we find among many composers in the early decades of the twentieth century. Whereas post-Romantic composers were interested in the intimate, personal, and intense expression of the artist's inner world (as we saw in our discussion of expressionism in Chapter 4), neoclassical styles are based on more objective, cooler musical idioms, often based on traditional formal types (such as binary, ternary, dance forms, sonata and rondo forms, and so on), sparser textures, smaller instrumental forces, and at times direct references to tonal idioms from the past.[1]

Interestingly enough, a neoclassical point of view is not at all incompatible with the modernist approach to style (that is, with the belief that artistic expression in the twentieth century should reflect the unique characteristics of the age and should thus depart from, if not break with, artistic expression of the past). Stravinsky summed up the neoclassical attitude by quoting a Verdi statement, "Torniamo all'antico e sarà un

---

[1]For a general discussion of neoclassicism in the context of early twentieth century music history, see Robert Morgan, "The Modern Age," in *Modern Times: From World War I to the Present,* ed. by Robert Morgan (Englewood Cliffs: Prentice Hall, 1993), pp. 1–32. For more detailed theoretical studies of neoclassic styles, see Joseph Straus, *Remaking the Past* (Cambridge, MA: Harvard University Press, 1990), and Martha Hyde, "Neoclassic and Anachronistic Impulses in Twentieth-Century Music," *Music Theory Spectrum* 18/2 (1996): 200–235.

progresso" ("Let's return to the old and it will be progress").[2] In fact, the same composers have often worn modernist or neoclassical hats either simultaneously or alternatively. After his modernist Russian period, for instance, Stravinsky adopted a neoclassical aesthetic stance patent in works from 1920 to the early 1950s such as *Pulcinella* (1920), the Octet (1923), *Oedipus Rex* (1927), the *Symphony of Psalms* (1930), and the Mass (1948). And we also speak of Schoenberg's "neoclassical period" to refer to his early serial years (although serialism is an openly modernist compositional technique), because of his preference in those years for genres of the past, such as the baroque dance suite or classical formal types such as sonata form, rondo, and variations. Some of Schoenberg's works from this period are the Piano Suite, op. 25 (1924), the Woodwind Quintet, op. 26 (1924), and the Suite for Chamber Ensemble, op. 29 (1926). Other composers who have espoused a neoclassical style at one point or another of their careers include Maurice Ravel, Paul Hindemith, Sergei Prokofiev, Francis Poulenc, Benjamin Britten, and Walter Piston. We should also mention that the term "neoclassical" is an often misleading general label. References in these composers are not only to the music of the classical period, but also, and most of all, to baroque music (and then we could speak of "neobaroque") or even to Medieval or Renaissance music (as in the case of Stravinsky's Mass, as we will see in the following section).

Neoclassical music features a play of tensions between the past and the present, between stylistic conflict and stylistic balance. These same issues and conflicts appear in music throughout the century, as we will see later in this book in Chapter 12, where we will study some more recent styles also based on borrowing and reinventing music from the past through quotation and collage. In the present chapter we will examine music by two composers who, at particular stages in their careers, embraced a neoclassical approach to composition: Stravinsky and Hindemith. In particular, we will discuss a movement from Stravinsky's Mass, and a movement from Hindemith's *Ludus Tonalis*. Our central questions in our study of neoclassical music will be the following: What elements from the past are present in these compositions? What, on the other hand, is characteristic of the twentieth century? How is the past incorporated and reinterpreted? How does this reinterpretation, or this recomposition, turn a past musical idiom into a twentieth-century composer's own language?

ANALYSIS 5.1: STRAVINSKY, *AGNUS DEI,* FROM MASS (ANTHOLOGY NO. 13)

Stravinsky's Mass was composed in 1944–48. Listen to Anthology no. 13 (the *Agnus Dei* from the Mass). To understand the stylistic realm of this composition, it will help if you can also listen to some four-voice sacred vocal polyphony by Renaissance composers. The following pieces are particularly suggested: Dufay, *Agnus Dei* from the *Missa L'homme armé*; Ockeghem, *Kyrie* from *Requiem*; Josquin Desprez, motet *Ave Maria,* and *Agnus Dei* from *Missa Pange lingua*; and Palestrina, motet *Lauda Sion,* and *Agnus*

---

[2]Igor Stravinsky, *Poetics of Music* (Cambridge, MA: Harvard University Press, 1970), p. 58.

Dei from *Missa brevis* in four voices. We should keep in mind that these composers represent a period and a style that has come to be considered (and studied) as one of the pinnacles of contrapuntal perfection in the history of music. You may also find it useful and interesting to listen to the *Agnus Dei* from Machaut's earlier *Messe de Notre Dame.*

Stravinsky is not necessarily imitating any of these composers or compositions, but in his Mass he is certainly evoking the sacred style of fifteenth- and sixteenth-century composers in general. Although Stravinsky's Mass has often been labeled as "neo-Medieval" or "neo-Gothic" (because of supposed associations with late-Medieval music, and particularly the music of Machaut), the *Agnus Dei* we are studying here can more appropriately be thought of as "neo-Renaissance" if we consider the stylistic parallels we find in it with the music of composers such as Dufay, Josquin, or Palestrina. In other words, Stravinsky's stylistic borrowings do not apply here to a specific work or composer from the past, but rather to a specific compositional style from the past (Renaissance sacred vocal polyphony). As you listen to the *Agnus Dei* and compare it with some of the Renaissance compositions previously suggested, try to make a list of elements of Renaissance style that you may find present in Stravinsky's piece.

The Design

The ternary text of the *Agnus Dei,* as is usually the case, determines the form of this movement. The three *Agnus Dei* textual stanzas are presented by the choir as three a capella sections, thematically independent from each other. The vocal sections are framed by an instrumental ritornello first presented as a prelude, then repeated twice as an interlude. The closing instrumental section is not musically equivalent to the previous ritornello sections, but rather represents a double cadential gesture. Each of the ritornellos ends with a clear cadential gesture, and so does each of the vocal sections. Each of the vocal sections, moreover, contains at least one inner articulation marked by a sonority of longer duration and corresponding with textual points of articulation. Articulations of this type occur in mm. 11 ("mundi"), 22 ("Dei"), 25 ("mundi"), 34 ("Dei"), and 38 ("mundi").

The vocal sections are clearly reminiscent of Renaissance vocal polyphony. Instrumental ritornellos, on the other hand, are often found in Baroque sacred polyphony, but not in either Renaissance or late-Medieval polyphony. There are no clear elements of pitch centricity in this movement. A logical place to look for elements of centricity would be cadences and inner points of articulation. The only consistent cadential sonority is the D major triad that we find at the end of each of the three complete ritornellos (mm. 3–4, 17–18, and 31–32), and also as a final sonority in the first closing cadential gesture (m. 43). The very final sonority (m. 45), on the other hand, consists of an open 5th on D to which a 7th and an 11th have been added (a C and a G), resulting in a (0257) set class.

The References

The vocal sections in the *Agnus Dei* are written in a style that can clearly be referred to Renaissance vocal polyphony. If, to begin with, we don't pay attention to sonority or counterpoint and we focus on melodic style, we can note that (1) melodies move mostly by steps and small leaps, (2) leaps as a norm are balanced by motion in the opposite direction of the leap, and (3) voices are independent and move following smooth contours, all of which is characteristic of Renaissance sacred vocal polyphony.

If, still not looking into the details of counterpoint, we examine the four-voice complex at a glance, we observe that (1) there are a number of syncopations, some of which look like possible suspensions, (2) sections 1 and 2 begin with paired imitation (a pair of voices is imitated by a second pair with the same thematic material, mm. 5–8 and 19–22), (3) imitation at the beginning of section 2 (mm. 19–22) includes rhythmic diminution in both voices (compare soprano-alto in mm. 21–22 to tenor-bass in mm. 19–20). These are all elements that, again, evoke the vocal contrapuntal style of the Renaissance.

Cadences in the Renaissance function linearly and contrapuntally rather than harmonically. The basic cadential motion, known as *clausula vera,* consists of a two-voice framework moving by contrary motion (often found in the duet formed by the discant voice—the soprano, in modern terms—and the tenor) in which a M6 opens to an octave (or, in its inversion, a m3 closes to a unison). Cadences in Stravinsky's *Agnus Dei* also function linearly and contrapuntally, and contrary motion is a determining factor in creating cadential gestures, as you can see in the ritornello cadence (mm. 3–4, repeated, essentially with the same voice leading, in mm. 17–18, and 31–32) and in the two closing instrumental cadential gestures (mm. 43 and 44–45). In the vocal sections, cadential approaches are more varied, but you can see this type of linear approach by contrary motion in the cadence closing section 1 (mm. 13–14). The linear approach to cadences is shown in Example 5.1.

In a more general way, we can also remark that the sparse textures, the use of brass and double reeds, and the a capella sound of the vocal sections are also evocations of older musical and performance styles. Having thus identified the elements that are reminiscent of Renaissance or late-Medieval styles, let us now focus on the details of pitch organization to identify how, far from simply imitating or absorbing those styles, Stravinsky actually reinterpreted and adapted them for his own expressive purposes.

The Stylistic Conflicts

Stylistic reinterpretations in the *Agnus Dei* affect some essential aspects of Renaissance vocal polyphony. The normative sonority in that style is the consonant triad. Dissonances are strictly controlled (prepared and resolved). Cadential sonorities are exclusively triadic (or open $\frac{8}{5}$ sonorities in earlier polyphony), and final cadences resolve to major triads (or open $\frac{8}{5}$ sonorities). Before you continue reading, examine cadential sonorities in the *Agnus Dei*. You can first determine what the sonorities are in the final chord for the ritornello and for each of the vocal sections, and then you can identify the inner cadential sonorities in the vocal sections (to the syllable "di" of "mundi"). Then, analyze the counterpoint in mm. 5–8 (the opening of the first vocal section), and determine how consonance and dissonance are used in these measures.

Example 5.1 provides an overview of cadential motion and of cadential sonorities. The cadential sonority in each of the three ritornellos is a DM triad in root position. The two closing instrumental cadences in mm. 43 and 45 feature a DM sonority (in

♪♪♪ Example 5.1   Stravinsky, *Agnus Dei* from Mass, cadential reduction

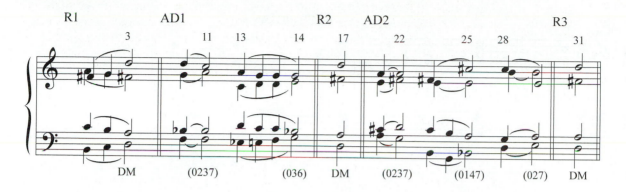

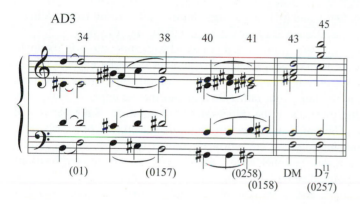

m. 43) and an open 5th on D with a 7th and an 11th, the (0257) set class so characteristic of Stravinsky. Not one of the inner or final cadences in the vocal sections features
simple consonant (that is, major or minor) triadic sonorities. Some of the sonorities
include a triad, but in these cases a dissonant pitch class has also been added. Thus, the
two cadential sonorities in *Agnus Dei* 1 (AD1) are a major triad with an added 4th, or
a (0237) set class, in m. 11, and a diminished triad in first inversion, (036), in m. 14. In
AD2, there are three cadential sonorities: a (0237) again in m. 22; a major triad with
an added m2 (placed, however, in the bass) in m. 25, resulting in a (0147) set class, and
a final, nontertian, (027) sonority in m. 28. The three equivalent sonorities in AD3 are
an open $\frac{8}{7}$, or set class (01), in m. 34, a nontertian (0157), and a final double sonority, a
C♯M triad in $\frac{6}{4}$ position with a m7 that turns into a M7, resulting in set classes (0258)
and (0158), respectively. In summary, Stravinsky's sonorities, far from being normative
Renaissance cadential sonorities, are Stravinsky's own dissonant sonorities that result
from reinterpretations of Renaissance cadences. Stravinsky's cadential sonorities, other
than the final major triad in the ritornellos, include nontertian and dissonant sets such

♪♪♪ Example 5.2   Stravinsky, *Agnus Dei* from Mass, mm. 5–8, counterpoint

as (027), (0257), (0157), (036), and (01), and tertian sonorities that result from adding a dissonant pitch class to a triad, such as (0237), (0147), (0258), and (0158).

The opening measures of AD1 (mm. 5–8, reproduced with annotations in Example 5.2) can illustrate how Stravinsky also reinterprets another essential element of Renaissance polyphony, counterpoint. In the first place, imitation between the upper and lower pair of voices is at the lower 9th, rather than the normative upper or lower 8ve, 4th, or 5th. Contrapuntal intervals in the initial duet are a mixture of normative and redefined counterpoint. The initial 4–7 intervals (both dissonant) are obviously non-normative, and the following 5–3–2–3 are "correct" counterpoint, including a correct 2–3 suspension. Mm. 7–8, on the other hand, contain only modern reinterpretations of Renaissance counterpoint. The two sonorities in m. 7 form (0257) and (0235) sets, both symmetrical, dissonant, and nontertian. Notice that the first set is the quartal or quintal set so often found in Stravinsky's music, whereas the second set is an octatonic set. The main contrapuntal feature in m. 8 is the syncopation that creates an illusion of suspensions. The apparent suspensions, however, are all reinterpretations of normative suspensions. First, an 8ve "resolves" down to a 7th, creating a consonance-dissonance inverted "suspension." The dissonant 7th then becomes the preparation for a 4th, which resolves up to a 5th, creating a 4–5 "suspension," while a 7th in the alto leaps up to a 9th in a 7–9 motion from dissonance to dissonance.

Conclusions

It now seems obvious that behind a superficial appearance of Renaissance style, Stravinsky's realization of cadences and counterpoint include a systematic reinventing of the essential tenets of Renaissance polyphony (use of consonant triadic sonorities and strict control of dissonance). Although Stravinsky's *Agnus Dei* can be seen as establishing a dialogue with a period of the past from which it borrows apparent elements of style, it is also, and above all, a twentieth-century composition using totally current twentieth-century aesthetics. Through stylistic reinterpretations, Stravinsky appropriates a style that has usually been considered as one of the high points of contrapuntal perfection in the history of music, and he uses it to create his own modern musical idiom. Thus this piece embodies (and resolves) particularly well the tensions between past and present that we have come to associate with modern neoclassicism.

HINDEMITH'S THEORETICAL AND COMPOSITIONAL PREMISES

Paul Hindemith (1895–1963) developed his own theoretical system, meant mostly to serve as a pedagogical curriculum to train student composers. Hindemith articulated his theories in a four-volume treatise, *The Craft of Musical Composition,* of which only the first three volumes were published (in 1937, 1939, and 1970, respectively).[3] Because of its complexity, we cannot attempt to provide a complete account or summary of Hindemith's theory here, but we will touch on some of its essential elements as a way to understand this composer's music from his own perspective. It should also be mentioned that Hindemith's theories (as well as his music) have generated substantial controversy and have had a number of detractors. Controversy, however, does not take anything away from Hindemith's stature as one of the leading composers of the first half of the twentieth century.[4]

The point of departure of Hindemith's theories are two orderings of the degrees of the chromatic scale that the composer calls **Series 1** and **Series 2.** Series 1, shown in Example 5.3a, presents an ordering of the chromatic degrees according to the relative strength of relationship to a tonic. Read from left to right, the series shows the degrees as they become further removed from the tonic. For ease of reference, we will use the traditional tonal terms to label the scale degrees, without necessarily implying a traditionally functional tonal framework. Thus, the dominant (which we will abbreviate as D) and the subdominant (S) are the closest degrees to the tonic (T), whereas the raised subdominant (TT, a tritone away), the leading tone (LT), and the upper leading tone ($\flat\hat{2}$, or ULT) are the most distant degrees.

Series 2 represents, reading from left to right, the relative harmonic force of intervals. Thus, the unison, the octave, the fifth, and the fourth are the most consonant and stable intervals from a harmonic point of view, and the tritone, the major seventh, and the minor second are the most dissonant intervals and also the most unstable ones. On the other hand, if we read Series 2 from right to left, it represents the relative melodic force of intervals, in such a way that the tritone, seconds, and sevenths are melodically strong (directed), whereas intervals to the left have less melodic strength.

The harmonic intervals at both extremes of Series 2 define the principal tonal functions: Tonic (T), dominant (D), and subdominant (S) on the one hand, and the

---

[3]The first two volumes have been translated into English: Paul Hindemith, *The Craft of Musical Composition,* vol. 1, *Theoretical Part,* trans. Arthur Mendel (New York: Associated Music, 1942; rev. ed., 1945); and vol. 2, *Exercises in Two-Part Writing,* trans. Otto Ortmann (New York: Associated Music, 1941).

[4]The main secondary source for the study of Hindemith's theory and music (as well as for our discussion on this composer and for the analysis of the Interlude in G) is David Neumeyer's *The Music of Paul Hindemith* (New Haven: Yale University Press, 1986).

Example 5.3   Hindemith's Series 1 and 2

a. Series 1

b. Series 2

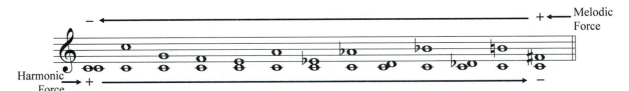

lower and upper leading tones on the other (LT and ULT). In a good composition, according to Hindemith, the essential melodic and harmonic framework can be found in a
two-voice framework. Hindemith classifies chords into two basic categories: those that
do not contain tritones and those that do. He also distinguishes, within both categories,
between chords that contain 2nds or 7ths and those that don't. All chords that contain
a tritone, a 2nd, or a 7th create tension that will eventually need to resolve. Chords that
do not contain tritones, 2nds, or 7ths (that is, M and m triads) are apt for relaxation or
resolution of tension. Hindemith's principle of **harmonic fluctuation** refers to the mix-
ing of consonant and dissonant chords and the process of eventual resolution of tension,
which he believes are necessary for a desirable musical flow.

Hindemith distinguishes **five stages in the compositional process.**[5] Stage I refers
to the level of interaction of tonal design and form. In other words, this is the stage of
definition of tonal areas, of cadences, and of formal design. Stage II defines the pillar
chords, in the form of a long-range progression which includes cadential sonorities and
other structural chords. Stage III focuses on significant melodic activity connecting the
pillar chords from the previous stage. Stage IV refers to surface harmonic activity, and
Stage V to surface melodic activity. Melodic activity is best when ruled by **step progression** or arpeggiation.

Hindemith did not intend his theory to be an analytical system, neither should we
view his mature compositions necessarily as illustrations of his theoretical/pedagogical
ideas. David Neumeyer, nevertheless, has shown that Hindemith's compositional stages

---

[5]See Neumeyer, *The music of Paul Hindemith,* Chapter 2.

can be used to good advantage to approach a lot of his pieces, and has proposed an analytical methodology for Hindemith's music that follows the composer's five stages and his basic theoretical tenets.[6] Neumeyer does not claim that the method results in the only or necessarily the best possible readings, especially when it comes to surface details (particularly for Stages III, IV, and V), but rather defines his method as an aid to interpreting technical, constructive features of Hindemith's music. In the following analysis we will adapt Neumeyer's analytical approach to study the structure of a piece by Hindemith, the Interlude in G from *Ludus Tonalis*.[7] By using the perspective provided by the composer's own principles, we should be able to obtain some historically and musically valuable insight into Hindemith's musical and compositional processes.

ANALYSIS 5.2: HINDEMITH, INTERLUDE IN G, FROM *LUDUS TONALIS* (ANTHOLOGY NO. 14)

Hindemith's *Ludus Tonalis* (*The Game of Tones*, 1942) is a collection of twelve fugues separated by eleven interludes, with an opening prelude and a closing postlude. The tonal centers of the twelve fugues are, respectively, C, G, F, A, E, E♭, A♭, D, B♭, D♭, B, and F♯, that is, the order of Series 1. The Interlude in G follows the second fugue, also in G. As is the case with much of Hindemith's music, both the complete *Ludus Tonalis* and this particular Interlude follow models from the past. Which composer and collection do you think *Ludus Tonalis* is modeled after? Before you continue reading, listen to the Interlude and determine its phrases, sections, formal design, and points of structural significance from a tonal point of view.

Formal and Tonal Design

We can easily identify a major point of articulation, clearly defined by a strong cadence, in m. 10. This cadence on D divides the piece into two sections, each of which can further be divided into two phrases each. Section 1 comprises the two phrases in mm. 1–4 and 5–10, respectively (phrases 1 and 2), and section 2 is made up of mm. 11–18 and 19–24 (phrases 3 and 4). You will have noticed that phrase 4 is the same as phrase 2, but transposed up a fourth. In other words, phrase 2 leads to a cadence on D (the dominant), and phrase 4 leads instead to a cadence on G (the tonic). From a formal point of view, then, this piece is in binary form, specifically of the type we usually call "balanced binary" (that is, the second phrase of reprise 2 contains the same material as the second phrase of reprise 1).[8] As a matter of fact, the Interlude is in the style of a baroque "siciliano" (and thus is in "neobaroque" style).

Example 5.4 shows the four phrases in the context of long-range tonal motion. If we take into account what we can consider structural chords (essentially the chords that

---

[6]Ibid., Chapter 3.

[7]An extended discussion of this piece, used to illustrate his analytical methodology, can be found in Neumeyer's Chapter 3.

[8]For a discussion of balanced binary, see Roig-Francolí, *Harmony in Context*, pp. 594–95.

begin and end phrases), we see that phrase 1 moves from G to C (tonic to subdominant, or T to S). Phrase 2 begins on a C♯ chord and ends on a D sonority (that is, ends on the dominant, D, and begins on the leading tone to the dominant, indicated as [LT]→D). Phrase 3 is the most equivocal area from a tonal point of view, and it begins and ends on sonorities on the mediant, M. Phrase 4 begins on a chord on the leading tone to G, F♯ (LT) and ends on a sonority on the tonic.

A couple of details in the graph in Example 5.4 are also significant. The approach to both cadences (mm. 10 and 24) first includes a pitch a tritone away from the cadential pitch (G♯ in m. 9, and C♯ in m. 23), and the upper leading tone (ULT) to each cadential pitch (D♯ leading to D in mm. 9–10, and G♯ leading to G in mm. 23–24). We know that the tritone is the interval that produces the highest melodic and harmonic tension, and that the lower and upper leading tones, a half step from the tonic, have a strong tendency to resolution. This is one of the means Hindemith uses to create a strong pull toward the cadence. The other significant detail is the chord in m. 16. We hear it as a climactic arrival, and this is a result of several processes. It is the end of a wedge motion between the two hands beginning in m. 13, the point covering the widest registral span in the whole piece, and the only spot marked *forte*. The intervallic content of the chord (namely the tritone in the two lowest voices, but also the ninth and seventh in the upper voices), moreover, makes it the point of highest harmonic tension in the piece.

As a final observation on long-range design in the Interlude, refer to Example 5.5. As is the case with many of Hindemith's compositions (and with many other twentieth-century composers), the main divisions of this movement are ruled by the Golden Section (GS), which we studied in Chapter 1. If we measure length, for instance, in eighth notes, we see that the complete piece is 144 eighth notes long, and that the climactic arrival of the chord in m. 16 is at eighth-note 91 from the beginning, which produces the ratio .631, a close approximation to the GS. Moreover, the cadence on D in m. 10 takes place on eighth-note 58, which divides the segment from the beginning to the climactic chord (ratio 58/91) at .637, again a close approximation to the GS.

Example 5.5   Proportional relationships in the Interlude in G

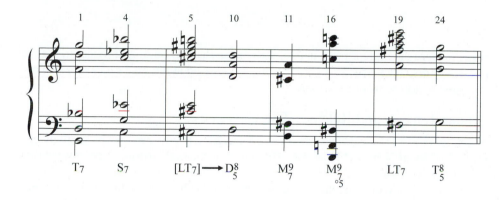

Example 5.6   Pillar chords in the Interlude in G

Harmonic Tension and Release: The Pillar Chords

In our next analytical stage we can examine the sonorities built on the structural degrees we identified in Example 5.4, and the resulting design of tension and release. These sonorities (resulting from reductions of the actual music surface) are represented in Example 5.6. What observations can you make on the sonority types, in the light of Hindemith's categorization of chords?

First, we can notice that the first three structural chords in phrases 1 and 2 are all minor triads with a minor seventh. That is, they are all dissonant chords (beginning with the very opening tonic), but they do not contain any tritone. Each of these chords, then, creates a tension toward a resolution. The resolution comes in m. 10, with a strictly consonant cadential sonority on D, an open $\frac{8}{5}$ sonority that does not even contain any 3rd. The process is similar for phrases 3 and 4, but in phrase 3 tension and dissonance are much heightened, first by an initial chord in m. 11, which contains both a 9th and a 7th (but still no tritone), and finally by the climactic chord in m. 16, which contains both a 9th and a 7th, but now also a tritone. The closing phrase 4 begins again with a

Example 5.7   Cadential progressions in the Interlude in G

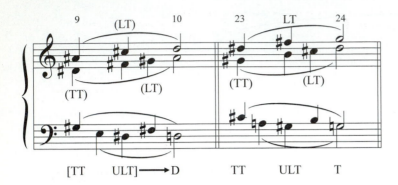

seventh chord on a minor triad, and all the tension that has built up through these two phrases of dissonant structural chords is finally released at the final cadence, again on an open $\frac{8}{5}$ sonority, now on the tonic, G.

Linear Tension and Release: The Cadences

Listen to (or play) the cadences in mm. 9–10 and 23–24. Why are they particularly effective cadential gestures? How does Hindemith achieve the strong drive toward the cadential resolution?

We previously saw that the tritone and the upper and lower leading tones are used at these cadences as a way to create intervallic tension toward the resolution. The same purpose is also often achieved in Hindemith's music by means of directed linear motion. Example 5.7 shows the linear progressions that make up each of the two cadences. We can identify four linear strands in each cadence, two in the right hand and two in the left hand. First, notice that both sets of linear strands move in contrary motion, creating a strong contrapuntal pull toward the open $\frac{8}{5}$ sonority. Moreover, all three pitches in the $\frac{8}{5}$ sonority are approached by leading-tone motion. In the first cadence, the D in the upper voice is approached from its LT, C♯; the D in the lower voice is approached from the ULT, D♯; and the A is approached from its own secondary LT, G♯. Two of the lines cover a span of a tritone (that is, they outline the interval that creates the highest melodic tension according to Series 2): the "tenor" line features a G♯–D span, and the "alto" line covers a D♯–A span. All these comments apply equally to the second cadence, with all pitches transposed at the upper 4th.

All in all, these are thus highly effective cadences: they create a strong sense of direction and tension toward the resolution by both intervallic and linear means, and they provide a distinctive consonant sound for the resolution. The resolution to an open $\frac{8}{5}$ sonority, the "double-leading tone" sound, and the parallel fifths and fourths in these cadences give them both an archaic character and a distinctly twentieth-century flavor.

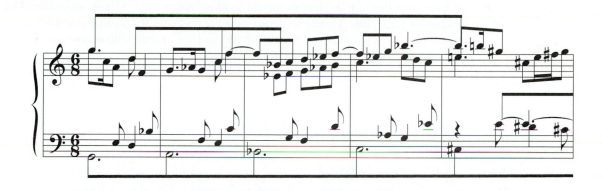

♪♪♪ Example 5.8   Step progressions in the Interlude in G, mm. 1–10

Long-Range Linear Design: Melodic Step Progressions

Melodic step progressions are one of the elements of musical design prescribed by Hindemith to provide coherence to composition. Example 5.8 shows some of the step progressions (but not the only ones) that can be identified in phrases 1 and 2 of the Interlude (see the pitches connected by beams). Phrase 1 is unified by two long progressions moving by contrary motion in the upper and lower voices. All pitches in the left hand are actually part of linear progressions moving parallel to the bass. Finally, a fourth, shorter progression is also marked in an inner voice in the right hand. The main melodic force in the second phrase, on the other hand, is the chromatic step progression in the tenor voice, and another step progression appears in the right hand as we approach the cadence.

Conclusions

As a summary of our study of the Interlude in G, discuss formal and tonal coherence in this piece. Then discuss the piece from the point of view of the interaction between past and present. What are the elements between past and present that create conflict in this short movement? What does Hindemith borrow from the past, and how does he imprint his own character in these elements from the past? The piece is indeed full of references to the past: think of its formal and long-range tonal designs, its cadential formulas, its genre. But Hindemith unquestionably reinterpreted these elements from the past and made them his own. Would anyone (at least anyone with a good enough ear) confuse this piece with a piece by Bach? Why not?

APPLICATION AND CLASS DISCUSSION

Would you say that the conflict between past and present is particularly a modern phenomenon (that is, characteristic of the twentieth century, but not so much of previous centuries), or can it also be found in the music of past centuries? Is the presence of the past an essential element in some of the music by major composers of the classical and Romantic periods, for instance? If so, can we speak of reinterpretations, and of what type?

What do you think is meant by Verdi's statement about the possibility of moving forward by returning to the past? Would you say that Stravinsky's Mass, for instance, points toward the future in the way it uses the past, or is it essentially a "conservative" piece that clings to the past to prevent motion toward the future? Where can we draw the line between what we could call a "reactionary" and a "progressive" use of the past? If you think Stravinsky's Mass is "progressive," what makes it so?

Do you know any other twentieth-century pieces that are inspired by the past in one way or another? How is the past used in these pieces? Can you think of some compositions that use the past in a particularly conservative way, in contrast to others that, by using the past create a "modern" and "progressive" musical idiom that actually points toward the future?

Further Listening

The following list provides suggestions for further listening to music by composers studied in this chapter or related to the styles and techniques we have studied (if possible, listen while following the score):

1. Hindemith, *Konzertmusik* for string orchestra and brass
2. Hindemith, Symphony *Mathis der Maler*
3. Hindemith, *Ludus Tonalis*
4. Prokofiev, Symphony no. 1, "Classical," op. 25
5. Ravel, *Le tombeau de Couperin* (for piano)
6. Stravinsky, *Symphony of Psalms*
7. Stravinsky, Octet
8. Stravinsky, Concerto in E flat, "Dumbarton Oaks"

Terms for Review

neoclassicism
Hindemith: Series 1 and Series 2
            two-voice framework
            harmonic fluctuation
            five stages in the compositional process
            step progression

CHAPTER 5 ASSIGNMENTS

I. Analysis

1. Hindemith, "Vom Tode Mariä I," from *Das Marienleben* (Anthology no. 15). Listen to this song, study the score, and answer the following questions.

   a. What is the overall formal type of this song?

   b. Two elements determine formal processes in this piece: first, the bass (in mm. 1–26 and again in mm. 59–78), and then the piano's top voice (in mm. 27–58). Explain.

   c. Comment on the voice leading used to approach the cadence on G in mm. 10 and 25–26.

   d. A melodic high point is reached in m. 14. Identify a long-range step progression following this high point and covering a complete descending octave. Do the same for mm. 62–76.

   e. The counterpoint in the opening measures contributes to a sense of relative repose and absence of tension. What exactly in the counterpoint produces this effect? How is this related to the text?

   f. The area of maximum harmonic tension occurs in mm. 40–55. What harmonic factors contribute to the creation of tension? What is the long-range, formal function of this area of harmonic instability? What does the text relate in this section?

   g. Hindemith did not write a meter signature for this song. What are the song's metric and rhythmic characteristics?

   h. Discuss pitch centricity in this piece. What is the pitch center, and why?

   i. What historical period or periods, and what composer or composers, do you think Hindemith is evoking here?

   j. Discuss the conflict and interaction between past and present in this movement and any reinterpretations of the past you may identify.

2. Stravinsky, *Octet*, I ("Sinfonia"). Listen to this movement and study the score (available in your music library). Then provide answers to the following questions.

   a. Discuss form in this movement. Does it follow or suggest some specific formal model?

   b. What is the role of motive in this movement? What are the most prominent motives?

c. What techniques of formal growth and formal development are used? What is traditional in the way Stravinsky deals with his thematic material in this piece, and what is not?

d. Discuss the role of counterpoint in this movement. Choose some particular passages for detailed study from a contrapuntal point of view, and explain the type of contrapuntal techniques used in these passages.

e. Discuss some specific rhythmic and metric features of this movement.

f. Discuss aspects of tonal organization. Is the music pitch centered, and how? What is the role of the key signature? What are the main long-range tonal relationships? Do you hear this music as "harmonic" or mostly "linear"?

g. What historical period or periods, and what composer or composers, do you think Stravinsky is evoking here?

h. Discuss the conflict and interaction between past and present in this movement and any reinterpretations of the past you may identify.

3. The following are possible pieces on which you may write brief analytical papers in application of the concepts and techniques you have learned in this chapter. Your discussions may cover any pertinent aspects of form, motivic and thematic relationships, harmonic techniques, pitch organization, tonality or pitch centricity, and salient aspects of meter, rhythm, and texture. Focus particularly on how past and present interact in these pieces, and on what elements of this interaction are a source of conflict. Discuss possible stylistic sources for these pieces, in the form of specific style periods or composers (or perhaps even specific compositions). How have these stylistic sources been misread?

a. Prokofiev, Symphony no. 1, "Classical," op. 25, movements I (Allegro) or III (Gavotte)

b. Ravel, *Le tombeau de Couperin* (for piano), "Forlane" or "Minuet"

c. Stravinsky, *Symphony of Psalms,* II

d. Stravinsky, Concerto in E flat, "Dumbarton Oaks," I

II. Composition

1. Write a brief piece in neoclassical or neobaroque style. Write for keyboard or for voice and keyboard. Suggestions for form or genre are a minuet, a sarabande, an invention, a passacaglia, or a short aria. You should model your piece after the style of a composer you choose (for example, Bach, Haydn, or Mozart), but you should at the same time make the piece your own and write in "twenty-first-century" style. In other words, your piece should be a reinterpretation of whatever model from the past you choose.

2. Write a piece for piano or voice and piano, incorporating Hindemith's style characteristics as we have studied them in this chapter. Here again, possible forms or genres are a minuet, a sarabande, an invention, a passacaglia, or a short aria. Plan your tonal and harmonic design to follow some aspects of series 2. Take into account elements of consonance and dissonance, of intervallic tension and release, in building both your counterpoint and your chordal progressions. Design your cadences linearly and your melodic lines following an underlying step progression.

Chapter 6

. . . And Inventing the Future

After having examined examples of neoclassical aesthetics, in this chapter we will study music by two composers who represent a contrasting stylistic position: Charles Ives and Ruth Crawford Seeger. The music of these composers can best be understood in the context of what we know as the American **ultramodern movement.** American composers in the late 1920s and 1930s were grouped around two major circles. The first group, centered around the League of Composers, included composers oriented toward Europe and European musical aesthetics. Among the composers in this circle were Aaron Copland, Walter Piston, and Roger Sessions. The second group, centered around the Pan American Association of Composers, included composers who had developed or sought more indigenous and particularly American musical idioms. Prominent members of this second group were Ives, Crawford, Edgard Varèse, Henry Cowell, Charles Seeger, and Carl Ruggles.[1]

In general, ultramodern composers sought to avoid European, or, more generally, traditional, compositional models. Joseph Straus identified the following characteristic aspects of the ultramodern position: integration of vernacular elements (such as quotations of American hymn tunes or folk songs) into the musical fabric; systematic avoidance of triadic harmony and melody and of any references to functional tonality; search for new harmonic combinations, new melodies, and new rhythms; avoidance of note repetition; commitment to dissonance; expansion of the timbral palette (either by using new instruments or sound sources, or by using traditional instruments in unconventional ways); and use of precompositional plans to organize pitch material.[2] A lot of these compositional principles, along with others, are presented in the treatise by Charles Seeger, *Tradition and Experiment in the New Music* (written in 1930–31, although not published until 1994).[3] We will not be able to illustrate all of the characteristic aspects

---

[1]Joseph Straus, *The Music of Ruth Crawford Seeger* (Cambridge: Cambridge University Press, 1995), p. 214.

[2]Straus, *The Music of Ruth Crawford Seeger,* pp. 216–220

[3]Charles Seeger, *Tradition and Experiment in the New Music,* in *Studies in Musicology II,* ed. Ann Pescatello (Berkeley: University of California Press, 1994).

of ultramodernism in this chapter, but we will at least focus on some examples by two representative composers of this group, Ives and Crawford.

IVES AND MUSICAL BORROWING

Charles Ives (1874–1954) is broadly considered one of the most idiosyncratic and original composers in the first half of the twentieth century. We find in Ives's music two particularly characteristic technical and stylistic trends. The first is the use of existing music, which Ives quotes or integrates into his own music in a variety of ways. The other trend, which best defines Ives as an ultramodern composer, results from his interest in experimentation, often into technical and compositional realms that turn Ives into a musical pioneer, a maverick who in many ways was well ahead of his time.[4] Within these two general trends, Ives's language varies broadly in matters of pitch organization, and it can use "frankly tonal, marginally tonal, tonally centric, and densely atonal idioms."[5]

NOTE

In Chapter 12 we will focus on the use of quotation and collage by composers after World War II. In that context, we discuss the use of quotation in similar terms as we have discussed neoclassicism: as a way to establish a creative dialogue with the past. From a technical point of view, Ives's extensive use of quotation is in the same compositional category as more recent uses of quotation found, for instance, in the music of George Rochberg and Luciano Berio. The music that is quoted in each case, however, is from broadly different sources. Composers such as Rochberg and Berio borrow mostly from the Western concert-music tradition (from composers such as Mozart, Berlioz, Brahms), and in this way establish a dialogue with the past. Ives, on the other hand, quotes mostly from American vernacular and traditional sources (hymn and Gospel tunes, popular, patriotic, and historical American songs, for example). Ives's dialogue with the past is thus established more through American popular culture and history than through references to major composers of the Western tradition.

A great majority of Ives's compositions include **musical borrowing** of some type. Peter Burkholder identified the following fourteen types of borrowing in Ives's music:

1. *Modeling* a work or section on some aspect of an existing piece.
2. *Variations* on an existing tune.
3. *Paraphrasing* an existing tune to form a new melody.
4. *Setting* of an existing tune with a new accompaniment.

---

[4]Ives's use of existing music has been studied in great detail by Peter Burkholder, especially in his book, *All Made of Tunes* (New Haven: Yale University Press, 1995). Ives the experimenter is the focus of Philip Lambert's *The Music of Charles Ives* (New Haven: Yale University Press, 1997).

[5]Lambert, *The Music of Charles Ives*, p. 2.

5. *Cantus firmus,* presenting a given tune in long notes against a more quickly moving texture.

6. *Medley,* stating two or more existing tunes one after another.

7. *Quodlibet* combining two or more existing tunes in counterpoint or in quick succession.

8. *Stylistic allusion,* alluding not to a specific work but to a general style.

9. *Transcription* of a work for a new medium.

10. *Programmatic quotation,* fulfilling an extramusical program.

11. *Cumulative setting,* in which the borrowed melody is presented complete only near the end of the movement, preceded by development of motives from the melody.

12. *Collage,* which uses a swirl of quoted and paraphrased tunes.

13. *Patchwork,* in which fragments of two or more tunes are stitched together.

14. *Extended paraphrase,* in which the melody for an entire work or section is paraphrased from an existing tune.[6]

The song "The Things Our Fathers Loved" (ca. 1917) is an excellent example of the technique Burkholder calls "patchwork" (no. 13 in the preceding list).[7] The complete song appears in the Anthology, no. 16. Ives's vocal line is reproduced in Example 6.1 (the line with text on this example). The text refers to the memories of old tunes and the associations to persons or places those tunes suggest. Toward the end of the song, with the line "I know not what are the words," Ives makes clear that the power of association comes from the tunes themselves, rather than the words. The poem creates an association between topics and song types: village and family life (the Main Street corner, Aunt Sarah) are thus associated with popular family songs, religious feelings (humming Gospels) with religious hymns, and patriotic feelings and sounds (the village cornet band, the town's Red, White, and Blue) with patriotic songs. Moreover, Ives also associates these topics with the timeless values that "our Fathers loved": hometown, family, religious faith, and patriotism.

All these associations become musically tangible in this song through a patchwork of appropriate borrowed tunes, as shown in Example 6.1 in the staffs above and below Ives's vocal line. The song opens with a brief quotation from the opening of "Nettleton" (a hymn tune attributed to Asahel Nettleton or John Wyeth), which immediately blends into a phrase from Stephen Foster's popular tune "My Old Kentucky Home," first in C major and then in F major. Beginning in m. 6 we hear a quotation of the popular tune "On the Banks of the Wabash," by Paul Dresser, to the words "I hear the organ on the Main Street corner," followed again by the hymn "Nettleton" ("Aunt Sarah humming Gospels"). A patriotic song from the Civil War era, George Root's "The Battle Cry of Freedom," is the quotation chosen by Ives to set the references to the village cornet band and to the colors of the flag. We hear the verse from this song in the vocal melody,

---

[6]Burkholder, *All Made of Tunes,* p. 3.

[7]This song is analyzed in Burkholder, *All Made of Tunes,* pp. 306–311. The present discussion is based on Burkholder's analysis.

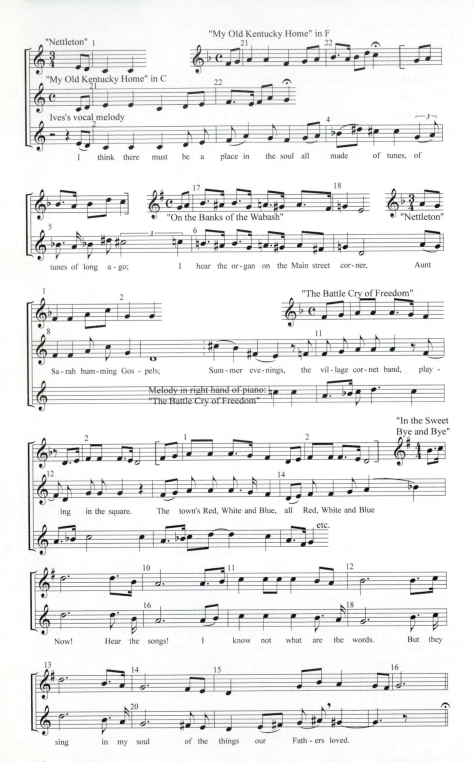

accompanied by its chorus in the top voice of the piano's right hand. The song closes with the melody from the hymn "In the Sweet Bye and Bye" in the voice, accompanied by a figure from "The Battle Cry of Freedom" in the piano. Through his use of quotation and patchwork, Ives achieves a closely knit set of connections between the specific references in the text, the underlying message of the poem, and the actual musical material.

ANALYSIS 6.1: IVES, "THE CAGE" (ANTHOLOGY NO. 17)

The song "The Cage" (1906) is an example of experimental composition by Ives, or, to use the term that Lambert prefers, "systematic" composition. Listen to the song while following the score, and read the text carefully. What is the text about? How many phrases does it have? How does the music portray the meaning of the text? What is the pitch material used in the melodic line? How about the piano chords—what kind are they? Before you read the following analysis, review the section in Chapter 2 titled "Interval Cycles and Equal Divisions of the Octave," especially the discussion on interval cycles.[8]

The Text and the Vocal Line

The poem describes the monotony of a leopard's life in a cage, pacing from one side to the other. The only event in the leopard's life that makes him stop his incessant pacing is the coming of the keeper with a meal of meat. A boy has patiently been observing this situation for three hours and wonders whether life is anything like it. We can divide the poem into five lines:

1. A leopard went around his cage
2. From one side back to the other side
3. He stopped only when the keeper came around with meat
4. A boy who had been there three hours began to wonder
5. "Is life anything like that?"

The vocal line reflects the monotony of the leopard's existence: it is mainly made up of whole tones and moves mostly in eighth notes. The constant flow of whole tones is interrupted by semitone motions at some significant points: first, between text lines 1 and 2 (between the words "cage" and "from"); second, after the word "stopped," which is also punctuated by a longer value. Ives thus stresses the arrival of the only event that will make the leopard stop: the meat. The next semitone comes between text lines 3 and 4, after the word "meat." Here the text changes focus and leads our attention from the leopard to the boy. This change is also punctuated by the only rest within the melody. The end of line 4 is also articulated by longer values to the word "wonder," and a leap of a minor 3rd (the only leap in the whole melody) introduces line 5, the boy's

[8]An analysis of "The Cage," on which the present discussion is based, can be found in Lambert, *The Music of Charles Ives*, pp. 150–159.

philosophical question. The melodic phrases correspond with the text lines, with the exception of melodic phrase 2, which continues until the word "stopped."

With each motion by semitone or minor 3rd, the pitch content of the melody switches from one whole-tone scale to the other. Thus, melodic phrase 1 is based on WT_0, phrase 2 (to the word "stopped") is based on WT_1, phrase 3 is based on WT_0, phrase 4 on WT_1, and phrase 5 again on WT_0. The exception is the high E5 in phrase 4, which belongs to WT_0, the opposite whole-tone collection from the rest of the pitches in this phrase. This alternation of whole-tone collections reflects the back-and-forth motion of the leopard within the cage, and the circularity of the animal's life. Notice that the pitch content of phrase 5 is identical to that of phrase 1 (both in the voice and in the piano). This represents again the idea of circularity and the connection between the text of lines 1 and 5: "A leopard went around his cage" and "Is life anything like that?"

The Piano Part

Because the vocal part is largely based on whole-tone scales, we can say that its pitch content is mainly derived from an interval cycle 2, represented (again as a circle!) in Figure 2.1b (Chapter 2). Similarly, most of the chords in the piano part result from segments of a pitch-space interval cycle 5 (a cycle represented in pitch-class space in Figure 2.1f). The complete pitch content of the piano part is reproduced in Example 6.2. We first hear a seven-chord introduction repeated mechanically two or three times. The first six chords, labeled A–B–C–D–E–C in the example, are all quartal chords (that is, resulting from interval cycle 5), whereas the seventh chord, labeled F (in Lambert's term, the "meal chord"), is made up of various intervals.

We have seen that pitch material and rhythm in the vocal part reflect the monotony of the leopard's life. The piano part equally depicts the meaning of the song in a variety of ways. First, we can think of the actual appearance and sound of the piano part, a succession of block chords, as the bars of the cage. The equally spaced pitches in the quartal chords further provide an image reminiscent of cage bars. On the score you can see that the first six chords are progressively shorter in rhythmic values, leading to the longer chord F. How does this introduction reflect the main topic of the song—the leopard's monotonous life, the pacing, the drive toward the meal, and the meal itself?

The piano accompaniment throughout the song is derived from the introductory chords. We first hear a T_5 transposition (itself a reference to interval cycle 5) of all seven chords in the original order: A–B–C–D–E–C–F. Then we hear a T_3 transposition of the first five chords, A–B–C–D–E, with some other chords interpolated in between. Note that chord 15 is indeed T_3 of the original chord D, but the pitch classes are now organized from top to bottom, and the resulting chord is quintal rather than quartal. Chord 19 is an extended version (not a transposition) of the meal chord (that is, a chord made up of a variety of intervals), and finally the last three chords bring back the original T_5 transposition of chords A–B–C.

The chords interpolated between the T_3 statements of chords A–B–C–D–E are mostly chromatic or whole-tone transpositions of the chords that precede them. Thus, chord 9 is T_1 of chord 8 (a chromatic derivation); chords 10–13 result from a three-step chromatic motion ($+1$, $+1$, $+1$) filling in the minor 3rd between chords 10 and 13; chord

Example 6.2   "The Cage," pitch content of piano part

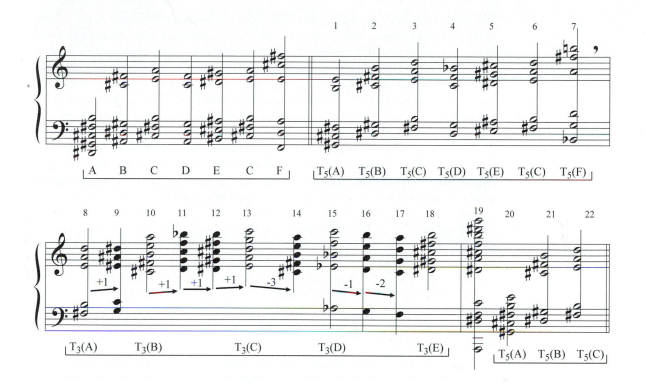

14 is a return to chord 10; and chords 15–16–17 are related by descending chromatic and whole-tone motions (−1 and −2) respectively.

As a final and interesting element of symbolism, Lambert points out Ives's use of pitch classes C–A–G–E in a variety of ways throughout this song. If you group these four pitch classes (which, of course, spell out "cage") into dyads pairing alternate letters, you come up with C–G and A–E, both members of interval cycle 5. Chord 13, for instance, features a five-note segment of interval cycle 5, C–G–D–A–E (reading from top to bottom), in which the dyads C–G and A–E "cage in" the note D that connects the two dyads within the cycle of fifths.[9]

As a summary of our study of "The Cage," review the following points: What are the basic principles of pitch organization in this song? How is the meaning of the poem reflected in the various musical parameters of the song, such as pitch, rhythm, pacing, and phrasing? What does all this tell us about Ives's approach to composing this type of piece?

[9]Lambert, pp, 158–59.

ANALYSIS 6.2: CRAWFORD, *DIAPHONIC SUITE* NO. 4, III (ANTHOLOGY NO. 18)

The music of Ruth Crawford Seeger (1901–1953) can best be understood in the context of the American ultramodern movement, whose characteristics were already explained in the introduction to this chapter. The compositional concepts presented in Charles Seeger's *Tradition and Experiment in the New Music* play a central role in Crawford's music, and in fact reflect her thinking as much as her mentor's thinking (Crawford studied with Seeger in 1929–30 and became his wife in 1932).[10] Seeger's compositional thinking is essentially melodic. Independent melodies are combined in polyphonic textures (following principles of "dissonant counterpoint"). Seeger's and Crawford's melodies feature extensive use of motives that are combined and transformed in many ways to generate melodic growth. Seeger called his motives or shapes "neumes." Seeger's **neume** is a collection of at least three elements that form a motive. A neume may be a collection of pitches, or it may also be a shape or a contour, without specific pitch content (as in "up-up" or <+, +>, "down-down" or <−, −>, "up-down" or <+, −>, and "down-up" or <−, +>). In our analysis we will focus particularly on the motivic aspects of Crawford's music. To simplify our terminology, however, we will use the familiar term "motive" instead of "neume" in our analyses.

Listen to Crawford's *Diaphonic Suite* no. 4, (Anthology no. 18), composed in 1930, and annotate some observations on texture, form, motivic content, and rhythm and meter.

Texture and Form

This piece consists of two melodic lines for oboe and cello. The lines are contrasting in timbre and register, and also in rhythm, thematic content, and character. The oboe is highly motivic and thematic, whereas the cello features a running bass line in a constant eighth-note motion. From a formal perspective, the piece is made up of four sections (mm. 1–13, 14–29, 30–50, and 51–74). Because each new section provides variations on the same motivic material that was first introduced in mm. 1–13, we can think of the form as varied strophic form, or strophic variations. The general character of the variations is improvisatory or rhapsodic, in what we hear as a free-flowing spinning out of a small number of motivic units. All four formal sections begin with the same thematic material originally presented in mm. 1–2, and the first three sections end with a cello glissando, followed by a rest in sections 1 and 2 and by a brief cadenza in section 3. The last section ends with a brief codalike restatement of the opening thematic idea (mm. 69–74).

The Oboe Part

In our discussion of themes and motives, we will focus mainly on section 1, mm. 1–13. The oboe's initial measures are based on two motives. The first motive, which we will call motive x, is presented in m. 1 (the two quarter notes ornamented with grace notes).

---

[10]For a general analytical study of Crawford's music, see Straus, *The Music of Ruth Crawford Seeger*.

♪♪ Example 6.3   Ruth Crawford, *Diaphonic Suite* no. 4, III, oboe line, mm. 1–4

a.

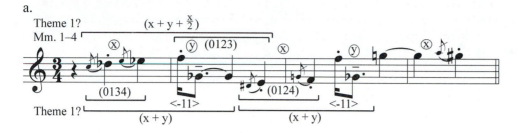

b. Mm. 3–4

c.

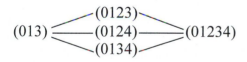

The second motive, motive y, is the descending major-seventh figure at the beginning of m. 2, or <−11>. These two motives together constitute the first theme of the piece. As we will see, several combinations of motives x and y are heard in mm. 1–6. The statement of motive y in beat 2 of m. 7 initiates a new theme. This second theme is made up of motive y followed by a scalar ascending figure in triplets, which we will label as motive z.

In its basic form, then, theme 1 consists of $(x + y)$, and theme 2 consists of $(y + z)$. The real length and identity of theme 1, however, is not so clear. Example 6.3 shows possible thematic segmentations of mm. 1–4. We hear mm. 1–4 as a phrase because in m. 5 there is a slightly varied return of the opening theme. By thematic parallelism, we would think of the two initial statements of the $(x + y)$ motivic complex in mm. 1–3 as two statements of theme 1: a statement and a slightly varied counterstatement. This grouping, however, is contradicted by the beginning of sections 2, 3, and 4, and by the closing statement of theme 1 in the coda. These later statements of theme 1 consist of $(x + y)$ followed by one more ornamented quarter note (that is, half of x), or $(x + y + x/2)$. This ambiguous beginning allows for several different readings of pitch-class relationships. If we think of mm. 1–3 as two statements of $(x + y)$, we can read the first

♩♪♪ Example 6.4   Crawford, *Diaphonic Suite* no. 4, III, oboe line, mm. 5–8

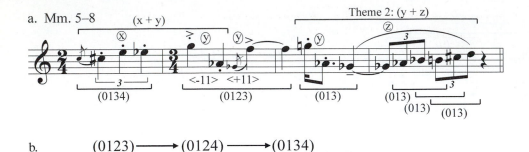

a. Mm. 5–8

b.   (0123) ──────▶ (0124) ──────▶ (0134)

one as a (0134) set followed by <−11>, and we can read the second one as a (0124) set also followed by <−11>. If, on the other hand, we hear all of mm. 1–2 as theme 1, we can read it as two consecutive tetrachords: (0134) in m. 1 and (0123) in m. 2. All these relationships are shown in Example 6.3a.

After the y motive in m. 3, beat 2, we hear an incomplete statement of motive x closing the initial phrase in mm. 1–4. This final pairing of (y + x) in this phrase, shown in Example 6.3b, forms set (01234). We can also read it as two overlapping (013) trichordal units or as a (0134) set, the same set we found in m. 1, with an inserted G. Note that, as shown in example 6.3c, (013) is a subset of each of the three tetrachords we have identified, (0123), (0124), and (0134), and each of these three tetrachords is a subset of (01234).

The second phrase (shown in Example 6.4a) begins in m. 5 with a restatement of theme 1 in its complete (x + y) form. Motive x is here varied rhythmically; motive y is both varied rhythmically and transposed by T_2 and is followed by an inverted form of itself, <+11>. The x motive in m. 5 forms the same (0134) set that we saw in m. 1, and the two y motives in m. 6 represent set (0123), also familiar to us from m. 2. Beginning in beat 2 of m. 7 we hear the new theme 2, made up of the descending <−11> gesture of motive y, followed by the ascending scalar fragment that we have called motive z. The first three pitches of this theme form a (013) set, and the scalar fragment breaks up into three overlapping (013) segments. This strong presence of (013) in the second theme provides a clear connection between themes 1 and 2. The two final statements of theme 2 in this opening section (mm. 9–12) can be broken up into the following combinations of motives y and z: (y + z + y) for the first statement, in m. 9 and beat 1 of m. 10; and (z + y) in the closing statement.

Notice that each of the three tetrachords we have identified in this section, (0123), (0124), and (0134), can be derived from another tetrachord in the group by chromatic expansion or contraction of one pitch class. We can refer to this relationship among set types as **linear transformation.** In other words, set (0123) is linearly transformed into

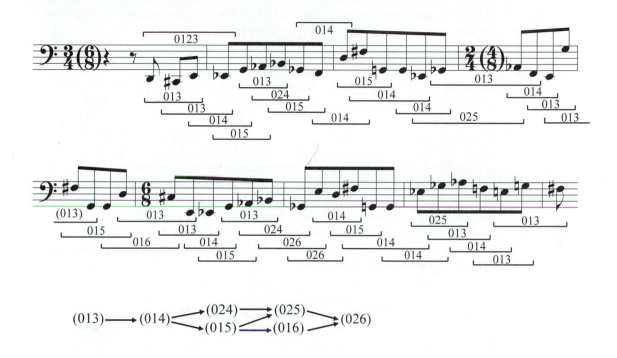

| Example 6.5 | Crawford, *Diaphonic Suite* no. 4, cello line, mm. 1–8 |

(0124) by chromatic expansion of the fourth pitch class, and set (0124) is linearly transformed into (0134) by chromatic expansion of the third pitch class, forming the network (0123)→(0124)→(0134), as shown in example 6.4b.[11]

The Cello Part

Because of the continuous flow of eighth notes in the cello part, motives in this line are less clearly delineated by distinctive rhythmic designs. A complete segmentation of this line into trichords, however, will help us understand its motivic nature. Example 6.5 shows a pc-set analysis of all adjacent and overlapping trichords in the cello's opening eight measures. The diagram under the example shows that there are only seven different set classes in these measures, and that the seven classes are related by a network of linear transformations: (013) is transformed into (014), which in turn can be transformed into either (024) or (015). (015) generates (016), and both (015) and (024) generate (025). Finally, both (025) and (016) can be transformed into (026). Thus, this cello

---

[11]This type of linear transformation of pitch-class sets is discussed in Miguel Roig-Francolí, "A Theory of Pitch-Class-Set Extension in Atonal Music," *College Music Symposium* 41 (2001): 57–90.

section is generated by linear transformation of the (013) set into six other trichords. Note, too, that the two instrumental lines (oboe and cello) are thus connected in this initial section by the structural significance of (013). Moreover, the opening tetrachord in the cello part, as shown in Example 6.5, is (0123), the same tetrachord that generates the linear transformation network for the oboe part.

Rhythm and Meter

The oboe and cello lines are also clearly differentiated rhythmically. The oboe part features distinctive rhythmic motives that contribute to the character of each of the three motivic gestures we have previously identified. Thus, motive x, in its original form, appears as two quarter notes with grace notes. The rhythmic figure associated to motive y consists of a sixteenth note followed by a dotted eighth, and motive z features the ascending run in triplets. Each of these rhythmic motives may appear in its original form or in a varied form. From a metrical point of view, there is no correspondence between these rhythmic motives and meter as notated. If you consider the first two statements of the complete (x + y) theme 1 in mm. 1–3, you will see that the first statement begins on beat 2 of a $\frac{3}{4}$ measure and is extended over a total of 4 beats. The second (x + y) statement, on the other hand, begins on beat 3 of measure 2, lasts for three beats, and then is extended for three more beats to the end of m. 4.

The nonmetrical nature of this music is further stressed by the cello line. The constant eighth-note pulse is punctuated by accents. First, we notice that these accents may fall on any of the eighth-note subdivisions of the measure. Moreover, we can observe that the grouping that results from the accents is totally irregular. If we consider the distance from one accent to the next in number of eighth notes, the resulting grouping pattern is as follows: 2 + 2 + 4 + 2 + 4 + 2 + 2 + 4 + 2 + 4 + 4 + 4 + 2 + 1 + 3 + 3 + 2 + 3 + 2 + 3 + 3 + 3 + 2 + 1 + 1. In the first part of this design we see a predominance of groupings in 2 and 4 notes (although without any particular pattern), whereas the second part turns to groupings in 1, 2, or 3 notes. Here again we observe a nonmetrical grouping that is in constant conflict with both the motivic grouping in the oboe line and the notated meter.

Conclusions

The fragment of Crawford's *Diaphonic Suite* no. 4 that we have analyzed displays two independent and, in principle, unrelated lines. The oboe line is clearly motivic, both in its pitch organization and in the presence of distinct rhythmic motives. The cello line consists of a constant flow of eighth notes which, although not as clearly motivic as the oboe part, is based on a network of trichords related by linear transformation. Trichord (013) plays a significant role in both lines and can be seen as the collection that provides a connection between both instruments. From a temporal point of view, both lines feature distinctive rhythmic profiles, and both are essentially nonmetric in that they avoid recurring groupings that would generate metric accents. Neither line features rhythmic patterns that correspond with the notated meter. We thus perceive the temporal aspect of this piece as a flowing, nonmetrical spinning out of motivically generated lines.

APPLICATION AND CLASS DISCUSSION

The neoclassical styles we studied in Chapter 5 reflect an interest in drawing on the past and incorporating it into present-day compositions. The ultramodern composers, on the other hand, were not so interested in actively drawing on the past as a compositional means. And yet one of the composers we have studied in this chapter, Charles Ives, also uses music from the past as a compositional element in many of his pieces. What is different between both uses of the past (neoclassicism and Ives's), and how do they generate highly contrasting stylistic results?

What musical style do you personally find more appropriate from the point of view of twentieth-century aesthetics, neoclassicism or ultramodernism?

Further Listening

The following list provides suggestions for further listening to music by composers studied in this chapter or related to the styles and techniques we have studied (if possible, listen while following the score):

1. Ives, *The Unanswered Question*
2. Ives, Fourth Symphony
3. Crawford, *Diaphonic Suite* no. 1 (complete)
4. Crawford, String Quartet no. 1
5. Varèse, *Octandre*
6. Varèse, *Intégrales*

Terms for Review

ultramodern movement
musical borrowing

neume
linear transformation of pc sets

 # CHAPTER 6 ASSIGNMENTS

I. Analysis

1. Analyze mm. 14–29 of Crawford's *Diaphonic Suite* no. 4 (Anthology no. 18). Your analysis should be based on the analysis of mm. 1–8 presented in this chapter (see Examples 6.3, 6.4, and 6.5). Discuss motivic and pitch-class set relationships in these measures.

2. Ives, *The Unanswered Question* (score and recording available in your music library). Listen to this composition and read Ives's "Foreword." Then answer the following questions, some of which refer to statements or instructions you will have read in the "Foreword."

    a. What are the three different instrumental groups? What programmatic meaning does each group have?

    b. Describe the pitch material and the general system of pitch organization for the string orchestra. Then do the same for the flute quartet and for the trumpet. Are the various elements of pitch organization related or unrelated to each other?

    c. How do the formal principles we learned with reference to the music of Stravinsky apply to this music? Explain particularly the role of stratification in this piece.

    d. Comment on aspects of spatial use of sound and sound sources stemming from performance instructions for this piece. What is particularly "modern" about this aspect of *The Unanswered Question*?

    e. Comment on metric and rhythmic matters in this piece. What issues are raised by the performance instructions in the "Foreword"? What is particularly "modern" about these issues as they affect synchronization, simultaneities, and tempo layers?

II. Composition

1. Compose a piece for voice or a melodic instrument and piano, using two or more interval cycles to generate your melody and your chordal sonorities. Although "The Cage" is a good model for this exercise, make sure you don't compose "The Cage" all over again!

2. Compose a piece for a solo melodic instrument of your choice, using some of the techniques of melodic growth and motivic transformations we have studied in our section on Ruth Crawford. You should compose one or more motives, and then use these motives as the basic cells for your lines. You may vary the motives as you want, and you may also create a network of pitch-class sets related by linear transformation from which you can draw for your motivic gestures.

Chapter 7

Twelve-Tone Music I: An Introduction

In Chapter 4 we analyzed several compositions in a style that we referred to as "free atonality." The type of compositional solutions we studied in that chapter in matters of pitch organization do not constitute a systematic compositional method. Rather, in that context composers devised ad hoc organizational principles for each piece and relied substantially on their musical intuition. Arnold Schoenberg, who for years followed this approach with successful and interesting results, was also aware that "free atonality" neither amounted to a systematic method nor provided a general, universal alternative to functional tonality as a means to organize pitch. From 1916 to 1923, Schoenberg did not compose any complete work, devoting himself instead to writing, teaching, and experimenting and researching a new method of composition. The result was what we know as the **twelve-tone** or **dodecaphonic method.** In general, we think of twelve-tone music as music based on one or more twelve-tone rows. A **twelve-tone row** or **twelve-tone series** is an ordered arrangement of the twelve pitch classes. Twelve-tone music thus involves a basic set that consists of the aggregate (the total chromatic) and that is presented in a particular ordering.[1]

---

[1]For Schoenberg's own discussion and historical justification of the twelve-tone method, see Arnold Schoenberg, "Composition with Twelve Tones," in *Style and Idea,* ed. Leonard Stein, trans. Leo Black (London: Faber and Faber, 1975), pp. 214–48. A thorough study of Schoenberg's method, including analyses of several of his serial compositions, can be found in Ethan Haimo, *Schoenberg's Serial Odyssey* (Oxford: Clarendon Press, 1990). Among the many important contributions to twelve-tone theory, the following are particularly recommended: Milton Babbitt, "Some Aspects of Twelve-Tone Composition," *Score* 12 (1955): 53–61; "Twelve-Tone Invariants as Compositional Determinants," *Musical Quarterly* 46 (1960): 246–59; and "Set Structure as a Compositional Determinant"; all three articles are reprinted in *The Collected Essays of Milton Babbitt*; see also *Milton Babbitt: Words about Music,* ed. Stephen Dembski and Joseph Straus (Madison: University of Wisconsin Press, 1987); Martha Hyde, "The Telltale Sketches: Harmonic Structure in Schoenberg's Twelve-Tone Method," *Musical Quarterly* 66/4 (1980): 560–80; and *Schoenberg's Twelve-Tone Harmony* (Ann Arbor, 1982); Andrew Mead, "Large-Scale Strategy in Schoenberg's Twelve-Tone Music," *Perspectives of New Music* 24 (1985): 120–57; Robert Morris, "Set-Type Saturation Among Twelve-Tone Rows," *Perspectives of New Music* 22/1–2 (1983–84): 187–217; *Class Notes for Atonal Music Theory,* and *Composition with Pitch Classes*; and Charles Wuorinen, *Simple Composition* (New York: Longman, 1979)

NOTE

*The twelve-tone method is also often called **serialism**. Serialism, however, refers to the compositional technique in which a row or series is used, no matter what the size of the row might be. Thus, serialism is not necessarily "twelve-tone serialism." A row may have five pitch classes (as it does sometimes in Stravinsky's music), nine pitch classes (in music of Ruth Crawford Seeger), or any number of pitch classes. If we want to make it clear that we are referring to the twelve-tone method, and not just to any serialism, we should use the term "twelve-tone serialism."*

Two works Schoenberg composed in 1923 are partially based on the twelve-tone method (Five Piano Pieces, op. 23, and the Serenade, op. 24), and his first twelve-tone piece is the Suite, op. 25, of 1924. We should keep in mind, however, that although in many ways the twelve-tone method represented a revolutionary step in the history of musical composition, it is also a logical consequence of Schoenberg's previous musical endeavors. His concern with motivic coherence and development, with the motive as an element of compositional cohesion, and with organic unity and integrity can be seen as leading to his discovery of the twelve-tone set as a "super-motive" of sorts that can provide the pitch material for a complete composition. Because the row can be read forward, backward (retrograde), upside-down (inversion), and upside-down backward (retrograde inversion), and still always be the same row, twelve-tone music allowed Schoenberg to realize the concept of "absolute and unitary perception of musical space" that he had always been so interested in.[2] Moreover, for years before the formulation of the twelve-tone method, Schoenberg's main source of pitch material was the twelve-tone collection, the aggregate. It is natural, from this perspective, that he should have investigated (and found) a way of organizing the aggregate into a single, ordered set with motivic implications.

Because the impact of serialism on twentieth-century composition is important and far ranging, we will devote three chapters to its study. Before World War II, the main twelve-tone composers were Schoenberg and his circle of students or former students in Vienna, including Webern and Berg. Other composers who practiced twelve-tone composition in the years before the war were the Spaniard Roberto Gerhard, the Frenchman René Leibowitz (both also students of Schoenberg), the Austrian Ernst Krenek, the American George Perle, and the Italian Luigi Dallapiccola. A young generation of European composers after World War II, including Pierre Boulez, Karlheinz Stockhausen, Luigi Nono, Bruno Maderna, and Luciano Berio, continued and developed the serial tradition. The method was also eventually adopted by composers with such well-established careers as Stravinsky and Aaron Copland. Although interest in serialism died out among most European composers after the 1960s and 1970s, an important school of twelve-tone composition developed (and continued into the beginning of the twenty-first century) in the United States, including composers such as Roger Sessions, Milton Babbitt, Charles Wuorinen, and Donald Martino.

---

[2]See Schoenberg, "Composition with Twelve Tones," in *Style and Idea*.

BASIC PRINCIPLES

A twelve-tone row or twelve-tone series is a particular ordering of the twelve pitch classes. The type of sets we have studied so far are unordered sets, that is, the pitch classes in the set can be presented in any order in the actual music (unless, as it sometimes happens, a set is used in association with a particular motivic shape, and then the pitch classes do appear in a certain order in the music, to preserve the motive). A row or series, on the other hand, is an **ordered pitch-class collection.** Changing the order of the pitch classes will change the row into a different row. Consider the passage shown in Example 7.1a. The right hand of the piano shows a particular ordering of the twelve pitch classes, that is, a row, in this case the basic row for Schoenberg's Suite, op. 25. You can count the twelve pitch classes in the row (a process we call a "twelve count") and assign each of them an **order number,** from 0 to 11, to show the position each pitch class occupies in the row (we could do it from 1 to 12, but we will count from 0 to 11 to keep the same numbering system as with pitch-class numbers, where we use integers 0 to 11). Note that we will use letters T and E to refer to 10 and 11, respectively, in a twelve-tone context (some authors use A and B for these two integers). This task is simple enough for the right hand because there is only one line involved. To number the left hand, however, we run into the problem of the two lines after order number 3. It helps to realize that the row in the left hand is a transposition (by T_6) of the row in the right hand (as it appears clearly by comparing the first four pitch classes of each hand). If we transpose the right-hand row to begin on B♭ instead of D, we come up with the row form shown in Example 7.1b. The order numbers of the left-hand row now become more apparent, as we can see in Example 7.1a. This example shows us that, although order is an important factor in building a row, the composer can alter that order to create a particular compositional texture.

As we have just seen, we may indeed transpose a row. We may, moreover, read it backward, upside down (that is, invert it), or read the inversion backward. These are the four **basic forms of a row:** the row may be read in its original order (**prime** or P), we may invert its intervals (**inversion** or I), we may read it in reverse order (**retrograde** or R), or we may read the inversion in reverse order (**retrograde inversion** or RI). Examine the melody reproduced in Example 7.2a. Mm. 1–5 present the original row form for Schoenberg's Variations, op. 31 (1926–28). If you read the melody in mm. 46–50, you will see the same pitch classes as in the original form, but now they are read backward. This is the retrograde of the row, R. In mm. 51–57 you can see the same intervals as in the original row, but their direction is now inverted. This is an inversion of the row, or I (which has also been transposed to begin on G instead of the original B♭). A retrograde reading of this I form of the row provides the pitch classes for mm. 39–45, the retrograde inversion of the row, or RI. Example 7.2b shows the four basic row forms for this row (for the sake of clarity, the I and RI forms in 7.2b are not transposed, and thus begin on the same pitch class as the original P form). Note that for the R and RI forms we simply read the P and I forms backward, as indicated by the arrows.

We can observe several things in Example 7.2b. Because R and RI forms are simply the backward versions of P and I, when we use order numbers for R and RI we will just use 11 to 0 in reverse order (E–T–9–8 . . . 2–1–0). In theoretical and analytical

Example 7.1a   Schoenberg, Suite op. 25, "Praeludium," mm. 1–3

Example 7.1b   The row forms from Example 7.1a

discussions, moreover, we will also use another numerical label for pitch classes, that we will refer to as **pitch-class number.** For pitch-class numbers, we will follow the standard "fixed do" system of integer notation, as we did in our study of pitch-class sets (that is, C = 0, and the remaining eleven pitch classes are numbered by their distance in semitones from C).

NOTE

In twelve-tone theory we work, as we did in pitch-class set theory, in pitch-class space. That is, enharmonic and octave equivalences apply. In other words, we may notate any note of the row in any octave and use any of its equivalent enharmonic spellings.

One more thing we can notice in Examples 7.1a and 7.2a is that, in a musical context, the row can be broken up into subsets in a variety of ways. The segments of the

♪♪ Example 7.2a   Schoenberg, Variations for Orchestra, op. 31, mm. 34–57

♪♪ Example 7.2b   The row for Example 7.2a

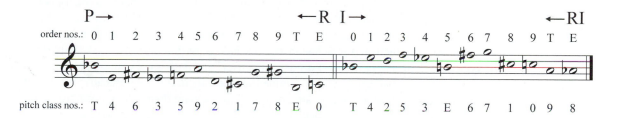

row may be equal or unequal. In Example 7.1a the texture and phrasing (as well as the imitative character of the passage) break up both row forms in both hands equally into tetrachords, as shown in Example 7.3. The line from Example 7.2a, on the other hand, breaks up into subsets of irregular size. In mm. 34–38, for instance, P is segmented into a pentachord, a tetrachord, and a trichord.

We can label the segments or subsets of a row as unordered sets and compare them in the same way that we compare pitch-class sets. The prime forms for the tetrachords in Example 7.3, for instance, are (0236), (0146), and (0123)—in other words, three different tetrachords. But because of the imitative structure of the passage, we hear an

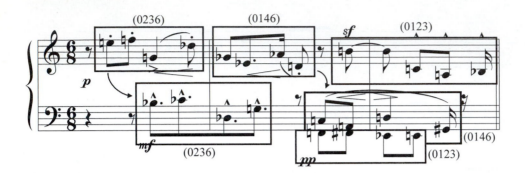

immediate motivic imitation of the (0236) tetrachord in the left hand, followed by a motivic imitation of the (0146) tetrachord as the upper line of the two-voice texture in the left hand (shown by arrows on the example). What imitative relationships can you discover among the three simultaneous lines that close this passage?

BUILDING A ROW

Writing a row is already part of the compositional process in twelve-tone music. Rows may be of very characteristic types, and particular composers have favored particular types of rows. The type of row may determine, or at least influence, some aspects of the composition, as we will see in our analyses later in the chapter. For the time being, let us examine a few examples of rows and their musical context. First, refer back to Example 7.2b, the row for Schoenberg's Variations for Orchestra, op. 31. This row is typical of Schoenberg in that it is not symmetrical and it does not contain any recognizable motives or patterns. Let us examine the intervals in this row. Because we need to measure intervals in a row in a consistent way to compare them, we will use the system we learned in Chapter 3 to calculate the adjacency interval series (AIS) of a set. The AIS lists ordered pitch-class intervals between adjacent pitch classes. We know from Chapter 3 that an ordered pitch-class interval is the distance between two pitch classes considered in a particular order (and, by convention, always in an ascending direction). To determine the ordered pc interval between two pcs, subtract the first pc from the second in *mod 12*. Thus, the AIS of the Variations row is <6,2,9,2,4,5,E,6,1,3,1>. We see from this series that the row includes a variety of intervals, but also that interval classes 1, 2, and 6 make up a majority of the intervals, with a total of seven. Schoenberg usually avoids outlines of major and minor triads in his rows because of their possible "tonal" implications. One triad is outlined in this row (order numbers 4, 5, and 6). But, in the musical context for this row shown in Example 7.2b, the three pitch classes that

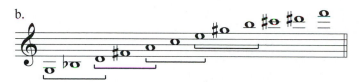

Example 7.4 (a) Berg, Violin Concerto, mm. 15–20, solo violin part.
(b) The row from (a).

a.

pp *ma espr.*

b.

outline the triad do not appear in the same phrase segment, so the sound of the triad is actually avoided in this way.

Examine now Example 7.4, which shows both the entrance of the solo violin in Berg's Violin Concerto (1935) and the row on which this passage is based. What is the difference between the way Berg built this row and the way Schoenberg built his for the Variations, op. 31? What does Berg's row tell us about Berg the composer? Why would it have been unlikely for Schoenberg to build such a row?

Example 7.5, on the other hand, shows one of several rows used by Berg in the *Lyric Suite* (1925–26), both in its musical context, and in abstract form. This is a type of row we call an **all-interval row.** An all-interval row can be written in pitch space in at least one form that contains all eleven intervals from the minor second to the major seventh (that is, all simple intervals, excluding the unison and the octave). In Berg's particular all-interval row, we can see that the row is symmetrical at the tritone (a fact easily verifiable if we write the row as in Example 7.5c). In its all-interval version (7.5b), the symmetrical intervals appear as the two different members of a same interval class (as in 1/11, 4/8, 3/9, and so on), all around the tritone axis of symmetry.

Any row whose AIS contains two instances of each interval class except for ic 6 (for which there will be a single instance) can be written as an all-interval row. Examine the Dallapiccola row shown in Example 7.8. The adjacency interval series for this row is <1,4,3,2,6,11,4,2,5,9,7>. In other words, all interval classes are represented twice, except for ic 6, which appears only once. This is, then, another all-interval row. Can you write a version of it that actually demonstrates the all-interval property for this row in pitch space?

Unlike Schoenberg, Webern favored what we know as derived rows, as well as row symmetry. A **derived row** is a row built from several forms of a single trichord or

discreet subsets
which are

♪♪ Example 7.5   **(a)** Berg, *Lyric Suite*, I, mm. 2–4 (first violin part). **(b)** The row from (a). **(c)** A symmetrical version of the row from (b).

tetrachord. Examine the discrete subsets for the row in Example 7.6 (from Webern's Concerto for Nine Instruments, op. 24; you can see the score for the opening passage of the Concerto, which uses this row, in Example 8.4 in the next chapter). **Discrete subsets** are those that divide the row into equal (adjacent and non-overlapping) segments. The set class for each of the four discrete trichords in this case is (014). Moreover, if we think of the first trichord as the P form of an ordered set, the second one is a transposed RI form of the original, the third set is a transposed R form, and the fourth set is a transposed I form.

The row in Example 7.7 illustrates Webern's interest in row symmetry. The row is not quite derived, because the discrete trichords are not all of the same class: (014), (013), (013), (014). We hear, however, motivic coherence because of the four overlapping (0134) tetrachords. The row, moreover, is constructed symmetrically in such a way that the second hexachord is arranged as a retrograde inversion of the first hexachord. The two hexachords actually feature inversional symmetry: the second hexachord is T_5I of the first hexachord, and T_5I is the one inversional level under which this set, (012345), maps onto itself. At the beginning of this piece from 1940, shown in Example 7.7a, Webern does not choose to emphasize any of the sets we have just discussed, but rather brings out musically the symmetrical arrangement of the three discrete tetrachords (see double basses, oboe, and trombone, respectively), whose prime forms are (0134), (0236), and (0134).

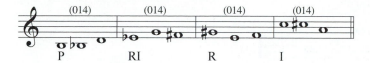

Example 7.6   The row for Webern's Concerto, op. 24

Example 7.7a   Webern Variations for Orchestra, op. 30, mm. 1–4

Example 7.7b   The row for Example 7.7a

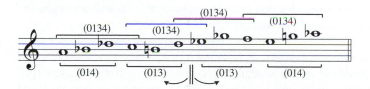

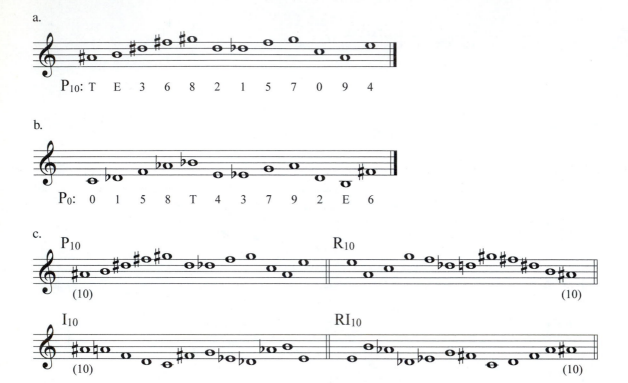

Example 7.8   The row for Luigi Dallapiccola's *Quaderno musicale di Annalibera*

a.

P_{10}: T   E   3   6   8   2   1   5   7   0   9   4

b.

P_0: 0   1   5   8   T   4   3   7   9   2   E   6

c.

P_{10} R_{10}

(10)   (10)

I_{10} RI_{10}

(10)   (10)

LABELING ROW FORMS

We will now learn how to label the various possible row forms. Example 7.8a shows the basic row form from Dallapiccola's *Quaderno musicale di Annalibera*. The integers under this example show pitch-class numbers for Dallapiccola's row. Because we label P forms after the first pitch class, this particular row form is P_{10}. P_0 will always be the P form that begins on C, as shown in Example 7.8b.

Example 7.8c illustrates how we will label the four types of row forms that result from the standard twelve-tone operations (P, I, R, and RI). As we just mentioned, a P or I form is labeled by means of an index number that indicates its first pitch class (pc). Thus, the P and I forms that begin on A♯ will be P_{10} and I_{10}, respectively, and the P and I forms that begin on C will be P_0 and I_0. R and RI forms, on the other hand, will be labeled from their *last* pc, allowing us to show in a simple and direct way that R_{10} is the retrograde of P_{10}, and RI_{10} is the retrograde of I_{10}. Observe, then, that the R form that begins on E and ends on A♯, shown in Example 7.8c as the retrograde of P_{10}, is actually

P_0:	0	1	5	8	T	4	3	7	9	2	E	6
Add:	11	11	11	11	11	11	11	11	11	11	11	11

P_{11}:	E	0	4	7	9	3	2	6	8	1	T	5

Figure 7.1 Transposing a row

R_{10} (for pc A♯) and not R_4 (for pc E). And the RI form that begins on E and ends on A♯ is also RI_{10} (for A♯) and not RI_4 (for E).

BUILDING A TWELVE-TONE MATRIX

Each of the four basic forms of a row (P, I, R, and RI) may be transposed twelve times. All together, there are forty-eight possible forms for each row. A **row class** is the set of row forms related to an original row by transposition, inversion, retrograde, or retrograde inversion. It is useful, both from a compositional and an analytical point of view, to have a list of all forty-eight forms for a particular row, and the best way to organize this list is through a 12×12 **twelve-tone matrix.** Before we build one such matrix, however, let us remember the basic operations for set transposition and set inversion.

To transpose a set (in this case a row) by a given index number (that is, a transpositional operator, as in the "n" of a T_n operation), add the index number to each of the members of the set (remember that we are performing our operations in *mod 12* arithmetic). Given P_0 for our sample row (Dallapiccola's row), we can determine P_{11}, for instance, by adding 11 to each member of P_0, as shown in Figure 7.1. Note that this is the same operation that we are familiar with (as the T_n operation) from our study of pitch-class set theory in Chapter 3.

To invert a set (in this case a row) by a given index number (that is, as in the "n" of a T_nI operation), subtract each of the members of the set from the index number. Given P_0, for instance, we can determine I_0 by subtracting each member of P_0 from 0 (that is, from 12), and we can determine I_1 by subtracting each member of P_0 from 1. Both operations are shown in Figure 7.2. Note that this is the same operation as the T_nI operation from our study of pitch-class set theory in Chapter 3.

A twelve-tone matrix is a 12×12 square in which P_0 is listed horizontally across the top row and I_0 is listed vertically down the leftmost column, as shown in Figure 7.3a. We can now complete the rest of the matrix as follows. All subsequent rows under P_0 will be transposed forms of P, and their first integer (given by each of the members of I_0 in the leftmost column) is the corresponding transpositional level or index number for each P form. Thus, the second row will be P_{11} (which we determine by adding 11 to each member of P_0), the third row will be P_7 (add 7 to each member of P_0), and so on. The complete matrix for the Dallapiccola row appears in Figure 7.3b.

After you have the complete matrix, you can read all twelve P forms by reading rows from left to right, and read all R forms by reading rows backward from right to

a.

Subtract from:	12	12	12	12	12	12	12	12	12	12	12	12
P_0:	0	1	5	8	T	4	3	7	9	2	E	6
I_0:	0	E	7	4	2	8	9	5	3	T	1	6

b.

Subtract from:	1	1	1	1	1	1	1	1	1	1	1	1
P_0:	0	1	5	8	T	4	3	7	9	2	E	6
I_1:	1	0	8	5	3	9	T	6	4	E	2	7

Figure 7.2 Inverting a row

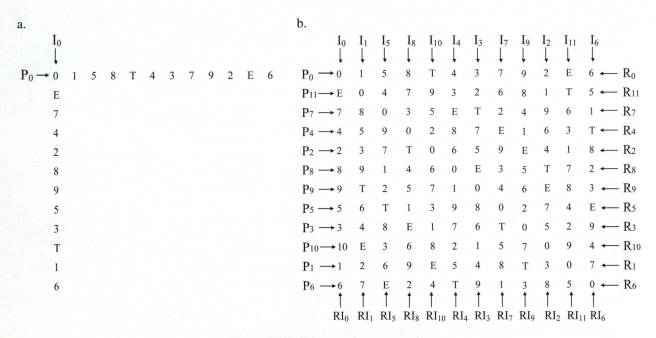

Figure 7.3 Building a twelve-tone matrix

left. I forms can be read as columns from top to bottom, and RI forms as columns backward, from bottom to top.

Keep in mind that if all you need is to calculate a few specific row forms given P_0, you need not go through the trouble of building a complete matrix. To calculate any P_n form, transpose P_0 by T_n (that is, add n to each member of P_0). To calculate any R_n

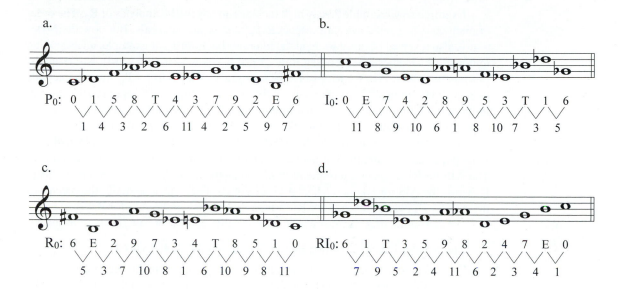

Example 7.9   Intervallic content for Dallapiccola's row

a.

P_0: 0 1 5 8 T 4 3 7 9 2 E 6

    1 4 3 2 6 11 4 2 5 9 7

b.

I_0: 0 E 7 4 2 8 9 5 3 T 1 6

    11 8 9 10 6 1 8 10 7 3 5

c.

R_0: 6 E 2 9 7 3 4 T 8 5 1 0

    5 3 7 10 8 1 6 10 9 8 11

d.

RI_0: 6 1 T 3 5 9 8 2 4 7 E 0

    7 9 5 2 4 11 6 2 3 4 1

form, first transpose P_0 by T_n, and then read the resulting row backward. To calculate any I_n form, invert P_0 by T_nI (that is, subtract each member of P_0 from n). And to calculate any RI_n form, first invert P_0 by T_nI, and then read the resulting row backward.

IDENTIFYING GIVEN ROW FORMS WITHOUT USING A MATRIX

A matrix can be a useful tool to identify a row form. At times, however, it is not worth building a whole matrix just to identify one or two row forms from a piece. We can easily do that also without a matrix, as we will learn right now. Because we will identify row forms by examining their interval content, we first need to understand the intervallic relationships between P, I, R, and RI forms. Example 7.9a shows the intervallic content of P_0 for the Dallapiccola row. The pc content of this row form is notated under the staff. We calculate the adjacency interval series for the row (AIS, measured in ordered pitch-class intervals) by subtracting the first integer from the second integer in each pair of adjacent pitch classes (we know that by doing so we will always list the corresponding interval in ascending direction). The result for P_0 is <1,4,3,2,6,11,4,2,5,9,7>.

Now look at I_0, shown in Example 7.9b. Because the intervals for I forms are the same as for P forms, but their contour is reversed, the ordered pitch-class intervals in I forms will be the inversions (that is, the intervallic complements) of the intervals for P. The AIS for I_0 indeed shows that intervals for I forms are the *mod 12* complements of intervals for P forms, <11,8,9,10,6,1,8,10,7,3,5> in our example. This makes sense because we have inverted the intervals (that is, subtracted their numerical value from 12).

Examine now Example 7.9c, which includes an intervallic analysis of R_0. The order of pitch classes is reversed with respect to P_0, and so are intervals. But now their contour is also reversed because we read the intervals backward (for example, an ascending minor third becomes a descending minor third if you read it backward). Numerically, this means that the AIS for R_0 will be the retrograde of the AIS for P_0, but the intervals in R_0 will be the *mod 12* complements of the corresponding intervals in P_0 (the ascending perfect fifth that closes P_0, ordered pc interval 7, becomes a descending perfect fifth in R_0, ordered pc interval 5). Thus, the AIS for R_0 is <5,3,7,10,8,1,6,10,9,8,11>.

A similar process applies to the AIS for RI forms, as shown in Example 7.9d. The order of pcs and the direction of intervals in RI forms is reversed with respect to I forms. The AIS for RI_0 is made up of the *mod 12* complements of the retrograded intervals in I_0. Thus, the AIS for RI_0 is <7,9,5,2,4,11,6,2,3,4,1>. This AIS is actually the reverse of the AIS for P_0 (that is, the AIS for RI forms is the reverse of the AIS for P forms).

We can summarize our discussion of intervallic content of row forms as follows:

1. The AIS for P forms in our sample row is <1,4,3,2,6,11,4,2,5,9,7>.

2. The AIS for I forms is made up of the *mod 12* complements of intervals for P forms (that is, we will subtract P intervals from 12). In our sample row, this will be <11,8,9,10,6,1,8,10,7,3,5>.

3. The AIS for R forms is made up of the *mod 12* complements of the retrograded intervals for P forms. This is the same as reading the AIS for I forms backward: <5,3,7,10,8,1,6,10,9,8,11> in our sample row.

4. The AIS for RI forms is made up of the retrograded intervals for P forms: <7,9,5,2,4,11,6,2,3,4,1> in our sample row.

In other words, because we can relate the AIS of all forms to the AIS of P forms, we need not actually figure out independently the AIS for each of the four row forms before we can identify any row form. It is sufficient to calculate the AIS for P forms and then apply the correspondences listed previously.

Now let's apply this knowledge to the identification of some given row forms, shown in Example 7.10. Let's identify the opening intervals for the first row form. The opening four pcs for this row form are 2, 1, 9, 6. The AIS for these pcs is <11,8,9>, which is the opening AIS for I forms. Because I forms are labeled from their first pitch class, D or 2 in this case, this form is I_2.

The second row form in Example 7.10 begins with pcs 5, 6, T, 1, with an AIS of <1,4,3>. This identifies the row as a P form beginning on F or 5, hence P_5. Similarly, the third row form begins with pcs 8, 1, 4, E, with an AIS of <5,3,7>, which identifies an R form. In an R form, the index number will be provided by the *last* pc, D in this case, hence R_2. Finally, the fourth row form begins with pcs T, 5, 2, 7, with an AIS of <7,9,5>. This is then an RI form, and the index number is provided by the *last* pitch class, E, hence RI_4.

As an exercise, you may now identify the row forms in Example 7.11, given P_0 for this row (from Schoenberg's String Quartet no. 4): C B G A♭ E♭ D♭ D B♭ F♯ F E A.

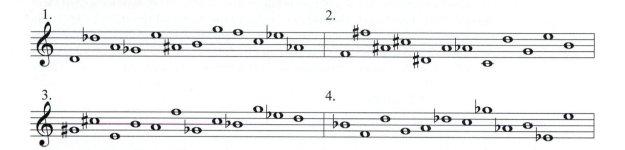

♪♪♪ Example 7.10   Row-form identification

♪♪ Example 7.11   Row-form identification exercise

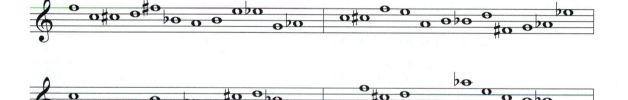

Although in our preceding discussion and in Example 7.9, we have provided, for the sake of clarity, the complete AIS for P, I, R, and RI forms, remember that you need not figure all of them out to identify row forms. Instead, determine the first two or three intervals for P_0 and the last two or three intervals of P_0 computed backward (as if reading R_0). Then you can compare the initial intervals of the row forms you are identifying with either the beginning or ending intervals of P_0, and that will be sufficient for you to identify the exact row form.

ANALYSIS 7.1: DALLAPICCOLA, "CONTRAPUNCTUS SECUNDUS," NO. 5 FROM *QUADERNO MUSICALE DI ANNALIBERA* (ANTHOLOGY NO. 19)

After building a twelve-tone row, a composer needs to decide which of the forty-eight row forms will be used in a particular composition, because it is highly unlikely that all of them will be used. Composers rely on a variety of musical reasons to choose the particular row forms for a composition. After they do so, they still need to compose the piece, that is, the actual musical surface, a task that requires many purely musical decisions. We will now look in some detail at a brief twelve-tone piece, "Contrapunctus secundus" (Anthology no. 19) by Luigi Dallapiccola (1904–1975), and our analysis will examine both this composer's choice of particular row forms for this piece and possible reasons for doing so. This is the fifth piece in the *Quaderno Musicale di Annalibera,* a collection of eleven piano pieces composed by Dallapiccola in 1952–53 and dedicated to his daughter Annalibera, for whom they were meant to be study pieces.

The Musical Surface

Listen to the piece while following the score. How are the two lines in this piece (right hand and left hand) related? How would you describe the general style of this piece?

This movement is a canon by contrary motion at a distance of an eighth note. It is divided into two parallel sections, indicated by the double slash between measures 4 and 5. In section 1, the left hand leads *(dux)* and the right hand imitates *(comes),* whereas in section 2 the order of the hands is reversed. Both sections are further related by rhythmic and motivic parallelisms. Can you identify some of these? Stylistically, this piece is a compositional miniature, featuring great economy of means. Texture is sparse, and the isolated points of sound, as well as the *staccato* markings, give it a "pointillistic" character.

Identifying Row Forms

Example 7.8a shows what is usually considered the basic row form for the *Quaderno musicale di Annalibera,* and 7.8b shows P_0 for this row. The complete matrix appears in Figure 7.3b. To identify row forms on the score, it is useful to realize a **twelve-count** of pitch classes, that is, to identify all twelve pitch classes and to number them with their corresponding order numbers. This process is illustrated in Example 7.12 for the first section of "Contrapunctus secundus." We already know how to identify row forms, so we can determine that the right hand begins with P_7 and the left hand with I_5. Using P and I forms simultaneously (or R and RI forms) is an obvious choice in a piece that is a canon by contrary motion. (P and I forms, as well as R and RI, are automatically related by inversion or contrary motion.)

A twelve-count is not always straightforward and obvious. Especially when the texture includes chords, identifying the exact order of pitch classes may require some guesswork and imagination because pitch classes may not necessarily appear in a predictable order. The identification of the second pair of row forms in our piece, R_3 and RI_9 in m. 2, is not quite as obvious as the opening pair of row forms because now two pitch classes are sounded simultaneously in each hand. Can you now do a twelve-count and row-form identification for section 2?

Row-Form Relationships and Large-Scale Pitch Structure

Example 7.13 shows the complete pitch-class content for the whole piece. The first thing we observe is that, as we already know, the two lines (or the simultaneous pairs of row forms) are mirror inversions of each other throughout. Two row forms related

Example 7.12   A twelve-count for Dallapiccola's "Contrapunctus secundus," mm. 1–4

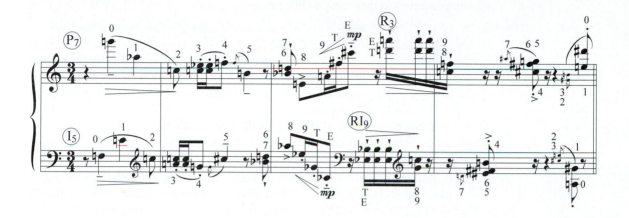

Example 7.13   Dallapiccola, "Contrapunctus secundus," pitch-class content

by inversion (P and I, or R and RI) will have an axis of symmetry (the "mirror" around which the inversion takes place). Inversionally symmetrical sets, such as the ones found in this piece, feature several interesting properties. The following is a discussion of two of these properties as they apply to this piece.[3]

a. *If the sum of index numbers of two row forms related by inversional symmetry is an even number* (for example, P_7 and I_5, whose sum of index numbers is 12), then two pitch classes a tritone apart function as axes of symmetry. We can determine the first pitch class by adding the index numbers for both row forms and dividing by two: $(7 + 5)/2 = 6$, or F♯. For the second axis, add 6 (a tritone) to the first pitch class: $6 + 6 = 0$, or C. Both axes of symmetry, F♯ and C in this case, will be invariant in the two row forms; that is, they will appear with the same order numbers in each row form, as you can verify in Example 7.8, where these pcs are connected with a solid line.

If the sum of index numbers is an odd number (for example, P_7 and I_8, whose sum of index numbers is 3), then the first axis is a dyad consisting of two half-step related pitch classes, and the second axis is another dyad a tritone away from the first one. If we add the index numbers of P_7 and I_8 and divide by two, the result is $(7 + 8)/2 = 7.5$, so the axis dyads are G–G♯ (the real axis, 7.5, runs between pcs 7 and 8, or G and G♯) and the dyad a tritone away, C♯–D (axis 1.5, between pcs 1 and 2).

b. Any two inversionally related row forms (P and I or R and RI) whose index numbers add up to the same number will have the same axes of symmetry. Thus, the pairs P_7/I_5 (sum of index numbers = 12) and R_3/RI_9 (sum of index numbers = 12) share the axes F♯–C, and the pairs P_{10}/I_8 (sum = 6) and R_6/RI_0 (sum = 6) share the axes E♭–A.

After Dallapiccola started with the pair P_7/I_5, why would he have chosen the pair R_3/RI_9 to continue? In the first place, because the two pairs share axes of symmetry, but moreover, because the pair R_3/RI_9 begins and ends with the dyad E♭–A, the two pitch classes that function as axes of symmetry for section 2. Similarly, after beginning section 2 with P_{10}/I_8 (axes E♭–A), Dallapiccola continues with R_6/RI_0, which not only extend the E♭–A axes, but begin and end with the same dyad, G♭–C, the two pitch classes which are also the axes of symmetry for section 1. The cadential gestures of both section 1 and section 2 feature these "structural dyads" as the lowest and highest pitches: A–D♯ at the end of m. 4, and C–F♯ at the end of m. 8.

We discuss other properties of inversionally symmetrical row forms in our analysis of Webern's Piano Variations, op. 27, II, in Chapter 8. For the time being, this discussion should suffice as an illustration of a possible set of criteria that can lead a composer to choose some particular row forms from the total set of forty-eight available forms, and how the choice of row forms is one of the essential elements that determine large-scale structure in twelve-tone compositions.

---

[3]See *Milton Babbitt: Words about Music*, pp. 38–41.

ANALYSIS 7.2: DALLAPICCOLA, "QUARTINA," NO. 11 FROM *QUADERNO MUSICALE DI ANNALIBERA* (ANTHOLOGY NO. 20)

The last piece in Dallapiccola's set is titled "Quartina," or "quatrain." A brief discussion of the pitch structure of this piece will help us practice the skill of identifying row forms and will provide us with further perspective on the types of process composers may follow to decide on the various row forms to use in a composition. First, listen to the piece and make some observations regarding phrases and form. Then identify the row forms for the complete melodic line. Try also to identify the row forms for the harmonic accompaniment, although these are not so clearly laid out as in the melody. The row for this piece is the same that we are already familiar with, and so is the matrix (see Example 7.8 and Figure 7.3).

Notice that the whole piece consists of a melody with chordal accompaniment. Moreover, the piece breaks up into four phrases, articulated by a variety of factors (such as melodic shape, rests, and register): mm. 1–5, 6–9, 10–13, and 14–18, respectively. These phrases, in turn, can be grouped into two contrasting pairs, phrases 1–2 (mm. 1–9) and phrases 3–4 (mm. 10–18), respectively. Contrast is provided mostly by rhythm, and the resulting formal design is a binary type with two contrasting sections.

Examine now Example 7.14a, which shows the complete pitch-class content for "Quartina." The identification of the melodic row forms is quite straightforward, but the identification of the row forms used harmonically is somewhat obscured by the four-note simultaneities that begin each phrase. The complete row-form content for the piece is thus I_{10}–R_0//RI_6–P_0 for the melody, and R_1–RI_6//P_9–I_4 for the harmonic accompaniment. (Identify all the pitch classes of these rows on the score if you have not done so yet.) The double bars in this listing refer to the division of the piece into two sections.

Let us now try to make some sense of this collection of row forms. An obvious row relationship is provided by the repetition of RI_6, first as a harmonic row form in mm. 6–9, and then immediately as a melodic row form in mm. 10–13. This repetition provides a connection not only between sections, but also between harmony and melody in two different phrases. There are also other, less obvious, connections. When you examine the boxed pitch-class collections in Example 7.14a, you see that I_{10} (the first melodic row in section 1) begins with the same set of pitch classes as P_9 (the first harmonic row in section 2), pitch classes T–9–5–2. Similarly, R_1 (the first harmonic row in section 1) begins with the same two pitch classes, 7–0, as RI_6, the first melodic row in section 2.

This exchange of pitch classes between melodic and harmonic rows at the respective beginnings of sections 1 and 2 provides for a connective pitch-class element between the two sections, as indicated by the arrows in Example 7.14b. This is made possible because the set made up of pcs 7–9–5–2 maps onto itself at T_7I, the operation that relates I_{10} and P_9. (Try it: if you invert I_{10} by T_7I, that is, if you subtract all the members of I_{10} from 7, you will end up with P_9, and with an invariant opening tetrachord

♪♪ Example 7.14   Dallapiccola, "Quartina," pitch-class content

a.

Mm. 1–5

Mm. 6–9

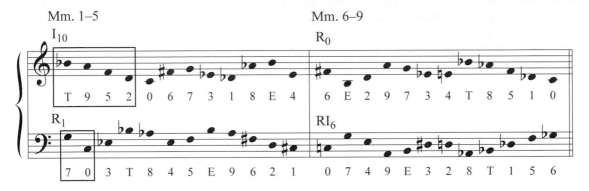

I₁₀

| T | 9 | 5 | 2 | 0 | 6 | 7 | 3 | 1 | 8 | E | 4 |

R₀

| 6 | E | 2 | 9 | 7 | 3 | 4 | T | 8 | 5 | 1 | 0 |

R₁

| 7 | 0 | 3 | T | 8 | 4 | 5 | E | 9 | 6 | 2 | 1 |

RI₆

| 0 | 7 | 4 | 9 | E | 3 | 2 | 8 | T | 1 | 5 | 6 |

Mm. 10–13

Mm. 14–17

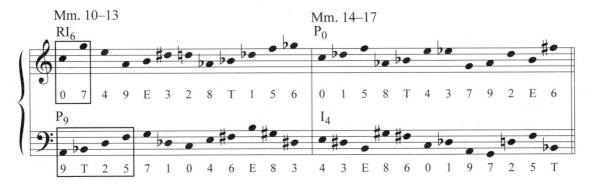

RI₆

| 0 | 7 | 4 | 9 | E | 3 | 2 | 8 | T | 1 | 5 | 6 |

P₀

| 0 | 1 | 5 | 8 | T | 4 | 3 | 7 | 9 | 2 | E | 6 |

P₉

| 9 | T | 2 | 5 | 7 | 1 | 0 | 4 | 6 | E | 8 | 3 |

I₄

| 4 | 3 | E | 8 | 6 | 0 | 1 | 9 | 7 | 2 | 5 | T |

b.

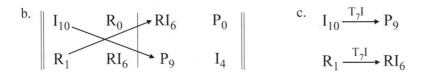

c.

$$I_{10} \xrightarrow{T_7 I} P_9$$

$$R_1 \xrightarrow{T_7 I} RI_6$$

between both row forms.) Not only this, but the same operation, $T_7 I$, also relates R_1 and RI_6, and now the opening dyad, 7–0, maps onto itself at $T_7 I$. Dallapiccola is thus taking advantage of the fact that a single operation, $T_7 I$, maps the initial pitch classes of both I_{10} and R_1 onto themselves, thus allowing him to establish a connection with the beginning of section 2 by using the row forms that result from this transformation, $T_7 I$, to begin section 2 (see Example 7.14c). The property we are discussing here, invariance in row forms under transposition or inversion, will be the focus of the first section of Chapter 8.

APPLICATION AND CLASS DISCUSSION

What do you think are the implications of twelve-tone serialism for the listener? In the absence of tonal points of reference, what aural elements is the listener likely to focus on? What musical elements might the composer use to provide a sense of aural unity to the music? Chapter 8 will help you answer this question, but you may attempt to provide answers to it now, at least to some extent. Try to refer your answers to the Dallapiccola pieces we have studied, and also to the types of characteristic rows we have discussed.

Further Listening

The following list provides suggestions for further listening to music by composers studied in this chapter or related to the styles and techniques we have studied (if possible, listen while following the score):

1. Dallapiccola, *Quaderno musicale di Annalibera* (complete)

2. Dallapiccola, *Sicut umbra*

3. Schoenberg, Suite, op. 25

4. Berg, Violin Concerto

Terms for Review

twelve-tone or dodecaphonic method
twelve-tone row, twelve-tone series
serialism
ordered pitch-class collection
order number
basic forms of a row
prime (P)
inversion (I)
retrograde (R)

retrograde inversion (RI)
pitch-class number
all-interval row
derived row
discrete subsets
row class
twelve-tone matrix
twelve-count

CHAPTER 7 ASSIGNMENTS

I. Theory

1. Study the following rows and determine in each case whether the row is (a) derived (if it is, provide the prime forms for the discrete subsets), (b) symmetrical, (c) all-interval, or (d) none of the above.

   a. Webern, Cantata no.1, op. 29:   A–F–A♭–G–B–B♭–D♭–C–E–D♯–F♯–D

b. Schoenberg, Wind Quintet, op. 26:   Eb–G–A–B–C#–Cʮ–Bb–D–E–F#–G#–F   √o

c. Webern, String Quartet, op. 28:   G–F#–A–Ab–C–C#–A#–B–Eb–D–F–E   yes (0123) RI symmetrical)

d. Luigi Nono, *Il canto sospeso*:   A–Bb–Ab–B–G–C–F#–C#–F–D–E–D#   R symmetrical, AIInterval.)

e. Webern (for a work never completed):   F#–G–Ab–F–E–Eb–B–Bb–A–C–C#–D

f. Schoenberg, Variations for Orchestra: Bb–E–F#–Eb–F–A–D–Db–G–G#–B–C

2. Write four different original rows. Try to make at least one of them derived and/or symmetrical.

3. Given the following row from Webern's Piano Variations, op. 27, supply pitch-class numbers for both the given row form and for P_0 of this row: G#–A–F–G–E–F#–C–C#–D–Bb–Bʮ–D#. Then build a complete 12×12 matrix for this row.

4. Looking at your matrix for the row from question no. 3, write out the first six pc numbers for the following row forms: R_7, I_5, P_9, and RI_{10}.

5. In the same matrix you just built, which pc is order no. 6 of P_6?

    And order no. 8 of RI_8?

    And order no. 4 of R_7?

    And order no. 7 of I_2?

6. The following row is from Elliott Carter's *Canon for 3*: 0 T 9 7 2 1 6 3 E 5 4 8

    Without using a matrix, write the following forms of this row:

    P_4:

    I_6:

    RI_7:

    R_8:

    Still without using a matrix, identify the following row forms:

    3 5 6 8 1 2 9 0 4 T E 7

    2 T E 5 9 0 7 8 1 3 4 6

    9 7 6 4 E T 3 0 8 2 1 5

    9 1 0 6 2 E 4 3 T 8 7 5

II. Analysis

1. Listen to and analyze Webern's "Wie bin ich froh," no. 1 from *Drei Lieder*, op. 25 (Anthology no. 21). This is a twelve-tone piece. The basic row is as follows: F#–F–D–E–D#–C–A–C#–G#–B–A#–G.

    a. Discuss the melodic style of this piece. What kind of contour does the melody display, and what is untraditional about it? What melodic intervals does Webern favor?

    b. Prepare and turn in a complete 12 x 12 matrix.

    c. Is there any consistency in the classes of discrete subsets in this row? Provide prime forms for each of the discrete trichords. Is this a derived row?

d. Identify all the row forms on the score. Most of the time, voice and piano have their own independent row forms, with the only exceptions of m. 5 and the end of m. 11, where they share a row form. Provide a copy of the score indicating all the row forms and including a twelve-count for the complete composition.

e. Rhythmic/harmonic figures. Notice that there are three characteristic rhythmic/harmonic figures in the piece: the sixteenth-note triplet, the eighth-note dyad, and the four-note chord.

   • Examine each of the triplets. Is there any consistency in their pitch-class content (provide prime forms).

   • With only two exceptions, all the eighth-note dyads outline the same interval class. Which one?

   • Is there any consistency in the spacing of the four-note chords? What intervals are emphasized, especially between the two lower pitches and the two upper pitches?

f. Form.

   • How many major sections does the piece have? How did you determine this?

   • Are there any characteristic pitches (not pc sets, but actual pitches, ordered collections, or motivic units) which Webern uses at the beginning of each section?

   • Are there any groups of pitch classes used at both the beginning and the end of each section? Show all these motivic connections very clearly on the score, in both voice and piano.

2. The following are some other twelve-tone pieces you may use for brief analytical papers:

a. Dallapiccola, "Linee" and "Fregi," from *Quaderno musicale di Annalibera* (scores available in Mary Wennerstrom, *Anthology of Musical Structure and Style,* pp. 518–521). The row for these pieces is the same Dallapiccola row we have already studied in this chapter.

b. Schoenberg, Menuett and Trio, from Suite for Piano, op. 25 (scores available in Mary Wennerstrom, *Anthology of Twentieth-Century Music,* pp. 175–77).[4] The row for this piece is E–F–G–Db–Gb–Eb–Ab–D–B–C–A–Bb.

III. Composition

Compose a short twelve-tone piece for piano or two melodic instruments of your choice. First, compose a row or use one of your original rows from Exercise I.2. Study the properties of your row and decide on what row characteristics you will particularly use in your composition. Then use Dallapiccola's "Contrapunctus Secundus" or one of the pieces you have studied for one of the previous analytical assignments as your model. Be as musical as possible in your actual composition and in all your compositional decisions.

---

[4]Wennerstrom, Mary. *Anthology of Twentieth-Century Music* (Englewood Cliffs, NJ: Prentice Hall, 1988).

Chapter 8

Twelve-Tone Music II: Invariance, Symmetry, and Combinatoriality

After studying the basic principles of twelve-tone music in Chapter 7, we are ready to explore some of the more complex aspects of twelve-tone theory and composition. In this chapter we will particularly focus on invariance, symmetry, and combinatoriality, especially as found in the works of Webern and Schoenberg.

INVARIANCE

In general, the term **invariance** refers to the preservation of some aspect of a row under transposition or inversion.[1] Some features of a row are always preserved under transposition (T) or inversion (I). We know that the intervallic structure of a row (the AIS) is always preserved under T, and it becomes a succession of its complementary intervals under I. The subset structure of a row, on the other hand, is preserved under both T and I. Think, for instance, of the derived row from Webern's Concerto, op. 24, that we discussed in Example 7.6. All four discrete trichords are members of the (014) set class, and they remain so in all forty-eight forms of this row.

A more particular type of invariance, however, is the preservation of one or more segments of a set (in an ordered or unordered form) under T or I. Figure 8.1 illustrates the case of *a row transformation that maps a subset of the row onto itself.* In Chapter 3 (in the section titled "Symmetry," which you may now want to review) we learned that a symmetrical set is a set that can map onto itself under transposition or inversion, and we learned the procedure to determine what exact T_n or T_nI operations map a set onto itself. Thus, to figure out which row transformations will map a subset onto itself (and will thus provide subset invariance), we determine which T_n and/or T_nI transformations map the subset onto itself.

---

[1] An essential source on invariance is Babbitt's article "Twelve-Tone Invariants as Compositional Determinants," cited in Chapter 7, footnote 1. The following two articles are also recommended: David Lewin, "A Theory of Segmental Association in Twelve-Tone Music," *Perspectives of New Music* 1/1 (1962): 89–116; and David Beach, "Segmental Invariance and the Twelve-Tone System," *Journal of Music Theory* 20 (1976): 157–84.

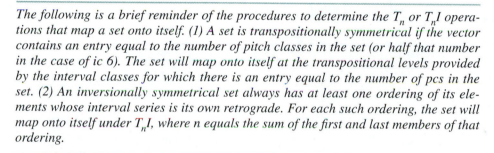

P₀: C G D D♭ B A♭ E♭ F A B♭ E F♯

I₂: D G C D♭ E♭ F♯ B A F E B♭ A♭

Figure 8.1 Invariant tetrachords under inversion in the row for Schoenberg's *Klavierstück*, op. 33a

P₀: 0 E 7 8 3 1 2 T 6 5 4 9

I₅: 5 6 T 9 2 4 3 7 E 0 1 8

Figure 8.2 Mapping of subsets onto each other under inversion in the row for Schoenberg's String Quartet no. 4

NOTE

The following is a brief reminder of the procedures to determine the T_n or T_nI operations that map a set onto itself. (1) A set is transpositionally symmetrical if the vector contains an entry equal to the number of pitch classes in the set (or half that number in the case of ic 6). The set will map onto itself at the transpositional levels provided by the interval classes for which there is an entry equal to the number of pcs in the set. (2) An inversionally symmetrical set always has at least one ordering of its elements whose interval series is its own retrograde. For each such ordering, the set will map onto itself under T_nI, where n equals the sum of the first and last members of that ordering.

The opening tetrachord in the row for Schoenberg's *Klavierstück,* op. 33a, is [0,1,2,7] in normal order. [0,1,2,7] is an inversionally symmetrical set that maps onto itself under T_2I, hence it is left invariant in the row under I_2. The other invariant segment between these two row forms, the tetrachord formed by pitch classes F, A, B♭, and E, or [4,5,9,T] in normal order, is also an inversionally symmetrical set that also maps onto itself under T_2I, and hence is also left invariant in the row under I_2.

In Figure 8.2, on the other hand, you can see an example of *a row transformation that maps a subset of the row onto another subset with identical intervallic content.* In this case, the row is from Schoenberg's String Quartet no. 4. Two nondiscrete trichords in this row, 0, E, 7 and T, 6, 5, are of the same set class, (015). This means that 0, E, 7 will map onto T, 6, 5 under some T or TI transformation. If we compare both sets in their normal order, [7, E, 0] and [5, 6, T], we can see that they are inversionally equivalent by T_5I (their AIS are <4,1> and <1,4>, respectively, and the sum of the first and last elements is 5). So 0, E, 7 will map onto T, 6, 5 under T_5I, and vice versa (that is, T, 6, 5 will also map onto 0, E, 7 under T_5I because the inversion operation goes both ways). This is shown in Figure 8.2.

🎵 Example 8.1   Schoenberg, String Quartet no. 4, I, mm. 27–28

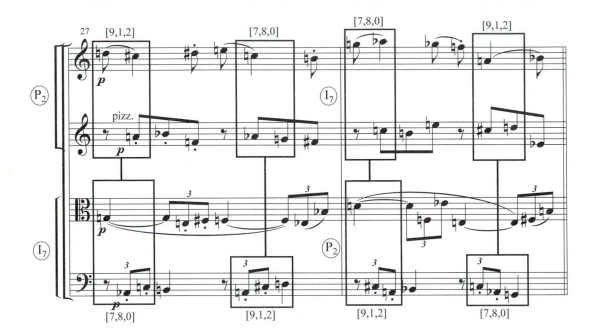

A musical rendition of these two row forms will show these invariant segments in context. Example 8.1 shows two measures from the first movement of Schoenberg's String Quartet no. 4 (1936). In m. 27, the two violins feature a complete statement of P_2, while the viola and cello are based on I_7. The two row forms are reversed in m. 28, where we hear I_7 in the violins, and P_2 in viola and cello. Notice that the relationship between P_2 and I_7 is the same as between P_0 and I_5 (both pairs are related by T_5I. The segments that exchange positions in P_2–I_7 are, in normal order, [9,1,2] and [7,8,0]. In this brief passage we hear four statements of the [9,1,2]–[7,8,0] pair of trichords, in such a way that every time we hear [9,1,2] we also hear a simultaneous [7,8,0], and vice versa.

Now try calculating a couple of invariant segments on your own: In the row from Schoenberg's String Quartet no. 4 listed in Figure 8.2, the segment 2, T, 6 remains invariant (maps onto itself) under three operations. Which are they? And under which I operation will the dyad 8, 3 in the same row map onto the dyad 4, 9 and vice versa?

Invariance in Webern takes on a particular character. Because of the very tight motivic and subset unity of some of Webern's derived rows, invariance may involve each of the four trichords or even complete hexachords. Consider, for instance, the row from the Concerto, op. 24, which we already discussed in Example 7.6. Example 8.2 shows P_0 for this row, and shows the four discrete trichords and the exact relationship of each of them to the original trichord. A consequence of this relationship among trichords

Example 8.2   The row for Webern's Concerto for Nine Instruments, op. 24

Example 8.3   Trichordal and hexachordal invariance in Webern's op. 24 row

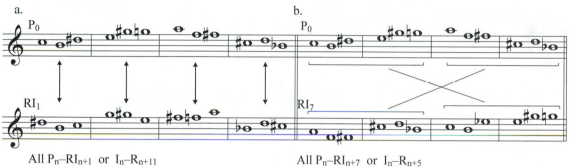

a.

b.

All P_n–RI_{n+1} or I_n–R_{n+11} All P_n–RI_{n+7} or I_n–R_{n+5}

is that all four trichords are preserved with exact pitch-class content, but in retrograde form, in all pairs of rows related as P_n–RI_{n+1} (for instance, P_0–RI_1) or I_n–R_{n+11} (for instance, I_0–R_{11}). This invariance is shown in Example 8.3a.

In yet another row relationship in Webern's op. 24 row, both hexachords in two row forms are exchanged and their exact pitch content and order are preserved (the first hexachord of the original row becomes the second hexachord of the second row, and the second hexachord of the original row becomes the first hexachord of the second row). This invariance takes place in row forms related as in P_n–RI_{n+7} (for instance, P_0–RI_7) or I_n–R_{n+5} (such as I_0–R_5), as shown in Example 8.3b.

The type of invariance in which all four trichords are preserved (as in Example 8.3a) appears in the opening measures of the concerto, reproduced in Example 8.4. (All instruments in this score are notated at concert pitch.) The row opens with P_{11}, followed by RI_0 (that is, a case of P_n and RI_{n+1}). The row presentation on the actual music surface clearly features the four trichords: in mm. 1–3, each trichord is stated by a different instrument, and in mm. 4–5 the grouping and articulation outline a segmentation of the row into trichords. What we are hearing in mm. 4–5 is an RI version of the row we first heard in a P form, but because of the P_n–RI_{n+1} relationship, we are actually

🎵🎵🎵 **Example 8.4**   Webern, Concerto for Nine Instruments, op. 24, I, mm. 1–5

hearing four trichords with the same pitch-class content as the original four trichords. In fact, every trichord in mm. 4–5 is an exact retrograde of the corresponding trichord in mm. 1–3. Thus, not only are we hearing set (014) eight times in these measures (as well as every time we hear a trichord throughout this piece!), but the four trichords in mm. 4–5 are at the same pitch level as the four trichords in mm. 1–3 because of the invariance properties of this row. Both of these facts contribute to the high level of motivic and pitch coherence in this passage.

Figure 8.3 A two-dimensional Latin palindrome

Some other aspects of these measures are worth mentioning. Webern thought of this row as a musical representation of the ancient Latin palindrome reproduced in Figure 8.3, and which can be translated as "the sower Arepo keeps the works turning." A **palindrome** is a word or sentence that reads the same forward or backward (such as "Madam, I'm Adam"). The palindrome in Figure 8.3 is a two-dimensional one that can be read in four different directions (as in a 5 × 5 matrix!). How do you think this palindrome is related to the row for the Concerto, op. 24? How is it related to mm. 1–5?

In mm. 13–21 (reproduced with annotations in Example 8.5), on the other hand, we observe several applications of the type of invariance in which the two hexachords of two row forms are exchanged, preserving the exact pitch-class content and order. The passage features R_6 beginning with the oboe and horn (mm. 13–14). The second hexachord of R_6, in the violin and viola, is also the first hexachord of I_1. The second hexachord of I_1, which we hear again in the oboe and horn (mm. 16–17), is identical with the first hexachord of R_6 that we heard in mm. 13–14. The remaining row overlaps in this section that are due to hexachordal invariance are all in the piano part and involve I_6 and R_{11} in mm. 14–17, and a chain of three overlaps involving R_1, I_8, and again R_1, in mm. 18–21. Verify these on the score. The two rows overlapping in mm. 13–17, I_1 and R_6, are related as I_n–R_{n+5}, the row relationship we saw in Example 8.3b. How are the overlapping rows in the piano in mm. 14–21 related?

In our analysis of Webern's Variations op. 27, II, later in this chapter, we discuss one final type of invariance that involves vertical dyads in pairs of row forms related by inversion.

WEBERN AND ROW SYMMETRY

Besides derived rows and invariance, we also often find symmetrical rows in Webern's twelve-tone music. Consider, for instance, the row shown in Example 8.6, from Webern's *Symphonie,* op. 21 (1928). The first hexachord (H_1) is symmetrical with the second hexachord (H_2) in such a way that H_2 is the retrograde of H_1 transposed at T_6, a relationship that we can express as $H_2 = R_6(H_1)$. All **symmetrical rows** can be read forward or backward and the intervals will be exactly preserved (that is, symmetrical rows are palindromic). In this case, the row can be read forward as P_0 and backward,

♪♪ Example 8.5   Webern, Concerto for Nine Instruments, op. 24, I, mm. 13–21

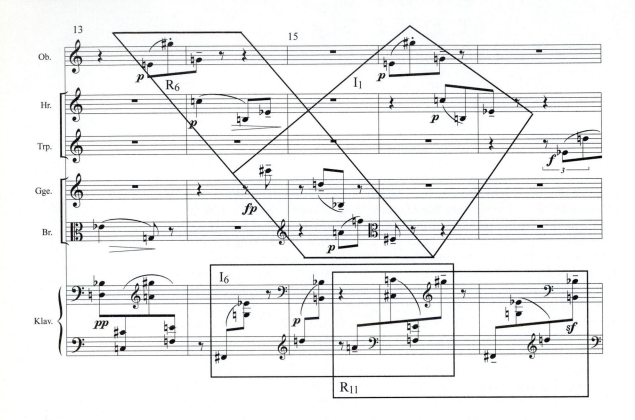

♪♪ Example 8.6   Webern's *Symphonie*, op. 21, P_0

of course, as R_0. But because of the retrograde tritone relationship between both hexachords, any R_n will be the same as the P form a tritone away, or P_{n+6}. In this case, R_0 is the same as P_6 (and, of course, reversing the formula, P_0 will be the same as R_6). In other words, in a symmetrical row, every row form can be identified with two row-form labels. A matrix for a symmetrical row will then include only twenty-four, in contrast to forty-eight, different row forms.

♪♪ Example 8.7   Webern's *Symphonie,* op. 21, the two rows of the *Thema*

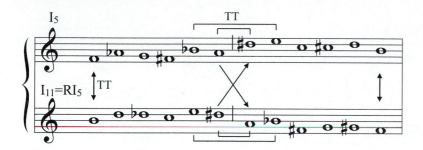

The symmetrical properties of this row are particularly brought out in the second movement of the *Symphonie,* a theme with variations. The two row forms used in the *Thema* (mm. 1–11 of the second movement) are shown in Example 8.7, and the theme itself (mm. 1–11 of movement II) is reproduced in Example 8.8 (where all instruments are notated at concert pitch).[2] The row form in the clarinet is I_5. The same as P_n is identical to R_{n+6} (and vice versa, R_n identical to P_{n+6}), I_n is also identical to RI_{n+6} (and RI_n is identical to I_{n+6}). This means that the retrograde of the clarinet row, RI_5 is the same as I_{11}. This is precisely the row form stated by the rest of the instruments in the *Thema* (harp and two horns).

This choice of row forms creates a multiplicity of tritone relationships throughout the *Thema*. First is the immediate T_6 transposition between I_5 and I_{11}. This is heard directly in the music only at the beginning and end of the phrase (B–F and F–B tritones in mm. 1 and 11) and in m. 6, the middle point (Eb–A and A–Eb tritones). As we already know, both hexachords of each row are related by R_6 (that is, a retrograde reading of T_6). This means that at the middle point (the axis of symmetry in m. 6) the hexachords between I_5 and I_{11} are literally reversed among themselves, while in each row the pitch classes symmetrical around the axis (order numbers 5–6, 4–7, 3–8, and so on) are related by tritone. As a result of the exchange of hexachords between I_5 and I_{11}, moreover, these two row forms feature only six different dyads, all related by tritone: the six vertical tritones in the combined first hexachords of both rows are the same as the six vertical tritones in the combined second hexachords, only that in the second hexachords their vertical (contrapuntal) and horizontal (melodic) orders are reversed with respect to the first hexachord.

Not surprisingly, in a piece in which pitch structure is saturated with symmetrical and palindromic relationships, Webern also created a multiplicity of other musical symmetrical relationships. Examine the score for the *Thema,* reproduced in Example 8.8. What other musical parameters are composed symmetrically? Investigate and comment on the following elements: rhythm, orchestration, articulation, and dynamics.

---

[2]An analytical and pedagogical discussion of the *Thema* can be found in John Rahn's *Basic Atonal Theory,* pp. 4–17.

In Example 8.7 we looked at pitch classes. But on the score you can examine the lines in pitch space and comment on exact intervallic relationships (you can do this particularly with the clarinet line). Is there intervallic symmetry? And how about register symmetry?

Some composers after World War II looked back at Webern as their point of departure. This applies especially to young composers, and particularly to those, such as Boulez, Stockhausen, Nono, Berio, and others, who practiced what we know as multiserialism (the serialization of other musical parameters besides, and along with, pitch). Why do you think compositions such as the Concerto, op. 24, and the *Symphonie,* op. 21, would have been particularly influential among such composers?

ANALYSIS 8.1: WEBERN, PIANO VARIATIONS, OP. 27, II (ANTHOLOGY NO. 22)

Listen to Webern's Piano Variations, op. 27, II, of 1935–36 (Anthology no. 22). First, comment on the style of this piece. Is there any trace of expressionistic postromanticism left in this music? Why and how is this piece so "modern," that is, so forward looking, so unlike most of the music that preceded it? What are the musical components of this piece, and how do they work? Is there a melody? Is there counterpoint? And harmony? And lines? If so, how are these components related to tradition, if they are at all? What is the form of this movement?[3]

General Observations

Because the basic compositional principles of this movement are closely derived from row-form relationships (as is often the case in twelve-tone compositions), it will be useful from the outset to examine the diagram with the complete pitch-class content of the movement which appears in Example 8.9. If you compare the diagram with the score, you will immediately discover that this is a canon by contrary motion (a mirror canon) at the metric distance of an eighth note. In this way, this piece is similar to Dallapiccola's "Contrapunctus secundus," which we analyzed in Chapter 7. The analogy, however, does not go very far. The mirror structure in Dallapiccola's piece is quite evident because the two lines are clear and independent and can be heard as lines. In op. 27, II, the row forms display clear mirror symmetry, as becomes evident by examining Example 8.9 even at a glance. But neither the lines nor the mirror symmetry are immediately obvious in the music surface. Try to perform a twelve-count on the score for the complete piece, and you will see that the two lines (and the hands) cross many times and that the actual pitch realization of the music surface contains numerous large leaps covering a very broad register.

The piece is, nevertheless, symmetrical and linear (that is, based on horizontal, melodic motion or lines), both in its surface and in its row structure. Two aspects provide particular links with tradition: it is a mirror canon (a very old contrapuntal genre), and its form is simple binary (as clearly shown by the two sections, both marked with repeat signs). Other than that, this is a highly modern piece. The rows provide melodic and linear material, but the very disjunct, pointillistic realization of the music surface does not lead to any concept of line and melody familiar to the listener of common-practice music. Example 8.9 certainly shows a strict contrapuntal structure underlying this movement, yet we hear it more as a succession of disjunct sound points grouped into twos and fours than as a traditionally contrapuntal piece. We will address the very interesting issue of harmony in this piece in a moment, but before we do so, listen to it again, and try to hear some harmonic coherence. Do the "sound points" sound random to you, or do they seem to have a coherent harmonic unity? Do you think you keep hearing the same harmonic and dyadic relationships, or do you instead hear what you might call random harmonic relationships?

---

[3]For an analysis of this movement, see Peter Westergaard, "Webern and 'Total Organization': An Analysis of the Second Movement of Piano Variations, Op. 27," *Perspectives of New Music,* 1 (1963): 107–20; David Lewin, "A Metrical Problem in Webern's Op. 27," *Music Analysis* 12 (1993): 343–54; and Andrew Mead, "Webern, Tradition, and Composing with Twelve Tones," *Music Theory Spectrum* 15/2 (1993): 172–204. Babbitt's commentary on this piece can be found in *Milton Babbitt: Words about Music,* pp. 33–38. A good general introduction to Webern's twelve-tone music can be found in Kathryn Bailey, *The Twelve-Note Music of Anton Webern* (Cambridge: Cambridge University Press, 1991).

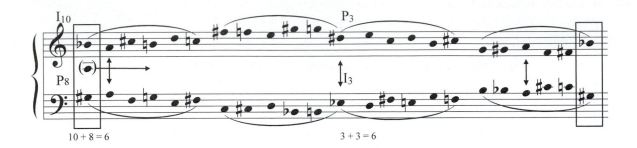

Example 8.9   Webern, Piano Variations op. 27, II, pitch-class content

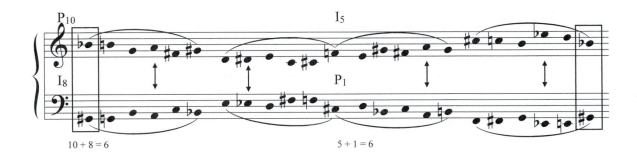

Pitch-Class Content and Row-Form Relationships: Symmetry and Invariance

We can now look at Example 8.9 in more detail. The row in itself is not particularly characteristic (P_0 = C C♯ A B G♯ A♯ E–F–F♯ –D–D♯ –G, or 0 1 9 E 8 T 4 5 6 2 3 7). It is neither symmetrical nor derived, and its four discrete trichordal subsets are all different. Compositional interest in this movement comes not so much from the row as from the set of row forms and the way Webern uses them. The piece begins with a pair of inversionally related row forms, I_{10} and P_8. We can easily calculate the two axes of symmetry for these two rows by applying the formula we learned in Chapter 7: add the index numbers and divide by two for the first axis, and then transpose by T_6 for the second axis: $(10 + 8)/2 = 3$, or pitch class E♭, and $3 + 6 = 9$, pitch class A. We also know that all inversionally related row forms whose index numbers add up to the same integer will have the same axes of symmetry. The index sum between I_{10} and P_8 is 6. The row pairs after this are P_3–I_3 (index sum = 6), P_{10}–I_8 (index sum = 6), and I_5–P_1 (index sum = 6). The dyad E♭–A will then function as the double axis for symmetry for the complete movement.

Because we know that the movement is a canon at the distance of an eighth note, every time we hear one of the axes of symmetry, E♭ or A, we should hear the same pitch class in the following eighth note. Does it work like this on the score? It does, clearly, for the four A4–A4 dyads, which we hear distinctly in mm. 1, 9, 13, and 19. The E♭–E♭ dyads are more disguised in the texture, as grace notes in mm. 6 and 21 and as part of two chords in m. 15. This seems to indicate that symmetry around A in this piece was more significant to Webern than symmetry around E♭. The whole piece is indeed symmetrical around A4. It is interesting to note that the A–A dyad in m. 9 marks the Golden Section (GS) from the end of the piece, and the A–A dyad in m. 13 marks the GS from the beginning. (The piece has a total of 90 eighth notes; the GS of 90 is 55; the A–A dyad in m. 9 falls on eighth-note numbers 53–54 counting from the end, and the dyad in m. 13 falls on eighth-note numbers 53–54 counting from the beginning.

Why do you think it makes sense to use the particular pairs of rows that we find after the initial I_{10}–P_8 pair? Within all the possible pairs whose index numbers add up to 6, why use P_3–I_3, then P_{10}–I_8, and finally I_5–P_1? Invariance is obviously a factor here. Webern simply chose to begin each row pair on the same pitch classes on which the previous row pair ended: E♭–E♭ in the first place, then G#–B♭, then C#–F, and finally G#–B♭ again. Each of these dyads becomes an element of overlap between adjacent row pairs, and thus invariance is the rationale for the connection of row pairs. Why does the dyad G#–B♭ appear three times with a connective function, at the beginning, middle, and end points of the piece? Do the repeat signs have anything to do with it? Note that indeed, because of the repeats, P_3–I_3 need to connect not only with P_{10}–I_8, but also back with I_{10}–P_8. And that I_5–P_1 also need to connect back with I_{10}–P_8, and these necessary connections with the opening explain the presence of the G#–B♭ dyad at the middle and end points.

Harmonic Aspects: Dyadic Invariance and the Viennese Trichord

Let us now address the issue of harmonic content in this movement. Inversionally related row forms feature two interesting properties that affect their vertical dyadic relationships. In the following definitions, by "dyad" we mean the pair of pitch classes that have the same order number between two row forms.

- Within a single pair of inversionally related row forms (P and I or R and RI) whose sum of index numbers is an even number, two dyads (the axis dyads) feature a single pitch class. Of the other ten dyads, five are always the inversion of the pitch classes of the other five.

  If the sum of index numbers is an odd number, six dyads are inversions of the pitch classes of the other six.

- Any two pairs of inversionally related row forms whose index numbers add up to the same number will preserve all their dyads.

Let us verify the first property. If you take the I_{10}–P_8 pair (whose sum of index numbers is even), we know that the two axis dyads feature repeated pitch classes (that is, a single pitch class each): A–A and E♭–E♭. Each of the other five dyads will appear twice in inverted order, as shown in Example 8.10: G#–B♭ appears in order number 0 and again in order number 9, inverted as B♭–G#; F–C# appears in order number 2 and again in order number 7 as C#–F. Now verify the remaining three dyads: G–B, E–D,

♪♪♪ Example 8.10   Dyadic inversion in Webern's op. 27 row pairs

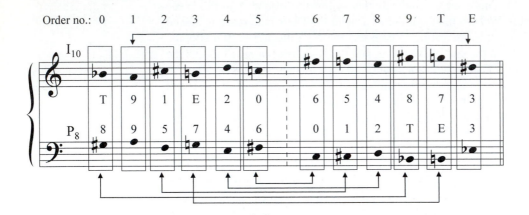

and F♯–C. This is a logical property: if the mirror inversion of, for instance, G♯ is B♭, then the mirror inversion of B♭ will be G♯ (that is, mirror inversions, as mirror images, are reciprocal). This means that in the I_{10}–P_8 pair, there are really only seven different dyads: the two axis dyads and the five dyads that appear again in inverted form. In this particular row, the five original dyads (and one of the axis dyads) appear in the combined first hexachords of a pair of row forms, and the five inverted dyads (and the other axis of symmetry) appear in the combined second hexachords of the same pair of row forms. You can verify the case of an odd sum of index numbers with the row pair P_3–I_8, and you will see that six dyads are inversions of the other six.

Now let us verify the second property. Compare each of the dyads for P_3–I_3 with the dyads for I_{10}–P_8, and do the same for P_{10}–I_8 and I_5–P_1. You will see that in all four pairs, all dyads are preserved (that is, they are invariant), because all four pairs feature index numbers that add up to the same number. But we also know that in I_{10}–P_8 there are only seven different dyads. This means, then, that throughout all this movement we only hear seven different dyads. Far from being random, the harmonic content of the piece is thus highly homogenous, and this is something that can easily be heard as we listen to the piece.

You may have noticed that in four places throughout the movement, we hear pairs of chords—trichords, to be exact. If you examine each of the eight trichords, you will see that they are all spaced as a type of quartal chord we learned in Chapter 4, the "Viennese trichord." This is a trichord made up of a perfect fourth and a tritone (spaced with either interval above or below), and its set class is (016). The reason why Webern can have eight of them in this twelve-tone context is that the pitch classes in order numbers 5, 6, and 7 in this row (and hence in each of the eight row forms in this piece) make up a (016) subset, which Webern then spaces as a Viennese trichord in the music.

Conclusions

In this piece we find again two of the characteristic traits of Webern's twelve-tone music: use of symmetry and invariance as essential compositional elements. As we listen to this movement, we experience a sense of sweeping coherence and unity. Both rhythm and meter contribute to this immediate perception. Rhythmically, we hear a constant and driving flow of eighth notes. Eighth-note attacks are grouped into two and four. Some of the two-attack groups include grace notes, and some are chordal rather than single notes. Groups of attacks are separated by rests. With only two exceptions, the duration of rests is of one eighth note. The two exceptions are m. 3 (three eighth notes) and mm. 21–22 (four eighth notes). Rhythm is thus greatly unified, although unpredictable. It is unified by the flow of eighth notes, by the groupings into two and four, and by the eighth-note rests. Unpredictability comes from the irregular order of two and four groupings, by the two rests longer than an eighth note, and by elements such as the grace notes and the chords. Even more unpredictable are the various and constantly changing dynamic markings, the articulations, and the widely disjunct registers of attacks.

From the point of view of pitch, strong coherence is provided by several factors. The row provides, as is always the case, intervallic invariance between row forms. Harmonic unity comes from dyadic invariance within row pairs and among row pairs, along with the use of the (016) Viennese trichord. Finally, and very significantly, symmetry around A (emphasized by the A4–A4 dyad at four points in the piece) provides a type of pitch centricity that we don't usually associate, at least as a norm, with twelve-tone music. In its conciseness, cohesion, extreme economy of means, and structural coherence, this movement is arguably one of Webern's compositional masterpieces.

HEXACHORDAL COMBINATORIALITY

In our studies of twelve-tone music so far, it has become apparent that Webern's rows often feature derivation and symmetry, and that he often took advantage of invariance in his structural designs involving complexes of row forms. We also find use of invariance, although perhaps to a lesser extent, in Schoenberg's twelve-tone music. But Schoenberg was even more interested in a property of some rows which we call **combinatoriality.**[4] **Combinatorial rows** are those that can produce some transposition, inversion, retrograde, and/or retrograde inversion in which the first six pitch classes will be completely different from the first six pitch classes in the original row. The first hexachord of the original row and the first hexachord of the transformed row will thus be complementary (that is, the combination of both first hexachords will contain

---

[4]An essential source for combinatorial theory is Babbitt's article "Set Structure as a Compositional Determinant," cited in Chapter 7, footnote 1. Two important sources for further study of combinatoriality are Daniel Starr and Robert Morris, "A General Theory of Combinatoriality and the Aggregate," *Perspectives of New Music* 16/1 (1977–78): 364–89, and 16/2: 50–84; and Robert Morris, "Combinatoriality without the Aggregate," *Perspectives of New Music* 21/1–2 (1982–83): 432–86. See also Morris, *Class Notes for Atonal Music Theory,* Chapters 12 and 13.

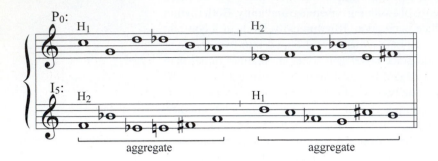

Example 8.11   Combinatoriality in Schoenberg's row from *Klavierstück,* op. 33a

the complete collection of twelve pitch classes, the aggregate). Because this type of combinatoriality involves the segmentation of the row into hexachords, we call it **hexachordal combinatoriality.**

NOTE

Other types of combinatoriality are possible, as we will study in Chapter 9: tetrachordal combinatoriality (in which the aggregate results from combining tetrachords from three different row forms), trichordal combinatoriality (the aggregate results from combining trichords from four different row forms), dyadic combinatoriality (the aggregate results from combining dyads from six different row forms), and unitary combinatoriality (the aggregate results from combining individual pitch classes from twelve different row forms). The segments combined to form the aggregate may also contain irregular numbers of pitch classes.

Take, for instance, the row for Schoenberg's *Klavierstück,* op. 33a, shown in Example 8.11. If we look at the pitch-class content of the first hexachord of P_0 we can see that it is totally different from the pitch-class content of the first hexachord for I_5 (hence the labels H_1 and H_2, which denote different hexachordal content). Consequently, the pitch-class content of the first hexachord of P_0 and the second hexachord of I_5 will be the same, although not necessarily in the same order (both are labeled as H_1), and the same applies to the second hexachord of P_0 and the first hexachord of I_5 (both are labeled as H_2). We can say, then, that this row is combinatorial, and that P_0 and I_5 (or any similarly related row forms, such as R_0–RI_5, P_2–I_7, R_2–RI_7, P_5–I_{10}, and so on) are combinatorially related.

We can now examine a musical application of this property in Example 8.12. In mm. 23–25, the right hand of the piano is based on the first hexachord of P_{10}, while the left hand presents the first hexachord of I_3. P_{10} and I_3 are combinatorially related, so there is no pitch-class invariance between both hexachords (or both hands). The same

♪♪♪ **Example 8.12**   Schoenberg, *Klavierstück*, op. 33a, mm. 23–26

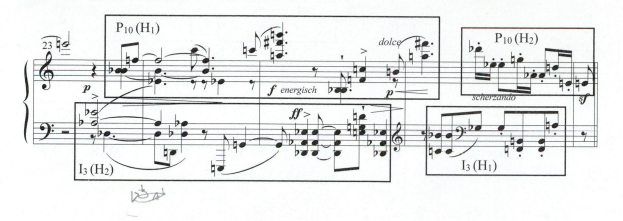

applies to m. 26, where we hear the second hexachord of P_{10} in the right hand and the first hexachord of I_3 in the left hand.

Looking back at Example 8.11, we see that a result of combinatoriality is that we hear the twelve pitch classes twice "horizontally" as rows (that is, as ordered sets), and twice "vertically" as the hexachordal combinations H_1–H_2 and H_2–H_1. The latter are unordered collections of twelve pitch classes (that is, aggregates). The complete combinatorial complex in Example 8.11 is called an **array,** and it contains two rows and two unordered aggregates. The musical consequences of such twelve-tone complexes are quite evident: in Example 8.12 we can see that by using an array of two combinatorially related rows, Schoenberg avoided any kind of invariance between row forms (contrary to what we saw Webern was doing in pieces such as the Concerto, op. 24, and the *Symphonie,* op. 21), and he presented the complete twelve-tone complex in two dimensions: we hear it twice (allowing for musical repetitions of some pitch classes) throughout mm. 23–26 in each of the hands, and twice more as the combined pitch-class content of both hands together in mm. 23–25 and 26, respectively.

Types of Combinatoriality

The type of combinatoriality most commonly found in Schoenberg's music is inversional combinatoriality, in which a row is combinatorial with an inverted form of itself. This is the type we have illustrated in Examples 8.11 and 8.12. There are, however, four types of combinatoriality: prime, inversional, retrograde, and retrograde-inversional. Before we examine each of these types, let us recall some properties of hexachordal complementarity that we studied in Chapter 3. Of the fifty hexachordal set classes, twenty are self-complementary (that is, the complement of each of these sets is the same set), and the remaining thirty sets are all Z-sets, related to their complements by the Z-relation. In all cases, a hexachord and its complement (which will be either the same hexachord or a Z-related one) have the same interval-class vector (that is, the

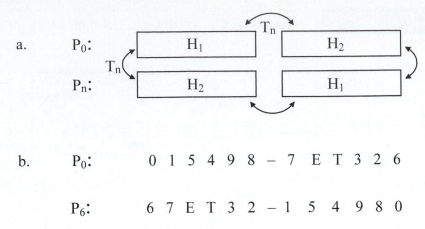

b. P_0:   0   1   5   4   9   8   –   7   E   T   3   2   6

       P_6:   6   7   E   T   3   2   –   1   5   4   9   8   0

Figure 8.4 Prime combinatoriality

same interval content). All self-complementary hexachords, moreover, can by definition map onto their complement under transposition or inversion (whereas this is not the case for Z-related complementary hexachords). Having reviewed these matters, let us now define the four types of combinatoriality.

Prime Combinatoriality

In **prime combinatoriality,** a row is combinatorial with a transposition of itself, as shown in Figure 8.4.

In P-combinatoriality, a hexachord (H_1) maps onto its complement (H_2) under T_n. H_2 is obviously the complement of H_1 (because H_1 and H_2 make up the complete row). But if P_0 and P_n are related by prime combinatoriality, as shown in Figure 8.4a, H_1 also maps onto H_2 (its complement) under T_n to form an aggregate that combines the first hexachords of P_0 and P_n, respectively. The row shown in Figure 8.4b is P-combinatorial at P_6. Verify the properties of P-combinatoriality as applied to this particular example.

Inversional Combinatoriality

In **inversional combinatoriality,** a row is combinatorial with an inversion of itself, as shown in Figure 8.5a.

In I-combinatoriality, a hexachord maps onto its complement under T_nI. H_1 maps onto H_2 (its complement) under T_nI to form an aggregate that combines the first hexachords of P_0 and I_n, respectively. Verify the properties of I-combinatoriality as applied to the I-combinatorial row forms shown in Figure 8.5b.

The fragment from Schoenberg's String Quartet no. 4 reproduced in Example 8.1 is also an excellent example of a musical application of inversional hexachordal combinatoriality. The fragment is reproduced again in Example 8.13. If you refer back to Figure 8.2 at the beginning of this chapter, you will find P_0 and I_5 for the row in this

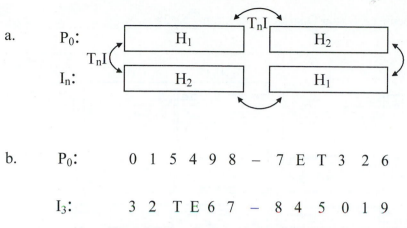

Figure 8.5 Inversional combinatoriality

piece. If you examine these two row forms for combinatoriality, you will see this row is indeed inversionally combinatorial at I_5. We already know that the fragment in Example 8.13 is based on P_2 and I_7. The two violins first state P_2 and then I_7, while the lower instruments reverse the order of presentation to I_7–P_2. In other words, we hear P_2 and I_7 simultaneously twice. Not only this, but we also hear each hexachord of P_2 simultaneously with the corresponding hexachord of I_7. Because P_2 and I_7 are inversionally combinatorial (they are related by T_5I, as P_0 and I_5 are), the first hexachords of each row form create the aggregate, and so do the second hexachords. In our passage, then, we hear four statements of the row (P_2 and I_7 in the violins, I_7 and P_2 in the cello and viola) and also four statements of the aggregate (because we hear four vertical simultaneities of H_1 and H_2, as shown in Example 8.13.

Retrograde Combinatoriality

In **retrograde combinatoriality,** a row is combinatorial with a retrograde form of itself, as shown in Figure 8.6a. All rows are trivially R-combinatorial with their own retrograde (P_0 is obviously combinatorial with R_0).

In R-combinatoriality a hexachord maps onto itself under T_n. Under T_n, H_1 of P_0 would map onto H_1 of P_n, and H_2 of P_0 would map onto H_2 of P_n (that is, both hexachords would map onto themselves under T_n). Because we read P_n backward as R_n, however, the mapping of H_1 onto itself becomes the second hexachord of R_n, and thus P_0 and R_n are combinatorial. Verify these properties in the R-combinatorial row forms shown in Figure 8.6b.

Retrograde-Inversional Combinatoriality

In **retrograde-inversional combinatoriality,** a row is combinatorial with a retrograde-inverted form of itself, as shown in Figure 8.7a.

Example 8.13   Schoenberg, String Quartet no. 4, I, mm. 27–28

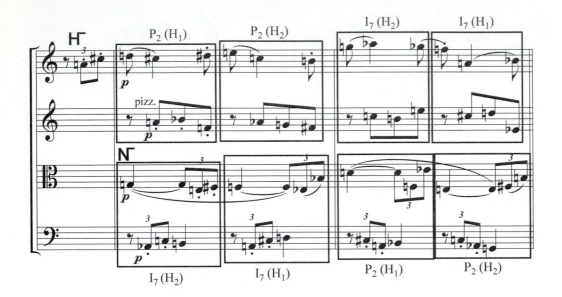

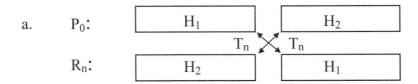

a. P_0:   [H_1] [H_2]

T_n ✕ T_n

R_n: [H_2] [H_1]

b. P_0:   0   1   5   4   9   8   –   7   E   T   3   2   6

R_8:   2   T   E   6   7   3   –   4   5   0   1   9   8

Figure 8.6 Retrograde combinatoriality

In RI-combinatoriality a hexachord maps onto itself under T_nI. Under T_nI, H_1 of P_0 would map onto H_1 of I_n, and H_2 of P_0 would map onto H_2 of I_n (that is, both hexachords would map onto themselves under T_nI). Because we read I_n backwards as RI_n, however, the mapping of H_1 onto itself becomes the second hexachord of RI_n, and thus P_0 and RI_n are combinatorial. Verify these properties in the RI-combinatorial row forms shown in Figure 8.7b.

a. P_0:

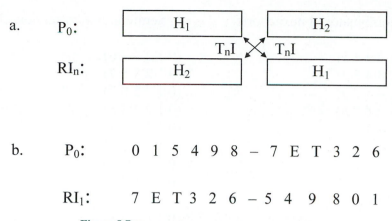

b. P_0:   0   1   5   4   9   8   –   7   E   T   3   2   6

        RI_1:   7   E   T   3   2   6   –   5   4   9   8   0   1

Figure 8.7 Retrograde-inversional combinatoriality

The All-Combinatorial and Semicombinatorial Hexachords

The most relevant type of combinatoriality (and the one normally used by Schoenberg and other composers) is inversional combinatoriality, in which a hexachord and its complement are inversionally related. All fifty hexachords are R-combinatorial even if it's only at R_0. Prime, inversional, and retrograde-inversional types of combinatoriality, on the other hand, do not apply to any of the Z hexachords. Of the twenty remaining hexachords (the self-complementary ones), six feature all four types of combinatoriality. These are the **all-combinatorial hexachords,** and they are listed in Figure 8.8a (where each of them is identified with a letter designation).[5] Thirteen hexachords are combinatorial only under one or two operations. These are the **semi-combinatorial hexachords,** and they are listed in Figure 8.8b. All of these hexachords are I-combinatorial, and one of them, (013679), moreover, is also combinatorial at R_6. None is P- or RI-combinatorial. Finally, one hexachord, (013458), is combinatorial only under T_6.

It is important to keep in mind that combinatoriality refers only to pitch-class content of hexachords, not to pitch-class order. Take, for instance, the row for op. 33a. The prime form for H_1 is (012367), which is listed as a semicombinatorial hexachord in Figure 8.8. Because in an I-combinatorial row, H_2 is always an inverted form of H_1 (a T_nI transformation), both H_1 and H_2 are of the (012367) set class. We already know that this row is combinatorial at I_5, which means that H_2 is T_5I of H_1. The first hexachord of I_5, on the other hand, also results from a T_5I transformation of the first hexachord of P_0, and although the pitch-class content of both T_5I transformations will be the same (the H_2 hexachord), the pc ordering will not be the same, as you can verify in Figure 8.9.

[5]The customary letter designation for all-combinatorial hexachords was originally used by Donald Martino in "The Source Set and Its Aggregate Formations."

a. All-combinatorial hexachords

A (0 1 2 3 4 5)
B (0 2 3 4 5 7)
C (0 2 4 5 7 9)
D (0 1 2 6 7 8)
E (0 1 4 5 8 9)
F (0 2 4 6 8 T)

b. Semicombinatorial hexachords

(0 1 2 3 4 6)
(0 1 2 3 5 7)
(0 1 2 3 6 7)
(0 1 2 4 5 8)
(0 1 2 4 6 8)
(0 1 2 5 7 8)
(0 1 3 4 6 9)
(0 1 3 5 7 9)
(0 1 3 6 7 9)
(0 1 4 5 6 8)
(0 1 4 5 7 9)
(0 2 3 4 6 8)
(0 2 3 5 7 9)

Figure 8.8 The all-combinatorial and semicombinatorial hexachords

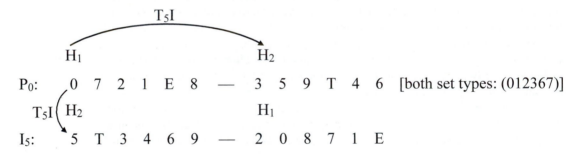

Figure 8.9 Pitch-class content combinatoriality in the row for Schoenberg's *Klavierstück,* op. 33a

Determining the Combinatorial Properties of a Hexachord or a Row

How can we determine if a given row is combinatorial, and how can we find out at what T, I, R, or RI levels it is combinatorial? Conversely, if we want to build a combinatorial row, how do we go about it?

Determining whether a row is combinatorial is simple enough given the list of combinatorial hexachords in Figure 8.8. All we need to do is figure out the prime form for the first hexachord and verify whether that set class is listed as a combinatorial hexachord in Figure 8.8. This does not tell us, however, at what index number or numbers the row will be combinatorial. Similarly, to build a combinatorial row we can start from

Set: (014589)   Summation square

Vector: [3 0 3 6 3 0]

	0	1	4	5	8	9
0	0	1	4	5	8	9
1	1	2	5	6	9	T
4	4	5	8	9	0	1
5	5	6	9	T	1	2
8	8	9	0	1	4	5
9	9	T	1	2	5	6

Figure 8.10 Interval-class vector and summation square for (014589)

any hexachord listed in Figure 8.8. But then we still don't know what exact operation we need to apply to the chosen hexachord to achieve a combinatorial form of the row.

General Procedure

We know that in P-combinatoriality, H_1 maps onto its *complement* (H_2) under T_n. In other words, the pitch classes in common between H_1 and such a T_n of H_1 (that is, H_2) will be zero (because the complement of H_1 contains "the other" six pitch classes). We need to find a T_n of H_1 with zero invariants with H_1.

In I-combinatoriality, H_1 maps onto its *complement* (H_2) under T_nI. H_1 and such a T_nI of H_1 (that is, H_2) will have zero pcs in common (because the complement of H_1 contains "the other" six pitch classes). We need to find a T_nI of H_1 with zero invariants with H_1.

In R-combinatoriality, H_1 maps onto *itself* under T_n. H_1 and such a T_n of H_1 will thus have six pcs in common. We need to find a T_n of H_1 with six invariants with H_1.

In RI-combinatoriality, H_1 maps onto *itself* under T_nI. H_1 and such a T_nI of H_1 will have six pcs in common. We need to find a T_nI of H_1 with six invariants with H_1.

We can do all this by applying the procedures to determine invariant tones under transposition or under inversion, which we studied in Chapter 3. Recall that the number of invariant pcs under transposition by interval n is equal to the number of times interval n occurs in the set (as shown in the set's interval-class vector), with the only exception of interval-class 6, for which the number of invariant pcs is twice the number of occurrences of the interval. The number of invariants under T_nI, on the other hand, will be equal to the number of times integer n appears in the summation square for that set.

Let's apply these procedures to a specific hexachord. We will choose an all-combinatorial hexachord, (014589), so we can demonstrate all four types of combinatoriality. First, we list the interval-class vector for this set and build a summation square, both shown in Figure 8.10.

For P-combinatoriality we need zero invariants under T_n. The second entry in the vector (for T_2 and T_{10}) and the last entry (for T_6) show zero entries. The hexachord is then P-combinatorial under T_2, T_{10}, and T_6.

$$P_0: \quad 0 \quad 1 \quad 5 \quad 4 \quad 9 \quad 8 \quad — \quad 7 \quad E \quad T \quad 3 \quad 2 \quad 6$$

$$P_2: \quad 2 \quad 3 \quad 7 \quad 6 \quad E \quad T \quad — \quad 9 \quad 1 \quad 0 \quad 5 \quad 4 \quad 8$$

$$I_{11}: \quad E \quad T \quad 6 \quad 7 \quad 2 \quad 3 \quad — \quad 4 \quad 0 \quad 1 \quad 8 \quad 9 \quad 5$$

$$R_4: \quad T \quad 6 \quad 7 \quad 2 \quad 3 \quad E \quad — \quad 0 \quad 1 \quad 8 \quad 9 \quad 5 \quad 4$$

$$RI_9: \quad 3 \quad 7 \quad 6 \quad E \quad T \quad 2 \quad — \quad 1 \quad 0 \quad 5 \quad 4 \quad 8 \quad 9$$

Figure 8.11 A combinatorial row built from hexachord (014589)

For I-combinatoriality we need zero invariants under T_nI. We need to find what integers do not appear at all in the summation square. Integers 3, 7, and 11 are absent, so the hexachord is I-combinatorial under T_3I, T_7I, and $T_{11}I$.

For R-combinatoriality we need six invariants under T_n. These are provided by the fourth entry in the vector (for T_4 and T_8). Moreover, all hexachords are R-combinatorial under T_0.

For RI-combinatoriality we need six invariants under T_nI. Three integers appear six times in the summation square, 1, 5, and 9. The hexachord is RI-combinatorial under T_1I, T_5I, and T_9I.

Building a Combinatorial Row

Now let's build P_0 of a combinatorial row using this hexachord. We can build the first hexachord from the prime form (014589), which, of course, we don't need to keep in the same order. Let's say 0 1 5 4 9 8. Now it will suffice to build H_2 as the complement of the first hexachord, and again we can choose any ordering, such as 7 E T 3 2 6. We thus have the row P_0: 0 1 5 4 9 8–7 E T 3 2 6. Both of these hexachords are of set class (014589), so we know that the preceding combinatorial relationships we have listed should apply. Let us verify one of the relationships for each of the combinatorial types. In Figure 8.11 we list P_0 along with P_2 (which features P-combinatoriality), I_{11} (I-combinatoriality), R_4 (R-combinatoriality), and RI_9 (RI-combinatoriality), and we see that indeed all these row forms are combinatorial with P_0.

Determining the Combinatorial Properties of a Given Row

We have thus learned how to build a combinatorial row. Let us determine the procedure to figure out the combinatorial levels of a given combinatorial row. Suppose that we try to find out whether and how the row from Schoenberg's op. 33a is combinatorial. P_0 is 0 7 3 1 E 8–3 5 9 T 4 6. We find out the prime form for H_1, which is (012367), and verify in Figure 8.8 that it is a combinatorial hexachord. Then we check its interval-class vector: [422232]. Because neither zero nor six (nor three in the case of ic 6) are entries in the vector, the row is not P-combinatorial nor R-combinatorial (except for the trivial R-combinatoriality with R_0).

```
        0   7   3   1   E   8
    ┌───────────────────────────
  0 │ 0   7   3   1   E   8
  7 │ 7   2   T   8   6   3
  3 │ 3   T   6   4   2   E
  1 │ 1   8   4   2   0   9
  E │ E   6   2   0   T   7
  8 │ 8   3   E   9   7   4
```

Figure 8.12 The summation square for the first hexachord of Schoenberg's *Klavierstück,*
op. 33a row

Now we need to build a summation square for the first hexachord. It is important
to keep in mind that to examine a specific row for I and RI combinatoriality, we need
to realize the summation square *from the actual pitch classes in the row, and not from
a prime form.* So our summation square in this case will be for 0 7 3 1 E 8, and not for
(012367), as shown in Figure 8.12.

One integer, 5, is missing from the square. So the row is I-combinatorial at I_5.
No integer, on the other hand, appears six times in the square, so the row is not RI-
combinatorial. These procedures verify what we already know: the row for op. 33a is
combinatorial only at I_5 and R_0.

ANALYSIS 8.2: SCHOENBERG, *KLAVIERSTÜCK,*
OP. 33A (ANTHOLOGY NO. 23)

We will conclude our analysis of "classical" twelve-tone music with a study of Schoenberg's *Klavierstück,* op. 33a (1929), a composition more complex and of larger proportions than the twelve-tone pieces we have analyzed so far.[6] First listen to the whole
piece, and as you listen, try to identify and mark any distinctive and characteristic musical event (particular textures, themes and their character, sections and other formal
issues). Then let's examine the two basic forms of the row on which much of the piece
is built. We already know that P_0 for this row is 0 7 3 1 E 8–3 5 9 T 4 6 (or C–G–D–
Db–B–Ab–Eb–F–A–Bb–E–F♯), and that this row is semicombinatorial at I_5.

---

[6]Recommended analyses of *Klavierstück,* op. 33a are Eric Graebner, "An Analysis of Schoenberg's *Kla-
vierstück,* Op. 33a," *Perspectives of New Music* 12 (1973–74): 128–140; George Perle, *Serial Composition
and Atonality,* 6th ed. (Berkeley and Los Angeles: University of California Press, 1991), pp. 111–116;
Joseph Straus, *Introduction to Post-Tonal Theory,* pp. 253–259; and Robert Morgan, *Anthology of
Twentieth-Century Music* (New York: Norton, 1992), pp. 68–70. See also *Milton Babbitt: Words about
Music,* pp. 75–79. For an analysis of op. 33a's "sister piece," *Klavierstück,* op. 33b, see Brian Alegant,
"Unveiling Schoenberg's op. 33b," *Music Theory Spectrum* 18/2 (1996): 143–166.

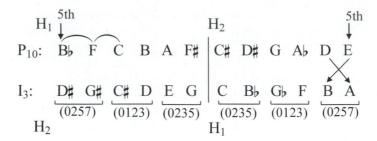

Figure 8.13 The two main row forms for Schoenberg's *Klavierstück,* op. 33a

The Row and the Row Forms

The two main row forms in this piece are P_{10} and I_3 (along with their respective retrogrades, R_{10} and RI_3). These two row forms appear in Figure 8.13. In this figure we can see some of the determining characteristics of both the row and this specific pair of rows. The row itself seems remarkable in that it begins with two ic 5 intervals (two P4s or P5s), which in principle we could think of as an unusual pair of intervals in a Schoenberg row, considering the strong tonal implications that successive perfect fifths might recall. The subset for these three pitch classes is (027). If we now look at the two combined tetrachords that open and close, respectively, the P_{10}/I_3 row pair, we will discover that ic 5 is further present in the pitch-class structure of this piece. P_{10} and I_3 are themselves related by an ic 5 transformation (I_3 is a T_5I transformation of P_{10}, and hence P_{10} and I_3 are combinatorial). Moreover, both the opening and closing tetrachords are of the (0257) class. That is, we can arrange each of these tetrachords into stacked fifths or fourths: F–B♭–D♯–G♯ for the opening tetrachord, and D–A–E–B for the closing tetrachord. We can also think of (0257) as two ic 5 dyads, [0,5] and [2,7], related by T_2. The opening and closing dyads, B♭–D♯ and E–A, are also members of ic 5. Otherwise, the complete set of discrete tetrachords for the combined P_{10}/I_3 row pair forms a symmetrical tetrachord design: (0257) (0123) (0235) // (0235) (0123) (0257).

Form

What did you come up with in your annotations on form as you listened to the piece? The opening two measures present some characteristic material. Does it come back? How is the material in mm. 14–18 also characteristic in its own way, and how does it differ from the material in mm. 1–2? Does the material in mm. 14–18 come back? How are measures 32–40 related to mm. 1–26, from a thematic/textural/formal point of view?

The theme in mm. 1–2 is indeed characteristic. It establishes a chordal texture that features tetrachords, and it features textural and intervallic symmetry (m. 2 is a strict mirror image of m. 1). Similar (but varied) tetrachordal textures appear in mm. 6, 8–9, and 10–11. The opening section (mm. 1–11) seems indeed unified by this theme and this texture, with the only exception of an episode in mm. 3–5. We can label the tetrachordal theme as "theme 1," and the opening section, mm. 1–11, as the "theme 1 area." A clearly contrasting theme and texture begins in m. 14. This is a *cantabile* section, with a more traditionally homophonic character. The elements here are a static upper line, a bass melody featuring large leaps, and a harmonic accompaniment in eighth notes. We will label this as "theme 2." Theme 2 continues through m. 18, and after a brief contrasting episode appears again in mm. 21–22. Mm. 14–22 are thus the "theme 2 area." Now compare mm. 12–13 with mm. 23–25. Their most audible and visible characteristic is their respective beginnings made up of ic 5 (P5s or P4s) successions in both hands by contrary motion (mm. 12 and 23). In mm. 12–13, this section serves as a transition between the theme 1 and the theme 2 areas, whereas in mm. 23–25 it closes the theme-2 area. In summary, we have two thematic areas (theme 1 and theme 2) connected by a transition and followed by a closing area or codetta.

By now we may be starting to recognize what could be the thematic and formal characteristics for a sonata-form exposition. It is indeed useful to hear this piece as an example of sonata form. From this perspective, mm. 1–26 are the exposition. The character of mm. 27–32 (to the fermata) is developmental, based mostly on theme 1 and on trichordal and tetrachordal textures. And mm. 32–40 can be understood as a shortened return of the material from the exposition, hence as the recapitulation. The tetrachordal theme 1 returns in mm. 32–34 (compare with mm. 8–9), the *cantabile* (now *dolce*) theme appears in mm. 35–36 (compare with mm. 14–15), and a final statement of theme 1 closes the movement in mm. 39–40 (compare with mm. 1–2). Although in this analysis we will think of this movement as a sonata form, we should keep in mind that other interpretations are also possible (we could think of it, for instance, as a ternary form rather than as a sonata form). In any case, op. 33a is a good example of the neoclassical approach to form that we find in many of Schoenberg's twelve-tone compositions, as we already mentioned in Chapter 5.

Issues of Pitch Organization

An analysis of the row-form content for the complete exposition (mm. 1–27) appears in Example 8.14. The first thing we may notice is that the only row forms used in the exposition are the members of the combinatorial pair P_{10}/I_3 and their respective retrograde forms, which also form a combinatorial pair, R_{10}/RI_3. We will now examine each of the subsections in some detail.

- Mm. 1–2. To achieve total symmetry in the opening statement of theme 1, in mm. 1–2, Schoenberg used a P and an RI form (so that the chordal texture for m. 1 is both inverted and retrograded in m. 2, P_{10} and RI_3. The tetrachords we hear in these two measures are the discrete tetrachords for each of the row forms, creating the symmetrical pattern (0127) (0258) (0146) // (0146) (0258) 0127).

- Mm. 3–5. The combinatorial forms R_{10} and RI_3 are used simultaneously in these measures. The resulting tetrachords we hear in these measures are thus the combined tetrachords for both rows that we studied in Figure 8.13, forming the symmetrical design (0257) (0123) (0235) // (0235) (0123) (0257). Otherwise, because these two row forms presented simultaneously are combinatorial, we hear both the rows and two aggregates. Can you identify and mark the two aggregates on the score?

- Mm. 6–13. These are a succession of theme-1 statements. P_{10} and RI_3 are again presented individually in mm. 6–7. The discrete tetrachords for P_{10} and I_3, respectively,

♪♫ Example 8.14   Schoenberg, *Klavierstück,* op. 33a, mm. 1–27, annotated

♪♪ **Example 8.14**   (continued)

are alternated between hands in mm. 8–9, again in m. 10, and finally in m. 11 (now in the form of R_{10} and RI_3). A simultaneous presentation of the combinatorial pair P_{10}/I_3 constitutes the pitch content for the transitional mm. 12–13.

- Mm. 14–18 and 21–22. The change of material (to theme 2) and of character comes along with a change of row segmentation. The right hand of mm.14–15 now features two statements of the first hexachord of P_{10} (H_1), while the left hand in the same measures features one statement of the first hexachord of I_3 (H_2). Mm. 16–18, on the other hand, present the second hexachord of P_{10} (H_2) in the two upper lines, and the second hexachord of I_3 (H_1) in the lower line. In other words, segmentation in theme 2 is hexachordal rather than tetrachordal, and Schoenberg is here taking clear advantage of the combinatorial relationship between P_{10} and I_3. The same can be said of the brief episode in mm. 19–20 and of the codetta in mm. 23–26.

Now examine and discuss the row form content and organization for the recapitulation, shown in Example 8.15. How is it related to what we have seen for the exposition? Do we find the same type of pitch organization and use of row forms in both sections?

Finally, let us examine row organization in the development. You will have noticed that so far, in both the exposition and the recapitulation, we have encountered only four row forms, P_{10}/I_3 and their retrogrades R_{10}/RI_3. The development also begins with the same row forms: in m. 27 we hear the two hexachords of R_{10} played simultaneously with their combinatorial counterparts, the second hexachord of I_3 and the second hexachord of RI_3, respectively. After this, however, the rest of the development is built on new row forms. Two new pairs of combinatorial rows are first introduced in m. 28: P_0/I_5 and P_5/I_{10}. The rest of the development is based on these two pairs, as you can verify in the annotated score for this section in Example 8.16.

The Large-Scale Pitch Organization: Twelve-Tone Areas

To understand the long-range pitch design for this composition, we will introduce the concept of twelve-tone areas.[7] A group of row forms made up of a row form and all the row forms that are combinatorially related with it constitutes a twelve-tone area. In the case of op. 33a, the basic twelve-tone area is made up of P_{10} and its combinatorially related row forms, I_3, R_{10}, and RI_3. We will call the area A_{10}, after the index number of the P form that generates it. The exposition and the recapitulation of op. 33a are exclusively based on A_{10}.

We have already seen, however, that the development features two new combinatorially related pairs, P_0/I_5 and P_5/I_{10}. The two row forms in the first of these pairs, P_0/I_5, are members of a new twelve-tone area, A_0, whereas the second pair, P_5/I_{10}, is part of the A_5 area. The three twelve-tone areas in this piece are, then, A_{10}, A_0, and A_5. If we think of these three index numbers, 10, 0, 5, as a pitch-class set, [10, 0, 5], we arrive

---

[7]The concept of twelve-tone areas was developed by David Lewin in "A Study of Hexachord Levels in Schoenberg's Violin Fantasy," *Perspectives of New Music* 6/1 (1967): 18–32, and "Inversional Balance as an Organizing Force in Schoenberg's Music and Thought," *Perspectives of New Music* 6/2 (1968): 1–21. For a discussion of other twelve-tone movements by Schoenberg imitating "tonal forms," see Andrew Mead, "'Tonal' Forms in Arnold Schoenberg's Twelve-Tone Music," *Music Theory Spectrum* 9 (1987): 67–92.

Example 8.15   Schoenberg, *Klavierstück,* op. 33a, mm. 32–40, annotated

at prime form (027). In other words, the relationship among twelve-tone areas in this piece reproduces, at a large scale, the same relationship that we found in the first three pitch classes of the row. As a matter of fact, the initial pitch classes for the P forms of each of the three areas are 10, 0, 5, or B♭, C, F, that is, the same three pitch classes that begin the basic row form for the piece, P_{10}, and which can be arranged in ic 5 order as B♭–F–C, as any (027) set can.

♪♪ Example 8.16   Schoenberg, *Klavierstück*, op. 33a, mm. 27–32, annotated

Conclusions

The traditional sonata-form design is based both on long-range tonal relationships and on thematic relationships. In a nontonal or post-tonal sonata form, it is still feasible to create the type of thematic relationships that are characteristic of sonata form and that define the genre's sections: primary theme, transition, secondary theme, closing section or theme, development, and recapitulation. We have identified such thematic relationships and the sections they generate in Schoenberg's op. 33a. The tonal relationships that define sonata form in the common-practice period (essentially, tonic key area, tonal transition or modulation, secondary key area, modulatory and tonally unstable development, and return to the tonic key in the recapitulation), on the other hand, are not possible in post-tonal music in the absence of functional tonal relationships. A composer in this context may choose to ignore long-range tonal relationships of this type and to focus on the thematic elements that can generate the sonata-form sections. Or the composer may also replace the functional tonal relationships with some other kind of long-range tonal relationships. This is exactly what takes place in *Klavierstück*, op. 33a. The relationship among twelve-tone areas creates a long-range tonal plan roughly equivalent to a traditional long-range formal plan of sonata form: the A_{10} area defines the exposition tonally (although here we don't find the traditional tonal motion to a secondary area within the exposition, which is characteristic in tonally functional sonata forms, and this could be seen as weakening the argument in favor of this movement being a sonata form). The A_0 and A_5 areas provide the tonal structure for the development and represent a tonal departure from the A_{10} area. And finally, the A_{10} area returns at the end to define the tonal content of the recapitulation. The three areas are bound together by fifth relationships (or by ic-5 relationships). Moreover, the long-range tonal plan reflects such smaller-scale tonal elements as the three beginning pitch classes of the row, the ic-5 relationships among the opening and closing combined tetrachords for combinatorial pairs, and the thematic and motivic surface events that outline, either melodically or harmonically, these ic-5 relationships. All of it (large-scale plan and its relationship to both small-scale structure and surface events) contributes to the strong unity of this piece and to its effective formal coherence.

APPLICATION AND CLASS DISCUSSION

With the perspective provided by this chapter, we can revisit some of the questions we asked in Chapter 7, and perhaps our answers will now be more complete and informed. What are some of the methods that composers can use to provide large-scale pitch coherence to their twelve-tone works (beyond the built-in coherence provided by the row)? With particular reference to the two pieces we have analyzed in this chapter, what compositional elements provide clear aural points of reference for the listener to focus on? Which of these elements allow the listener to trace a path of large-scale coherence in these compositions?

Further Listening

The following list provides suggestions for further listening to music by composers studied in this chapter or related to the styles and techniques we have studied. If possible, listen while following the score:

1. Berg, *Lulu*
2. Schoenberg, Variations for Orchestra, op. 31
3. Schoenberg, String Quartet no. 4
4. Webern, *Symphonie,* op. 21
5. Webern, Concerto for Nine Instruments, op. 24

Terms for Review

invariance	prime combinatoriality
palindrome	inversional combinatoriality
symmetrical rows	retrograde combinatoriality
combinatoriality	retrograde-inversional combinatoriality
combinatorial rows	all-combinatorial hexachords
hexachordal combinatoriality	semicombinatorial hexachords
array	

CHAPTER 8 ASSIGNMENTS

I. Theory   3, 5A

1. The following is the row (P_0) for Webern's *Symphonie,* op: 21: 0 3 2 1 5 4 T E 7 8 9 6.

   Under which operation will the segment 5, 4 map onto itself?

   And the segment T, E?

   Under which operations will the tetrachord 0, 3, 2, 1 map onto 7, 8, 9, 6, and vice versa?

2. The following is the row (P_0) for Schoenberg's String Quartet no. 3: 0 9 8 2 5 6 3 1 T E 4 7.

   Under which operation does the dyad 6, 3 map onto itself?

   And the segment 0, 9?

   And the segment T, E?

3. The following is the row (P_0) for Schoenberg's Wind Quintet, op. 26: 0 4 6 8 T 9 7 E 1 3 5 2.

   What segments remain invariant under T_4?

4. The following is the row (P$_0$) for Webern's Variations, op. 30: 0 1 4 3 2 5 6 9 8 7 T E.
   a. This row is symmetrical. Each form of the row is identical with another form of the row. Which operation maps the complete row onto itself?
   b. The first seven pcs of P$_0$, 0 1 4 3 2 5 6, appear again in the same order as the last seven pcs of another row form, in such a way that the two row forms can be connected by overlapping the seven invariant pcs. Which is the row form that has this property? Provide the two labels that apply to this row form because of the symmetry.

Suggestion: You should first determine under what operation the segment 0 1 4 3 2 5 6 maps onto itself (you can do so by examining the prime form of this set and applying the procedure we learned in Chapter 3 for inversionally symmetrical sets). That will give you an I form that will begin with the same seven pcs but in reverse order: 6 5 2 3 4 1 0. What we want, though, is a row form that ends with 0 1 4 3 2 5 6, and that will be the retrograde (RI form) of the I form we just determined.

5. The following two rows are symmetrical. Each form of each row is identical with another form. Which operation maps each of the rows onto itself?
   a. 0 E 2 1 5 6 3 4 8 7 T 9 (Webern, String Quartet, op. 28)
   b. 0 1 2 E T 9 5 4 3 6 7 8 (Webern)

6. Answer the following questions (circle the correct answers).
   a. A row is P-combinatorial if its first hexachord maps onto *itself / its complement* under some T_n/T_nI.
   b. A row is R-combinatorial if its first hexachord maps onto *itself / its complement* under some T_n / T_nI.
   c. A row is I-combinatorial if its first hexachord maps onto *itself / its complement* under some T_n / T_nI.
   d. A row is RI-combinatorial if its first hexachord maps onto *itself / its complement* under some T_n / T_nI.

7. Each of the following rows is combinatorial. First, determine whether it is all-combinatorial or semicombinatorial. If it is all-combinatorial, determine all the P, I, R, and RI operations that produce row forms combinatorial with P$_0$. If it is semicombinatorial, determine the I operation(s) that result in combinatorial row form(s).
   a. 0 1 4 3 2 5 6 9 8 7 T E (Webern, Variations, op. 30)
   b. 0 E 1 9 3 7 T 8 2 6 4 5 (Schoenberg, "Der neue Klassizismus," no. 3 from *Three Satires*, op. 28)
   c. 0 E 8 2 1 7 9 T 4 3 5 6 (Schoenberg, "Unentrinnbar," no. 1 from Four Pieces for Mixed Choir, op. 27)
   d. 0 2 9 5 7 3 T E 1 8 4 6 (Schoenberg, "Der Wunsch des Liebhabers," no. 4 from Four Pieces for Mixed Choir, op. 27)
   e. 0 1 9 E 8 T 4 5 6 2 3 7 (Webern, Piano Variations, op. 27)

8. Compose four different combinatorial rows. Two of them should be all-combinatorial, and two semicombinatorial. For each of them, explain what operations result in combinatorial row forms, and why.

II. Analysis

1. Refer to Example 8.17 (from Webern's Cantata no. 1, op. 29, I). This is a fragment of a twelve-tone piece. The basic row for this piece is as follows: A–F–A♭–G–B–B♭–C♯–C–E–D♯–F♯–D

Example 8.17   Webern, Cantata no. 1, op. 29, I, mm. 14–19

The Row

Study the row carefully, and answer the following questions:

  a. Provide pitch-class numbers for P_0.

  b. What are the prime forms of each of the 4 discrete trichords? Is this a derived row? Why?

  c. The matrix for this row contains only 24 different row forms. Why?

  d. Which operation maps this row onto itself?

  e. How many (and which) different interval classes are used between adjacent notes?

  f. Is this row combinatorial? If so, under what operation(s)?

The music

  a. The given fragment contains four statements of the row, one per voice. Identify each of the four row forms, and provide pitch-class numbers for each of them. Use P and R forms (instead of I and RI).

  b. The next group of row forms (not included in the example) are

Soprano:	P_6 _____
Alto:	R_6 _____
Tenor:	P_4 _____
Bass:	R_4 _____

In the spaces above, write the pitch-class numbers for each of these four forms. What is the connection that makes these rows suitable to be used after the ones in the example? Does invariance play any role in this connection?

c. Vertical sonorities (tetrachords). There are twelve vertical sonorities in the passage (counting the corresponding order numbers among rows as simultaneous pitches among all four voices, even when they are not exactly presented simultaneously, as in mm. 16–19). How many different prime forms are there among them, and what are they?

d. You can think of the vertical tetrachords in this passage as forming two groups of six tetrachords each (arranged symmetrically). By what T-equivalence(s)—that is, by what transposition(s)—are the two groups related among themselves? (Note: because of the symmetrical design, the correspondences will be between the first and the last, the second and the second-to-last, and so on.)

2. Refer to Example 8.18 (a fragment of the cadenza for Mov. I of Schoenberg's Violin Concerto). The basic row for this piece is as follows: A–B♭–E♭–B–E–F♯–C♯–G♯–D–F

The row

a. Provide pitch-class numbers for P_0.

b. What are the prime forms of each of the four discrete trichords? Is this a derived row? Why?

c. What specific operation relates the first and third trichords of P_0?

d. How are the two hexachords related (circle one)? *self-complementary/Z-related*

e. Is this row combinatorial? If so, under what operation(s)?

f. Complete the blanks or circle "doesn't map," as appropriate.

In this specific row,

1. H_1 maps onto itself at T___/doesn't map.

2. H_1 maps onto itself at T___I/doesn't map.

3. H_1 maps onto its complement at T___/doesn't map.

4. H_1 maps onto its complement at T___I/doesn't map.

Study of invariance

a. Identify the row forms (there are only two and the R of one of them) used in the cadenza, from the *Lento* in m. 233 to A♭ right before the *Lento sul G*. Are these forms combinatorial? Is combinatoriality emphasized in any way in the music?

b. In mm. 230–233 (to the fermata) there is a statement of P_2. Identify it. Then identify the first row form at the *Lento sul G*.

c. You now have four row forms for this example: two from question a and two from b. Provide a detailed study of invariance among all these forms, using a graph to compare them. Begin by comparing the two forms from question a: find invariant dyads, trichords, tetrachords, pentachords, and hexachords, and devise a way to represent the relationships clearly. Then find any invariant segments between the two rows from question a and the two from question b.

d. Are any of the invariant segments that you have identified in question c emphasized in any way in the music? Explain clearly and specifically where and how (you may mark relationships on the score if you want).

♪♪♪ **Example 8.18**   Schoenberg, Violin Concerto, I, fragment from the cadenza

3. The following are some other twelve-tone pieces you may use for brief analytical papers:

   a. Webern, Variations, op. 30. P_0 for this piece is 0 1 4 3 2 5 6 9 8 7 T E.

   b. Schoenberg, "Tot," no. 2 from Three Songs, op. 48. P_0 for this piece is 0 1 7 E 8 2 6 5 T 9 3 4.

III. Composition

1. Compose a short twelve-tone piece for piano or two melodic instruments of your choice. First, compose a row or use one of your original rows from Exercise I.2 in Chapter 7. Study the invariance properties of your row and plan your composition in some ways that will take advantage of these properties. Use any of Webern's pieces we have studied in this chapter as your model. Be as musical as possible in your actual composition and in all of your compositional decisions.

2. Compose a short twelve-tone piece for piano or two melodic instruments of your choice. First, compose a combinatorial row. Study the combinatorial properties of your row and plan your composition in some ways that will take advantage of these properties. Although Schoenberg's op. 33a is likely to be longer and more complex than the piece you will compose, you can use some aspects of that composition as your model. Be as musical as possible in your actual composition and in all your compositional decisions.

Chapter 9

Serialism: Developments after 1945

After the world emerged from the generalized destruction and historical trauma caused by World War II, the young generation of composers that appeared in Europe and the United States in the late 1940s and early 1950s saw the opportunity to effect a radical break with a past they tended to distrust. These composers sought to create new types of music that would open up the doors to the future and to new ways of musical expression and perception. As a result, the two decades after World War II (marked by musical *avant-gardes* and experimentation) are one of the most stylistically diverse periods not only in the twentieth century, but also in the whole history of music.

Despite the great diversity, two broad trends can be identified in the early years after the war. The first of these parallel and contrasting trends includes a variety of compositional approaches that aim at rigorous, rational control of the musical material on the part of the composer. This category includes composers such as Pierre Boulez, Karlheinz Stockhausen, and Milton Babbitt, who practiced various extensions of serial techniques, including integral serialism. The other trend is based on the principle of indeterminacy, through which the composer introduces elements of chance into the compositional process, and hence relinquishes control of the musical materials, partially or totally. This trend began as a purely American movement in the early 1950s and is best represented by John Cage and a group of composers known as the New York School, who worked closely with Cage in those years, and that included Morton Feldman, Earle Brown, Christian Wolff, and David Tudor. These two trends merged and interacted progressively by the end of the 1950s, particularly in Europe, and in great part because of the strong influence that Cage exerted on European *avant-garde* composers. As we will see in Chapter 11, simultaneous aspects of compositional control and freedom are indeed to be found in many compositions beginning in the late 1950s and early 1960s.

In this chapter we continue and complete our study of serialism, and we focus on some representative examples of serial techniques after 1945. We first examine Stravinsky's use of serial methods in his late compositions. Then we study some of the serial techniques used by French composer Pierre Boulez and by American composer

Milton Babbitt. Both composers are representative of post-World War II serialism, including the various compositional methods usually referred to as multiserialism or total serialism.

STRAVINSKY AND SERIALISM

In the last sixteen years of his active compositional life, and beginning at a time when he was already seventy years old, Stravinsky turned to serialism as the main compositional method for his music. This unexpected stylistic move was even more surprising if we consider that for decades, Stravinsky and Schoenberg had been widely considered as representing antithetical positions in musical aesthetics and composition, and the personal animosity between the two composers was quite notorious. Stravinsky's opinion of Schoenberg's music changed after the latter's death in 1951. At that time, not only did Stravinsky study Schoenberg's music (and, with particular admiration, Webern's music), but his interest in what he found was such that, for reasons that are still debated, beginning with his *Cantata* of 1952, he started experimenting with his own serial methods. Stravinsky's serial period includes his twenty last compositions, from the *Cantata* and the Septet (1953) to his last major work, *Requiem Canticles* (1966). Stravinsky's serialism, however, is idiosyncratic. As could be expected from such a major and original composer, he devised his own methods to transform and use the row, in ways that set his serial practices apart from those of other serial composers, as we will discover in the discussion that follows. In some of Stravinsky's earlier serial pieces, Stravinsky uses rows made up of less than twelve pitch classes, as in the case of *In memorian Dylan Thomas* of 1954, based on a five-pitch-class row. After 1960, however, Stravinsky focused on a serial technique known as rotation, which we will now study.[1]

Stravinsky's Rotational Arrays

The procedure known as **rotation,** found in a majority of Stravinsky's serial works, is the most characteristic element in the composer's approach to serial composition. Stravinsky starts from a prime form of his row (P) and three untransposed row forms: the retrograde of P (or R), the inversion of P starting on the same pitch class as P (or I), and the inversion of R starting on the same pitch class as R (inversion of the retrograde, or IR, not to be confused with the familiar operation of retrograde inversion, or RI). These four basic forms are shown in Example 9.1, applied to the row from *Requiem Canticles.*

Then Stravinsky builds a **rotational array** for each of the four forms. To build a rotational array, we first divide the row into two hexachords. In the first step of the rotation process, each hexachord is independently rotated, first to begin on its second pitch

---

[1]The most important study to date of Stravinsky's serial period is Joseph Straus's *Stravinsky's Late Music* (Cambridge: Cambridge University Press, 2001).

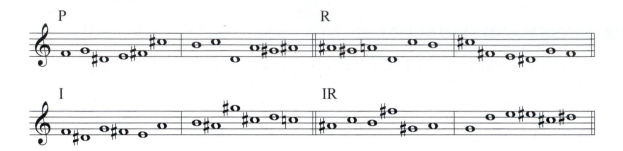

♪♪♪ Example 9.1   The four basic row forms for *Requiem Canticles*

class, then on the third, and so on. This results in **rotational arrays α (alpha) and β (beta).** The α and β arrays for the P form of the *Requiem Canticles* row are shown in Example 9.2a, where each of the rotations is labeled with a Roman numeral, I through V (we won't use a Roman numeral to refer to the original form of the row, P in this case, in a rotational array). In a second step in the rotation process, we transpose each of the rotations to begin on the first pitch class of the original untransposed hexachord. In our Example 9.2b, we transpose each rotation of the first hexachord to begin on F, and each rotation of the second hexachord to begin on B. We will refer to the arrays of transposed rotations as **rotational arrays γ (gamma) and δ (delta).**[2]

If we follow the same process for each of the other three row forms (R, I, and IR), we come up with a complete rotational chart for this row, as shown in Example 9.3. All of Example 9.3 is based on γ and δ arrays because all the rotations are transposed to begin on the same pitch class as the corresponding original hexachord. We can identify each of the rotations in this chart by combining the various labels. Thus, Pγ is the first hexachord of the original P row; P_{III} δ is the third rotation of the second hexachord of P; I_I γ is the first rotation of the first hexachord of I; and IR_V δ is the fifth rotation of the second hexachord of IR.

Besides using the rows and their hexachordal rotations, Stravinsky also uses the sets made up of the vertical columns in the rotational arrays. These **rotational array "verticals"** are numbered 1 through 6 for each of the hexachords of the IR array in Example 9.3. We will use the labels v1, v2, v3, and so on to denote verticals. Thus,

---

[2]An analytical study of *Requiem Canticles* and the rotational arrays involved in its composition can be found in Claudio Spies, "Some Notes on Stravinsky's Requiem Settings," *Perspectives of New Music* 5/2 (1967): 98–123; reprinted in *Perspectives on Schoenberg and Stravinsky,* ed. Benjamin Boretz and Edward Cone (Princeton: Princeton University Press, 1968), pp. 223–50. More general discussions of rotational arrays can be found in Robert Morris, "Generalizing Rotational Arrays," *Journal of Music Theory* 32/1 (1988): 75–132, as well as in Morris, *Class Notes,* Chapter 15, and Wuorinen, *Simple Composition,* Chapter 8.

♪♪♪ Example 9.2   The rotational arrays for the P row from *Requiem Canticles*

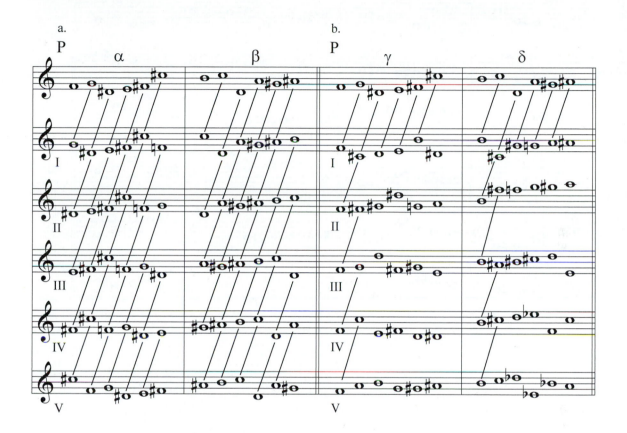

IR$_{v1}$ γ is the first vertical for the γ hexachord of IR, while IR$_{v5}$ δ is the fifth vertical for the δ hexachord of IR.

ANALYSIS 9.1: STRAVINSKY, "LACRIMOSA," FROM *REQUIEM CANTICLES* (ANTHOLOGY NO. 24)

We will now study a specific compositional realization of a rotational array. Listen to the "Lacrimosa" from *Requiem Canticles*. Before we figure out its pitch structure, let us discuss this piece from a general musical point of view. How does the piece work formally? What are the textural/instrumental blocks in this movement, and what role do they have in shaping its form? Are there any principles of formal growth characteristic of early Stravinsky, and which we have studied previously, that still apply to this late piece?

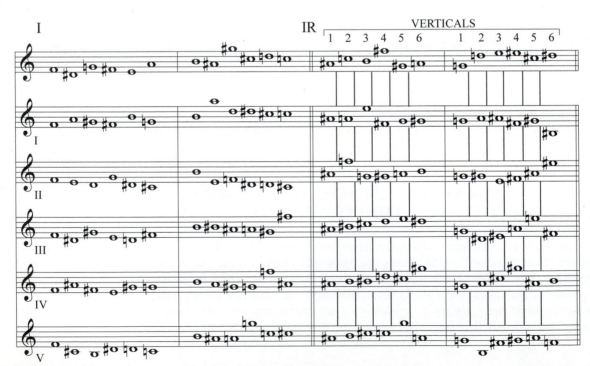

The Textural/Instrumental Blocks

In this movement we can identify a number of textural/instrumental blocks that are the basic form-building elements. In Chapter 2 we discussed the formal technique of juxtaposition in Stravinsky's *Rite of Spring*. The same formal principle is present in the "Lacrimosa": the different and independent sound blocks are juxtaposed; that is, they are presented side by side with no overlap or minimal overlap, and the motion from one block to the next is often effected by abrupt interruption. Let us define the various textural/instrumental blocks in this movement.

1. The main texture in the movement, and the first one we hear, is made up of the vocal line (the vocal phrases determine the length of these blocks) accompanied by sustained chords in the flute quartet, with double basses and harp providing either sustained tones or brief rhythmic figures.

2. Vocal phrases are closed by brief chordal punctuations provided by flutes and strings (violins, violas, and cellos).

3. A connective or transitional element between phrases is provided by brief figures by three trombones.

4. Harp, violas, and cellos perform an accompaniment to the last two vocal phrases ("*dona eis requiem*" and "*Amen*") in isolated sixteenth-note dyads.

Pitch Organization

Having identified the textural blocks in the movement, we can now examine how Stravinsky organized the movement's pitch structure. The complete pitch content can be traced to the rotational arrays we presented in Example 9.3. We will explain the specific compositional realization of rotational arrays in each of the textural groups.

1. The voice solo features the complete IR arrays in "spiral" order: begin with $IR_V \delta$ read in reverse order (that is, in retrograde, which we will indicate with an "r" following the usual rotation label, $IR_V \delta$–r), then go up the δ array alternating forward and reverse readings:

Mm.	229	235	238	240	245	246
	$IR_V \delta$–r	$IR_{IV} \delta$	$IR_{III} \delta$–r	$IR_{II} \delta$	$IR_I \delta$–r	$IR\delta$

Then start again at the top of the γ array and go down in the same way:

Mm.	250	255	256	257	259	262
	$IR\gamma$–r	$IR_I \gamma$	$IR_{II} \gamma$–r	$IR_{III} \gamma$	$IR_{IV} \gamma$–r	$IR_V \gamma$

2. The flute chords and the punctuations by flutes and strings following the vocal phrases feature an almost complete set of IR verticals, beginning with six δ-array verticals:

Mm.	229	233	235	236	238	243
	$IR_{v2} \delta$	$IR_{v3} \delta$	$IR_{v4} \delta$	$IR_{v5} \delta$	$IR_{v6} \delta$	$IR_{v1} \delta$

And then five γ-array verticals:

Mm.	245	248	250	255	260
	$IR_{v2}\gamma$	$IR_{v3}\gamma$	$IR_{v4}\gamma$	$IR_{v5}\gamma$	$IR_{v6}\gamma$

3. Double basses and harp (and, in mm. 256–265, the harp with violas and cellos) feature their own cycle of rotations, a complete Rγ spiral in the following order:

Mm.	229	238	250	257	258	262
	$R\gamma$–r	$R_I\gamma$–r	$R_{II}\gamma$	$R_{III}\gamma$–r	$R_{IV}\gamma$	$R_V\gamma$

4. Finally, the trombones feature a complete Iγ cycle in the following order:

Mm.	234	237	244	249	254	264
	$I_I\gamma$	$I\gamma$	$I_{III}\gamma$	$I_{II}\gamma$	$I_V\gamma$	$I_{IV}\gamma$

Conclusions

If you trace all of these rotational cycles on the score and mark each of them with circles, you will be able to verify that Stravinsky derived his complete pitch materials for this movement from his rotational arrays, and that he did so in a systematic and logical way. Now discuss in class the orchestration for this movement. What is unusual about it? What is particularly interesting? What is typically Stravinskian about it? Then discuss any aspects of rhythm and meter that you may find significant in this movement. Considering all aspects of this composition, how would you say it is related to the other compositions by Stravinsky that we have studied in this book? How does it depart from those compositions? In which ways does this piece reflect a thoroughly "modern" style, and also Stravinsky's amazing adaptability to historical musical developments?

ANALYSIS 9.2: BOULEZ, *STRUCTURES Ia* (ANTHOLOGY NO. 25)

Pierre Boulez (born 1925) represents, perhaps better than any other composer of his time, the compositional attitudes and approaches characteristic of the young post-World War II generation in western Europe (a group which also includes composers such as Luciano Berio, Karlheinz Stockhausen, Luigi Nono, Bruno Maderna, and Henri Pousseur, among others). Two of the most salient aspects of Boulez's compositional techniques in the 1950s and 60s are his serialization of musical elements other than pitch (in what is known as **multiserialism, total serialism,** or **integral serialism**) and the use of an operation that he called **multiplication** to generate his pitch structures.[3] Both

---

[3]Boulez's multiplication (which we will not cover in this book) and its application in *Le marteau sans maître* have been studied by Lev Koblyakov in *Pierre Boulez: A World of Harmony* (New York: Harwood Academic Publishers, 1990) and Stephen Heinemann in "Pitch-Class Set Multiplication in Boulez's *Le Marteau sans maître*" (D.M.A. diss., University of Washington, 1993). See also Heinemann, "Pitch-Class Set Multiplication in Theory and Practice," *Music Theory Spectrum* 20/1 (1998): 72–96.

aspects of Boulez's serialism (multiserialism and multiplication) stem from his wish, shared by many composers in his generation, to exert control over the compositional material (as well as over the *precompositional* material) in a way as rigorous and rational as possible, and as a means to create a new musical language that would represent a complete departure from traditional musical structures. Boulez considered Webern as his point of departure and strove to break away from Schoenberg's thematic use of the row and from his post-Romantic conception of composition. The row for Boulez becomes instead an abstract, intervallic source for a composition's pitch material, and he derives this material from the row through a variety of complex processes, as we will learn in the following discussion.

Listen to *Structures Ia* (1952). This was the first fully multiserial work, and one that had a substantial impact not only on Boulez's own immediate compositional output, but also on a variety of other contemporary composers. The four musical elements serialized by Boulez in this composition are pitch, durations, intensities, and modes of attack. An earlier piece by Boulez's mentor, Olivier Messiaen, ("Mode de valeurs et d'intensités," from *Quatre études de rythme,* 1949) was based on a series that associates specific rhythms, intensities, and modes of attack to specific pitch classes. Although Messiaen thus achieved integrated control of all four musical elements, his compositional method itself is not serial, inasmuch as it does not use the usual row transformations and other serial conventions. As an acknowledgment of his mentor's compositional achievement toward integral serialism, the point of departure for Boulez's *Structures Ia* is the same pitch-class row and the same series of durations, intensities, and attacks as in Messiaen's work. The compositional process, however, is much more rigorous in Boulez's piece. Because precompositional processes (that is, the preparation of the compositional material before actually starting to write the musical surface on score) are so essential in a multiserial work, a lot of our analysis will be the explanation of "precompositional" processes (which, in integral serialism, are hardly "precompositional," but constitute a lot of the compositional process itself).[4]

The main row form for *Structures Ia* is E♭–D–A–A♭–G–F♯–E–C♯–C–B♭–F–B, or, in C = 0 notation, 3 2 9 8 7 6 4 1 0 T 5 E (P_0 is then 0 E 6 5 4 3 1 T 9 7 2 8). Instead of building a single matrix based on P_0 of this row, however, Boulez builds two matrices, one for P and R forms only (built on the main row form, P_3) and one for I and RI forms only (built on I_3). These two matrices are shown in Example 9.4.[5] In 9.4a, the matrix for P and R forms, P_3 is listed horizontally as the uppermost row, and also vertically as the leftmost column. This means that the matrix is totally symmetrical around its NW/SE diagonal (upper left to lower right). The matrix for I and RI forms, shown in Example 9.4b, similarly lists I_3 both as the uppermost row and the leftmost column.

[4]An essential source for the study of compositional processes in *Structures Ia* is the analytical (and also highly critical) article by György Ligeti, "Pierre Boulez: Decision and Automatism in *Structure Ia*," *Die Reihe* 4 (1960): 36–62.

[5]Although Boulez does not use the C = 0 notational convention, and hence his matrices are different numerically from ours, the results will end up being the same in both systems, under an appropriate transformation.

🎵 **Example 9.4**   The matrices for Pierre Boulez's *Structures Ia*

a.

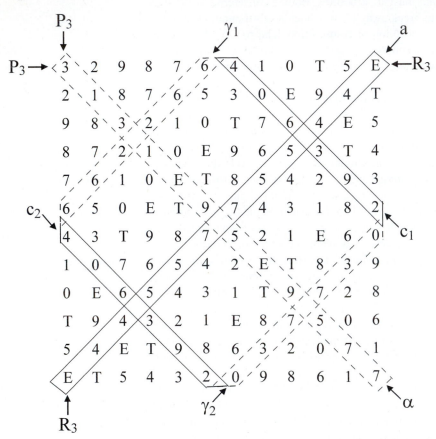

Compositional Processes

Boulez derives all pitch classes, rhythms, intensities, and attack modes for *Structures Ia* by means of these two matrices. We will now examine the exact processes he follows to derive all of these musical elements from the row.

Pitch Classes

Pitch classes in piano 1 are derived from a complete succession of all twelve P row forms presented in the order provided by the pc numbers of I_3 (that is, 3, 4, 9, T, E, 0, 2, 5, 6, 8, 1, 7, which generate the row succession P_3, P_4, P_9, P_{10}, and so on).

♪♪♪ Example 9.4 (continued)

b.

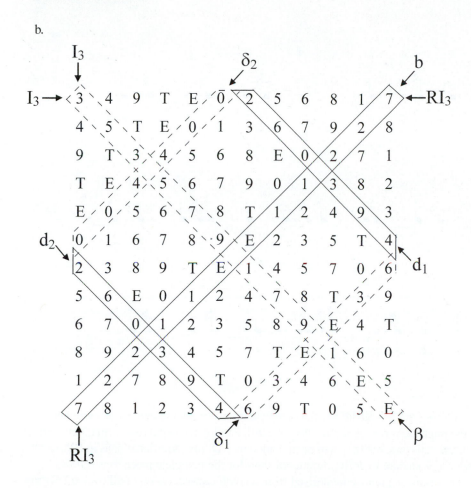

Pitch classes in piano 2 are derived from a complete succession of all twelve I row forms presented in the order provided by the pc numbers of P_3 (that is, 3, 2, 9, 8, 7, 6, 4, 1, 0, T, 5, E, which generate the row succession I_3, I_2, I_9, I_8, and so on).

Durations

To serialize durations, Boulez first builds a basic series of twelve durations, beginning from a thirty-second note and arranged by values that increase by one thirty-second note each. This basic durational series is shown in Example 9.5a. He then associates this basic durational series to the pitch-class numbers from his basic pitch-class row (that is, P_3 in our C = 0 notation, or 3 2 9 8 7 6 4 1 0 T 5 E). This association (also

Example 9.5   Examples of durational rows in Boulez's *Structures Ia*

a.

b.

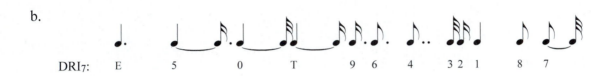

c.

shown in Example 9.5a) allows the composer to use the same two matrices he had built for the pitch-class row (Example 9.4). We will employ the usual row-form labels to refer to durational rows, but they will be preceded by a D (for "durational"), as in DP_3 or DI_3. Boulez's procedure to derive durational rows for the complete piece is as follows:

Durations in piano 1 are derived from a complete succession of all twelve DRI row forms presented in the order provided by the pc numbers of RI_3 (that is, 7, 1, 8, 6, 5, 2, 0, E, T, 9, 4, 3, which generate the row succession DRI_7, DRI_1, DRI_8, DRI_6, and so on). Example 9.5b shows the first durational row for piano 1, DRI_7.

Durations in piano 2 are derived from a complete succession of all twelve DR row forms presented in the order provided by the pc numbers of R_3 (that is, E, 5, T, 0, 1, 4, 6, 7, 8, 9, 2, 3, which generate the row succession DR_{11}, DR_5, DR_{10}, DR_0, and so on). Example 9.5c shows the first durational row for piano 2, DR_{11}.

Intensities

As he did with durations, Boulez first builds a basic series of twelve intensities in increasing order, from *pppp* to *ffff*. He then associates this basic series of intensities to the pitch-class numbers from his basic pitch-class row (P_3), as shown in Example 9.6a.

♪♪♪ **Example 9.6**   Intensity rows in Boulez's *Structures Ia*

a.

order no.:	1	2	3	4	5	6	7	8	9	10	11	12
	pppp	*ppp*	*pp*	*p*	quasi *p*	*mp*	*mf*	quasi *f*	*f*	*ff*	*fff*	*ffff*
P₃:	3	2	9	8	7	6	4	1	0	T	5	E

b.

a:	*ffff*	*mf*	*mf*	*fff*	*fff*	quasi *p*	quasi *p*	*fff*	*fff*	*mf*	*mf*	*ffff*
	E	4	4	5	5	7	7	5	5	4	4	E

b:	quasi *p*	*ppp*	*ppp*	quasi *f*	quasi *f*	*ffff*	*ffff*	quasi *f*	quasi *f*	*ppp*	*ppp*	quasi *p*
	7	2	2	1	1	E	E	1	1	2	2	7

c:	*ppp*	*pp*	*pppp*	*mp*	*f*	*mf*	*mf*	*f*	*mp*	*pppp*	*pp*	*ppp*
	2	9	3	6	0	4	4	0	6	3	9	2

d:	*mf*	*pp*	*pppp*	*f*	*mf*	*ppp*	*ppp*	*mp*	*f*	*pppp*	*pp*	*mf*
	4	9	3	0	6	2	2	6	0	3	9	4

To derive the intensity rows for the complete piece, he refers back to the pitch-class matrices (see Example 9.4), and he generates four rows (labeled a, b, c, and d in Example 9.4) by reading the pitch-class successions diagonally in each matrix from top right to bottom left (rows a and b), and as shown in Example 9.4 for rows c and d (which break up into two halves each, c_1–c_2 and d_1–d_2). The resulting four intensity rows are shown in Example 9.6b.

Modes of Attack

Boulez generates his rows of modes of attack in a similar way as he generated his intensity series. He first builds a basic series of ten (not twelve) attack modes, in which he leaves out order numbers 4 and 10. He then associates this series of attack modes to the pitch-class numbers from the basic pitch-class row (P_3, leaving out pitch classes 8 and T), as shown in Example 9.7a. To derive the attack rows for the complete piece, he

♪♪ Example 9.7   Mode-of-attack rows in Boulez's *Structures Ia*

a. P₃:

>	>·	•		normal	⌒	▼	*sfz* ∧	>·		⁒	⌒
3	2	9	(8)	7	6	4	1	0	(T)	5	E

b. α:

normal	normal	⁒	•·	⌒	⁒	•	⌒	*sfz* ∧	>	*sfz* ∧	>
7	7	5	9	E	5	9	E	1	3	1	3

β:

⌒	⌒	*sfz* ∧	•	normal	*sfz* ∧	•	normal	⁒	>	⁒	>
E	E	1	9	7	1	9	7	5	3	5	3

χ:

⌒̇	⌒̇	>·	>·	⌒̇	⌒̇	>▼	>	normal	normal	>	>▼
6	6	2	2	6	6	0	3	7	7	3	0

δ:

⌒̇	>	⌒	⌒	>	⌒̇	>▼	>▼	▼	▼	>▼	>▼
6	3	E	E	3	6	0	0	4	4	0	0

refers back to the pitch-class matrices (see Example 9.4), and he generates four rows (labeled α, β, γ, and δ in Example 9.4) by reading the pitch-class successions diagonally in each matrix from bottom right to top left (rows α and β), and as shown in example 9.4 for rows γ and δ (which break up into two halves each, γ₁–γ₂ and δ₁–δ₂). The resulting four attack rows are shown in Example 9.7b.

Navigating the Rows on the Score

After we know which rows Boulez used for each of the elements, it is not difficult to identify them on the score. Piano 1 begins with the pitches of P_3 coupled with the durations of DRI_7. In m. 8 he moves to the second set of rows, P_4 and DRI_1. These appear in the right hand of piano 1, while the left hand presents the next set, P_9 and DRI_8. Can you complete the piano-1 pitch/duration analysis of the fragment given in the anthology? The next set of rows would be P_{10} and DRI_6. Where do they begin? Piano 2, on the other hand, begins with the pitch/duration pair I_3/DR_{11}, followed by I_2/DR_5 in the right hand in m. 8, and I_9/DR_{10} in the left hand. You may now complete the analysis of the rest of the fragment (the next pair will be I_8/DR_0).

Boulez applies intensities and attack modes to sections rather than to individual pitches. Thus, piano 1 begins with the intensities from row a: *ffff, mf, mf, fff, fff,* and so on. The first intensity, *ffff,* applies to mm. 1–7; the second intensity, *mf,* to mm. 8–11; the third intensity, again *mf,* to mm. 12–16, and so on. The intensities for piano 2 follow row b: *quasi p, ppp, ppp, quasi f, quasi f, ffff,* and so on. You can easily identify these intensities on the score, applied to the same sections as the intensities for piano 1. Similarly, you can verify that the attack modes for piano 1 follow row β, and that the attack modes for piano 2 follow row α.

Style and Aesthetics

As a conclusion of your study of *Structures Ia,* discuss issues of style and aesthetics in this piece. What elements define the particular style of this music? Does Boulez succeed in his intention of creating a new musical style? How does the piece break away from traditional (that is, classical and romantic) Western styles, if you think it does? What aesthetic challenges does this music present for the listener?

MILTON BABBITT'S SERIAL METHODS

As a final step in our study of serialism, we will examine some of the serial techniques used by Milton Babbitt (born 1916) in his music. Babbitt has been the leading exponent of serialism in the post-1945 American compositional scene.[6] His serial methods are multiple, complex, and rich in both their theoretical scope and their compositional applications. In this section we will limit our study to Babbitt's trichordal arrays and to some of his techniques to serialize durations.[7]

Trichordal Arrays

As we know from our studies of hexachordal combinatoriality, by combining the first two or the second two hexachords of two combinatorial row forms, we create aggregates. Now examine the four row forms shown in Example 9.8a. The row, from Babbitt's *Composition for Twelve Instruments* (1948), is 0 1 4 9 5 8 3 T 2 E 6 7, and the row forms listed are P_0, RI_9, I_9, and R_0. First, these rows display hexachordal combinatoriality: P_0 is combinatorial with RI_9 (and also with R_0), and I_9 is combinatorial with R_0 (and also with RI_9). Moreover, if you break each of these rows into discrete trichords and then combine the corresponding trichords in each row (all first trichords, all second trichords, and so on), you will come up with four aggregates (shown by the boxes in Example 9.8a).

---

[6]Other prominent American serial composers are Roger Sessions, George Perle, Donald Martino, Stefan Wolpe, Mario Davidovsky, and Charles Wuorinen.

[7]The major source for the study of Babbitt's music (as well as for the present discussion) is Andrew Mead's *An Introduction to the Music of Milton Babbitt* (Princeton: Princeton University Press, 1994). See also Joseph Dubiel, "Three Essays on Milton Babbitt," Part 1: *Perspectives of New Music* 28/2 (1990): 216–61; Part 2: *Perspectives of New Music* 29/1 (1991): 90–123; Part 3: *Perspectives of New Music* 30/1 (1992): 82–121; and Babbitt's own writings, in *The Collected Essays of Milton Babbitt.*

♪♪ Example 9.8 Trichordal array for Milton Babbitt's *Composition for Twelve Instruments*

a.

P_0	0	1	4	9	5	8	3	T	2	E	6	7
RI_9	2	3	T	7	E	6	1	4	0	5	8	9
I_9	9	8	5	0	4	1	6	E	7	T	3	2
R_0	7	6	E	2	T	3	8	5	9	4	1	0

b.

	a			b			c			d	
0	1	4	9	5	8	3	T	2	E	6	7

c.

a	b	c	d
c	d	a	b
b	a	d	c
d	c	b	a

d.

a	b	c	d
c	d	a	b
b	a	d	c
d	c	b	a

In other words, you can combine this row with three other forms of itself to come up with four rows and four trichordal aggregates. This is the type of trichordal array that Babbitt uses in many of his compositions. A **trichordal array** combines four row forms that feature both hexachordal and **trichordal combinatoriality.** If we label the trichords of P_0 with the letters a, b, c, and d, as shown in Example 9.8b, we can easily see how these trichords form a 4 × 4 matrix of trichords, which features both hexachordal combinatoriality (Example 9.8c) and trichordal combinatoriality (Example 9.8d).[8]

---

[8]For extensive studies of the types and properties of arrays (including not only trichordal arrays, but also those that result from other-and all-partitions of the aggregate), see Morris *Composition with Pitch Classes,* Chapter 5; Robert Morris and Brian Alegant, "The Even Partitions in Twelve-Tone Music," *Music Theory Spectrum* 10 (1988): 74–101; and Brian Alegant, "The Seventy-seven Partitions of the Aggregate: Analytical and Theoretical Implications," Ph.D. dissertation, University of Rochester, 1993.

♪♪♪ Example 9.9   Trichordal array for Babbitt's *Composition for Four Instruments*

In the trichordal array we have just discussed, the trichords are of two types: a and b are (014) set classes and c and d are (015) set classes. This trichordal array is derived from one single row (that is, all four row forms result from performing operations on the same row). At other times, Babbitt builds his trichordal arrays from derived rows. This is the case with the array shown in Example 9.9, from *Composition for Four Instruments* (1948), where the array contains only trichords of the (014) set class. Babbitt combines the four original trichords, labeled a, b, c, and d in Example 9.9, to form the same type of 4 x 4 matrix we saw in Example 8.8c, and, unlike in Example 9.8, the resulting row forms in 9.9 are not all derived from the same row: the top two rows are a P and an I form of the same row, which we label as row P (hence the labels P_6 and I_1P, or "I_1 of P"), and the two bottom rows are P and I forms of a second row, which we label as row Q (hence the labels Q_8 and $I_{11}Q$, or "I_{11} of Q").

Durational Rows

Babbitt has used a variety of techniques to serialize his rhythmic structures (**durational rows**).[9] One of these approaches is the serialization of durations grouped into short patterns, most often of four durations. In *Composition for Four Instruments,* for instance, he uses a basic pattern of four durations, 1 4 3 2, where the numbers represent durations in units of sixteenth notes. If this arrangement constitutes the prime ordering P, simply reading it backward will be the R form, or 2 3 4 1. To invert the values,

---

[9]See Mead, pp. 38–53.

 **Example 9.10**   The four forms of a durational row

 **Example 9.11**   A durational row from the String Quartet no. 2

Babbitt subtracts them from 5 (that is, 1 inverts into 4, 4 into 1, 2 into 3, 3 into 2). The resulting I form is 4 1 2 3, which reads backward as RI, 3 2 1 4. Example 9.10 shows the musical notation for these four forms of the durational row.

Babbitt's durational rows may also include twelve durations, as in the case of Boulez's *Structures Ia* durational row. Unlike Boulez's, however, Babbitt's rhythmic rows are durational translations of the actual pitch-class numbers from the corresponding pitch-class rows; moreover, these numbers represent actual durations in some pre-established measuring unit. For instance, in the melody from the String Quartet no. 2 reproduced in Example 9.11, the durational row E–2–T–3–12–1–7–9–4–8–6–5 signifies durations in thirty-second note units. But if you assign the pc number 1 to B♭ (and you count from 1 to 12 instead of 0 to 11, because 0 has no duration), you will see that the same numerical row also represents the pitch content for this phrase. In this way, Babbitt establishes a closer relationship between pitch and durational rows than Boulez did in his method.

The Composer as an Isolated Specialist?

Milton Babbitt is both one of the most influential and one of the most controversial composers in American music in the past fifty years. A great part of the controversy comes from the fact that his work has either been hailed as a pinnacle of intellectual achievement in the musical realm or decried as the result of pedantic and elitist academicism. Babbitt himself has addressed these issues (as well as the gap created by much twentieth-century music—including his own—between the general musical public and contemporary composers) in a variety of articles.[10] It is helpful to understand that far from lamenting this gap, and far from refuting the accusations of elitism and isolation on the part of the experimental composer, Babbitt believes that this situation is not only unavoidable, but also desirable and positive. In a well-known and mistitled article ("The Composer as Specialist," which an editor infamously retitled "Who Cares if You Listen?" for publication), Babbitt argues that the role of the experimental composer of "serious" music is similar to the role of the scientific researcher (particularly a mathematician or physicist) whose scientific discoveries are usually presented in language that only a limited circle of specialists can understand or appreciate, but which eventually may be absorbed into practical applications of scientific knowledge.

Common-practice musical compositions share numerous common stylistic factors that can be easily processed, from a perceptual point of view, by a listener. The music Babbitt refers to as "advanced" contemporary music, on the other hand, is truly new music. The extreme stylistic contextuality and individuality of each composition mean that the general, lay, listeners do not have the means and knowledge to understand this music; neither does Babbitt expect them to do so. "I dare suggest," he writes, "that the composer would do himself and his music an immediate and eventual service by total, resolute, and voluntary withdrawal from this public world to one of private performance and electronic media, with its very real possibility of complete elimination of the public and social aspects of musical composition. By so doing, the separation between the domains would be defined and beyond any possibility of confusion of categories, and the composer would be free to pursue a private life of professional achievement, as opposed to a public life of unprofessional compromise and exhibitionism."[11]

[10]See particularly "Who Cares if You Listen?" *High Fidelity* 8/2 (1958): 38–40, 126–27, reprinted as "The Composer as Specialist" in *The Collected Essays of Milton Babbitt,* pp. 48–54; and "Past and Present Concepts of the Nature and Limits of Music," *International Musicological Society Congress Report* (New York, 1961), 398–403; reprinted in *Perspectives on Contemporary Music Theory,* ed. Benjamin Boretz and Edward Cone (New York: W. W. Norton, 1972), pp. 3–8, and in *The Collected Essays of Milton Babbitt,* pp. 78–85. See also Martin Brody, "'Music for the Masses': Milton Babbitt's Cold War Music Theory," *Musical Quarterly* 77/2 (1993): 161–92.

[11]Babbitt, "Who Cares if You Listen?" p. 126.

In a third method to serialize durations, found in his later works, Babbitt used **time-point rows.**[12] To understand this method, let us first imagine a measure divided into twelve equal time points, as shown in Example 9.12a. The attack for each of the durations represented by a row will then take place in the beat subdivision represented by the numbers shown in Example 9.12a. For instance, the row 0 9 1 8 5 4 2 6 7 3 T E (used by Mead in his illustration of time point rows) will be realized as a time-point row, as shown in Example 9.12b, where pc 0 will appear in measure 1, attack point 0; pc 9 will appear in m. 1, attack point 9; pc 1 will appear in m. 2, attack point 1; pc 8 will appear in m. 2, attack point 8, and so on. Note that we include as many time points as possible in a measure, and then we move on to the next measure, where counting begins

[12]The time-point system is discussed in Milton Babbitt, "Twelve-Tone Rhythmic Structure and the Electronic Medium," *Perspectives of New Music* 1/1 (1962): 49–79; reprinted in *The Collected Essays of Milton Babbitt,* pp. 109–140. See also Morris, *Composition with Pitch Classes,* Chapter 7, and Wuorinen, *Simple Composition,* Chapter 10.

♩♪♪ Example 9.12   Realizations of time-point rows

a.

b.

c.

all over again from time point zero. The inversion of this row, 0 3 E 4 7 8 T 6 5 9 2 1, will be realized as shown in Example 9.12c.

ANALYSIS 9.3: BABBITT, *COMPOSITION FOR TWELVE INSTRUMENTS* (ANTHOLOGY NO. 26)

We will now study the pitch and rhythmic organization in the opening fragment of Babbitt's *Composition for Twelve Instruments* of 1948 (mm. 1–23), reproduced in Anthology no. 26.[13] Listen to the complete piece, and as you do take some notes about its style and main musical characteristics.

Pitch-Class Content

As we already saw, P_0 in this piece is 0 1 4 9 5 8 3 T 2 E 6 7. The piece opens with twelve simultaneous linear statements of the row, organized in three groups of four instruments each: flute, oboe, clarinet, and bassoon (P_4, R_4, I_1, and RI_1, respectively); horn, trumpet, harp, and celesta (RI_9, I_9, R_0, and P_0, respectively); and violin, viola, cello, and bass (P_8, R_8, I_5, and RI_5, respectively). Each of these groups states four

---

[13]The pitch organization of this piece has been discussed by Babbitt in his article "Set Structure as a Compositional Determinant." See also Peter Westergaard, "Some Problems Raised by the Rhythmic Procedures in Milton Babbitt's Composition for Twelve Instruments," *Perspectives of New Music* 4 (1965): 109–18, and David Hush, "Asynordinate Twelve-Tone Structures: Milton Babbitt's Composition for Twelve Instruments," *Perspectives of New Music* 21 (1982–83): 152–205.

♪♪♪ Example 9.13   The opening pitch-class complex for Babbitt's *Composition for Twelve Instruments*

Inst.	Form												
FL.	P_4	4	5	8	1	9	0	7	2	6	3	T	E
OB.	R_4	E	T	3	6	2	7	0	9	1	8	5	4
CL.	I_1	1	0	9	4	8	5	T	3	E	2	7	6
BN.	RI_1	6	7	2	E	3	T	5	8	4	9	0	1
TPT.	I_9	9	8	5	0	4	1	6	E	7	T	3	2
HRN.	RI_9	2	3	T	7	E	6	1	4	0	5	8	9
CLSTA.	P_0	0	1	4	9	5	8	3	T	2	E	6	7
HRP.	R_0	7	6	E	2	T	3	8	5	9	4	1	0
VN.	P_8	8	9	0	5	1	4	E	6	T	7	2	3
VA.	R_8	3	2	7	T	6	E	4	1	5	0	9	8
VC.	I_5	5	4	1	8	0	9	2	7	3	6	E	T
CB.	RI_5	T	E	6	3	7	2	9	0	8	1	4	5

row forms that display trichordal (as well as hexachordal) combinatoriality. In other words, the pitch-class content for each of these groups taken independently constitutes a trichordal array. In fact, the trichordal array we have studied in Example 9.8 shows precisely the pitch-class content for the second of the groups listed previously (horn, trumpet, harp, and celesta).

The combinatorial properties of this pitch-class complex, however, go beyond hexachordal and trichordal combinatoriality to include also dyadic and unitary combinatoriality. The complete opening pitch-class complex is shown in Example 9.13. Some of the combinatorial properties in this complex are shown by squares. For instance, squares enclosing hexachords of adjacent row forms indicate hexachordal combinatoriality: P_4 and R_4 are combinatorial, and so are I_1, and RI_1, and so on. What we cannot show on the chart, however, is that each P form is combinatorial with *each* R form and with *each* RI form, and that each I form is combinatorial with *each* RI form and with *each* R form (you can easily double-check some of these relationships). The squares enclosing four trichords show some of the many cases of trichordal combinatoriality

♪♪ Example 9.14   Durational rows for the opening of *Composition for Twelve Instruments*

a.

b.

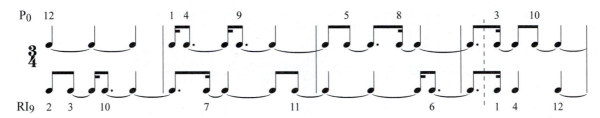

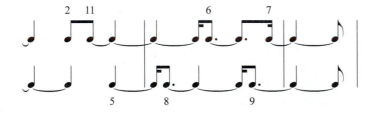

among three rows in the complex (those involving adjacent row forms). **Dyadic combinatoriality** takes place when we can combine the corresponding discrete dyads of six row forms to create aggregates, and **unitary combinatoriality** occurs when the combination of corresponding individual pitch classes among twelve row forms create aggregates. The squares enclosing dyads in groups of six rows in Example 9.13 show dyadic combinatoriality in this complex. To verify unitary combinatoriality you simply read each of the columns in the complex to verify that indeed it forms an aggregate.

Composition for Twelve Instruments is divided into two movements. The pitch content for movement 1 is all based on the row listed earlier and is organized into four twelve-row complexes (of which the complex in Example 9.13 is the first). Movement 2 is based on eight row complexes, each complex being generated by a different row trichordally derived from the row in movement 1.[14]

---

[14]The complete pitch-class content of each of these complexes can be found in Hush, "Asynordinate Twelve-Tone Structures."

Durational Rows

Babbitt's derivation of durations for *Composition for Twelve Instruments* follows a straightforward method: pitch-class numbers for specific row forms are turned into durations measured in the number of sixteenth notes. Time-point 0 becomes time-point 12 in the durational row, so that duration can be assigned to it. The piece opens with a single statement of the durational row represented by P_2: 2–3–6–E–7–T–5–12–4–1–8–9. If these integers represent numbers of sixteenth notes, the resulting rhythmic row is the one shown in Example 9.14a (here shown as a model in $\frac{3}{4}$, although the actual musical realization includes meter changes).

   If you take the rhythmic pattern that results from all the individual instrument attacks in mm. 1–6, you will see that it is exactly the pattern provided by P_2. In mm. 7–13, the rhythmic pattern results from combining two row forms, P_0 and RI_9. Example 9.14b shows these two simultaneous durational row forms (also presented here as a model in $\frac{3}{4}$, regardless of the meter changes in the actual music), from which you can verify the rhythmic design for mm. 7–13 (beginning on the second eighth note of m. 7). The complete durational-row design for *Composition for Twelve Instruments* is provided in both the Westergaard and Hush articles cited in footnote 13. Immediately following m. 13, for instance, the durational rows are I_3/RI_7, I_1, R_8/I_5, P_{10}/R_6, and RI_5.

   As you did with Boulez's *Structures Ia,* discuss any pertinent issues of style and aesthetics in this piece. How are Babbitt's and Boulez's compositions related stylistically? How do they relate to, or depart from, established styles in Western music?

APPLICATION AND CLASS DISCUSSION

An issue that is often pointed out regarding multi-serialism is the perceptual and performance difficulties that result from the serialization of various musical elements. Both Ligeti and Westergaard address these matters in their respective articles on Boulez and Babbitt cited in footnotes 4 and 13. What do you think are the perceptual challenges created by the serialization of rhythm, dynamics, and modes of attack? What are the aspects of a pitch-class row that remain invariant when the row is transformed? Is it possible to perceive different transformations of a pitch-class row, and why? What about durational rows when used in the various ways we have seen in this chapter? How are different transformations of durational rows related?

Are there any elements that can be identified by a listener that would relate the various transformations among themselves? And what about intensity and attack rows? Moreover, what kind of performance problems are created by intensity and attack rows of the type we have seen in Boulez's music?

   From a compositional point of view (rather than a perceptual one), what are the advantages that multi-serialism may afford a composer? What did composers in the 1950s and 1960s achieve by using the methods we have studied in this chapter? Did they succeed in what they were trying to do? Did they have to give up something for the sake of achieving their ends?

Further Listening

The following list provides suggestions for further listening to music by composers studied in this chapter or related to the styles and techniques we have studied (if possible, listen while following the score):

1. Stravinsky, *Threni*
2. Stravinsky, *Abraham and Isaac*
3. Stravinsky, *Variations*
4. Boulez, *Le marteau sans maître*
5. Boulez, *Pli selon pli*
6. Babbitt, *Composition for Four Instruments*
7. Babbitt, *All Set*
8. Stockhausen, *Kreuzspiel*
9. Stockhausen, *Gruppen*
10. Nono, *Il canto sospeso*

Terms for Review

rotation
rotational array
rotational arrays α (alpha) and β (beta)
rotational arrays γ (gamma) and δ (delta)
rotational array "verticals"
multiserialism, total serialism, integral
  serialism

multiplication
trichordal array
trichordal combinatoriality
durational rows
time-point rows
dyadic combinatoriality
unitary combinatoriality

 CHAPTER 9 ASSIGNMENTS

I. Theory and Analysis

1. The basic row for Stravinsky's *Abraham and Isaac* is F–F♯–E–D–D♯–B–A–G–G♯–A♯–C–C♯. First, provide a complete chart of the γ and δ rotational arrays for all four forms of the row. Then analyze the complete pitch content for Example 9.15 (the vocal part for the first two verses of *Abraham and Isaac*), and identify the exact arrays and rotations used in this fragment.

2. The row for Stravinsky's *Variations* is D–C–A–B–E–A♯–G♯–C♯–D♯–G–F♯–F. First, provide a complete chart of the γ and δ rotational arrays for all four forms of the row. Then, analyze the pitch content for Variation 2 (mm. 23–33) and identify the exact arrays and rotations used in this fragment (you can find the score for this piece at your music library). This variation is written in twelve-part counterpoint for twelve solo violins.

Example 9.15   Stravinsky, *Abraham and Isaac,* mm. 12–45, voice part only (text omitted)

To help you understand its pitch organization, first think of violins 1 and 12 as being switched on the score (that is, think of the line for violin 1 as being at the bottom, and the line for violin 12 as being at the top). Then divide the instruments into three groups of four adjacent violins each (violins 1–4, 5–8, and 9–12). The pitch-class content for each of the three groups is derived from a single array.

3. Example 9.16 reproduces the opening eight measures of Babbitt's *Three Compositions for Piano.* This work is based on both a pitch row and an attack row. The pitch row is 0 5 7 4 2 3 9 1 8 E T 6, and the row of attacks is P: 5 1 4 2, inverted as I: 1 5 2 4. These numbers refer to number of attacks in sixteenth notes, with attack groups being separated by longer notes or rests. For instance (for the lower line in the left hand, mm. 1–2): five attacks—long note/one attack—rest/four attacks—long note/two attacks—long note. Identify the complete row content for the given passage, both for pitches and attacks, and determine whether there is any correlation between pitch and attack rows.

♩♪♪ Example 9.16   Babbitt, *Three Compositions for Piano*, mm. 1–8

II. Composition

Write a short multiserial composition for four instruments of your choice (or two melodic instruments and a piano), using some of the techniques used by Boulez or Babbitt that we have studied in this chapter. First, build a pitch-class row. You need not, but may, try to build a row that allows you to derive a trichordal array. Then decide how you are going to serialize durations, and how your durational series are going to be related to your pitch-class series. Decide whether you want to serialize other elements (such as intensities and attack modes) and how you will do so. Finally, write your composition using all the material you have generated in your precompositional planning. In this final compositional stage you will have to decide on aesthetic, stylistic, and purely musical matters.

Chapter 10

Expanding the Limits of Musical Temporality

In previous chapters we have referred to a variety of issues pertaining to particular uses of rhythm and meter by twentieth-century composers. We have particularly examined examples of changes of meter, metric displacement, rhythmic layers, polymeter, irregular accentual patterns, and nonmetric notation in the music of Stravinsky, Bartók, and Ives. More recently, we have studied examples of rhythmic symmetry in Webern and serialized rhythm in Boulez and Babbitt. Some composers in the second half of the century, however, have been particularly concerned with aspects of rhythm, meter, and time in their music, and have been actively interested in expanding the limits of musical temporality. In this chapter we will focus on some highly innovative and idiosyncratic uses of musical temporality by three of these composers. We will explore Olivier Messiaen's rhythmic structures, Elliott Carter's use of tempo as a structural element in his music, and Karlheinz Stockhausen's new concepts of musical time. Before doing so, however, let us review some of the most salient issues pertaining to rhythm and meter in post-tonal music before 1945.

RHYTHMIC AND METRIC IRREGULARITIES IN POST-TONAL MUSIC

Following conventional definitions, the term **rhythm** refers to the *grouping, patterning, and partitioning of musical events,* whereas **meter** refers to the *measurement of the number of pulses between regularly recurring accents.* **Pulses** are regularly recurring time points, and we will refer to pulses in a metric context as **beats.** In other words, the standard definition of meter takes into account the regular nature of both the basic units that make up meter (the beats) and the grouping of these beats. Although tonal music is greatly based on metric regularity, this regularity has often been offset by irregular rhythmic groupings or by the conflict between meter and rhythm. Asymmetrical phrases, for instance (made up of five or seven measures, for example, or of a grouping of 4 + 5 measures) create a sense of rhythmic irregularity, and so does the use of irregular divisions of the beat (triplets, quintuplets, and so on). Other types of rhythmic irregularities can create a sense of conflict between the beat and the meter on the one hand, and the actual perceived rhythm on the other. This type of irregularity is particularly created by **syncopation** (the rhythmic contradiction of a metrical pattern of strong and weak beats) and by **hemiola** (the juxtaposition of, or interplay between, three and two beats). All these metric and rhythmic irregularities are often found in tonal music, as, for instance, in the music of Mozart, Beethoven, Schumann, Brahms, and others.

Rather than focusing on this type of temporal event that is familiar to us from the tonal repertoire, we will now examine some types of rhythmic and metric irregularities favored by some post-tonal composers in the twentieth century. Although syncopation, hemiola, and irregular or asymmetrical phrase structure are common in post-tonal music, twentieth-century composers went far beyond these techniques as they created complex musical textures that at times featured sharply articulated metric/rhythmic conflicts and irregularities.

Asymmetrical and Additive Meters

Most standard meters (such as $\frac{4}{4}$, $\frac{3}{4}$, $\frac{6}{8}$, $\frac{9}{8}$, and so on) are **symmetrical or divisive.** That is, we think of them in terms of their divisions, and the divisions form symmetrical patterns. Other meters, however, are **asymmetrical or additive.** We think of them as two or more combined metric units, and the resulting metric structure is asymmetrical. This is the case of meters such as $\frac{5}{8}$, $\frac{7}{8}$, $\frac{11}{8}$, and so on. When we think of $\frac{5}{8}$, for instance, we think of two possible combinations of metric units (3 + 2 or 2 + 3). Because of their asymmetry, additive meters are conducted in unequal beats (in the case of $\frac{5}{8}$, the value of beats is a dotted quarter and a quarter, in either order).

Additive meters produce metric regularity, but their irregular, asymmetric beat patterns create a sense of unevenness and irregularity that has been favored by twentieth-century composers. The passage shown in Example 10.1a, in $\frac{7}{8}$ (2 + 2 + 3), illustrates this sense of irregularity in an additive meter. The sense of irregularity is further stressed in the fragment from Bartók's String Quartet no. 5 (1934) shown in Example 10.1b. Bartók's notated meter for this passage is 3 + 2 + 2 + 3 over 8 (that is, $\frac{10}{8}$ resulting from combining 3 + 2 + 2 + 3). This is the meter and grouping that we hear indeed in the first violin (this is an additive meter, but it is symmetrical). The viola, however, contravenes this grouping by performing a different version of $\frac{10}{8}$, now as 2 + 3 + 3 + 2.

Changing Meters

A direct and simple way of creating metric irregularity is by **changing (or mixed) meters.** This is a procedure widely found in post-tonal music and particularly used in the early part of the twentieth century by Stravinsky. The passage from *Les noces* (1914–17) reproduced in Example 10.2 (piano I only) changes meter every measure (after the initial two measures in $\frac{3}{4}$). The meters involved are simple, compound, symmetrical, and asymmetrical, and all they have in common is an underlying eighth-note pulse that provides a rhythmic connection throughout the passage.

♪♪♪ Example 10.1a   Bartók, Bulgarian Rhythm no. 1, from *Mikrokosmos* IV, mm. 4–5

mf, *legato, leggero*

♪♪♪ Example 10.1b   Bartók, String Quartet no. 5, III, Trio, mm. 24–26

Irregular and Displaced Rhythmic Grouping

Temporal irregularity can also be achieved by **irregular rhythmic groupings** (created, for instance, by an irregular pattern of accents), regardless of whether the meter changes, or is symmetrical or asymmetrical. Consider the passage from Bartók's Piano Concerto no. 1 (1926) shown in Example 10.3. The meter does change, though not every measure. If you take into account only the two violin parts, however, you will see that the accentual pattern creates a totally irregular grouping that does not correspond with the metric divisions: 2 + [5 + 3 + 5 + 4 + 4] + 6. The violas and cellos, on the other hand, also have their own irregular accentual pattern that creates a rhythmic

♪♪♪ Example 10.2   Stravinsky, *Les noces,* scene II, reh. 27–29 (piano I only)

♪♪♪ Example 10.3   Bartók, Piano Concerto no. 1, I, reh. 13–14

grouping different from that of the violins, [5 + 3 + 5 + 4 + 4] + 4 + 7 (the brackets in these lists of rhythmic divisions show that the beginning of this pattern, 5 + 3 + 5 + 4 + 4, creates a rhythmic canon with the same groupings in the violins). The notated meter in this passage is only a tool to notate in a simple way what is otherwise a complex interplay of irregular rhythmic groupings among the parts.

At times the accentual pattern contravenes the notated meter, but nevertheless creates a regular pattern of equal rhythmic groups. This is the case in Example 10.4, where

♩♪♪ Example 10.4   Bartók, *Music for Strings, Percussion, and Celesta*, II, mm. 106–110

the accents and phrasing create regular groups of three eighth notes that do not correspond with the $\frac{2}{4}$ meter and hence result in **metric displacement.** Note that each group
of three notes is metrically displaced with respect to both the notated meter and the
groups that precede and follow it. The texture in this example, moreover, results from a
three-part rhythmic canon (each part comes in two eighth notes after the previous part),
in such a way that metric displacements are different in each of the three parts that create the canon.

Additional metric and rhythmic complexity and irregularity can be achieved by
combining some of the techniques we have previously described. The example from
The Soldier's Tale (1918) shown in Example 10.5a features constant meter changes. The
violin follows the notated meter, and hence the metric changes. But the double bass, on
the other hand, performs a repeated ostinato pattern of four eighth notes that disregards

Example 10.5a   Stravinsky, *The Soldier's Tale,* "Music to Scene I," mm. 86–95

Example 10.5b   Bartók, String Quartet no. 5, III, Scherzo da capo, mm. 44–48

the metric changes. As a result, this pattern features constant metric displacement with respect to the notated meters. Now study Example 10.5b, which is notated in an additive, asymmetrical meter (4 + 3 + 2 over 8). First, explain the instances of metric displacement in the first violin. Notice particularly that in mm. 45–48, this instrument features metric displacement due to the repetition of a six eighth-note long motive in the

♪♪ Example 10.6a   Bartók, String Quartet no. 2, II, 7 mm. after reh. 41

context of a nine eighth-note long measure. Then notice the syncopated nature of the two middle voices. And finally, explain the rhythmic characteristics of the cello part.

Polymeter

Polymeter is the simultaneous presentation of more than one meter. In our discussion of *The Rite of Spring* in Chapter 1, we saw an example of a section in which we hear three different meters (see Example 1.19), although the section is actually notated in a single meter. In other cases, however, the composer notates the different meters in the music. In Example 10.6a we see a polymetric fragment from Bartók's String Quartet no. 2 (1915–17) where two different, simultaneous meters are notated ($\frac{6}{4}$ and $\frac{4}{4}$). In this case, the length of a measure in each meter is the same, so we hear six quarter notes against four (or three against two), that is, a hemiola. Example 10.6b, on the other hand, shows a more complex polymeter. In this reduction of Ives's orchestral score for *The Fourth of July* (1911–13), we hear two groups of instruments, each of which features different meters. One group is made up of percussion instruments (timpani, cymbals, bass drum, and xylophone), and it is notated in $\frac{4}{4}$ throughout. The xylophone in this passage quotes two Irish tune dances, "Garryowen" in mm. 82–83, and "Saint Patrick's Day" in mm. 88–90. The other group, made up in our example of flute, violins, cellos, and double basses, also begins in $\frac{4}{4}$, but then continues alternating $\frac{4}{4}$ and $\frac{7}{8}$, creating a lack of metric synchrony between the two groups (measures in $\frac{7}{8}$ are one eighth-note shorter than measures in $\frac{4}{4}$). The cellos and flute in this passage feature imitative and developmental material on "Columbia, the Gem of the Ocean."[1] In other words, this passage illustrates polymeter in which measures in each meter have different lengths.

[1] Burkholder identifies these quotations in *The Fourth of July* in *All Made of Tunes*, pp. 376–79.

Example 10.6b   Ives, *The Fourth of July,* mm. 86–91 (reduction)

Polyrhythm

Polyrhythm is the simultaneous presentation of different rhythmic groupings or divisions. The difference between polymeter and polyrhythm is not always a clear one, but in general we will think of polymeter as referring to different simultaneous groupings of beats, whereas polyrhythm affects groupings or elements other than beats, or also beat subdivisions. Consider, for instance, the Bartók passage in Example 10.7a. It involves a canonic presentation of a theme in four voices. The theme is made up of two units: first, a four sixteenth-note segment, and then a six sixteenth-note segment. This asymmetrical 4 + 6 grouping creates metric displacement of the repeated theme in each voice. That, combined with the staggered canonic entries, results in simultaneous statements of the theme beginning on different parts of the beat. In this example, the different groupings heard simultaneously create polyrhythm.

In the following example from Debussy's *Prelude to "The Afternoon of a Faun"* of 1892–94 (Example 10.7b), polyrhythm is first created by different groupings within equivalent subdivisions of the beat. The two moving inner voices in mm. 63–66 share the same type of subdivision of the beat (triplets in one case, sextuplets in the other). Notes in the voice in triplets, however, are grouped in pairs, creating a cross-rhythm with the voice in sextuplets. Over the span of two measures, we hear six sextuplets against nine pairs of triplet eighth-notes. We thus hear these two voices as independent

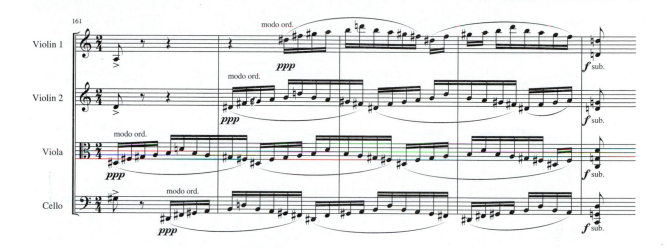

♩♪ Example 10.7a   Bartók, String Quartet no. 4, II, mm. 161–65

rhythmic layers that create a polyrhythm. In mm. 67–70, the situation is slightly different. We still have an accompanying pattern in sextuplets, but the melody, now in the inner voices, features duple and quadruple divisions of the beat. We thus hear polyrhythm
as different simultaneous subdivisions of the beat that create a pattern of 6 against 4.

TEMPORAL ISSUES IN THE MUSIC OF MESSIAEN

It is not far-fetched to consider Messiaen (1908–1992) one of the most complex, rich,
and individualistic musical personalities in the twentieth century. A lot of the components of his musical language were explained by the composer in his 1942 book
Technique de mon langage musical.[2] From the point of view of pitch organization, the
most significant aspect of Messiaen's language is his use of symmetrical pitch-class
collections based on the division of the octave into equal segments, and which he called
modes of limited transposition (because each of these collections allows for only a
limited number of transpositions that do not map the collection onto itself). Messiaen
considers seven such modes, as shown in Example 10.8. Note that modes 1 and 2 are
the familiar whole-tone and octatonic scales, respectively. The rest of the modes result
from repetition of particular intervallic patterns. Mode 3, for instance, is formed by

---

[2]Translated into English by John Satterfield as *The Technique of My Musical Language* (Paris: Alphonse
Leduc, 1956).

 **Example 10.7b**   Debussy, *Prelude to "The Afternoon of a Faun,"* mm. 63–71 (piano reduction)

repeating a pattern of tone-semitone-tone three times. The resulting scale allows for four different transpositions that do not map the collection onto itself.

 NOTE

Not all existing "modes of limited transposition" are included in Messiaen's list. The hexatonic scale we studied in Chapter 2, for instance, is not included.

♪♪♪ Example 10.8   Oliver Messiaen's modes of limited transposition

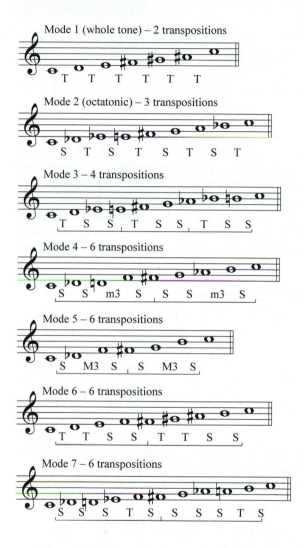

Messiaen often derived added-note chords from the modes. Some added-note chords derived from the modes (following Messiaen's own interpretation) are shown in Example 10.9. Example 10.9a, derived from mode 2, can be interpreted as a CM triad with an added augmented 4th. The chord in Example 10.9b, from mode 3, is a Cm triad with an added +4 and an added m6; the chord in Example 10.9c (mode 4) is a Bm triad with an added 2nd; the chord in Example 10.9d (mode 6) is an augmented triad on C with an added 2nd; and the chord in Example 10.9e (mode 7) is a DM_7 chord with a diminished 5th and an added 6th.

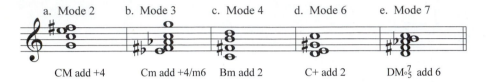

♩♪♪ Example 10.9   Added-note chords

a. Mode 2   b. Mode 3   c. Mode 4   d. Mode 6   e. Mode 7

CM add +4   Cm add +4/m6   Bm add 2   C+ add 2   DM∘⁷₅ add 6

Later in his life, Messiaen became interested in the relationship between sound and color. Messiaen claimed that he saw colors when writing or listening to music, and in some compositions he associated chords or sonorities to particular colors (for instance, in his orchestral work from 1960, *Chronochromie*). An expert ornithologist, he collected and incorporated into his compositions hundreds of birdsongs (for instance, in his 1958 piano piece *Catalogue d'Oiseaux*). Always a devout Catholic, and always interested in mathematics and numerology, his works include complex religious and numerical symbolism built in to his pitch and rhythmic structures.

Rhythmic Techniques in Messiaen's Music

The most distinctive and peculiar element of Messiaen's music, however, is his use of rhythm, and this is what we will focus on in the rest of our discussion. Before we examine in some detail an example from the *Turangalîla Symphony,* we will review and define some of the main rhythmic techniques we find in Messiaen's music in general.[3] As it will become obvious in the following discussion, for Messiaen, rhythm arises by addition and extension of durations, rather than by division of time.

Indian Tālas

In Indian music, a ***tāla*** is a specific time or rhythmic cycle. In the late 1920s Messiaen came across excerpts from a thirteenth-century Indian treatise, the *Saṅgīta-ratnākara,* by Śārṅgadeva, which included a list of 120 rhythmic patterns from the provinces of India called *deśītālas* (or "regional *tālas*"). These *tālas* had a strong appeal for Messiaen, to the point that he either incorporated many of them into his music or based many of his rhythms and rhythmic ideas on their properties. Example 10.10 shows three of the *tālas* that can be found most often in Messiaen's music, the *rāgavardhana* (*tāla* no. 93), the *candrakalā* (*tāla* no. 105), and the *lackskmīça* (*tāla* no. 88).

Several properties of these *tālas* were particularly attractive to Messiaen. In the first place, they are fundamentally ametrical. That is, they are not defined by consistent, equal beats, (and by regular groupings of such beats), but rather by the shortest

---

[3]Two general studies of Messiaen's music that include good discussions of his rhythmic practices are Harry Halbreich, *Olivier Messiaen* (Paris: Fayard/SACEM, 1980) and Robert Sherlaw Johnson, *Messiaen* (London: Dent, 1989).

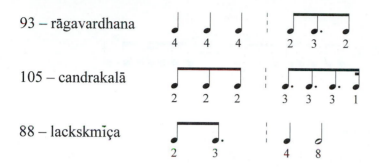

♪♪♪ Example 10.10   Three *deśītālas*: *rāgavardhana*, *candrakalā*, and *lackskmīça*

note value on which each rhythmic pattern is built, in an additive process. The shortest note value on which we can build all the durations in Example 10.10 is the sixteenth note. We can notate each of these *tālas* by means of number sequences that represent durations in multiples of sixteenth notes. Thus, *rāgavardhana* can be represented as 4 4 4 2 3 2, *candrakalā* as 2 2 2 3 3 3 1, and *lackskmīça* as 2 3 4 8.

Another property that interested Messiaen was the inexact processes of augmentation or diminution involved in the generation of these *tālas,* and the principle of "added values" on which this inexact process is based. To understand this, let's divide each of these *tālas* into two parts or patterns. Thus, *rāgavardhana* becomes 4 4 4 / 2 3 2, *candrakalā* 2 2 2 / 3 3 3 1 (or 2 2 2 / 3 3 4), and *lackskmīça* 2 3 / 4 8. In the first case, 4 4 4 would be diminished by half to become 2 2 2, but by adding one sixteenth note to the middle value, we end up with an inexact diminution, 2 3 2. Similarly, in *candrakalā* 2 2 2 can be augmented to 3 3 3 (multiplying each 2 by 1.5), but the augmentation in this case includes an added sixteenth note at the end, turning it into 3 3 3 1 (or 3 3 4). Finally, 2 3 can be augmented to 4 6 (multiplying the original values by 2), but an addition of two sixteenth notes turns the augmentation into 4 8. That is, in all these cases, the augmentation or diminution is altered by means of an added value.

Rhythms with Added Values

A characteristic rhythmic technique in Messiaen's music is the use of **rhythms with added values** (rhythms in which a short value is added by means of a note, a dot, or a rest), which reflects the asymmetrical additive processes we find in the *deśītālas*. Example 10.11, for instance, shows a possible standard division of a $\frac{4}{4}$ measure (hence a metrical pattern), followed by four transformations of this model that result from adding one or more values to the original pattern (each added value is marked with an x). The rhythms with added values shown in Examples 10.11b–d are all ametrical (they do not feature beat regularity), and are all taken from the "Danse de la fureur, pour les sept trompettes," from Messiaen's *Quatuor pour la Fin du Temps* (1940).

Example 10.11   Rhythms with added values

a.   b.   c.   d.

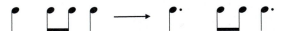

Example 10.12   Rhythmic augmentations

a. Augmentation by a ratio

b. Augmentation by a fixed value

c. Inexact augmentation

Augmented and Diminished Rhythms

Messiaen uses various types of augmentations and diminutions to transform his rhythms. Here again, the basic principle is addition (or subtraction) of values. **Rhythmic augmentation or diminution** in Messiaen's music may be proportional, by a fixed value, or inexact. Example 10.12a shows two examples of **proportional augmentation,** in which all the values of a given rhythm are augmented by the same ratio (¼ of the original value in the first case, and ⅓ in the second case). Example 10.12b illustrates **augmentation by a fixed value** (all the values in the original rhythm are equally augmented by a sixteenth note). Finally, Example 10.12c shows an example of **inexact augmentation** (two values are augmented by ½, two values are not augmented at all).

Example 10.13   Nonretrogradable rhythm

Nonretrogradable Rhythms

Nonretrogradable rhythms are symmetrical, palindromic rhythmic patterns that are the same whether they are read in original form or in retrograde. A nonretrogradable rhythm is shown in Example 10.13.

Other Rhythmic Techniques

Messiaen's music uses a variety of other techniques. These include **rhythmic pedals** or **ostinatos** (repetition of a rhythmic figure or a rhythmic cycle), polyrhythms (superposition of rhythms of unequal length), and **rhythmic canons** in which the *comes* features some augmentation of the *dux*'s values, and in which the pitch content of each line is often based on a different mode.

ANALYSIS 10.1: MESSIAEN, INTRODUCTION, FROM *TURANGALÎLA SYMPHONY* (ANTHOLOGY NO. 27)

We will now study a passage from the Introduction to Messiaen's *Turangalîla Symphony* (1946–48) as a musical illustration of the rhythmic principles we have previously discussed.[4] Listen to the Introduction and focus on the texture from rehearsal 12 to rehearsal 21 (Anthology no. 27). What are the rhythmic and formal elements in this section? What are the main compositional principles and techniques that you can identify? Go back to Chapter 1 and review our discussion of form in Stravinsky's *Rite of Spring,* in particular the concepts of stratification, interruption and continuation, and juxtaposition. Do these principles apply to Messiaen's fragment?

Texture and Formal Growth

The passage from reh. 12 to reh. 21 is made up of a variety of textural layers. The principle of stratification does indeed apply to this texture. Let us first define the main layers in this texture:

---

[4]Analyses of the rhythmic structure of this movement can be found in Johnson, *Messiaen,* pp. 84–85, and very particularly in Julian L. Hook, "Rhythm in the Music of Messiaen: An Algebraic Study and an Application in the *Turangalîla Symphony,*" *Music Theory Spectrum* 20/1 (1998): 97–120.

Layer A

A first layer, which we will call layer A, is made up by the rhythmic motives separated by rests in the oboes and clarinets. This layer functions as an ostinato or rhythmic pedal that continues uninterrupted, except for the rests that separate each statement of the rhythmic motive, throughout the passage.

Layer B

A second layer (layer B), which is present throughout the passage without any interruption, is provided by the continuous, syncopated lines in second violins and violas.

Layers C and D

The snare drum (layer C) and the Chinese cymbal (layer D) provide two additional layers, which also appear throughout the passage without interruption.

The Gamelan Group

Finally, and most prominently, we also hear a large textural group, itself made up of several layers, which we can call the "gamelan group." This group is made up of the tuned percussion instruments (celesta, glockenspiel, vibraphone, and piano, and hence its sound and timbre affinities with a Balinese gamelan), the flutes and bassoons, the *ondes Martenot,* the first violins, and the cellos and basses. Although we will focus on the rhythmic structure of the four layers we have identified and the gamelan group, other elements or layers are also present in this passage. What are they?

We can see that while the layers we have labeled as A, B, C, and D continue throughout the passage without interruption, the gamelan group forms a unified textural block that is subject to the process of interruption and continuation. Thus, this block is suddenly interrupted four measures after reh. 12, is started again at reh. 13, is interrupted four measures later, and so on for the rest of the passage (it appears briefly five more times before the longer statement four measures after reh. 18, and only once briefly after this final longer statement). Thus, the formal technique of juxtaposition also applies in this passage.

The Rhythmic Layers

The elements we have identified as textural and timbral layers are also distinctive rhythmic layers. We will discuss again each of these elements, now from the point of view of rhythmic structure.

Layer A

If you count the durations in the rhythmic motive in layer A in numbers of sixteenth notes, you come up with a pattern of five durations, 2 3 4 4 <4>, where the four sixteenth-note rest is indicated by angle brackets. This pattern is used as a rhythmic ostinato (with a total cyclic length of seventeen sixteenth notes), with no alteration throughout the passage. If you compare the pattern to the *tālas* in Example 10.10, you will see that this is indeed a form of *tāla* 88, *lackskmīça.* The pitch content of this layer is provided

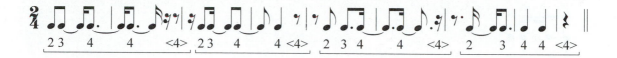

Example 10.14   Layer A, rhythmic reduction

Example 10.15   Layer B, rhythmic reduction

by a repeated sequence of fourteen chords derived from Messiaen's mode 6. Example 10.14 shows a rhythmic reduction of this layer as it appears from reh. 12 to reh. 13.

Layer B

Here again we can count the durations in numbers of sixteenth notes, and we come up with a pattern of six durations, 4 4 4 2 3 2 (with a total cyclic length of nineteen sixteenth notes), repeated throughout the passage with no interruption. A comparison of this pattern with the *tālas* in Example 10.10 reveals that this is *tāla* 93, *rāgavardhana*. The pitch content of layer B is provided by a repeated sequence of 13 chords, now derived from Messiaen's mode 4. As in layer A, the chord cycle does not coincide with the cycle of durations. This compositional situation is akin to medieval isorhythm, in which a rhythmic pattern (*talea*) and a pitch pattern (*color*), which provided the basic compositional materials, normally had a different number of elements, and thus their repetition followed unequal cycles. Example 10.15 shows a rhythmic reduction of the initial fragment of layer B (reh. 12–reh. 13).

Layer C

A complex and very interesting rhythmic process takes place in the snare drum layer. In the first place, this line illustrates what we call a **generative rhythm.** This is a rhythm that grows from a small initial segment following some systematic process of repetition, addition, expansion, and so on. We will call the initial cell from which a generative rhythm is constructed a **seed.** Example 10.16a shows the basic seed for layer C, which we will call seed x: 2 1 1 1 2. This cell in itself is a nonretrogradable rhythm. Example 10.16b shows the first segment that is generated from this seed, and which can be described by the formula (x 3 x). That is, seed x is repeated twice, and a value

♪♪♪ Example 10.16   The basic cells for layer C

a.

x:

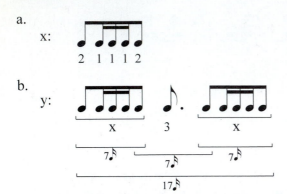

b.

y:

of three sixteenth notes is inserted between the repetitions. This segment, which opens the snare drum line at reh. 12, is also a nonretrogradable rhythm, but moreover illustrates Messiaen's taste for prime numbers (numbers that can be evenly divided only by one and by themselves). The total length of the segment is seventeen sixteenth notes (a prime number that we already saw as the length of the durational cycle for layer A), and the segment breaks up into three symmetrical and overlapping cells of seven sixteenth notes each.

Now we can examine how the complete cycle for layer C is generated from these initial segments. The process illustrates what Julian Hook has called recursive progressions.[5] A **recursive progression** results when a seed generates a longer segment, which in turn becomes the seed from which a longer segment is generated, which in turn generates a still longer pattern, and so on. Example 10.17 shows the complete recursive progression for the snare-drum line, beginning with the (x 3 x) segment, which in turn generates a (4 / x 3 x / 4) segment, and then a (2 1 2 / 4 x 3 x 4 / 2 1 2). In these segments, which we have labeled as y_1, y_2, and y_3, durations have been added symmetrically at the beginning and the end of the previous segment. For the next segment, y_4, a (1 1 1 1) segment is added at the beginning and end of y_3, and the central 3 duration is expanded into a (3 9 3) pattern. Each of the four y segments are nonretrogradable rhythms. The complete snare-drum cycle consists of a concatenation of all four y segments, $y_1 + y_2 + y_3 + y_4$, and it has a total length of 132 sixteenth notes.

Layer D

The Chinese cymbal line illustrates what Hook calls progressive rhythms. In a **progressive rhythm,** an initial seed is expanded (or contracted) by the addition (or subtraction)

---

[5]The terms "generative rhythm," "seed," and "recursive progressions" (as well as "progressive rhythm" and "chromatic progression") are all borrowed from Hook (see footnote 4 in this chapter). The snare drum rhythm we are now discussing is indeed Hook's example of a recursive progression.

Example 10.17   The complete recursive progression for layer C

17 16 15 14 ... 10 9 8 (7) 8 9 10 ... 14 15 16 (17) 16 15 14 ... 10 9 8 (7) 8 9 10 ... 14 15 16 (17)

Figure 10.1 The progression of durations for layer D

of a fixed value. If the value added or subtracted each time is 1 (in our example, a single sixteenth note), the progression is said to be a **chromatic progression.** Layer D begins with a duration of seventeen sixteenth notes. This original seed generates a contracting chromatic progression: each subsequent duration is a sixteenth note shorter, until we reach a duration of seven sixteenth notes. At that point, the process changes into an expanding chromatic progression, with durations increasing from seven to seventeen. The length of the complete cycle of contraction from seventeen to seven and then expansion from seven to seventeen is 240 sixteenth notes, or thirty measures. The passage from reh. 12 to reh. 21 includes two complete statements of the cycle (30 measures each) plus an incomplete cycle (the first 9 measures), or 30 + 30 + 9 measures. Note that every time a contracting or expanding process is completed in this cycle, an elision takes place at either 7 or 17 to begin the new process. Figure 10.1 illustrates two rotations of the cycle, with the elisions marked in parentheses. Note, of course, that 7 and 17 are again the same prime numbers which we have already found in layers A and C.

The Gamelan Group

The gamelan group features a simple rhythmic structure in comparison with the four layers discussed earlier. The texture is made up of a continuous stream of sixteenth notes that are grouped into cycles of 10 by a ten-pitch ostinato pattern, and a continuous stream of eighth notes, grouped into cycles of 5 by a five eighth-note pitch ostinato.

As a conclusion to the study of Messiaen's music, you may discuss how and why the perceptual aspects of this music are so different from the perceptual aspects of total serialism. Although this music features rhythmic structures of great complexity, and although several of these complex structures are presented simultaneously, the result presents a more immediately comprehensible whole from a perceptual point of view. Why is it so?

TEMPO AS A STRUCTURAL ELEMENT IN THE MUSIC OF ELLIOTT CARTER

Temporal issues are central to understanding the music of Elliott Carter (born 1908). Following a line of rhythmic innovations by American composers (especially by Charles Ives, Henry Cowell, and Conlon Nancarrow—three composers whose work Carter admired), Carter developed a variety of highly elaborate and innovative rhythmic methods in his music. Perhaps the most characteristic among Carter's temporal techniques is his use of tempo as an essential compositional element. Our study will focus on successive tempo processes, tempo simultaneities, and the use of "musical characters" or personalities, especially as found in Carter's first and second string quartets.[6]

Metric Modulation

The term **metric modulation** refers to a process widely found in Carter's compositions, by which the music moves from one precise metronomic marking to another through a series of intermediate steps. Although Carter preferred the term "tempo modulation," the term "metric modulation" has become standard to refer to this procedure. Tempo markings are frequent and very exact in Carter's music, and they are normally related by precise and complex ratios. An exact, accurate performance of these tempo processes would be virtually impossible if it were not because of metric modulation. Metric modulation is actually a built-in, written-in procedure that allows the performer to effect, and the listener to perceive, complex tempo changes with relative ease and with total accuracy.

Let us examine the metric modulation shown in Example 10.18a, from Carter's String Quartet no. 1 (1951). The passage takes us from a tempo of beat (dotted quarter) = MM

[6]The standard general study of Carter's music is David Schiff, *The Music of Elliott Carter* (Ithaca, NY: Cornell University Press, 1998). A more detailed study of Carter's rhythmic methods can be found in Jonathan Bernard, "The Evolution of Elliott Carter's Rhythmic Practice," *Perspectives of New Music* 26/2 (1988), 164–203. Both sources include discussions of temporal processes in the first and second string quartets. Issues of pitch structure in these two quartets have also been discussed by Jonathan Bernard in "Problems of Pitch Structure in Elliott Carter's First and Second String Quartets," *Journal of Music Theory* 37 (1993): 231–66. See also Andrew Mead, "Pitch Structure in Elliott Carter's *String Quartet No. 3*," *Perspectives of New Music* 22/1 (1983): 31–60; and "Twelve-Tone Composition and the Music of Elliott Carter," in *Concert Music, Rock, and Jazz since 1945: Essays and Analytical Studies,* ed. by Elizabeth West Marvin and Richard Hermann (Rochester, NY: University of Rochester Press, 1995), pp. 67–102. Carter's own writings can be found in *The Writings of Elliott Carter,* ed. by Else Stone and Kurt Stone (Bloomington: Indiana University Press, 1977), and *Elliott Carter: Collected Essays and Lectures,* 1937–1995, ed. by Jonathan Bernard (Rochester, NY: University of Rochester Press, 1997). See also Carter's own study of post-tonal harmony (including his own) in his *Harmony Book,* ed. by Nicholas Hopkins and John F. Link (New York: Carl Fischer, 2002).

♪♪♪ Example 10.18b   Metric reduction of 10.18a

84 to beat (quarter) = MM 189. The ratio between the new and the old tempos is 9:4 (that is, the tempo has accelerated by a 2.25 factor). In itself, performing such a tempo change with exactly accurate precision would be quite a challenge. With the metric modulation that Carter writes between the two tempos, however, the challenge disappears almost totally. First, we move from beat (dotted quarter) = MM 84 to beat (half note) = MM 63. This is still a complex 3:4 ratio, but one which is highly simplified by the quarter note = quarter note equivalence at the meter change in m. 200 (from $\frac{9}{8}$ to $\frac{3}{2}$). Then we move from beat (half note) = MM 63 to beat (quarter note) = MM 189. Here again, a complex 9:4 ratio is highly simplified by a half note = dotted half-note equivalence in m. 205 (meter change from $\frac{2}{2}$ to $\frac{3}{4}$). Example 10.18b shows a metric reduction of this passage, which should clarify the process of modulation from the original MM 84 to MM 189.

A second example from the same composition will help you understand the process of metric modulation. In this case, shown in Example 10.19a (with a metric reduction in Example 10.19b), the modulation takes us from beat (quarter note) = MM 96 to beat (quarter note) = MM 120, an increase of 5:4 (or 1.25). The intermediate steps include first a move to a beat (dotted quarter) = MM 80, a 5:6 ratio which, however, poses no problem because of the sixteenth-note equivalence between the two tempos (at the meter change from $\frac{5}{16}$ to $\frac{12}{16}$ in m. 134). A second step takes us from beat (dotted quarter) MM 80 to beat (quarter note) = MM 120, a 3:2 ratio that presents no difficulty because of the sixteenth-note equivalence at the meter change from $\frac{6}{8}$ to $\frac{3}{4}$ in m. 137. The original tempo increase by a 5:4 ratio, from MM 96 to MM 120, can thus be accurately performed through this metric modulation.

Simultaneous Speeds

Metric modulation refers to the connection between successive tempos. At other times, however, we find the use of **simultaneous speeds** or tempos in Carter's music. This

Example 10.19a   Carter, String Quartet, no. 1, III, mm. 130–138

♪♪ Example 10.19b   Metric reduction of 10.19a

is the case, for instance, in the passage from the first string quartet reproduced in Example 10.20. All four instruments share the same notated metronomic marking, quarter note = 120. The actual tempo that we perceive for each instrument, however, is not determined in this case by the collective beat, but by the rate of speed at which each instrument actually moves. The slowest moving instrument is the first violin, whose prevailing duration is a dotted half note plus a triplet eighth note. As you can see on the example, this duration is prevailing, but not exclusively regular. The second violin moves mostly at a speed of quarter note plus sixteenth note, with some shortening of values in mm. 27–28. The initial speed for the cello is quarter note, replaced by a longer value of half note plus eighth note in mm. 27–30. Finally, the fastest-moving instrument, the viola, moves in consistent quarter-note triplets. What we hear in this passage, then, is a complex of tempo layers, or "tempo stratification."

ANALYSIS 10.2: MUSICAL CHARACTERS IN CARTER'S STRING QUARTET NO. 2, I (ANTHOLOGY NO. 28)

Carter at times thought of his instruments as representing characters or personalities. Each of the instrumental layers could thus embody some distinctive personality traits which, through their interrelationships (such as companionship or confrontation), give the music a dramatic aspect. A good example of character layers is provided by the String Quartet no. 2 (1959), of which we will examine the first movement (Anthology no. 28). Carter thought of each of the instruments in this quartet as representing different personalities and psychological types. Thus, the first violin in this quartet represents a virtuoso character with a manic psychological type. This character lives in a time world of contrasting fast and slow motions. The viola, representing a depressive psychological type, is doleful and moody, and lives in a time world of expressive rubatos where time changes along with moods. The cello represents a self-indulging romantic character, of a hysterical psychological type, living in a world of uneven tempos

| Example 10.20 | Carter, String Quartet no. 1, I, mm. 22–30 |

marked by accelerandos and ritardandos. Finally, the compulsive second violin tries to create some sense of order and continuity, and lives in a world of regular, steady motion.[7] Each of the instruments in turn is assigned a soloist's role in one of the quartet's movements. In the first movement the soloist is the first violin.

---

[7]See Schiff, *The Music of Elliott Carter,* pp. 71–78, and Bernard, "The Evolution of Elliott Carter's Rhythmic Practice," 183–87.

First violin: m3, P5, M9, M10 (intervals 3, 7, 14, and 16)

Second violin: M3, M6, M7 (intervals 4, 9, and 11)

Viola: TT, m7, m9 (intervals 6, 10, and 13)

Cello: P4, m6, compound TT (intervals 5, 8, and 18 or 30)

Figure 10.2 The intervallic repertoires in Carter's String Quartet no. 2

The Intervallic Repertoires

The stratification of these four characters is brought about through specific repertoires of intervals, rhythms, and musical gestures assigned to each instrument. These repertoires are not exclusive: instruments do interact and share materials among each other, and one can find numerous intervals or elements other than the ones listed as characteristic for each instrument, although the characteristic elements are indeed what defines each instrument's part in a most distinctive way.

The **intervallic repertoires** for each of the instruments are shown in Figure 10.2. You can see to what extent these intervals determine each of the lines by examining Example 10.21. Only the intervals from the repertoire have been labeled in this example. Other intervals are present (especially major and minor seconds, which are not listed in the repertoire list as being characteristic of any instrument, and appear in all of them), but the intervals from the repertoire make up most of the intervallic relationships in the music. As a further sample, examine the intervals in each of the instruments in the closing measures of the movement (mm. 130–134). Do you find that the interval repertoires form the basic intervallic material for this passage, too?

The Four Rhythmic Characters

Besides their intervallic content, the four personalities are also represented by their rhythmic and tempo characteristics. The first violin features virtuosic, fast-moving outbursts in which quintuplets abound (as in mm. 35–40, 51–53, 57–60, and so on), as do groups of six sixteenth notes (in such compound-meter passages as mm. 69–74 or 117–134). Such passages contrast with other slow-moving phrases, such as mm. 80–86, 92–96, or 110–115. The role of the second violin in this movement, on the other hand, is subdued and low key. Its appearances are limited to single-note, double-stop, or chordal isolated punctuations until mm. 75–80, where it features a passage of regular, on-the-beat pulses, which, however, begin disintegrating by m. 81. The second violin's brief attempt at providing some tempo and rhythmic stability to the shifting, mercurial temporal world of his companions seems to have been futile, at least for the time being (the second violin will eventually be more successful at it in the second movement).

Both "romantic" characters, viola and cello, begin the movement with fairly consistent speeds provided by eighth-note and triplet figures. Soon, however, the cello falls into its pattern of written-in accelerandos and ritardandos, as in mm. 54–72 or 79–86.

Example 10.21   Carter, String Quartet no. 2, I, mm. 80–83

The viola's figures, on the other hand, continue mostly in groupings of three notes, but with written-in rubato effects. See, for instance, the figures in mm. 62–63, 68–70, and 74–83. Little by little throughout the movement, the three lower instruments assert themselves against the supremacy of the first violin. By the end of the movement, all four instruments are actively contributing to a complex rhythmic texture in which they all (except for the second violin) seem to be competing for leadership.

ANALYSIS 10.3: STOCKHAUSEN, *STIMMUNG* (ANTHOLOGY NO. 29)

The examples we have studied so far in this chapter illustrate the expansion by some composers of concepts and techniques related to rhythm, meter, tempo, and tempo relationships. The work we are going to discuss now stretches the concept of musical time itself. Anthology no. 29 reproduces a few representative pages of an unconventional score by Karlheinz Stockhausen (born 1928), *Stimmung* for six vocalists (1968). Rather than "analyzing" this score, we will discuss some of the temporal and aesthetic issues raised by it. But let us first understand how the score, the performance, and the structure of this composition work.

The Score and the Performance

The main pitch element of this composition is a B♭ Mm 9th chord, which is sustained by the voices (complete or incomplete, and with occasional minor variations) throughout the duration of the piece. The chord is also played electronically behind the singers (and not heard by the audience), as an aural tonal reference. The duration is open, but performances usually last at least 70 or 75 minutes.

The *Formschema*

The compositional plan for the piece is laid out in the *Formschema* which is reproduced in Anthology no. 29. The composition is divided into 51 sections, each led by a different singer (indicated on the *Formschema* by a darker line for the leading singer in each section). Each singer has a different set of eight or nine "models" for his or her performance. The model sheet for one of the singers, showing the nine models this particular singer can choose from, is reproduced in Anthology no. 29. When a singer has the leading role, he or she chooses, and starts performing, one of the models in his or her sheet. The rest of the singers progressively adapt their own performances to the leader's chosen model (they do so by ear), until they all reach "identity," and then they move on to the next section, where a new leader will begin the process again by choosing one of his or her models.

The Models

The models essentially contain a set of phonetic instructions and some rhythmic patterns on which phonetic collections are delivered. Singers are required to learn a special vocal technique, by which they can produce different overtones while singing the vowels of the international phonetic alphabet. The **international phonetic alphabet** is a set of symbols used in phonetic transcription that contains a different symbol for every speech sound that can be distinguished in any language. Stockhausen uses these symbols on his model sheets to indicate the exact sound the singer will sing. Moreover, by changing the position of the lips, mouth, or tongue, one can bring out specific overtones within each sound (a process for which the singer needs particular training before attempting to perform this piece). The desired overtones are indicated by numbers above or below the phonetic symbols. Singers are required to sing softly, without vibrato, and with a microphone (one per singer) placed very close to the mouth.[8]

Other Compositional Elements

Some of the models call for the recitation of poems. These are love poems with an intense erotic content, written by Stockhausen (in German) in what he has described as an "amorous interlude" at Sausalito, California, in 1967.

The letter "N" in some of the sections in the *Formschema,* moreover, indicates that in that section the voices may call one of the names that Stockhausen refers to as

---

[8]For a study of the central role of text and phonemes in the compositional process of *Stimmung,* see Emily Snyder Laugesen, "Construing Text as Music in Berio's *Thema (Omaggio a Joyce)* and Stockhausen's *Stimmung*" (Ph.D. dissertation, Columbia University, 2003).

"magic names." Each of the singers receives a sheet with eleven such names, which are actually names of divinities in a variety of cultures and traditions of the world. The sheet of "magic names" reproduced in Anthology no. 29, for instance, contains names only from the ancient Greek and Roman mythologies.

In some sections in the *Formschema,* particular singers, marked by the symbol "var.", are instructed to deviate from the main model in pitch, tempo, rhythm, timbre, or distribution of accents. These are the only possible pitch deviations from the pervading B♭ Mm 9th chord, and they should "move away and come back to the model in continuous fashion," as stated in the performance instructions.

Listen to the piece, or at least to a fragment ten or fifteen minutes long. Before we move on to interpret and discuss the issues involved in this composition, try to address some of them. How does this piece depart (in quite a few ways) from conventional composition? What are the temporal issues involved in performing or listening to this piece? How would you characterize the aesthetic characteristics of the piece and the types of temporality created by the piece's syntax? What would you say are the main differences between the temporal aspects of listening to, say, a Beethoven symphony or listening to *Stimmung*?

Linearity and Nonlinearity in Musical Time

In his study of musical time, Jonathan Kramer distinguishes between musical linearity and nonlinearity.[9] Understanding these two concepts is essential to a discussion of temporality in *Stimmung*. **Musical linearity** takes place when some musical events are determined by implications that arise from earlier events in the piece. Musical linearity results in linear time, in which events are a consequence of earlier events. Most of the music of the common-practice period, ruled by the principles of functional tonality, is linear. Some degrees in the tonal system create a sense of stability, others create a sense of instability and direction. Instability and direction create a drive toward a goal (the resolution to stability), and thus a linear sense of time. We have all experienced this linearity of musical time when, during an extended dominant pedal or prolongation (perhaps at the end of a sonata-form development or toward the end of a fugue), we have been aware of the harmonic tension creating a directed motion toward a resolution. When the resolution comes, in the form of a return of the tonic, we feel that the goal has been reached, and the tension has resolved into stability. Linearity is also often present in post-tonal music, although in this case it is created more by specific contexts than by a preestablished system of tensions and resolutions. A frequent contextual source of linearity in post-tonal music is voice leading. In Chapter 5 we have seen, for instance, how both Hindemith (in the Interlude in G) and Stravinsky (in the Mass) create a drive to the cadence by means of linear voice leading. Although there are no functional harmonic tensions in these examples, we can hear the cadential resolution as a goal because of the contextual linearity that results from voice leading. Normally, however, this type of linearity is present only at the local level (as we approach the cadence, for instance) rather than at a large-scale level, and for this reason Kramer calls it **nondirected linearity.**

[9]Jonathan Kramer, *The Time of Music* (New York: Schirmer, 1988).

Musical nonlinearity, on the other hand, takes place when musical events are determined by principles that govern the entire composition or section, rather than by earlier events. In nonlinear time we don't hear an event as a consequence of a previous event, but rather as part of a whole that is governed by some principles. Nonlinearity is common in twentieth-century music. We have studied a number of compositions that featured harmonic stasis, and where events succeeded one another, but did not necessarily imply one another. Think, for instance, of the Introduction to *The Rite of Spring* that we analyzed in Chapter 1. How would you argue that that is an example of musical nonlinearity? Can you think of other examples from among the pieces we have studied in which musical time could be said to be nonlinear?

Moment Time and Vertical Time

In his article "Moment Form," Stockhausen proposes the concept of moment form, from which Kramer derives his own concept of **moment time.**[10] In moment form, music is made up of a series of events ("moments") that may be related (for instance, motivically or rhythmically), but not connected by transitional processes. That is, in moment time, "moments" succeed each other in a discontinuous, nonlinear way. A moment does not imply the next moment. A moment is self-contained, independent, and static (in that it does not create an implication or directed motion to the next moment). The motion to the next moment is marked by discontinuity, not by the linear realization of an implication. Moment forms can be found in numerous works by Stockhausen (for instance, in *Kontakte* and *Momente*), but also in the music of many other twentieth-century composers.[11] The technique of juxtaposition of musical blocks, which we have discussed in Stravinsky and Messiaen, lends itself particularly well to moment time. The concept of moment time can indeed help us understand the temporal processes and discontinuities in works such as *The Rite of Spring* and *Turangalîla Symphony,* and especially in later works by Messiaen such as *Couleurs de la cité céleste.* How do the concepts of moment time and moment form apply to the Introduction of *The Rite,* the "Lacrimosa" from *Requiem Canticles,* and the Introduction to *Turangalîla Symphony* (Anthology nos. 4, 24, and 27, respectively)?

Beyond, and as an extension of, moment time, Kramer develops the concept of **vertical time.** When the moment becomes the whole piece, we can speak of music (and musical time) in which not only there is no linearity, but moreover, there are no discontinuities or divisions (such as phrases, sections, cadences, and the like), but only a continuum of static time. In Kramer's words, "a vertically conceived piece, then, does not exhibit large-scale closure. It does not begin but merely starts. It does not build to a climax, does not purposefully set up internal expectations, does not seek to fulfill any expectations that might arise accidentally, does not build or release tension, and does not end but simply ceases. . . No event depends on any other event."[12] Both moment

[10]Karlheinz Stockhausen, "Momentform," in *Texte zur elektronischen un instrumentales Musik,* vol. 1 (Cologne: DuMont, 1963), pp. 189–210. See also Kramer, *The Time of Music,* pp. 201–04, as well as the rest of his Chapter 8.

[11]For a general introduction to the music of Stockhausen, see Robin Maconie, *The Works of Karlheinz Stockhausen* (Oxford: Clarendon Press, 1990).

[12]Kramer, p. 55.

and vertical times are concepts we can find in non-Western music and other cultural manifestations (particularly, but not only, within the Buddhist realm). The stress in both types of temporality is on "being" rather than "becoming," to use traditional philosophical terms. Vertical music simply "is." It comes from nowhere (other than from itself) and goes nowhere (other than to itself). It is static, it exists only in the present moment, in a perpetual "now" that is preceded and followed by an infinitude of equal or very similar "nows."

To appreciate to their full extent the temporal aesthetics of vertical music, listeners would ideally drop all expectations of goal-oriented, directed motion. They would enter this timeless present with no projections of future, and would listen to what the present "now" has to offer, as if becoming part of the music, and as if letting their own emotional and mental activity be stopped (and replaced) by the vertical stasis of musical time. In John Cage's words, "the wisest thing to do is to open one's ears immediately and hear a sound suddenly before one's thinking has a chance to turn it into something logical, abstract, or symbolical."[13]

The Time of *Stimmung*

Listen again to a substantial fragment of *Stimmung* and, in the light of our discussion of different types of musical temporality, make some observations about time in this composition. The following discussion provides some possible ideas (although certainly not the only possible ones—you are welcome to argue differently or even to the contrary if you want to do so) on *Stimmung*'s temporality.

The first thing that strikes us when we listen to *Stimmung* is the nonlinear character of it musical time. Although the general impression we get from this piece may be one of stasis, we actually hear both stasis and activity. The stasis is provided by the unchanging B♭ chord. The activity is provided by the various timbres, rhythms, syllables, and other events that result from the performance of the models. But although at times we hear substantial activity, we cannot detect implications that would result from an event necessarily generating another event. We don't really know what will be next after we hear an event (taking into account, especially, that every performance will be different). One could argue that once a leader begins, the other singers will follow, sooner or later, with the same material as the leader, and that this process could signify implication. But this process is improvisatory: in most cases singers will slowly transform whatever they were singing into the model the leader is singing. This process of transformation is unpredictable. And, in any case, we can also argue that these processes of adaptation to the current model "are determined by principles that govern the entire composition or section, rather than by earlier events," quoting from the definition of nonlinearity we have previously studied.

If time in *Stimmung* is nonlinear, can we say that it illustrates moment time or vertical time? We can indeed think of the whole piece as being a single moment. Each of the fifty-one sections could be considered a division, but the transition from one section to the next is seamless, and moreover all the models are similar enough that we cannot

---

[13]Kramer, p. 384. Originally quoted in Michael Nyman, *Experimental Music: Cage and Beyond* (New York: Schirmer, 1974), p. 1.

perceive any clear change from one to the next. Thus, although we could think of moment time as relating the different events taking place in the piece, its overwhelming continuity points at vertical time. The unchanging B♭ is another element of verticality, and so is the essentially unchanging character of the music and its total lack of linear expectations. We can indeed say that *Stimmung* does not begin or end (but rather starts and stops). Any moment in the piece is a "now" that is essentially the same as any other moment in the piece. The music never builds to a climax, neither is the listener led to expect the arrival of one. In the liner note for the recording of *Stimmung* by *Collegium Vocale*, Stockhausen writes: "Certainly *Stimmung* is meditative music. Time is suspended. One listens to the inner self of the sound, the inner self of the harmonic spectrum, the inner self of the vowel, *THE INNER SELF*. Subtlest fluctuations, scarcely a ripple. *ALL THE SENSES* alert and calm. In the beauty of the sensual shines the beauty of the eternal."[14]

Conclusions

In our discussion of *Stimmung* we have introduced several concepts of time that are relevant not only to a lot of music written in the twentieth century, but also to many non-Western musical styles. The aesthetic experience of listening to this type of music changes dramatically when we take these temporal types into consideration, and we place our listening in the "correct" mode. Listening to *Stimmung* with a linear mindset (that is, with the expectation of tensions that will lead to a climax, or of harmonically shaped phrases, or of events that follow each other according to predictable implications) will almost certainly lead to boredom and rejection of the static nature of the music, where nothing of what was expected is actually happening. Listening, on the other hand, with awareness of nonlinearity and temporal verticality should lead to an enjoyment of the music for what it really has to offer, and it will afford the listener a perceptual and temporal experience remarkably different from the one afforded by linearly conceived music.

---

[14]Stockhausen, liner notes for the LP *Stimmung,* by *Collegium Vocale Köln* (Deutsche Grammophon 2543–003, 1971).

APPLICATION AND CLASS DISCUSSION

In this chapter we have studied a variety of complex temporal techniques (involving rhythm, meter, tempo, and time) in the music of three representative twentieth-century composers. How does the knowledge of these techniques affect the way you listen to the music we have studied in this chapter? How does your knowledge of linearity and nonlinearity enrich the way you can understand and appreciate musical time? Chronometric, or physical, time is measurable and quantifiable. Psychological time is not and may have a strong subjective component (you may experience both general time and musical time as passing very slowly or very quickly, depending on many circumstances). How do chronometric and psychological time interact in music? Musical time is hardly just chronometric. How do the concepts of moment time and vertical time contribute to your understanding of nonchronometric musical time?

Further Listening

The following list provides suggestions for further listening to music by composers studied in this chapter or related to the styles and techniques we have studied (if possible, listen while following the score):

1. Messiaen, *Quartet for the End of Time*
2. Messiaen, *Chronochromie*
3. Messiaen, *Couleurs de la cité céleste*
4. Carter, *Variations for Orchestra*
5. Carter, *Double Concerto*
6. Stockhausen, *Mixtur*
7. Stockhausen, *Momente*
8. Morton Feldman, *Three Voices*
9. Feldman, *Why Patterns?*
10. Conlon Nancarrow, selected Studies for player piano
11. György Ligeti, *Lontano*
12. Ligeti, selected Études for piano

Terms for Review

rhythm
meter
pulses
beats
syncopation
hemiola
symmetrical or divisive meters
asymmetrical or additive meters
changing (or mixed) meters
irregular rhythmic groupings
metric displacement
polymeter
polyrhythm
modes of limited transposition
tāla
rhythms with added values
rhythmic augmentation or diminution
proportional augmentation
augmentation by a fixed value

inexact augmentation
nonretrogradable rhythm
rhythmic pedal
ostinato
rhythmic canon
generative rhythm
seed
recursive progression
progressive rhythm
chromatic progression
metric modulation
simultaneous speeds
intervallic repertoire
international phonetic alphabet
musical linearity
nondirected linearity
musical nonlinearity
moment time
vertical time

CHAPTER 10 ASSIGNMENTS

I. Theory

1. Write a whole-tone melody in $\frac{7}{8}$.

2. Write a Lydian melody in 3 + 2 + 2 + 3 over 8.

3. Write an octatonic melody with changing meters.

4. Write a chordal passage (in repeated block chords) for piano, in $\frac{4}{4}$, with irregular rhythmic groupings created by accents. Use a repeated added-note chord derived from one of Messiaen's modes of limited transposition.

5. Write a passage for a single melodic instrument featuring metric displacement of a melodic cell.

6. Write a passage for two instruments featuring polymeter. The line for each instrument will be a repeated, simple whole-tone melodic ostinato, and each instrument will be in a different meter.

7. Write a passage for three instruments featuring polyrhythm. The line for each instrument will be a repeated, simple octatonic melodic ostinato. All three instruments will be in the same meter, but their rhythms will be different, either because of groupings of different lengths among them or because of different beat subdivisions among each of the instruments.

8. Write a musical passage made up of three rhythmic pedals for three different instruments. Two of the pedals will be based on the repetition of two of the *deśītālas* listed below. The third layer will be a continuous stream of sixteenth notes grouped into a seven-pitch ostinato pattern. Choose a different mode (from Messiaen's pitch modes) to provide the pitch material for each of the three layers.

    Three *deśītālas* :

    no. 37, *rangābharana,* 3 2 2 <2>

    no. 77, *gajajhampa,* 2 2 3 4 <4>

    no. 105, *candrakalā,* 2 2 2 3 3 3 <1>

9. Write five different, brief, nonretrogradable rhythmic patterns.

10. Choose one of your nonretrogradable patterns from Exercise 2, and starting from it as a seed, use it to generate a recursive progression following the procedures illustrated in Example 10.16 and 10.17. Then do the same with another one of your nonretrogradable rhythms.

II. Analysis

1. Analyze the rhythmic techniques in the following passages from Messiaen's *Turangalîla Symphony*:

    a. Movement 2, "Chant d'amour 1," reh. 29–40

    b. Movement 3, "Turangalîla 1," reh. 9–13

    For both of these passages, identify the main rhythmic layers or pedals, and discuss the patterns, groupings, and possible characteristic rhythmic techniques used in them. Write a brief essay explaining your findings in each of these passages.

2. Study and explain the exact process of metric modulation that takes place in the following passages by Elliott Carter: String Quartet no. 1, I, mm. 210–216, and mm. 222–230. For both passages, provide a brief narrative similar to the explanations of Examples 10.18 and 10.19 in this chapter, and provide also metric reductions similar to the ones found in Examples 10.18b and 10.19b.

3. Study and explain the tempo relationships among voices in the following passages by Carter: String Quartet no. 1, I, mm. 312–351; and String Quartet no. 1, III, mm. 282–300.

4. Analyze the second movement of Carter's String Quartet no. 2 (II, Presto scherzando) in terms of intervallic repertoires and rhythmic characters. Write a brief essay explaining your observations.

5. Choose one piece from each of the two groups listed below. Listen to the pieces you choose (or at least to part of them), following the score if one is available, and write a brief essay explaining the temporal characteristics of each piece. Do these pieces feature linear or nonlinear temporal modes? If they are nonlinear, are they examples of moment time or of vertical time? Provide reasons for your observations.

   a. Messiaen, *Chronochromie,* Introduction, or Stockhausen, *Mixtur*

   b. Any of the three following pieces by Morton Feldman: *Three Voices, Why Patterns?,* or *For Frank O'Hara*

III. Composition

1. Compose a piece for four different instruments, using the compositional techniques we have studied in Messiaen's *Turangalîla Symphony.* The texture of the piece will be layered, layers will be based on rhythmic pedals, and each instrumental line will be based on a characteristic rhythmic technique. Use one or two of the *deśītālas* we have learned in this chapter. Your rhythmic layers should also feature nonretrogradable rhythms, rhythms with added values, or augmented and diminished rhythms, and you should use several of Messiaen's rhythmic techniques, such as recursive progression, progressive rhythm, chromatic progression, and so on. Draw your pitch materials from Messiaen's modes of limited transposition. Write a brief essay explaining the techniques you have used in your composition.

2. Compose a piece for three or four different instruments using some kind of tempo relationships in the style of Carter. You may decide to connect different tempo sections by metric modulations, or you may instead decide to write instrumental layers of simultaneous tempos in which each instrument moves at its own speed. Your instrumental lines should also reflect musical personalities, defined by particular intervallic repertoires and rhythmic characters. Write a brief essay explaining the techniques you have used in your composition.

3. Compose a piece in which you will apply the concept of vertical time as we have studied it in this chapter. Your music should be nonlinear, essentially static, and whatever activity there is should be determined by the principles of the whole composition and not implied by some previous event.

Chapter 11

Aleatory Music, Sound Mass, and Beyond

As we suggested in Chapter 9, the 1960s and 1970s are among the most diverse and richest years in the history of musical composition in the twentieth century. Numerous compositional trends and new techniques appeared in both Europe and America in these two decades. As we have already mentioned, there were, at first, two general approaches to composition among the young generation of composers after World War II. The first approach, which we studied in Chapter 9, arose from the wish to exert rigorous control over musical materials. The second approach arose from the wish to relinquish such control and allow elements of chance to intervene in the act of composition.

The term **aleatory** refers to any compositional process in which some elements are not exactly determined by the composer and are either left indeterminate (a process we refer to as **indeterminacy**) or are determined by some process in which chance plays a definitive role (the Latin term *alea* means die—as in "the die is cast"). In aleatory music, some of the final decisions as to the exact materials used in a composition or the way they are used are often left to the performer, who makes the decision at the moment of the actual performance. Scores in this type of music may include instructions that leave some choices to the performer, or may include some kind of graphic notation that may be interpreted in various ways by the performer. Indeterminate music thus not only presupposes that the composer gives up some of the compositional control, but also builds in a certain level of improvisation on the part of the performer. The leading exponent of indeterminacy and aleatory composition, as well as an early practitioner of compositional methods that involved chance (beginning in the early 1950s) was John Cage. Following Cage's powerful influence in avant-garde musical circles, most major American and European experimental composers in the 1960s used aleatory procedures at one level or another.

By the end of the 1950s, both general trends (control and chance) merged in the works of some composers, and various styles, including various types of sound-mass composition, resulted from the combination of partial control and partially aleatory procedures. In **sound-mass composition,** or **textural composition,** individual pitches and lines are integrated into complexes of sound ("sound masses"). In sound masses we do not perceive individual pitches, but rather chromatically filled complexes of sound.

These sound blocks may result from multiple, minutely notated chromatic lines that fuse into each other (and then the sound masses are dynamic, in constant motion and transformation), as in György Ligeti's *Atmosphères* (1961), or they may result from more static **clusters** (blocks of sound made up of adjacent chromatic or microtonal steps), as in Krzysztof Penderecki's *Threnody for the Victims of Hiroshima* of 1960. (The term **microtonal** refers to music that includes quarter-tone accidentals for which special quarter-tone symbols are used.) At times, clusters are notated pitch by pitch in conventional notation, whereas at other times they are indicated graphically, usually by means of solid black bands on the score. In sound-mass compositions, musical elements such as texture, density, register, dynamics, and instrumental color replace such musical parameters as rhythm, meter, lines, chords, and harmony, usually considered as "primary" in a more traditional compositional context.

In this chapter we will first discuss some of the compositional techniques used by John Cage, with particular focus on his piece *Winter Music*. This will be followed by a movement from a work that demonstrates both aleatory techniques and sound-mass composition, Lutosławski's *Jeux vénitiens*. We will then study an example by Ligeti that illustrates his use of harmonic and spatial processes in some of his works of the late 1960s and early 1970s.

NOTE

The same diversity of styles and techniques that are covered in this chapter (and in the following chapters) also explains the need for analytical eclecticism. We will use, in each case, the analytical technique that best suits the particular music we are studying, among a variety of possible analytical approaches.

JOHN CAGE'S CREATIVE JOURNEY

Widely recognized as one of the most influential American composers in the twentieth century, John Cage (1912–1992) has also been one of the most controversial and misunderstood composers in the century's history. His early years as a composer (1933–1948) were mostly devoted to composing for percussion instruments and for **prepared piano** (a piano with various objects inserted between and over the strings to create percussive sounds and altered timbres). Toward the late 1940s, Cage progressively discovered and studied Eastern spiritual philosophies, an interest that had a deep and lasting impact in his life, in his thinking, and in his approaches to composition. He was indeed deeply influenced, at various stages in his life, by Indian spirituality (in particular by the teachings of Sri Ramakrishna and the philosophy of art expounded by Ananda K. Coomaraswamy), by the writings of Meister Eckhart (a Medieval Christian gnostic), and by Zen Buddhism, particularly the Zen master Huang Po. Understanding the influence of these sources on Cage's thought is essential to understanding his music. The teachings of all these masters have in common an emphasis on silence and unselfconsciousness (negation of the self) as a means to attain spiritual realization. One of Cage's formulations of the purpose of music, coming directly from Indian philosophy, is "To sober and quiet the mind thus rendering it susceptible to divine influences." Similarly, Cage learned from Eckhart that "It is in stillness, in the silence, that the word of God is to be heard." And, from Huang Po, Cage learned the doctrine of "no-mindedness," according to which spiritual realization requires unity with the Universal Mind, which in turn requires detachment from the sphere of phenomena and of individual thoughts.[1]

These ideas are central to Cage's musical development after 1951. In a first stage of this development, Cage turned to **chance operations** for his compositional processes. By turning to chance, Cage was practicing the act of silencing his mind of musical thoughts and was opening it to the influence of the "universal idea" (as opposed to the individual's idea or creative act). The musical material for one of the most important compositions of this period, *Music of Changes* for piano (1951), is based on charts of musical events. Each chart contains 64 cells (in 8×8 arrangements) of either pitch sonorities, durations, or dynamics. Cage chose particular items in his charts by associating them to the 64 hexagrams of the *I Ching,* the ancient oracle contained in the Chinese *Book of Changes.* Each hexagram is made up of six lines, some of which are broken and some solid, and each hexagram provides an answer to various situations in life (three of these hexagrams are shown in Figure 11.1). The consultation of the *I Ching* as an oracle involves tossing coins to find a particular hexagram, and with it, a particular answer to a problem. This is exactly the way Cage used the *I Ching* as a compositional tool in *Music of Changes* and other pieces of this period. By tossing coins (to decide on solid or broken lines) he arrived at particular hexagrams, which were then matched with the corresponding musical events in the precomposed charts, in a laborious and time-consuming process (*Music of Changes* took nine months to complete). The resulting score was a totally determined score (that is, it is fully notated as it must be performed), but important aspects of the compositional process, such as the particular successions of pitch events, durations, and dynamics, are left to chance.

The concepts of silence, stillness, and no-mindedness also help us understand the context of what is probably Cage's best-known piece, *4′ 33″* (1952). In this composition, a performer (usually, but not necessarily, a pianist) remains totally silent during the duration of the piece (four minutes and thirty-three seconds). The piece is in a way the ultimate instance of creative non-action and stillness. It is the musical realization of Cage's introductory statement to his book *Silence* (p. xii):

> nothing is accomplished by writing a piece of music
> nothing is accomplished by hearing a piece of music
> nothing is accomplished by playing a piece of music
> our ears are now in excellent condition.

---

[1]These influences of Eastern and Medieval mystic philosophies on Cage's thought are thoroughly discussed in James Pritchett's *The Music of John Cage* (Cambridge: Cambridge University Press, 1993). This book—which was the main source for the present discussion—is particularly recommended as a general introduction to Cage's music, thought and compositional life. Cage's own lectures and writings are also essential to understanding his thought and are collected in several volumes. See, particularly, *Silence* (Middletown, CT: Wesleyan University Press, 1961), and *A Year from Monday* (Middletown, CT: Wesleyan University Press, 1967).

Chun   Mêng   Hsü

Figure 11.1 Three hexagrams from the *I Ching*

4′ 33″, moreover, is consistent with Cage's focus on music as *the art of time* (in contrast to the art of organized sounds in time). The structure of *4′ 33″* lies in its duration, not in its sound. Unlike what one may think, however, the piece is also based on sound (though not organized sound). Cage was also interested in the sounds of everyday life and the environment, and in breaking the barrier between life and art, or between the sounds of "concert music" and the common sounds of life. That is achieved in *4′ 33″,* where the attentive listener will hear numerous sounds (of coughing, of seats creaking, of program rustling, of fans and room ventilation, perhaps even of people leaving the hall in impatient annoyance).

This fusion of life and music is even more patent in Cage's pieces of action music. Cage's scores of **action music** are often textual instructions in which Cage proposes an action or a number of actions (sometimes specific, at other times to be freely chosen by the performer) to be performed in front of the audience. The score of *0′ 00″* (1962) consists of a single sentence: "In a situation provided with maximum amplification (no feedback), perform a disciplined action." In Cage's first performance of this piece, he sat on a landing of a museum staircase writing letters on a typewriter. Microphones captured all the sounds produced by the action (chair squeaks, gulping sounds of Cage drinking water, the clacks of the typewriter, and so forth). The (puzzled) audience in the museum could hear these sounds loudly amplified by the museum's sound system. When Cage finished writing his letters, the piece was over.

Cage's action pieces are among the earliest examples of **performance art** (a form of art in which some particular actions of an individual or group constitute the work). Cage's breaking of boundaries between life and art, on the other hand, also reflects Cage's interest in the work of French–American artist Marcel Duchamp (1887–1968), a close friend of his. Duchamp proposed (and practiced) the elevation of everyday items or *objects trouvés* ("found objects," such as a bicycle wheel, a kitchen stool, or, in his highly influential work of 1917, *Fountain,* a urinal) to the status of works of art, by exhibiting them at museums and art galleries.

The term "chance," in the context of Cage's music, refers to the use of compositional procedures that involve randomness in the choice of musical events. The term "indeterminacy," on the other hand, refers to a process in which a piece allows the performer a variety of choices (left indeterminate by the composer). The piece will thus be different every time it is performed. The concept of indeterminate composition was particularly developed through the 1950s by a group of composers we know as **The New York School,** and which included John Cage and three younger composers who were close to him: Morton Feldman, Christian Wolff, and Earle Brown. A piece such as *Music of Changes* includes the element of chance as an essential component of the compositional process. Nevertheless, the final result is a minutely notated and determinate score. A turn toward more indeterminate scores required the use of different types of notation. To this effect, Cage adopted a variety of **graphic and spatial notations** that, rather than imposing specific pitch and temporal structures on performers, required interpretation and a decision-making process (as well as possible improvisation) on their part.

An example of indeterminate notation is shown in Example 11.1. The score for Cage's *Concert for Piano and Orchestra* (1957–58) consists of a "Solo for Piano" made up of sixty-three large and loose pages, and separate solos for each of the instruments that make up the ensemble. The piano part contains a large number of individual events notated in a variety of ways and grouped into eighty-four different notation types identified by letter combinations. The general instructions for the piano part are as follows: "Each page is one system for a single pianist to be played with or without any or all parts written for orchestral instruments. The whole is to be taken as a body of material presentable at any point between minimum (nothing played) and maximum (everything played), both horizontally and vertically: A program made within a determined length of time (to be altered by a conductor when there is one) may involve any reading, i.e., any sequence of parts or parts thereof." Example 11.1 shows one event of the AY notational type. The directions for this type are as follows: "Graph music. ¹⁄₁₀ inch square = time unit. Numbers within are of tones that may complete their appearance within any amount of time area given them by graph. Vertical graph is frequency, the treble and bass areas mobile as indicated." Read these two sets of instructions carefully, and discuss their elements of indeterminacy. What options is Cage giving the performer, and what decisions does the performer need to make? If you were to perform this piece (and this particular passage), how would you go about it?

NOTE

In Chapter 6 we studied the music of some composers who were part of the American ultramodern movement, and we mentioned Henry Cowell as one of them. The ultramodern tradition of experimentation (in areas such as new instruments, new tunings, new textures, and borrowing instruments and techniques from non-Western musical traditions), of which Cowell is an excellent representative, was continued by several composers of the following generation, including two of Cowell's students: John Cage (who studied with Cowell), Conlon Nancarrow, and two West Coast composers, Harry Partch and Lou Harrison (also a Cowell student).

♪♪♪ Example 11.1   John Cage, *Concert for Piano and Orchestra,* "Solo for Piano," p. 40, notation type AY

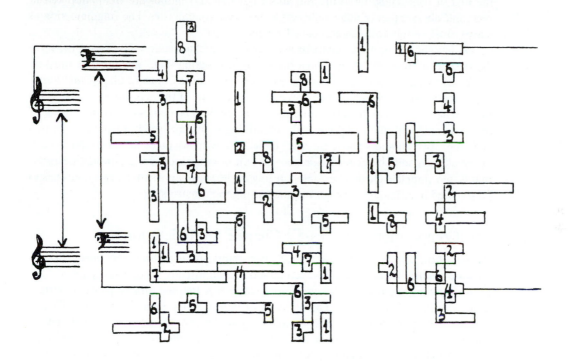

ANALYSIS 11.1: CAGE, *WINTER MUSIC* (ANTHOLOGY NO. 30)

Anthology no. 30 reproduces one page of Cage's *Winter Music* (1957). The complete score of the piece, "To be performed in whole or part, by 1 to 20 pianists," consists of twenty loose pages (all similar to the page reproduced in the anthology, with smaller or greater density of the same type of events).

The Score and the Performance Instructions

The instructions for the piece read as follows: "The 20 pages may be used in whole or part by a pianist or shared by 2 to 20 to provide a program of an agreed upon length. The notation, in space, 5 systems left to right on the page, may be freely interpreted as to time. An aggregate must be played as a single ictus. Where this is impossible, the unplayable notes shall be taken as harmonics prepared in advance. Harmonics may also be produced where they are not so required. Resonances, both of aggregates and individual notes of them, may be free in length. Overlappings, interpenetrations, are also free. The single staff is provided with two clef signs. Where these differ, ambiguity obtains in the proportion indicated by the 2 numbers notated above the aggregate, the first of these applying to the clef above the staff. Dynamics are free. An inked-in rectangle above a pair of notes indicates a chromatic tone-cluster. The fragmentation of staves arose simply from an absence of events."

A few matters in these instructions may require clarification. Cage uses the term "aggregate" to refer to "chordal sonorities." By instructing that "an aggregate must be played as a single ictus," he means that the complete sonority must be played simultaneously and at once, not in an arpeggiated or broken form. If the sonority is too large for the two hands to reach, then the unplayable notes should be depressed silently ahead of time and held with the pedal while the remaining notes are struck. In staves with two clef signs, two numbers above the staff indicate how many notes must be read in each of the clefs. A solid black rectangle above a pair of notes indicates a chromatic cluster, that is, the complete chromatic content filling in the space between the two notes has to be sounded in a single attack (for instance, using the forearms).

The Compositional Processes: Chance and Indeterminacy

Winter Music is an example of both chance composition and indeterminacy. To determine pitches, Cage used a chance method he had already used in other pieces, the **point-drawing method.** In this procedure, Cage first marked minute paper imperfections with points. After he had a collection of points on the page, he added staffs and clefs to turn these points into pitches, and then, in the case of our piece, he notated the result as we see on the page in the example. This same method was the origin of Cage's use of **musical tools** in many of his compositions after the late 1950s. A musical tool is some object that is usually superimposed on some other object that includes some kind of notation, to allow for a variety of possible readings of the same notation. In *Music Walk* (1958), for instance, Cage provides the performers with ten pages on which a number of points are marked. A transparency with a large set of five parallel lines (a "musical tool") is also provided, and performers are asked to superimpose the transparency on each of the sheets to provide a musical interpretation of the points. The dots are read as musical events, and each of the lines in the transparency represents a different timbral or attack category for the performance of the dots (such as notes plucked on muted strings, notes played on the keyboard, or noises made by striking the piano on the outside or the inside).

Many aspects of *Winter Music* are left indeterminate. First, the piece can be performed by one to twenty pianists, can be performed in whole or in part, and the duration of the piece is free. Second, although pitch is notated, the notation can be interpreted in many ways. Each event may or may not be performed, and events on a page can be performed in any order. Pitches in events that include two clefs can be read in a variety of ways. Although Cage indicates how many notes must be played in each clef (the numbers 1–2 in the first event in the second system of our example page mean that one note will be read in bass clef and two in treble clef), he does not specify which notes should be played in which clef. That is, in our example, any note can be played in bass clef, and then the remaining two notes will be played in treble clef. Pitch is thus not fixed in this piece, despite the apparent exact pitch notation. Other than pitch, no other musical elements are notated at all. Thus, durations and rhythm, dynamics and attack types are all left to the decision of the performer.

Conclusions

An analysis of this piece cannot go much beyond what we have already done. Because we are not dealing with any fixed musical elements at all (each performance will be based on different orders of pages and sound events, different readings of the actual pitches for events, different durations, dynamics, and so on), we have no fixed material that we can focus on for discussion. Cage, in his own words, wanted to allow "sounds to be themselves." That is, to let sounds be what they are, free of any relationships to other sounds, of conventional or preestablished linear or functional conventions. Chance and indeterminacy provide the means for the composer to get out of the way in the compositional process, as Cage intended to do. By doing so, and by not determining the compositional materials, Cage achieved true nonlinear temporality in his aleatory music.

ANALYSIS 11.2: LUTOSŁAWSKI, *JEUX VÉNITIENS*, I (ANTHOLOGY NO. 31)

Witold Lutosławski's *Jeux vénitiens* (1960–61) represented a breakthrough in the Polish composer's career after years of composing more traditionally oriented pieces. After listening to Cage's *Concert for Piano and Orchestra* on the radio in 1960, and beginning with *Jeux vénitiens,* Lutosławski (1913–1994) incorporated a number of new compositional elements in his music. *Jeux vénitiens,* which consolidated Lutosławski's position as one of the world's leading composers, is usually considered the first work in his period of compositional maturity. Some of the techniques that Lutosławski developed for this composition were to become essential elements in many of his works from the 1960s and 1970s. In particular, the concept of limited aleatory composition became an essential component in Lutosławski's music from this period. In **limited aleatory composition,** some essential elements are determined by the composer, and others are left undetermined. In the case of Lutosławski's music, form is usually predetermined, and so is the general, overall harmonic result, while exact simultaneities are not. In other words, the realization of contrapuntal and harmonic details is left to chance in performance. The term **aleatory counterpoint** is indeed also used to refer to this same technique. Precisely because of its indeterminate character, aleatory counterpoint results in a type of sound mass, although one in which the overall harmonic content, as we will soon see, is controlled. We will now discuss some of the compositional principles found in the first movement of *Jeux vénitiens.*[2] First, listen to

---

[2]The following sources provide good introductions to the music of Lutosławski: Steven Stucky, *Lutosławski and His Music* (Cambridge: Cambridge University Press, 1981), and Charles Bodman Rae, *The Music of Lutosławski* (London: Faber and Faber, 1994).

the movement and read the performance instructions. How are sections differentiated? How many different types of section are there? Can you describe the type of pitch material and musical process in each of the sections? Can you hear any spatial processes taking place throughout the movement?

Performance Instructions and Form

The score of this movement consists of eight boxed-in musical events labeled with capital letters. In his performance notes, Lutosławski provides the following order for the performance of the eight events: A–B–C–D–E–F–G–H. There are essentially two types of events in this group. A-type sections (A, C, E, and G) function as a refrain. The core of these sections is provided by the first box (labeled A–C–E–G), a set of very lively lines for the woodwinds that always begins with a punctuation by four percussion instruments (fourth box, also labeled A–C–E–G). Some instruments are added every time the A-type section recurs. Thus, the three timpani are added for sections C–E–G (third box), three brass instruments are added for sections E–G (second box), and the piano is added in section G (fifth box). With the exception of section E, each of the A-type sections increases in duration with respect to the previous one. Thus, the durations required by the composer for each section are A–12″, C–18″, E–6″, and G–24″.

The principle of aleatory counterpoint applies fully to the A-type sections. Each instrument is supposed to play its part independently from what the other instruments do. Lines are not metered, and dotted vertical lines simply mean a brief caesura, the duration of which is determined by the performer. Simultaneities are thus in no way determined by the composer and in fact will be different in every performance. Rhythmic values are only approximate and relative, and the general tempo should be around 140–150 for the eighth note. Each new A-type section (that is, sections C, E, and G) should not be started with the first phrase, but rather each performer chooses one of the subsequent phrases (determined by the caesuras) to begin. When performers get to the end of their parts, they must start again from the beginning.

Sections B, D, F, and H, on the other hand, function as contrasting interludes between the A-type sections. Each of these B-type sections is static, soft, and consists of string clusters (in contrast to the more active and louder A-type sections). Each begins with the same percussion punctuation as the A-type sections, and here again dotted bars and rhythmic values are only approximate and are used merely for orientation. The first violin part in section D is to be played freely and independently from the rest of the ensemble. Section F is the shortest of all (surprisingly so, as sections B and D had prepared us to expect a longer static section after section E), and can be heard as being grouped with sections E (which is also short) and G in an E–F–G formal unit.

Pitch Material and Spatial Relationships

The A-Type Sections

The basic pitch structures for this movement are twelve-tone chords and clusters. A-type sections feature twelve-tone chords, a characteristic type of sonority in Lutosławski's music. A **twelve-tone chord** is, in the first place, a harmonic collection that contains

♪♪♪ Example 11.2   Twelve-tone chords in *Jeux vénitiens*

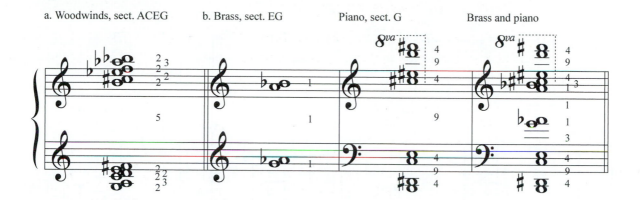

a. Woodwinds, sect. ACEG   b. Brass, sect. EG   Piano, sect. G   Brass and piano

all twelve tones (that is, a harmonic aggregate). Lutosławski's twelve-tone chords are spatially symmetrical and are usually constructed using a limited number of intervals. Examine, for instance, the chord that results from a pitch reduction of the woodwind lines in section A of our movement, reproduced in Example 11.2a. The chord is a twelve-tone aggregate, and it consists of two spatially symmetrical collections, separated by a central interval [5], and each of which contains only intervals [2] and [3]. (We use numbers to denote interval size in semitones, and we reduce compound intervals to simple intervals.) The complete intervallic structure, from bottom to top, is thus: 23222 / 5 / 22232. This chord is present in sections A, C, E, and G. A four-note collection in the brass is added to this aggregate in sections E and G (with an intervallic structure of 111), and an eight-note chord in the piano is added in section G (intervallic structure 494 / 9 / 494). The combined brass/piano collection forms a second twelve-tone chord, with the intervallic structure 494 / 3 / 111 / 3 / 494. The brass and piano collections are shown (both separately and combined) in Example 11.2b. In other words, the type of compositional technique we have described above for A-type sections (aleatory counterpoint) results in a sound mass, but one in which the full chromatic spectrum is not covered. The twelve tones are heard harmonically, but as a symmetrically spaced chord rather than as a cluster.

The B-Type Sections

The B-type sections, on the other hand (and with the only exception of section F), feature sound masses made up of fully chromatic sound blocks. The main defining characteristics of sound masses and clusters are their density, width, register, and timbre. These are all elements that function in musical space. That is, we can imagine a three-dimensional space in which sound masses exist and are transformed. We will picture such space by means of the type of bi-dimensional graph shown in Example 11.3. The vertical axis of the grid in this example represents pitch, going from

♪♪♪ **Example 11.3**   Witold Lutosławski, *Jeux vénitiens,* spatial reduction

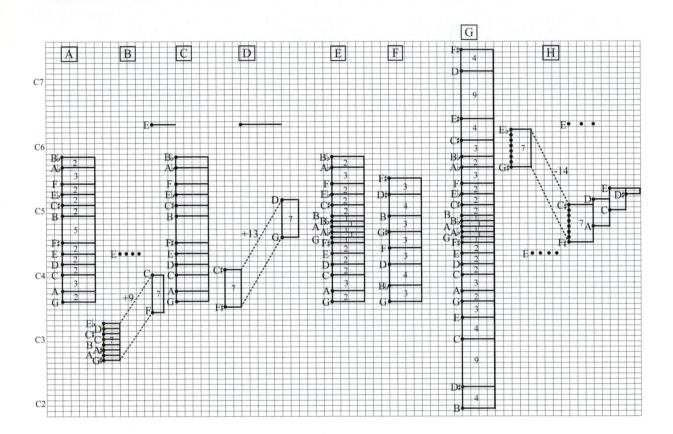

lowest at the bottom to highest at the top. Each square equals one semitone, and octaves are indicated by their usual numerical labels (C4 equals middle C). Time is read from left to right on the horizontal axis, which, however, has no constant value (that is, length in the horizontal axis does not indicate proportional duration in the actual music).[3] In his spatial analyses of Varèse's music, Jonathan Bernard used the term **projection** to refer to the transference of a structure (a pitch, an interval, a complex of pitches, and

---

[3]This type of spatial grid graph was first used by Robert Cogan and Pozzi Escot in *Sonic Design : The Nature of Sound and Music* (Englewood Cliffs, NJ: Prentice-Hall, 1976), and then adopted by Jonathan Bernard in his studies of Varèse's music, and later to represent spatial relationships in the music of Ligeti and Bartók. To consult Bernard's use of this graphic technique, see his article "Pitch/Register in the Music of Edgard Varèse," *Music Theory Spectrum* 3 (1981): 1–25, and his book *The Music of Edgard Varèse* (New Haven, Yale University Press, 1987).

so forth) to a new pitch/registral level. The same concept will be useful in our study of Lutosławski's spatial processes.

Each of sections B, D, and H begins with a cluster with a span of a perfect 5th. Each of these clusters is projected, voice by voice and pitch by pitch, to another higher or lower cluster also spanning a P5. Example 11.3 shows a complete spatial graph for the whole movement. After the twelve-tone chord from section A, in section B we first hear a cluster from G#2 to E♭3, with a span of [7]. A [+9] projection places the cluster at F3–C4, where the section ends. Note that some pitches are projected directly up [9], whereas in some voices the projection is effected in two steps rather than directly. G#2 in the double bass II, for instance, is projected up to F3 through an intermediate projection down to D2 (G#2↘D2↗F3). The only pitch class that is not present in the clusters, pitch class E, appears as E4 and E6 in the solo first violin. The cluster texture is interrupted by the return of the twelve-tone chord, now as section C. Section D returns to the cluster of a [7] span, now up [1] from where we left it before, at F#3–C#4. A projection of [+13] takes it to G4–D5, while we still hear E6 in the solo first violin.

Section E brings back the twelve-tone chord, now thickened by the addition of the brass cluster closing the gap of [5] at the center of the chord. The brief section F follows. It is the only B-type section that does not feature clusters, but rather an eight-pitch symmetrical chord closer to the A-section type of chord. The final return of the A-type chord is in section G, now greatly expanded registrally by the piano chord (we now have two overlapping twelve-tone chords, as we saw in Example 11.2). The closing section H begins with the familiar [7] cluster, now as G#5–E♭6, a projection of the original G#2–E♭3 up three octaves, and also again a [+13] projection from the closing cluster in section D (the G4–D5 cluster). A [−14] projection of the new G#5–E♭6 cluster places it at F#4–C#5, which itself is an octave projection of the previous F#3–C#4 that we heard in section D. All along in section H we keep hearing the solo E4 and E6 in the first violin. To close the movement, the cluster gets narrower, first to [5] A4–D5, then to [4] C5–E5, and finally to [1] D#5–E5, where we finally hear the "solo" pitch class E as part of a fading cluster.

Conclusions

In summary, we can see that the A-type sections are texturally active, but they are spatially passive: they expand registrally by addition of pitches, but the basic twelve-tone chord comes back always in the same register. The B-type sections, on the other hand, are static texturally, but the clusters are in constant process of spatial projection, so they are spatially active. Figure 11.2 traces the complete path of spatial transformation of the [7] clusters, which are identified only by their lowest pitch. Thus, a projection of [+9] in section B is followed by a [+13] projection in section D. The clusters between sections B and D are related by a [+1] projection, and the clusters between sections D and H are related by [+13], that is, a compound [+1]. The final cluster projection in section H is [−14]. Both of the section H clusters, moreover, are spatially connected with sections B and D: the first cluster in section H is a projection up three octaves of the first cluster in section B, and the second cluster in section H is a projection up an octave of the first cluster in section D. Spatial relationships among sound masses thus seem to play a central role in the large-scale compositional plan for this movement.

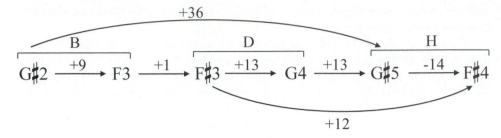

Figure 11.2 Spatial projections of [7] clusters in *Jeux vénitiens,* I

ANALYSIS 11.3: LIGETI, *RAMIFICATIONS,* MM. 1–44 (ANTHOLOGY NO. 32)

After György Ligeti (1923–2006) fled his native Hungary in 1956, his compositional style underwent a highly personal process of development. Through several stages in his career, Ligeti's music has always been distinctive in its individuality and its character. In his early period after fleeing Hungary, Ligeti's works featured a type of texture that he called **micropolyphony,** made up of webs of minutely notated, interweaving chromatic lines. If you listen to and examine the score of *Atmosphères* (1961) or the *Requiem* (1963–65; see particularly the *Kyrie*), you will note that, as part of such micropolyphonic textures, pitches and intervals are neutralized and integrated into overall chromatically filled complexes (that is, into sound masses). Beginning with works such as *Lux Aeterna* (1966) and *Lontano* (1967), pitch and interval recover their distinctive identity. In these two pieces Ligeti uses a polyphonic technique, **microcanon,** in which pitch successions are treated canonically in multiple voices at short time intervals. Microcanonic procedures in these works result in harmonic/spatial processes in which intervallic units (small intervallic collections) are subject to gradual and continuous transformation.

In yet one further step beyond the building of sound masses and in the development of his personal harmonic language, in compositions such as *Ramifications* (1968–69), the *Second String Quartet* (1968), and the *Chamber Concerto* (1969–70) Ligeti turned to a technique through which he recovered a fully harmonic thought, although of a type fundamentally different from traditional harmony, in that there is no direct succession or progression of harmonies, but rather what Ligeti himself has referred to as "progressive metamorphosis of intervallic constellations." By "intervallic constellations" he means harmonic intervallic collections, and by "progressive metamorphosis" he is referring to the type of harmonic transformation that we will discuss in the following analysis. We will refer to the harmonic technique used in these pieces as **net-structures.** A net-structure is a continuous web of finely woven lines or repeated patterns in a constant, interactive process of transformation. The following analysis of *Ramifications* will illustrate and clarify this technique with specific examples.[4]

The Musical Surface

Ramifications, scored for two groups of strings tuned a quarter-tone apart, is largely constructed on the technique of net-structures. At the immediate surface level, which determines the texture of a net-structure, the unfolding of the same harmonic processes by all instruments is not simultaneous. Intervallic transformations are displaced metrically, in more or less strict canonic form, and are often presented in layers of diverse rhythmic groups moving at different speeds. Example 11.4 illustrates a case of intervallic transformation unfolded "diagonally" by the different instruments. The first violin, for instance, progressively expands the linear intervals of a harmonic cell. In each of the circled trichords, one of the outer boundaries of the previous trichord has been expanded by a semitone or a tone, the upper voice following an ascending motion and the lower voice a descending motion. The same process occurs in the remaining instruments, except that each instrument is temporally delayed with respect to the instrument immediately above it in the score. This twining of the harmonic strands, together with the constant metric overlap of the harmonic cells, creates both the effect of interweaving and the flowing, nonmetrical textures so characteristic of net-structures.

Mm. 1–10: Chromatic Fluctuation of Melodic Microstructures

Pitch reductions of the melodic-harmonic processes common to all instruments reveal the next compositional level of net-structures. At this level, the pitch content defines different types of net-structures. In the first type, the harmonic process is produced by *constant chromatic fluctuation of melodic microstructures* (short melodic patterns moving within a range no larger than a tritone). A pitch reduction of the opening section of *Ramifications* (mm. 1–10, Example 11.5a) illustrates such a technique. The outer boundaries of the harmonic cells expand from [2] to [4], while inner chromatic fluctuation within the cells covers all of the possible subdivisions for each outer interval. The interval [4], for instance, is broken up into the following microstructures: 121, 112, 211,

---

[4]Ligeti's microcanonic compositions have been studied by Jane Clendinning (who first used and defined the term "microcanon") in "Structural Factors in the Microcanonic Compositions of György Ligeti," *Concert Music, Rock, and Jazz since 1945: Essays and Analytical Studies,* ed. Elizabeth West Marvin and Richard Hermann (Rochester: Rochester University Press, 1995), 229–56. Jonathan Bernard has discussed the spatial aspects of Ligeti's music (including his micropolyphonic and microcanonic pieces) in the following articles: "Inaudible Structures, Audible Music: Ligeti's Problem, and His Solution," *Music Analysis* 6 (1987): 207–36; "Voice Leading as a Spatial Function in the Music of Ligeti," *Music Analysis* 13 (1994): 227–53; and "Ligeti's Restoration of Interval and Its Significance for His Later Works," *Music Theory Spectrum* 21/1 (1999): 1–31. Studies of net-structure compositions can be found in Jane Clendinning, "The Pattern-Meccanico Compositions of György Ligeti," *Perspectives of New Music* 31 (1993): 192–234; Michael Hicks, "Interval and Form in Ligeti's *Continuum* and *Coulée,*" *Perspectives of New Music* 31 (1993): 172–90; and Miguel Roig-Francolí, "Harmonic and Formal Processes in Ligeti's Net-Structure Compositions," *Music Theory Spectrum* 17/2 (1995): 242–67. The present analysis of *Ramifications* is borrowed from the latter article.

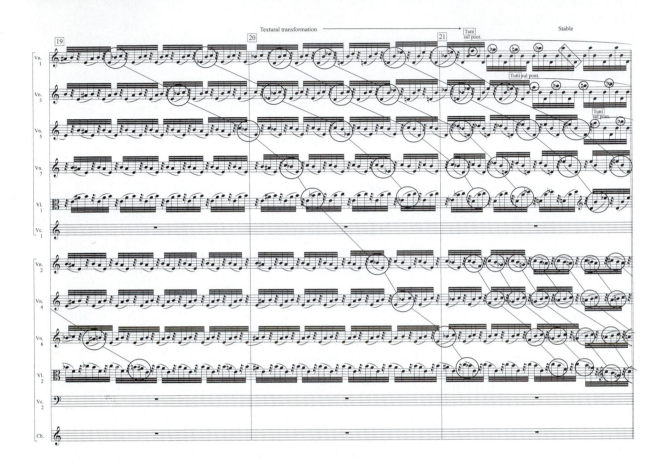

♪♪♪ Example 11.4   György Ligeti, *Ramifications*, mm. 19–21, annotated score

1111, 31, 13, 22 and 4. A complex set of symmetrical relationships governs the passage: group cardinality (that is, number of pitches in each cell) as shown in the reduction is symmetrical (creating the pattern 2–3–4–5–4–3–2); the arrangement of microstructures is symmetrical around [4]=1111, the only group with a cardinality of 5; the equal divisions of [2], [3], and [4] (11, 111, 1111, and 22, respectively) are arranged symmetrically (see Example 11.5b); and finally, the structural cluster of the passage displays a symmetrical configuration: the piece begins with the pitches A–G, connected in m. 2 by A♭, and expanded a half step above and below to the outer boundaries of the passage, B♭ and F♯ (Example 11.5c). The section is supported by a triple pedal on the pitches A–A♭–G, the inner cell of the structural cluster.

Example 11.5	Ligeti, *Ramifications*, mm. 1–10; a. Pitch reduction; b. Equal divisions of [2], [3], and [4]; c. Structural cluster

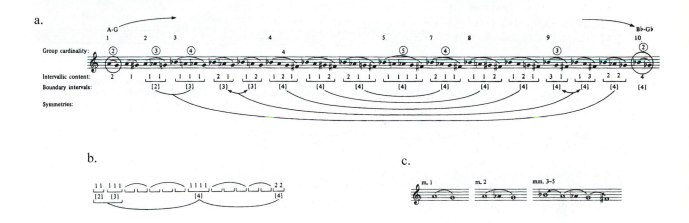

Mm. 10–24: Intervallic Expansion or Contraction of Harmonic Cells

The second type of net-structure is illustrated by mm. 10–24 of *Ramifications*. Example 11.6 displays a pitch reduction for the complete passage, showing that harmonic transformation results from constant *intervallic expansion or contraction of harmonic cells*. Expansion and contraction are here again effected chromatically, following the model of chromatic transformation previously described: harmonic cells change by half-step motion (or occasionally by whole step), one pitch and one voice at a time. The pitch space of an interval pair (that is, a trichord) is represented by two superposed numbers—one for each interval—in brackets. The spatial position of the intervals within the pair is preserved in this notation: $[^2_3]$ is thus a spatial inversion of $[^3_2]$.

On the graph in Example 11.6, we can see that the interval [4], reached in m. 10, is subject to two parallel transformations by the two instrumental groups (an example of the type of "ramification" to which the title of the piece refers). In group 1, [4] is constantly expanded until it reaches a stable $[^9_{10}]$ in m. 23 (by referring to a sonority as "stable" in this context, we mean that it remains in an untransformed state for a period of time, even if it is only a brief one). A section of textural transformation (mm. 20–21) is delimited by $[^2_8]$ and $[^6_8]$, while in mm. 21–22 a passage of relative harmonic stability is based on $[^{10}_8]$ and then on $[^9_{10}]$. Group 2, meanwhile, presents an extension of the harmonic material by means of a series of expansions and contractions. An initial expansion leads from [4] to $[^2_2]$ in m. 20, followed by a contraction to $[^2_6]$ (m. 21), a symmetrical and spatially inverted expansion from $[^1_2]$ to $[^6_2]$ (m. 22), and a series of fluctuations, also symmetrical, around boundary interval [8] (mm. 22–23). Finally, in

♪♪ Example 11.6   Ligeti, *Ramifications,* mm. 10–26, pitch reduction

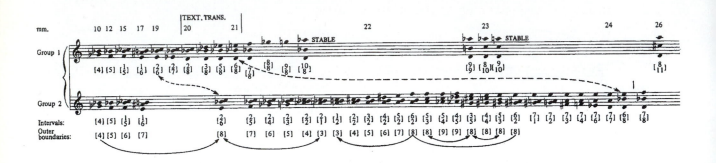

mm. 23–24, [⁶₂] expands to [⁶₈], the same pitch configuration which was reached in m. 21 by group 1.

In the program notes to the 1967 Donaueschingen premiere of *Lontano,* Ligeti explained that harmonic processes in that piece contained several strata: "Inside the harmonies we find other subharmonies, which in turn contain new subharmonies, and so on. There is not a single process of harmonic transformation, but rather several simultaneous processes moving at different speeds. These layered processes are translucent, and by means of varied refractions and reflections they create an imaginary perspective." In mm. 10–24 of *Ramifications,* the two translucent processes moving at different speeds are defined by the two instrumental groups. The more complex process of group 2 expands the harmonies of group 1 and covers the same ground as the latter in a more elaborate way. Translucence is achieved by keeping one group static while the other moves at a faster harmonic rhythm: the [²₆] reached in m. 19 by group 1 is delayed for a full measure in group 2, and the [⁶₈] that closes the harmonic phrase in group 1 in m. 21 is not reached by group 2 until m. 24, after the fast chromatic development that we hear through the transparency of more stable harmonies in group 1.

Rhythm

Along with harmonic motion, rhythm is one of the determining factors in the shaping of a net-structure's surface. The sections of *Ramifications* that we have studied provide several examples of rhythmic intertwining of musical strands, as well as of rhythmic transformation. The following rhythmic factors, for instance, contribute to the building of interweaving patterns in mm. 1–6:

1. Various instruments present identical processes of chromatic transformation with a temporal displacement with respect to each other.
2. Strands are further interlaced by means of layers of contrasting beat subdivisions (that is, polyrhythm). In mm. 1–6 the layers are made up of triplets, sixteenth notes, quintuplets, and sextuplets, respectively.

3. All possible expectations of rhythmic regularity are broken by the irregular grouping of the pitches that constitute the fluctuating chromatic microstructures.

4. Rests of different values are irregularly placed within the melodic cells, further differentiating the layers already moving at different speeds.

As a result of all these factors, *Ramifications* is perceived as totally ametric music: We perceive a flow of sound, we hear layers intertwining and displaced patterns, but we don't hear any kind of metric regularity.

In mm. 6–17 we hear both a process of written-in acceleration and a process of rhythmic transformation. Acceleration is effected first by the occasional introduction of smaller beat subdivisions (septuplets and thirty-second notes within the layer of sextuplets, for instance), and, after m. 12, by a systematic motion through successions of progressively smaller subdivisions. The transformation leads to m. 17, where all the voices join in a rhythmic continuum in thirty seconds, which is sustained, with minimal disturbances, until m. 32.

APPLICATION AND CLASS DISCUSSION

What is your impression of the various compositional techniques we have studied in this chapter? What aesthetic issues do these techniques raise? For instance, what are the aesthetic implications of aleatory composition? How do the composer/performer/listener relationships change in the context of aleatory music? What do you think is the best way for the listener to approach aleatory and sound mass compositions?

What is the importance of Ligeti's style and techniques we have studied in this chapter in the context of the music of the 1950s–60s? How is Ligeti's net-structure music different from sound-mass music and textures?

How important do you think it is to understand the music we have studied in this chapter in order to appreciate and like it? Do you appreciate and like it better after you understand the compositional processes and techniques involved? Can you hear these processes as you listen to the music, and does knowing about them help you make sense of the music as you listen to it?

Further Listening

The following list provides suggestions for further listening to music by composers studied in this chapter or related to the styles and techniques we have studied (if possible, listen while following the score):

1. Cage, *Concert for Piano and Orchestra*
2. Cage, *Winter Music*
3. Earle Brown, *Available Forms II*
4. Lutosławski, *Paroles tissées*

5. Lutosławski, *Livre pour orchestre*

6. Penderecki, *Threnody for the Victims of Hiroshima*

7. Penderecki, *De natura sonoris*

8. Ligeti, *Requiem*

9. Ligeti, *Lontano*

10. Ligeti, Chamber Concerto

Terms for Review

aleatory	The New York School
indeterminacy	graphic and spatial notations
sound-mass composition	point-drawing method
textural composition	musical tools
clusters	limited aleatory composition
microtonal	aleatory counterpoint
prepared piano	twelve-tone chord
chance operations	projection
I Ching	micropolyphony
action music	microcanon
performance art	net-structures

CHAPTER 11 ASSIGNMENTS

I. Analysis

1. Choose one of the following pieces by Cage: *Atlas eclipticalis,* for orchestra; *TV Köln,* for piano; *Aria,* for solo voice; or *Theatre Piece*. Study the score and the performance instructions, and then write a brief essay discussing issues involved in the performance of this piece. What is determined by the composer, and what is not? What are the options for performers, and what decisions will they have to make? To what extent is the performer involved in the composition of this piece, and how?

2. Choose one of the following two fragments from Lutosławski's *Jeux Vénitiens,* fourth movement: Introduction (mm. 1–58), or sections a₁ through F. Study the fragment you choose, and write a brief analytical essay on the compositional, textural, and temporal techniques used. Provide brief explanations (using graphs as needed) of the pitch structures used in each of the sections or subsections, and realize a general spatial graph for the complete fragment you choose.

3. Analyze and write an essay on "*Et surgens omnis multitudo,*" movement 13 from Penderecki's *St. Luke Passion*. First study and discuss the text and the dramatic action represented in the text. Study the score carefully, and identify all unusual notational symbols. Discuss how the dramatic characters and action in the text are represented in the music. In particular, discuss the various vocal techniques used in this movement as

well as the use of clusters. With the help of some kind of graph or diagram, study and discuss the spatial and registral characteristics of the opening section, mm. 1–12.

4. Analyze in detail the net-structure in Ligeti's *Ramifications,* mm. 24–38 (Anthology no. 32). Study the type of sonorities involved in this section and determine the type of transformation that these sonorities go through. Write an essay on this passage, and provide any graphs or reductions you may need to clarify and illustrate your discussion.

5. Write a brief analytical paper on Penderecki's *De natura sonoris.* Discuss any pertinent aspects of pitch and temporal organization, form, notation, texture, orchestration and timbre, compositional techniques, spatial and registral issues, and so forth. Accompany the paper with any graphs you may consider useful or necessary to illustrate and explain your analytical points.

6. Write a brief analytical paper on Ligeti's Chamber Concerto, I. Study the form and compositional techniques in this movement. Are there any sections in which Ligeti uses net-structures? If so, provide a more detailed discussion of at least one of these sections, and accompany your discussion with graphs or reductions showing the transformation of pitch patterns throughout the section.

II. Composition

1. Compose a piece using sound-mass and/or aleatory techniques for an instrumental and/or vocal ensemble of your choice. If you use aleatory techniques, limit the aleatory possibilities somehow, while leaving some of the compositional elements to chance or performer's choice (for instance, you may choose to determine the pitch content of your music but not the exact rhythmic/metric simultaneities, or the other way around). If you use sound-mass techniques, decide whether you want to write out the lines that make up the sound masses, or whether you want to use some graphic notation to refer to clusters. In any case, plan your spatial/registral structure, as you would plan the form of a composition, before you start writing the actual piece.

2. Compose a movement for string quartet using net-structures in a style similar to Ligeti's. Begin from a sonority of your choice. Then make a plan of how this sonority is going to be transformed in a harmonic process. Write a "reduction" of the process of harmonic transformation, and when you reach what you decide will be the point of arrival of the process, you may want to begin a new and different process. After you have a good plan for the sections of the movement and the various harmonic processes involved, you will have to decide on the rhythmic process you will use to realize the actual net-structure. Make sure that your rhythmic designs break the sense of beat and measures in the music so that we hear a seamless, nonmetric flow of intertwined harmonic and rhythmic patterns.

Chapter 12

Where Past and Future Meet . . .

In Chapter 5 we discussed neoclassicism, and we saw that through this style a creative dialogue is established between the past and the present, by incorporation and reinterpretation of musical idioms of the past as active elements in the music of the present. The complex interactions between past, present, and future continued in the decades after World War II, and they often generated more polarized positions than in the decades before the war. Some composers, of whom Boulez (who did not hesitate to extol historical amnesia) is the main representative, have thought of music history as a linear, evolutionary process (or "progress") in which the past should be left behind as much as possible, and in which composers would ideally create new musical idioms that would fulfill the need for present, current musical expression while opening the door toward the future.

A different perspective, however, was adopted by other composers beginning in the 1960s and 1970s. In general, the term **postmodernism** has been used to refer to a variety of compositional and aesthetic trends that are particularly difficult to define. Postmodern composition usually shows no interest in, or even respect for, the traditional concept of structural unity, and it may instead be based on sharp stylistic discontinuities. Postmodern composers are pluralistic and eclectic in the techniques and musical idioms they use. Postmodern music establishes no boundaries between past and present, tonal and post-tonal, or progressive and conservative (as a matter of fact, postmodern thinking particularly distrusts binary oppositions).[1] In particular, some composers have sought to establish a new, direct dialogue with the past in a variety of ways, some of which we will study in this chapter. The historical time model resulting from this position would be more circular than linear or evolutionary, inasmuch as it implies uses of, or return to, styles and materials of the past, rather than a linear motion away from them.

---

[1] For an interesting comparison of modernist and postmodernist aesthetics, see Jonathan Kramer, "Beyond Unity: Toward an Understanding of Musical Postmodernism," in *Concert Music, Rock, and Jazz since 1945: Essays and Analytical Studies,* ed. by Elizabeth West Marvin and Richard Hermann (Rochester: University of Rochester Press, 1995), pp. 11–33.

Quotation: A Long and Old Musical Tradition

Far from being a new compositional technique, quotation of existing music (originally in the form of a borrowed tune used as a *cantus firmus*) is as old as polyphony itself, and was a common procedure in Medieval and Renaissance music. Beyond cantus firmus, quotation in the Renaissance took many forms, such as the borrowing of polyphonic textures in what we know as *parody,* the alteration and variation of borrowed material in what we know as *paraphrase* techniques, or the building of complete polyphonic textures by means of a collage of many different existing tunes in a genre we know as *quodlibet.* After the Renaissance, borrowing and quotation became more sporadic practices. Well-known uses of existing material after the sixteenth century are J. S. Bach's reinstrumentations of Vivaldi concertos, Mozart's dinner scene in *Don Giovanni,* Berlioz's and Liszt's uses of the *Dies irae* tune, and the numerous examples of sets of variations based on themes borrowed from other composers. Much closer to our time, and as we discussed in Chapter 6, the concepts of quotation and collage were at the core of many compositions by Charles Ives. In pieces such as the *Holidays Symphony, Three Places in New England* or the Fourth Symphony, Ives fully foreshadowed the compositional styles and techniques we will study in this chapter.

Not until the second half of the twentieth century, however, does the use of these techniques become as widespread as it was in the sixteenth century. What is remarkable about quotation in recent decades is thus not its novelty (there is nothing new about the use of quotation), but the fact that it became a widely used technique, that quotations often took on a structural function in compositions, and that they often produced jarring stylistic contrasts with the musical contexts in which they appeared.

The presence of the past in the music of recent decades has often taken the form of **quotations** from particular works and composers. The juxtaposition of multiple quotations in the course of the same work creates a polystylistic patchwork or **collage.** Collages are usually integrated into broader musical contexts in which they become one more element in the overall complex of sound, along with the composer's original music, and the resulting aesthetic is one of stylistic pluralism, and not of stylistic unity or uniformity. An excellent example of this type of texture based on quotation and resulting in a highly integrated, multistylistic collage is provided by one of the pieces we will study in this chapter, Berio's *Sinfonia.* Among the many other composers who have used some type of quotation are George Rochberg, George Crumb, Donald Martino, Lukas Foss, Jacob Druckman, William Bolcom, and Joan Tower in the United States, and Bernd Alois Zimmermann, Luigi Nono, Hans Werner Henze, Peter Maxwell Davies, Alfred Schnittke, and Mauricio Kagel in Europe.

Another salient aspect in much of the music written in postmodern styles is its adoption of some kind of tonality or pitch centricity, whether it be functional tonality, some nonfunctional, consonant (and normally tertian) harmonic idiom, or at times simply pitch centricity stemming from the use of symmetrical referential collections (such as pentatonic, whole tone, or octatonic). Tonal references may result from the borrowing of a passage from a tonal work of the past, but the tonal passage or movement may also be newly composed. Both cases can be found in works by Rochberg, as we will discuss in this chapter. Other composers whose music has featured references to tonal structures at one level or another include David Del Tredici, John Corigliano, Ellen Taaffe Zwilich, John Harbison, Joan Tower, Henryk Górecki, Penderecki, Schnittke, and Sofia Gubaidulina. The musical movement centered on the adoption of tonal or pitch-centered idioms in recent decades has often been called **neo-Romanticism** or **neotonality.** The use of consonant or neotonal structures, moreover, at times has come along with a great simplification of musical materials (in music by composers such as

Arvo Pärt, Louis Andriessen, Steve Reich, Philip Glass, or John Adams). We will focus on this simplification of compositional means in the next chapter.

NOTE

It is not uncommon to find references to the "return to tonality" in the type of styles and composers we have just mentioned. This characterization, however, is somewhat misleading, inasmuch as it implies that tonality and pitch centricity were actually abandoned at some point. They were not. There has been a continued use of extended tonal idioms and pitch centricity throughout the twentieth century (and this without even taking into account the obvious use of tonal syntax in the pop, rock, jazz, and musical theater repertoires). Composers such as Aaron Copland, Dmitri Shostakovitch, Benjamin Britten, Leonard Bernstein, Percy Grainger, Heitor Villa-Lobos, Samuel Barber, Walter Piston, David Diamond, and Gian Carlo Menotti, among others, are good representatives of the extended tonal tradition in the twentieth century. The significance of the supposed "return to tonality," or of the "neotonal" movement, comes from the fact that it often came from composers who had previously established a solid reputation as atonal, avant-garde, experimental, or serial composers (as is the case of Rochberg, Górecki, and Penderecki), or who at least had successfully explored atonal and serial styles (as in the case of Tower, Zwilich, or Harbison).

GEORGE ROCHBERG AND THE USE OF THE PAST

George Rochberg (1918–2005) embodies in many ways the attitudes toward the past that we are studying in this chapter. For years the composer practiced a serial musical idiom in which he absorbed specific influences from Schoenberg and Webern. After 1963, however, Rochberg's stylistic path took an unexpected turn best described by his own words: "I engaged in an effort to rediscover the larger and more sweeping gestures of the past, to reconcile my love for that past and its traditions with my relation to the present and its often-destructive pressures. This has been an almost impossible task; it has taken many forms; all of them have led me back to the world of tonal music."[2] As a consequence of this turn toward the past, Rochberg abandoned the notion of originality (one of the basic principles of modernist and avant-garde composers in the 1950s and 60s) as a driving premise in his compositional processes. In his own rewording of the Verdi maxim that, as we saw in Chapter 5, Stravinsky liked to quote ("Torniamo all'antico e sarà un progresso"), Rochberg wrote, in the same liner notes we previously quoted: "Music can be renewed by regaining contact with the tradition and means of the past, to re-emerge as a spiritual force with reactivated powers of melodic thought, rhythmic pulse, and large-scale structure." Works of this period that incorporate extensive quotations or sections newly composed in a fully tonal language include *Music for the Magic Theater* (1965), the Third String Quartet (1971–72), and *Ricordanza* (1972) for cello and piano.

---

[2]George Rochberg, liner notes to LP "String Quartet no. 3," by the Concord String Quartet (Nonesuch Records, H 71283, 1973).

Before we study some passages from *Music for the Magic Theater* in detail, let us discuss a possible analytical process to approach this music. In a general way, we can expect that music that makes use of quotations or collage techniques includes both borrowed passages and newly composed music. The two types of music (borrowed and original) may be presented simultaneously, may be juxtaposed, or both. Often the newly composed music extends or elaborates the quoted music. When that is the case, we say that the original music provides (or is) a "commentary" to the borrowed music. Moreover, we can also expect that various quotations taken from various sources will display disparate stylistic elements, often in very close succession. We can thus spell out the following steps for our study of collage music:

1. Identify (at least as much as possible) the quotations and their origin, and identify the newly composed music.

2. Examine whether, and how, the quotations show any relationship to the original music adjacent to them, and also to other adjacent quotations.

3. Identify any procedures that may be used to connect (and/or unify) disparate stylistic elements among themselves in the collage and also to connect quotations and newly composed passages.

In her studies of collage in the music of Rochberg and Berio, Catherine Losada uses the term **modulation** to refer to a variety of techniques through which the transition between disparate stylistic and compositional elements is effected. These techniques of modulation may be used to bridge the discontinuity between the different musical fragments of a collage.[3] Losada identifies three types of modulation in the music of Rochberg and Berio. The first type, the most common of the three, is **overlap:** some elements at the end of one quotation intersect with some elements at the beginning of the next quotation. In **chromatic insertion,** the second type of modulation, some chromatic structures are inserted between quotations as a way to connect them. Finally, in the third type of modulation, **rhythmic plasticity,** the connection is effected by means of alteration or transformation of rhythmic figures to achieve a gradual transition between adjacent quotations. We will now turn to the analysis of passages from Rochberg's *Music for the Magic Theater* to illustrate various collage techniques.

ANALYSIS 12.1: ROCHBERG, *MUSIC FOR THE MAGIC THEATER,* REH. 1–17 (ANTHOLOGY NO. 33)

Music for the Magic Theater, composed in 1965, is one of Rochberg's most celebrated pieces, and one of the first two in which he started to experiment with the integration of music from the past through quotation and collage (the other piece, from the same year, is *Contra mortem et tempus*). *Music for the Magic Theater* is structured in three

---

[3]See Catherine Losada, "A Theoretical Model for the Analysis of Collage in Music Derived from Selected Works by Berio, Zimmermann and Rochberg" (Ph.D. dissertation, City University of New York, 2004). The following analyses of Rochberg's *Music for the Magic Theater* and Berio's *Sinfonia* are indebted to Losada's pioneering work in the field of analysis of musical collage. See also Michael Hicks, "The New Quotation: Its Origins and Functions" (DMA diss., University of Illinois, 1984).

movements, which the composer calls "acts." In brief notes written on the score at the beginning of each act, Rochberg states the philosophical program underlying this composition. Thus, at the beginning of act I he writes: "In which the present and the past are all mixed-up . . . and it is difficult to decide or to know where reality is . . ." Act II is introduced by the following words: "In which the past haunts us with its nostalgic beauty . . . and calls to us from the deeps of inner spaces of heart and mind . . . but the past is all shadow and dream and insubstantial . . . and we can't hold on to it because the present is too pressing . . ." Finally, the introduction to act III is as follows: "In which we realize that only the present is really real . . . because it is all we have . . . but in the end it too is shadow and dream . . . and disappears . . . into what? . . ." In other words, the whole composition can thus be seen as a reflection on the relationship and complex interactions between past, present, and future in music and in life.

The Quotations

The presence of the past takes the form of very specific quotations from a wide range of composers and styles. Whereas in acts I and III the quotations are more or less brief and are usually framed by original music, act II contains very little original music, and consists mostly of a transcription and reinstrumentation of Mozart's Adagio from the *Divertimento* K. 287. Besides this piece by Mozart, Rochberg has identified the following sources for his quotations and references in *Music for the Magic Theater*: Beethoven, String Quartet op. 130; Mahler, Symphony no. 9, Adagio; Webern, Concerto for Nine Instruments, op. 24; Varèse, *Déserts*; Stockhausen, *Zeitmasse* no. 5; Miles Davis, *Stella by Starlight*; and Rochberg, String Quartet no. 2 and Sonata-Fantasia for solo piano. In act I, where "the present and the past are all mixed-up," clear quotations from the past interact and alternate with Rochberg's own music and with his musical commentaries to the quotations. Act II is mostly made up of the past, and only toward the end does the past disintegrate into the present. Act III, on the other hand, is mostly made up of the present (Rochberg's original music), although the past continues to appear in the form of more or less veiled quotations and references to Mozart and Mahler.

As a first step in our analysis of act I, reh. 1–17 (Anthology no. 33; note that all instruments are notated at concert pitch), let us identify the quotations in this passage (mark these quotations on the score as we identify them). Several of the quotations are literal renditions of passages by Mahler, Varèse, and Mozart. The measure in $\frac{4}{4}$ in the strings right before reh. 2 is a literal borrowing of m. 13 from the Adagio of Mahler's Symphony no. 9. After a brief interruption by Rochberg's own commentary, the following measure from Mahler's Adagio (m. 14) appears right before reh. 3. The $\frac{7}{4}$ measure at reh. 4 comes literally from Varèse's *Déserts*. And, finally, a literal quotation from Mozart's *Divertimento* K. 287, I , begins at reh. 12 (for only one $\frac{3}{4}$ measure), and then continues two measures before reh. 13, all the way to reh. 15.

Besides these literal quotations, a great deal of Rochberg's own commentary is based on motives borrowed from Mahler or Varèse. Example 12.1 shows four motives, which we will label W, X, Y, and Z, as they appear in their original sources.[4] Exam-

---

[4]These motives, listed by Losada, were originally noted by Lisa Brooks Robinson in "Mahler and Postmodern Intertextuality" (Ph.D. diss., Yale University, 1994).

Example 12.1 Motives from Mahler and Varèse used in *Music for the Magic Theater*

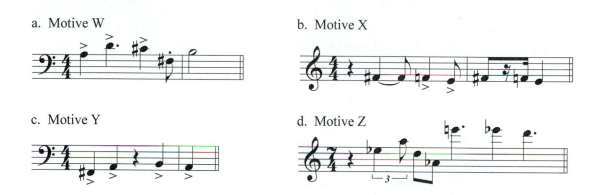

a. Motive W

b. Motive X

c. Motive Y

d. Motive Z

ple 12.1a features motive W as it first appears in the second horn in F in Mahler's Symphony no. 9, I, mm. 4–5. Example 12.1b shows motive X, taken from trumpet 1 in the same Mahler movement, mm. 44–45. Motive Y, as shown in Example 12.1c, is taken from the second harp in mm. 3–4 of the same movement. Finally, motive Z appears in Varèse's *Déserts* (as quoted in *Music for the Magic Theater,* reh. 4, oboe and piccolo). The following fragments from Rochberg's piece are based on these motives: (1) the complete pitch and interval content of reh. 3 (piano, B♭ clarinet, oboe, and trumpet) follows the pitch content of motive Z; (2) the trombone solo at reh. 5 is a transposition of motive X; (3) the cello solo at reh. 6, continued through reh. 7, is an adaptation of motive Y; and (4) the horn solo at reh. 7 is a rendition of the exact pitches from motive W.

Motivic Relationships

Rochberg uses motivic relationships as the essential procedure to interconnect the diverse quotations, along with his own original commentaries. The chromatic trichord, (012), has a central role in unifying the disparate musical materials in this piece. In the first place, the set permeates the two measures from the Mahler Adagio quoted in reh. 1–2. The two measures from Mahler (mm. 13–14) are reproduced in Example 12.2a (the viola part, which doubles the first violin, has been omitted). All instances of the (012) trichord and its subset (01) are shown by boxes in this example. We can see that each line has at least one case of (012) or (01). Moreover, the actual pitch–class content of these sets, shown as bracketed sets, is limited to three collections or subsets of these collections: [10,11,0], [2,3,4], and [7,8,9].

Example 12.2b features motive X as played by the trombone in reh. 5. As you can see, the set for this motive is (012), and the specific pc content is one of the three listed previously, [10,11,0]. In Example 12.2c we can see the intervallic characteristics of motive Z, the Varèse motive, which can be broken into two parts. The first part is a (0167) tetrachord presented as two successive tritones, E♭–A and D–A♭. The second part is the

♪♪♪ Example 12.2   Motivic interconnections in *Music for the Magic Theater*

a.

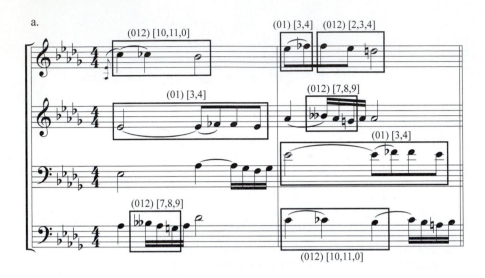

b. Motive X   c. Motive Z

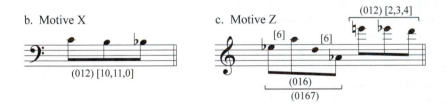

familiar (012) set, now with the content [2,3,4], again one of the three normal orders listed earlier. Note also the particular (016) set that results from pitches E♭–A–A♭ (with the contour <+6, −13>), a trichord to which we will soon come back.

Is the chromatic trichord (012) similarly relevant in the Varèse and Mozart quotations that we have identified in this section of *Music for the Magic Theater*? First, refer to the Varèse passage in reh. 4. We already know that the trichord in the piccolo (the second part of motive Z) is (012) [2,3,4]. Focus now on the complete pitch-class content of each of the following groups: (1) oboe and clarinet, (2) bassoon and two horns, (3) piano, upper staff, and (4) piano, lower staff. How are the sets in these groups related to the sets in the Mahler quotation? Do not read on until you have answered this question.

The pitch classes in the oboe and clarinet duo can be grouped into a trichord and a dyad. The trichord is (012) [2,3,4], and the dyad is (01) [8,9], a subset of the [7,8,9] trichord. The trichord formed by bassoon and horns is (012) [10,11,0]. The upper staff in the piano is again a combination of (012) [2,3,4] and (01) [8,9], whereas the lower staff

♪♪♪ Example 12.3   Modulatory process in *Music for the Magic Theater*, reh. 1–4

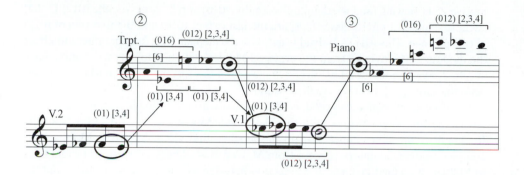

also combines a trichord and a dyad, now (012) [10,11,0] and (01) [5,6]. In other words, the trichords and dyads we have identified are all of the (012) and (01) type, and the only actual pc collection that was not present in the Mahler measures is the dyad [5,6]. Otherwise, the Mahler and Varèse quotations share the same pc material.

It would be excessive to expect the Mozart quotation to be mostly based on such chromatic sets as (012) and (01), and yet, Rochberg managed to both introduce and leave the Mozart quotation also by means of (012). Refer to the first appearance of the Mozart *Divertimento,* at reh. 12. You will recognize, in the viola line, the collection (012) [3,4,5]. Now go to the end of the Mozart quotation, at reh. 14. First, check the end of the bass line, beginning two measures after reh. 14. You will find again the set (012) [3,4,5]. Finally, the very last measure of the Mozart quotation, one measure before reh. 15, also features the same set, (012) [3,4,5] in the first violin, along with (012) [0,1,2] in the second violin. Note that the [3,4,5] that ends this quotation is actually presented as an exact retrograde of the [3,4,5] in the viola that opened the quotation at reh. 12, thus providing an element of symmetrical balance between the beginning and the end of the quotation.

Connecting the Quotations: Processes of Modulation

We have now identified the quotations in our example, and we have demonstrated the motivic relationships that provide musical coherence to these otherwise seemingly disparate fragments from three different style periods. How does Rochberg effect the actual connections between quotations? A particularly striking example of modulation using the overlap technique is provided by the transition from the Mahler quotation at reh. 1–2 to the Varèse quotation at reh. 4. This passage, moreover, illustrates the use and function of Rochberg's original commentary that frames the quotations. The modulatory process in this passage is summarized in Example 12.3.

The original commentary at reh. 2 begins with a statement of the motive A–E♭–E, a motive we can refer to the Varèse quotation. In the first place, the tritone A–E♭ is the opening tritone from motive Z, the Varèse motive. Moreover, the complete A–E♭–E motive (now presented with the contour <−6, +13>) is itself an inversion (by T_0I) of the (016) set which, as we saw in Example 12.2c, is a subset of the opening (0167) in motive Z. Following (and overlapping) with this (016) at reh. 2, we see the (012) [2,3,4] trichord. Note that pitch classes [3,4] are the last two of (016) and the first two of (012) in this passage. This (01) [3,4] dyad is actually the element that Rochberg uses to effect the modulation by overlap from the previous Mahler quotation to his own commentary at reh. 2. Observe that the last two pitch classes of the second violin in Mahler are indeed the same [3,4] dyad we are discussing.

The same elements also produce the overlap with the following Mahler measure, where the first violin begins with the [3,4] dyad. Moreover, the [2,3,4] set from the Rochberg commentary appears again in the same first violin line from Mahler, thus completing the modulatory process from Mahler to Rochberg's commentary and back to Mahler. As a final element of connection between Rochberg's commentary and the second Mahler measure, note that the last D5 of the Rochberg passage (circled in Example 12.3) forms the (012) [2,3,4] trichord with the initial two pitch classes of the first violin, the [3,4] dyad.

We already saw that the material of Rochberg's commentary at reh. 3 is drawn directly from the pitch content of motive Z, the Varèse motive. This commentary functions as a modulating passage between the Mahler quotation and the Varèse quotation that follows. The connection with the Mahler measure is provided again by the same D5 that already served as a connection into the same measure. Here, the D5 is an element of overlap linking the end of the first violin line with the motive in the piano (both pitches are circled in the example). Moreover, the (012) [2,3,4] trichord that closes the same violin line in the Mahler measure is replicated by the clarinet, oboe, and trumpet (012) [2,3,4] in the Rochberg passage, providing another element of overlap. Notice also, as a means of connecting both of Rochberg's passages at reh. 2 and reh. 3, that the exact pitch content of the (016) trichord at reh. 2, A–E♭–E, is replicated as an E♭–A–E (016) trichord at reh. 3. Finally, the modulating overlap between Rochberg's commentary at reh. 3 and the Varèse quotation that follows at reh. 4 obviously results from the fact that the complete pitch-class and motivic content of the commentary at reh. 3 is taken from the oboe, clarinet, and piccolo lines in the ensuing Varèse quotation.

Conclusions

In this brief discussion of *Music for the Magic Theater*, we have demonstrated in the first place that Rochberg's choice of quotations was determined by the closely related motivic content of the quotations, in particular by the multiple presence in each of them of set (012). Moreover, we have shown that different quotations are connected among themselves, as well as with the inserted original commentaries by Rochberg, by means of the modulatory technique of overlap. In particular, we have studied the very close connections among the two Mahler measures quoted in reh. 1 and 2, the Varèse quotation at reh. 4, and the two original commentaries inserted between these quotations. As a final observation in this discussion, note that the (016) motive, which we saw was derived from motive Z, has a central role in many of the passages of newly composed music in this piece. As an example, refer to the beginning of the passage at reh. 1, where you will see that the first violin, second violin, and viola lines begin with (016) motives, or to reh. 15, where you will recognize a variety of overlapping (016) motives in the oboe part and elsewhere (see, for instance, the trumpet part).

ANALYSIS 12.2: BERIO, *SINFONIA*, III ("IN RUHIG FLIESSENDER BEWEGUNG"), MM. 1–120 (ANTHOLOGY NO. 34)

The third movement of *Sinfonia* (1968) by Luciano Berio (1925–2003), "In ruhig fliessender Bewegung" (Anthology no. 34), is one of the richest and most complex examples of musical collage in the literature. The movement consists of a kaleidoscope of textual and musical references, allusions, and quotations, organized in multiple and interconnected layers. We will examine some of the references and their interconnections in mm. 1–120, up to reh. F.[5]

NOTE

In this type of "cut-away" score, staff segments that hold measures of rest are either fully deleted (for long segments) or replaced with a single line (for shorter segments).

The Sources

The main source for Berio's text in this movement is Samuel Beckett's novel *The Unnamable.* This novel consists of an artist's monologue who, following his death in the previous novel, is trapped up to his neck in a jar, where he is constantly assailed by voices from the past, which he is tricked into believing are his own. As Michael Hicks writes, "obviously such a work has a rich potential for quotation and parody: fragmented references to characters and events of earlier books, allusions to scripture, Shakespeare, even Joyce."[6] Thus, the basic story in this novel is precisely the tortured and obscure relationship between the past and the present, and how the past informs and enriches the present in a way that the character in the novel (in a similar way as the modern artist) is not even or necessarily aware of.

A less direct, but not less strong, literary influence in Berio's *Sinfonia* is exerted by the works of James Joyce. Joyce's texts, and in particular his *Ulysses,* are interweaved with quotations and allusions, both from literary or liturgical sources and from popular culture, often in several languages. *Ulysses* is certainly a model for Berio, and the

[5]The main studies of textual and musical quotation in this movement can be found in Michael Hicks, "Text, Music, and Meaning in the Third Movement of Luciano Berio's *Sinfonia,*" *Perspectives of New Music* 20 (1981–82): 199–224, and David Osmond-Smith, *Playing on Words: A Guide to Luciano Berio's Sinfonia* (London: Royal Musical Association, 1985). The present commentary is indebted to both of these sources.

[6]Hicks, p. 209.

third movement of *Sinfonia* includes a number of direct quotations from or passing references to Joyce. Besides the literary references to Beckett and Joyce, Berio's text includes references to the titles or tempo indications of music being quoted, passages of solfège (usually following the melody of a quoted musical passage), fragments of personal dialogues with friends and family, student slogans painted on walls in the Sorbonne during the riots of May 1968, and phrases spoken by undergraduates at Harvard (where Berio taught in the 1960s).

The main musical quotation in the movement is the scherzo from Mahler's Second Symphony. We start hearing it in m. 8, and it is always present thereafter, although at times it disappears (or becomes inaudible) momentarily, only to return at the exact point where it would be had the music never stopped being audible. Osmond-Smith refers to a process of progressive "obliteration" of the Mahler scherzo. We first hear the complete scherzo in an almost literal rendition (ending six measures after reh. E). The Mahler sections after that (Trio 1, Reprise 1, Trio II, Reprise II, Trio I reprise, and Reprise III) are not heard in their entirety, but only as reemerging fragments (separated by the "inaudible" continuation of the scherzo we just referred to). These fragments do not necessarily include the complete Mahler texture, but may instead consist of only one or two lines from the Mahler original.

The choice of the Mahler scherzo is highly significant. This movement is itself an adaptation of an earlier Mahler song, "Des Antonius von Padua Fischpredigt," from *Des Knaben Wunderhorn,* on a text from an old German song which narrates how St. Anthony preaches to the fishes for lack of a better audience. The layers of allusion to the past are multiple: Berio quotes Mahler (the scherzo) who quotes his own use (in the *Wunderhorn* song) of an old German text. Moreover, the image of the unheeded preacher establishes a link between this movement and the second movement of *Sinfonia, O King,* a homage to Martin Luther King.

Besides Mahler's scherzo, a large number of compositions by an equally large number of composers are quoted in the third movement of *Sinfonia*. We will identify and examine some of them in some detail in our following discussion, but for now it should suffice to mention some of the composers and works quoted: Schoenberg (*Fünf Orchesterstücke,* op. 16, nos. 4 , "Péripétie," and 3, "Farben"), Debussy (*La mer*), Ravel (*Daphnis et Chloé, La valse*), Strauss *(Der Rosenkavalier),* Hindemith (*Kammermusik* no. 4), Stravinsky (*The Rite of Spring, Agon*), Berlioz (*Symphonie fantastique*), Brahms (Violin Concerto, Fourth Symphony), Beethoven (Sixth Symphony), Bach (First Brandenburg Concerto), Webern (Cantata, op. 31), Boulez (*Pli selon pli*), Stockhausen (*Gruppen*), Berg (Violin Concerto, *Wozzeck*), and Mahler (Ninth Symphony, Fourth Symphony).[7] Note that several of these quotations contain direct references to water: "Farben" (subtitled "Summer Morning by a Lake"), *La mer,* Beethoven's Sixth Symphony (of which the "Scene by the Brook" is quoted), and *Wozzeck* (of which the drowning scene is quoted). These passages provide semantic associations with the image of St. Anthony preaching to the fishes in the water.

---

[7]A complete and detailed inventory of quotations in this movement appears in Osmond Smith, pp. 57–71. See also Hicks, pp. 200–207 and 212–21.

Musical Quotations and Textual Interrelations in the Opening Sections

We will now examine in detail the musical and textual references in the opening sections of this movement. Example 12.4 shows the quotations in the first page of Berio's score. Follow the same procedure illustrated in this example (that is, boxing quotations as they are identified in the analysis that follows) to mark the quotations on the rest of the score in Anthology no. 34.

Mm. 1–7 (to reh. A)

The opening of the movement contains three simultaneous musical quotations:

1. Schoenberg's *Fünf Orchesterstücke,* op. 16, no. 4, "Péripétie," mm. 2–3 (abbreviated as S–P in Example 12.4), appears in the trumpets and trombones (mm. 1–2) and in the complete strings (mm. 2–3, with the only exception of violins A, which borrow from Debussy's *La mer,* III, reh. 54:5).

2. The opening measures of Debussy's "Jeux de vagues," second movement from *La mer* (abbreviated as D–LM in Example 12.4), appear in clarinets, oboes, bassoons, harp, and strings (mm. 4–5).

3. The opening measures of Mahler's Fourth Symphony, I (abbreviated as M–4 in Example 12.4), appear in flutes and sleigh bells (*grelots,* played by the snare drum player, mm. 2–7), and violins B (mm. 6–7).

The singers in these measures refer to the quotes with titles, movement numbers, and tempo or performance indications. Thus, we hear the titles of the three quotations: "Péripétie," "Les jeux de vagues," and both "quatrième symphonie" and "deuxième symphonie" (the latter announcing the immediate beginning of Mahler's scherzo). We also hear simultaneous references to the movements: "deuxième partie" (for *La mer*), première partie" (for Mahler's Fourth), "quatrième partie" (for Schoenberg's piece), and "troisième partie" (for Mahler's Second). The phrases "nicht eilen, bitte" and "recht gemächlich" are both performance indications from the score of Mahler's Fourth.

Mm. 8–42 (to reh. C)

Mahler's scherzo from the Second Symphony (abbreviated as M–2 in Example 12.4) first appears in the woodwinds (clarinets, English horn, bassoons) in mm. 7–10, and then in the strings (violins A and B, and cellos/double basses) in mm. 10–18. In the measures after that, numerous fragments of the scherzo can be traced in various instruments, as, for instance, the clarinets and flutes in mm. 18–28, the harp and piano in mm. 12–29, or the saxophones in mm. 29–34. A prominent theme from *La mer,* III (reh. 54:7) is heard in the flute and oboe in mm. 27–32, and Hindemith's *Kammermusik* no. 4 (*Violinkonzert*) appears in the solo violin in mm. 26–31 (after its beginning was previewed in the violins B in m. 18).

The texts in the vocal parts continue some of the practices established in the opening measures. Thus, the indication "In ruhig fliessender Bewegung," which is also the title of this movement, is the tempo indication for the Mahler scherzo ("in quiet,

Luciano Berio, *Sinfonia,* III, quotations in first page of score. Abbreviations: M–2 (Mahler's Second), M–4 (Mahler's Fourth), S–P (Schoenberg, "Péripétie"), and D–LM (Debussy, *La mer*)

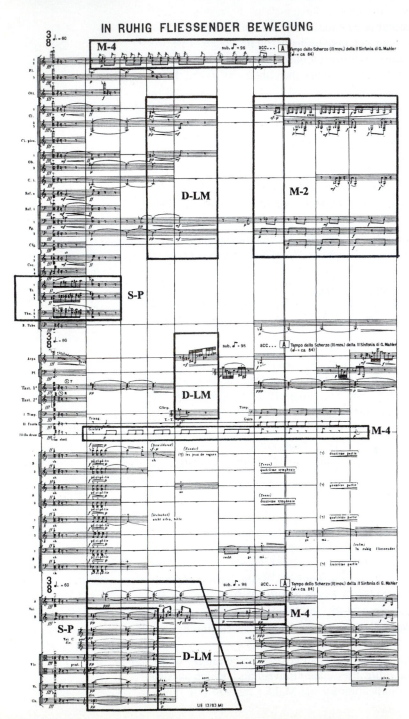

flowing motion"). A new textual element in the section we are now considering is the passages of solfège (in "fixed do"). The first one (sol–mi–do–re–mi–fa–fa–sol–si–do–re) is the solfège for the Mahler melody sounding simultaneously in the violins A, and so is the passage in m. 16. Later solfège phrases (mm. 27–33) refer to either the Mahler or the Hindemith melodies sounding simultaneously with them.

The opening words of Beckett's novel ("Where now? Who now? When now?") are heard several times beginning in m. 15. One of *The Unnamable*'s central concepts is the need to "keep going," a motto throughout the book (which, moreover, is directly related to a very common indication in Mahler's scores, "Vorwärt," "forward"). The book's character admits at the beginning that he is "afraid as always of going on," and the ambiguous closing words of the book are "you must go on, I can't go on, I'll go on." The idea appears for the first of many times in *Sinfonia* in m.17 ("Keep going"). All of it is related to Mahler's own program for the Second Symphony, which included the following lines: "Our hearts are gripped by a voice of awe-inspiring solemnity, which we seldom or never hear above the deafening traffic of mundane affairs. 'What next?' it says. Have we any continuing existence? Is it all an empty dream or has this life of ours, and our death, a meaning? If we are to go on living, we must answer this question."[8]

Finally, the sentence "nothing more restful than chamber music" in mm. 22–23 is a variation on Beckett's line "nothing more restful than arithmetic" (Beckett, p. 105). It introduces the *Kammermusik* quotation, whereas the textual extensions to this sentence in mm. 24–25 (". . . than flute" and "than two flutes") point at the Mahler passage for two flutes quoted in mm. 25–28. Note also that the *Kammermusik* quotation is interrupted at m. 44 (reh. C) with the scornful comments "no time for chamber music . . . you are nothing but an academic exercise."

Mm. 43–121 (to reh. F)

The commentary to the previous two sections should be a good introduction to the complexity and richness of Berio's text. Continuing a detailed and extensive discussion of the movement might not be necessary at this point, because the interested student can do so by consulting Osmond-Smith's list of quotations. We will just point out some of the most significant references in the remaining passages included in the anthology. Besides the ubiquitous Mahler scherzo, the main musical quotations in this passage are the following:

1. A line from the Berg Violin Concerto (solo violin, mm. 52–56) which is directly connected to a line from the Brahms Violin Concerto (mm. 57–60).

2. A passage from Ravel's *La Valse,* reh. 26 (bassoon and contrabassoon, mm. 62–69), continued by saxophone and bassoons in mm. 82–83, and followed by a reference to Strauss's *Der Rosenkavalier*'s waltz in the bassoons in mm. 86–87.

3. A line from Ravel's *La Valse,* reh. 32 (flute 1, mm. 77–86) with a chromatic accompaniment from the same source (flutes 2–3, mm. 77–83).

4. A flute line from Ravel's *Daphnis et Chloé,* reh. 176 (flute, mm. 87–92).

---

[8]Quoted in Hicks, p. 210.

5. A passage from "Jeux de vagues" (oboe and solo violin, mm. 97–103).

6. A line from Berlioz's *Symphonie fantastique* (flute, mm. 106–111).

Beginning at reh. C, extensive quotations from *The Unnamable* appear in the vocal parts. One of them, which in Beckett is "So after a period of immaculate silence there seemed a feeble cry was heard by me . . ." turns into "So after a period of immaculate silence there seemed to be a violin concerto being played in the other room, in $\frac{3}{4}$," in reference to the Berg Violin Concerto quote, extended by the exclamation "two violin concertos" when Berg turns into Brahms. Both *La Valse* and *Der Rosenkavalier* are "neoclassical" works that evoke musical styles of the past, so their presence contributes to the concept of "voices from the past," which is evoked in Beckett's novel. The same concept of culling from the memory is directly alluded to by the quotation from Beckett that appears in mm. 106 and following: "I feel the moment has come for us to look back, if we can, and take our bearings, if we are to go on," followed by "I must not forget this, I have not forgotten it, but I must have said this before, since I say it now." Here again, past and present get confused by virtue of a memory that cannot quite determine which is which.

Connecting the Quotations

In our preceding discussion of modulation between quotations, we identified three common types of modulation. Using Losada's terms, these three types are overlap, chromatic insertion, and rhythmic plasticity. All three types are used by Berio in the passages we have just studied, and we will now examine some examples of quotation connections following these three criteria.

Overlap

In our preceding discussion of modulation, we defined overlap as a technique in which "some elements at the end of one quotation intersect with some elements at the beginning of the next quotation." Berio uses overlap in a broader way. The essential principle of overlap is the use of common elements between quotations. In literal overlap, the common elements connect the end of a quotation with the beginning of the next. In a broader sense, overlap connects two quotations by using common elements that do not necessarily need to be at their beginning or end. Compare, for instance, the Mahler line in violins A, mm. 11–18, and then moving to the clarinets, mm. 18–25, with the Hindemith line in the solo violin, mm. 26–31. Two fragments from the Hindemith passage (taken from mm. 26 and 27) appear, overlapping with the Mahler line, in mm. 18 (violins B) and 20 (tenor saxophone). Example 12.5 shows the detail of the overlap in these measures.

In both Hindemith fragments, we identify two motives. Motive a is made up of a P4 motion and back, and motive b consists of a neighbor figure. Both motives are common elements with the Mahler line. The opening of the Mahler passage in m. 11 features motive a, and the neighbor figure, motive b, is prominent throughout the passage. In m. 18 in particular, the two fragments quoted exchange motives: the a–b motivic structure in Hindemith finds its parallel in the corresponding and simultaneous b–a struc-

Example 12.5   Berio, *Sinfonia,* III, details from mm. 11–21

Example 12.6   Berio, *Sinfonia,* III, details from mm. 52–61

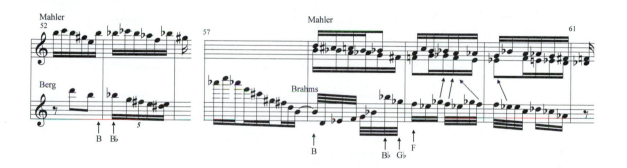

ture in Mahler. In m. 20, moreover, the two quotations are connected by common pitch classes: both begin on F and end on A♭.

A second fragment illustrating the same type of overlap through common tones, now linking three quotations, is shown in Example 12.6, taken from mm. 52–61. First, the Berg Violin Concerto quote intersects with the Mahler scherzo through two common simultaneous tones, B and B♭. Second, the Berg and Brahms Violin Concerto fragments are connected through overlap of a common B over bar 58. Third, the Brahms is itself connected to the Mahler line by four simultaneous common tones (B, B♭, G♭, and F in mm. 58–59) and by four almost simultaneous common tones in mm. 59–60 (G♭, F, F again, and E♭).

Chromatic Insertion

As we saw earlier, in the type of modulation we call chromatic insertion, "some chromatic structures are inserted between quotations as a way to connect them." Examine

Example 12.7   Berio, *Sinfonia,* III, details from mm. 77–87

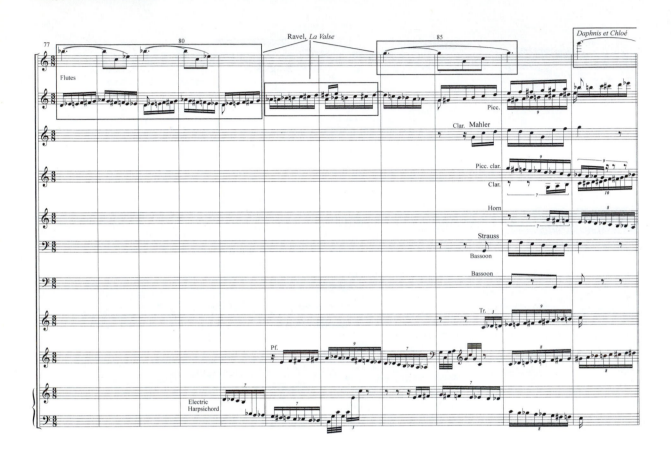

Example 12.7, which presents a reduction of mm. 77–87 of Berio's score. Through mm. 77–86, we hear a fragment from reh. 32 of Ravel's *La Valse* in the flutes. The Ravel passage is made up of a melody and an accompaniment of ascending and descending chromatic scales. At m. 87, however, the Ravel quotation in the flute turns into a melody from reh. 176 of *Daphnis et Chloé.*

The modulation between both quotations is effected in two ways. First, we see that a common pitch-class G links the flute melodies in mm. 86–87. Second, beginning with the electric harpsichord and the piano in mm. 81–82, a set of independent ascending and descending chromatic scales begins taking shape, starting at the same pitch, D, as the chromatic scale from *La Valse* in the flute at m. 81. That is, an independent chromatic insertion is derived from the chromatic material in the Ravel

♪♪♪ Example 12.8   Berio, *Sinfonia*, III, details from mm. 94–100

quotation. Then, woodwinds and brass join the keyboard instruments for a general chromatic wash that connects and blends together the four quotations present in these measures: the two Ravel fragments, the ever-present Mahler scherzo (clarinet 1, mm. 85–87), and Strauss's *Der Rosenkavalier* (bassoons, mm. 85–87). Notice that the Mahler and Straus fragments combine in perfectly correct counterpoint and that in m. 87 the Ravel, Mahler, and Strauss quotations all come together on a C–E–G chord, a CM triad!

Rhythmic Plasticity

In our preceding definition of rhythmic plasticity we saw that, through this technique, "the connection is effected by means of alteration or transformation of rhythmic figures in order to achieve a gradual transition between adjacent quotations." An example of rhythmic plasticity, coupled with chromatic insertion, appears in Example 12.8, a reduction of mm. 94–100 of Berio's score. Clarinets 2 and 3, along with strings, carry the quotation from Mahler's scherzo. Out of this quotation grows a second quotation, now from *La mer*, II, reh. 24, in the solo violin and oboe. The connective element between the two quotations is a chromatic insertion in clarinet 1. This insertion grows from the descending chromatic lines in the Mahler fragment in mm. 96–99. But it also introduces an element of rhythmic acceleration that builds rhythmic momentum toward the Debussy quotation, which features quicker rhythmic figurations than the Mahler fragment before it. Thus, the clarinet-1 line functions as a modulating element through transformation of rhythmic figures or rhythmic plasticity.

Conclusions

Obvious similarities exist between the collage techniques used by Rochberg and Berio. A significant difference, however, is the number of quotations used. The Rochberg fragment we have analyzed is based on many fewer quotations than the Berio example. Moreover, Berio's piece includes vocal parts, which allows him to incorporate textual collage besides its musical counterpart. We have seen that Berio weaves a complex and rich text in which textual and musical references interact and are actually treated as parts of a single collage. Moreover, we have seen that Berio, as Rochberg did before him, is very careful in crafting the connections among different musical quotations by means of a variety of modulation techniques. The resulting text, which incorporates so many fragments from the past, both musical and literary, is unquestionably the product of a present-day composer who is looking toward the future by establishing a creative dialogue with the past.

APPLICATION AND CLASS DISCUSSION

Listen to the second movement of Rochberg's *Music for the Magic Theater,* and discuss in class the aesthetic and compositional issues that arise from it. Is this "contemporary music"? Is Rochberg just copying Mozart's music? Is this music by Mozart or by Rochberg? What does a movement like this one do to the notion of originality? Is this a valid aesthetic for a late-twentieth-century composition? Would you say that total serialism is more or less appropriate as a late-twentieth-century aesthetic than this type of integration of the distant past, or perhaps that both aesthetics are perfectly appropriate to express different aspects of twentieth-century creative expression?

Further Listening

The following list provides suggestions for further listening to music by composers studied in this chapter or related to the styles and techniques we have studied (if possible, listen while following the score):

1. George Rochberg, String Quartet no. 3
2. Berio, *Sinfonia* (complete)
3. Berio, *Folk Songs*
4. Alfred Schnittke, Concerto grosso no. 1
5. Peter Maxwell Davies, *Eight Songs for a Mad King*
6. Crumb, *Ancient Voices of Children*
7. Joan Tower, Piano Concerto
8. David Del Tredici, *Final Alice*

Terms for Review

postmodernism
cantus firmus
parody
paraphrase
quodlibet
quotation
collage

neo-Romanticism
neotonality
modulation
overlap
chromatic insertion
rhythmic plasticity

 CHAPTER 12 ASSIGNMENTS

I. Analysis

1. Analyze George Crumb's "Dream Images (Love-Death Music)," no. 11 from *Makrokosmos,* vol. 1 (Anthology no. 35). First, identify the quotations in the piece. Then provide a complete analysis of motivic and formal aspects of the piece, including a discussion of pitch-class sets where appropriate. Finally, explain how the quotations and Crumb's original material are connected.

    Discuss also the allegorical aspects of this piece. The initials at the end of the piece, F.G.L. are a reference (or dedication) to Federico García Lorca (the symbol II that follows the initials is the symbol for Gemini). Who was García Lorca? What role does he have in Crumb's compositional output? How would you say that the figure of García Lorca is evoked in this piece?

2. Analyze the style of movement III of Rochberg's Third String Quartet. This movement is a set of variations on an original theme, and it contains no literal borrowings. In a brief essay, discuss what the stylistic borrowings are. How is the past reinterpreted? What is "traditional" and what is not?

3. Analyze the style of movement V of Rochberg's Third String Quartet. In a brief essay, discuss the various styles and tonal idioms used in this movement. What is the general formal design of the movement? What is the character of each of the large sections? What are the elements of contrast among sections? Explain in some detail (providing specific examples) the criteria for pitch and temporal organization used by Rochberg in each of the large sections.

4. Listen to, and study the score of, Joan Tower's Piano Concerto. Although there are no exact quotations in this composition, there are numerous stylistic borrowings, particularly from Beethoven and Stravinsky. What passages are inspired or based on passages by Stravinsky? What particular Stravinsky pieces are evoked in these passages? If you are not very familiar with Beethoven's Piano Sonatas op. 53 ("Waldstein"), I, and op. 31, no. 2 ("The Tempest"), I, listen to these movements. Tower has declared that there are influences from both of them in her Piano Concerto. What, and where, are these influences?

5. Listen to, and study the scores of, Peter Maxwell Davies' *Eight Songs for a Mad King,* songs nos. 6 and 7. How does the presence of the past manifest itself musically in these songs? Can you identify any specific references to specific composers and pieces? What are the dramatic and historic contexts for this interaction with the past?

6. Besides the quotations and references we have studied in Berio's *Sinfonia,* III, an element of textural cohesion is provided by Berio's own commentary in the form of clusters and punctuating cluster chords, especially from the beginning of the movement to reh. D. Study these chords and clusters. Write a brief paper explaining the textural relationship between the clusters and the quotations. Provide some kind of graphic depiction (either on staff paper or on a grid) of the spatial development of clusters in this section, and comment on your graph. How do the clusters interact with the quotations? How do they contribute to the final musical result in this movement?

II. Composition

Compose a piece for piano and four other instruments of your choice, using collage and quotation techniques of the type we have studied in this chapter. You may choose to include a vocal part in your ensemble, and if you do so you may use some kind of collage technique for your text, too. Otherwise, choose several tonal musical pieces from the past from which you will borrow most of your quoted material.

For instance, you may want to choose a Mozart or Beethoven piano sonata (or a sonata for other instruments) or quartet, and some baroque pieces (perhaps by Bach or Handel), or you may instead (or besides) decide to choose more chromatic, post-Romantic materials by composers such as Wagner, Mahler, Hugo Wolf, or Strauss. Find passages in these pieces that you may be able to connect using some of the techniques of modulation we have studied in this chapter. You may also connect various passages by means of your own newly composed commentary.

Alternatively, you may also quote large passages from a piece from the past, and add other quotations and original material on top of that quotation. In any case, try to write a coherent piece within the context of stylistic diversity and "stylistic incoherence," emulating as much as possible the excellent collage compositions by Rochberg and Berio we have studied in this chapter.

Chapter 13

Simplifying Means

As a response to both the rigorous complexity of serialism and, on the composer's part, the relative loss of control over the final sounding product in aleatoric music, a number of composers in both America and Europe turned, beginning in the 1960s, to styles based on radical simplifications of the compositional materials. The term **minimalism,** often used to refer to these styles, was defined by composer La Monte Young as "that which is created with a minimum of means." Both the term and the definition, however, can be misleading. Simplicity and economy of means do not necessarily mean use of minimal materials. Even when some of the musical parameters are greatly reduced (pitch and harmony, for instance), other parameters may be organized according to complex processes (for instance, rhythm). Having said this, and because the term minimalism has become widely accepted in the musical community, we will use it in this chapter as a general label to be broadly applied to musical styles based on the reduction of compositional means.[1]

The term "minimalism" originated in the visual arts, in reference to paintings and sculptures by artists in the 1960s (such as Frank Stella, Tony Smith, Donald Judd, Robert Rauschenberg, and Richard Serra), consisting of elemental, simple forms, normally used in repetitive and symmetrical geometric patterns. In a parallel process, musical minimalism originated in the United States, also in the 1960s, as a style based on the repetition of simple patterns featuring a steady pulse and slow, gradual changes. The main American composers in the early stages of minimalism were La Monte Young, Terry Riley, Steve Reich, and Philip Glass. Among the most significant composers in the United States and Europe who have branched out from early American minimalist

---

[1]Interesting introductions to minimalism and the major minimalist composers can be found in K. Robert Schwarz, *Minimalism* (London: Phaidon Press, 1996) and Keith Potter, *Four Musical Minimalists* (Cambridge: Cambridge University Press, 2000). The basic aesthetic issues and analytical challenges presented by minimalism are perceptively discussed by Jonathan Bernard in the following two articles: "The Minimalist Aesthetic in the Plastic Arts and in Music," *Perspectives of New Music* 31 (1993): 86–132, and "Theory, Analysis, and the 'Problem' of Minimal Music," *Concert Music, Rock, and Jazz since 1945: Essays and Analytical Studies,* ed. Elizabeth West Marvin and Richard Hermann (Rochester: Rochester University Press, 1995), 259–84.

♪♪ Example 13.1   Philip Glass, *Music in Fifths,* nos. 13–17

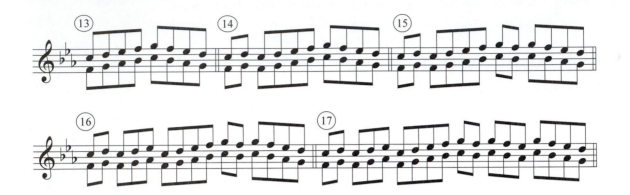

styles into various types of postminimalist idioms, besides Reich and Glass, we can mention Michael Nyman in the United Kingdom, Louis Andriessen in Holland, and John Adams in the United States.

Early minimalist pieces normally featured simple, usually diatonic, and mostly consonant pitch patterns. The two basic compositional principles of early minimalism are repetition (which normally results in a steady pulse) and a slow, gradual process of change. This style can be seen, for instance, in the fragment from Glass's *Music in Fifths* (1969) shown in Example 13.1. An initial scalar figure of eight notes (four ascending and four descending) performed in parallel fifths is repeated and progressively expanded until it becomes a figure of 200 notes. The fragment in Example 13.1 shows the initial figure and four successive steps in the process of expansion. In the first two steps, the initial two notes in the ascending subgroup, and then the initial two notes in the descending subgroup, are repeated. In the next two steps, repetitions of the initial three notes in each subgroup are added to the previous patterns, and so on.

Although American minimalism is a Western musical style, fully integrated into Western musical traditions, it has also incorporated influences from a variety of non-Western traditions (such as Indian *rāga,* Balinese gamelan, or West-African drumming), both aesthetically, philosophically, and technically (particularly in the rhythmic and instrumental realms). Similarly, pop music and American popular culture have exerted a significant influence on American minimalist composers, as reflected in the pervasive, steady beat of early minimalist music, and in the fact that this music was usually performed by the composers' own ensembles, on loudly amplified electronic instruments, often in nontraditional venues that attracted large numbers of younger listeners, including numerous rock fans.

This brings us to the controversies that have raged around minimalism for several decades. Detractors of minimalism criticize its simplicity and its apparent stasis and lack of direction, whereas its supporters praise its accessibility and clarity, and its capacity to reestablish a connection between contemporary music and audiences (it is indeed undeniable that minimalism has enjoyed a remarkable level of public and commercial success). In his essay "Music as a Gradual Process," Reich explained that in his early minimalist pieces, the compositional process and the sounding musical product were identical.[2] In other words, Reich argued that, while in serial music there is a hidden structure disconnected from the sounding music (and this is one of the causes for the subsequent disconnection between the music and the listener), in his own music the listener can hear the actual compositional process as part of the final sounding product, in a way that makes the music more accessible. The simple surfaces, along with this type of commentary from a leading minimalist composer like Reich, have usually discouraged analysis of minimalist music beyond mere description of surface processes, following the assumption that there is nothing to be found below the audible surface. In recent years, however, a number of scholars have demonstrated that despite the apparent surface simplicity in minimal music (particularly in the realm of pitch), the underlying rhythmic structures in this music often feature rich and complex relationships, which we can understand only through perceptive and sophisticated analytical approaches.[3] Jonathan Bernard, moreover, has argued that minimal music is not static. Although repetition and simplicity of pitch collections may be interpreted as elements of stasis, the unrelenting and gradual processes of change featured in most minimalist music are anything but static and create a sense of directed motion or progression.[4]

Following the analytical models proposed by some of these scholars, in this chapter we first study fragments of representative pieces by Reich and Andriessen. In the third analysis of the chapter we examine a complete composition by Estonian composer Arvo Pärt. Pärt is one of several European composers (along with the Polish Henryk Gorecki and the British John Tavener) whose music features a severe reduction of compositional means, yet whose style is radically different from the pattern-oriented, rhythmically active style of American minimalists. Each of these composers achieves serene, spiritually intense musical idioms whose economy of means and quiet utterances bespeak of fervent religious and mystical artistic temperaments.

ANALYSIS 13.1: REICH, *VIOLIN PHASE* (ANTHOLOGY NO. 36)

In his early minimalist experiments (such as *I Can't Stop, No,* and *Mescalin Mix,* both of 1963), Terry Riley used and manipulated **tape loops,** fragments of recorded sound that were endlessly repeated. In his 1964 composition *In C,* for an indeterminate

[2]See Steve Reich, *Writings about Music* (Halifax: The Press of the Nova Scotia College of Art and Design, 1974), pp. 9–11.

[3]See, in particular, Paul Epstein, "Pattern Structure and Process in Steve Reich's *Piano Phase," The Musical Quarterly* 72/4 (1986): 494–502; Richard Cohn, "Transpositional Combination of Beat-Class Sets in Steve Reich's Phase-Shifting Music," *Perspectives of New Music* 30/2 (1992): 146–77; Timothy Johnson, "Harmonic Vocabulary in the Music of John Adams: A Hierarchical Approach," *Journal of Music Theory* 37/1 (1993): 117–56; and John Roeder, "Beat-Class Modulation in Steve Reich's Music," *Music Theory Spectrum* 25/2 (2003): 275–304.

[4]Jonathan Bernard, "Theory, Analysis, and the 'Problem' of Minimal Music," pp. 262–63.

♪♪ Example 13.2   Terry Riley, *In C,* figures 1–6

number of performers, usually considered the first truly minimalist instrumental composition, each player repeats each of fifty-three brief melodic modules (the first six of which are shown in Example 13.2) as many times as he or she wishes before moving on (individually) to the next one.

This piece ushered the techniques of repetition and phasing into instrumental composition. In a **phase shifting** process, two or more performers begin repeating a pattern in unison. At one point, one of the players increases his or her tempo very slowly and gradually until his or her pattern is one rhythmic unit ahead of the other player's pattern. The process of progressive acceleration may continue at will, and the repeated patterns may further become out of sync by two, three, four, or more notes. While the horizontal component of phase-shifting music is static and repetitive, the vertical or contrapuntal component is ever changing (and so are the rhythmic relationships among the different parts) as long as at least one of the parts follows a process of tempo acceleration. Some early minimal pieces by Steve Reich (born 1936), such as *It's Gonna Rain* (1965) and *Come Out* (1966) feature both tape loops and phase shifting, and some of his best-known instrumental compositions of this early period, including *Piano Phase* (1967), *Violin Phase* (1967), *Phase Patterns* (1970), and *Drumming* (1971) are essentially based on phase-shifting techniques.

Beat-Class Sets in the *Violin Phase* Cycle

Richard Cohn has developed a methodology to explore the metric and rhythmic relationships in phase-shifting compositions.[5] Establishing an analogy between beats in a cyclic (that is, repeated) pattern and pitch classes, Cohn has used the concept of beat-class set, which has the same formal properties as its analogous pitch-class concept, the pitch-class set.[6] A **beat-class set** (abbreviated as "bc set") is a set made up of the beats that are attacked in a pattern. If the cycle has a total of twelve beats, as is often the case in Reich's patterns, we can arrange the beat classes in a *mod-12* system, just as we do with pc sets. Take, for instance, the basic pattern for *Violin Phase,* reproduced in Example 13.3. The total cycle for this pattern is made up of twelve beats (eighth notes), of which ten are attacked (all but beat-classes 5 and 6). Because we perceive the pitches

---

[5]See Cohn, "Transpositional Combination of Beat-Class Sets in Steve Reich's Phase-Shifting Music." The present analysis of *Violin Phase* is based on Cohn's work.

[6]The concept of "beat-class set" was originally developed by David Lewin in *Generalized Musical Intervals and Transformations.*

♪♪♪ Example 13.3   Beat-class sets for the *Violin Phase* pattern

beats: 0   1   2   3   4   5   6   7   8   9   T   E

Low:	0					7			PF: (05)
High:		2	4				9	E	PF: (0257)
High+Low:	0	2	4		7		9	E	PF: (024579)

♪♪♪ Example 13.4   Pitch-class sets for the *Violin Phase* pattern

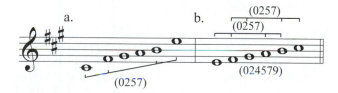

a.

b.

(0257)

(0257)

(024579)

(0257)

in the high and low registers as grouped by register into significant subsets, we can use register as a criterion of segmentation. The low register is made up of two C♯ attacks on beat-classes 0 and 7, whose prime form is (05). The high register consists of four high E attacks (the beats with double stops) on beat classes 2, 4, 9, E, whose prime form is (0257). The set that results from the union of both registral extremes (high plus low) is 0,2,4,7,9,E, prime form (024579).

    This segmentation allows for several interesting observations that illustrate the close relationship between the rhythmic and pitch components of the *Violin Phase* pattern. Let us examine the pitch structure of the pattern, as shown in Example 13.4. In the first place, we see that the pattern is generated by a chain of perfect fourths, C♯–F♯–B–E. That is, the generating interval is 5 (or its complement, 7), the same interval that generates the low subset of beat classes. The complete chain of P4s, C♯–F♯–B–E, has a prime form of (0257), the same as the prime form for the high subset of beat classes. Finally, the pc set for the complete pc content of the pattern is (024579), as shown in Example 13.4b. This is, again, the same prime form as the bc prime form for the combined high and low attacks. Moreover, this set is also generated by interval 5: it can be organized as a chain of ascending P4s beginning on G♯, and the set actually results from two overlapping (0257) subsets, as shown in Example 13.4b. In other words, not only are the

main sets for both the beat-class pattern and the pitch-class pattern the same, but they are all generated by one single pc or bc interval, 5.

The Large-Scale Design: Prolongational Regions

Phase-shifting processes begin with patterns played in unison. The process includes two steps: a **phase-shifting progression,** in which one of the voices accelerates and actually effects the phase shifting, and a **prolongational region,** in which the new displaced relationship between the patterns is locked in, and we hear a canon at a certain number of beats. At reh. 3, after the first acceleration, the first canon is locked in and the first prolongational region starts, until the next acceleration begins and we move on to the next progression. Example 13.5 shows the location of the pattern in each of the two voices at reh. 3. The pattern in violin 1 is in its original position, which we call T_0. The same pattern in violin 2 appears displaced forward by eleven eighth notes. The second pattern thus results from a transposition by eleven beats, or T_{11}. The prolongational region represented by this canon can be expressed as $T_{0,11}$, where the two subscript integers define the position of the pattern in each of the voices within the twelve-beat module.

The first section of *Violin Phase* (reh. 1–6) consists of a series of five prolongational regions in alternation with four phase-shifting progressions. The sequence of prolongational regions is $T_{0,0}$–$T_{0,11}$–$T_{0,10}$–$T_{0,9}$–$T_{0,8}$, as shown in Example 13.6.

The original two voices (the upper two voices on the score) become fixed at $T_{0,8}$ for the rest of the piece, performed by either violins 1 and 3 or by a tape track. From reh. 9 through reh. 11b, the phasing process stops, and violin 2 performs a series of "resulting patterns." These are new patterns derived from the notes of the combined pattern that results when the two patterns of $T_{0,8}$ sound together. This whole section (reh. 9–11b) is thus a further prolongation of $T_{0,8}$. At reh. 12, however, the phasing process resumes. The upper two voices still hold the $T_{0,8}$ canon (and do so through the end of the piece), but a third voice (played by violin 2) begins a phase-shifting process moving through T_8, T_7, T_6, T_5, and T_4. The prolongational regions through this section (reh. 12 to reh. 16),

Example 13.6   The prolongational regions in the opening section of *Violin Phase* (reh. 1–6)

taking all three voices into account, are $T_{0,8,8}$–$T_{20,8,7}$–$T_{0,8,6}$–$T_{0,8,5}$–$T_{0,8,4}$. At reh. 17, $T_{0,8,4}$ is fixed on a tape track, and violin 2 begins a new process of resulting patterns until the end of the piece. The sequence of prolongational regions for the complete piece is thus as follows: $T_{0,0}$–$T_{0,11}$–$T_{0,10}$–$T_{0,9}$–$T_{0,8,8}$–$T_{0,8,7}$–$T_{0,8,6}$–$T_{0,8,5}$–$T_{0,8,4}$.

The Large-Scale Design: Density of Attack Points

Cohn has demonstrated that the density or frequency of attack points in the composite of all the voices in *Violin Phase* (that is, the resulting patterns that the listener actually hears when the voices are performed together) features a well-planned, large-scale

Regions:	$T_{0,0}$	$T_{0,11}$	$T_{0,10}$	$T_{0,9}$	$T_{0,8,8}$	$T_{0,8,7}$	$T_{0,8,6}$	$T_{0,8,5}$	$T_{0,8,4}$
Attack points:	4	8	6	7	8	9	10	8	12

Figure 13.1 Attack points for the high bc set in each of the *Violin Phase* regions

design. Although we could focus on any of the registral beat-class sets we identified earlier, let us examine the frequency of attacks for the "high" bc set, the high-E/double-stop pattern that we identified with the (0257) prime form as it appears in the original cycle. In the $T_{0,0}$ region, this register is attacked four times per measure. In the composite pattern for the $T_{0,11}$ region (reh. 3) we hear eight attacks for this register. The $T_{0,10}$ region features six attacks, the $T_{0,9}$ region features seven, and the $T_{0,8,8}$ region features eight. Figure 13.1 shows the number of attack points for this register in each of the regions for the complete piece.

We can make several observations from this design. First, we see that no two consecutive regions feature the same number of attack points per measure. Second, the sequence of attack points is inversionally symmetrical around the 8 axis (you can verify this by adding the first and last members of the sequence, then the second and second to last, third and third to last, and so on, and you will note that the result of each of these sums is always the same, 16). Finally, and perhaps more significantly, the sequence moves from the minimum number of attacks (four) to the maximum (twelve, or total saturation, where every beat is attacked). Other than the two eights, in regions $T_{0,11}$ and $T_{0,8,5}$, the sequence follows an ascending progression from 4 to 12 (with integers 5 and 11 replaced by the two eights we have just noted). The piece begins with the minimum number of attacks for the high-register (0257) bc set, then moves through an ascending sequence toward saturation, and when it reaches the maximum possible number of attacks, the phase-shifting process ends, and so does, eventually, the piece.

Conclusions

Our discussion of *Violin Phase* allows for several reflections on the nature of so-called minimal music. On the very surface, this music uses, or appears to use, minimal compositional materials. But, as we have discovered, even the surface processes in *Violin Phase* cannot be thought of as minimalistic, especially because they result in complex, rich rhythmic relationships among the voices. Moreover, we have identified several levels of "hidden" structural relationships that are not likely to have arisen in a coincidental way: First the basic bc sets and pc sets for the original pattern are not only the same, but they are all generated by interval 5. Second, a large-scale formal plan exists for the piece, mostly defined by a scheme of transpositional regions. Third, this particular scheme of transpositional regions results in a large-scale design of attack points that features an ascending progression (with some diversions) from minimum density to maximum density of attacks for the register we have focused on (the high-register attacks). And fourth, this progressive sequence of attacks provides a large-scale plan that implies motion toward a goal (in this case, total saturation of high-register attacks).

In other words, *Violin Phase* is neither static nor devoid of linear direction: both motion and direction are provided by the combined designs of transpositional regions and attack-point density. Minimalism, as we see in this analysis, should not be interpreted (as it often has by its critics) as "simplistic," "simple-minded," or unworthy of systematic, serious study because of a supposed lack of structural content and depth.

ANALYSIS 13.2: ANDRIESSEN, *DE STAAT,* MM. 1–161 (ANTHOLOGY NO. 37)

Dutch composer Louis Andriessen (born 1939) is one of the foremost representatives of European minimalism. After some early experimentation with serialism and with post-serial avant-garde techniques in the late 1950s and early 1960s, Andriessen became disillusioned with the gap between the musical avant-garde's progressive ideals and its failure to communicate with a large audience. His commitment to Marxist ideology, moreover, led him to reject conventional performance venues, such as established concert halls, and professional symphony orchestras, which he viewed as focuses of bourgeois and elitist culture, and to search for both a performance medium and a musical language that would serve as vehicles for his social and political principles. He solved the former by founding his own ensemble, De Volharding (Perseverance), just as both Reich and Glass did in the United States. The discovery of Riley's and Reich's early minimalist compositions was a breakthrough in Andriessen's career and led to his adoption of a repetitive, minimalist musical idiom in pieces such as *De Volharding* (1972), *Worker's Union* (1975), *Hocketus* (1975–77), and *De Staat* (1972–76), Andriessen's major composition from the 1970s. Other significant influences on Andriessen's music came from Stravinsky and from jazz, particularly Charlie Parker, Count Basie, and Stan Kenton.[7]

Listen to the opening section of *De Staat* (Anthology no. 37). The influence of American minimalists will be obvious to you, but you will also note that this music is different from American minimalism. What are the differences between the two styles? As you listen to our example, identify its main sections. How would you define the characteristic elements for each of these sections? Focus now on the pitch and pitch-class content for each section. What collections can you identify?

De Staat

Andriessen considers composers (and artists in general) as part of a social and cultural context, of which they should be active and committed members through their art. To Andriessen, the act of composing is a social and cultural activity, and the musical composition is a social construct. This is precisely, in essence, the message of *De Staat*

---

[7]For a general introduction to Andriessen's life and music, see Maja Trochimczyk, ed., *The Music of Louis Andriessen* (New York: Routledge, 2002). Robert Adlington's *Louis Andriessen: De Staat* (Burlington, VT: Ashgate, 2004), on the other hand, is a monographic study of Andriessen's best-known composition.

("The Republic"). The text for this work is made up of passages from Plato's *Republic,* which address the relationship between the individual and the community, in particular the artist and the state, and the conditions and limitations that the state sets for artistic expression.

De Staat is scored for a large and distinctive instrumental ensemble (*not* a symphony orchestra): four each of oboes/English horns, trumpets, horns, trombones, and violas; two electric guitars, one electric bass guitar, two harps, two pianos, and four female voices. All these forces are amplified (and loudly so) and are distributed on both sides of the stage in the form of two symmetrically arranged, identical groups. *De Staat* is structured into three large choral sections, with instrumental sections used in the introduction preceding the first chorus, to separate the choral sections, and to conclude the piece, respectively. The formal plan for the complete piece is roughly symmetrical, with shorter first and third choruses and a longer second chorus. The fragment that we will discuss includes the opening instrumental introduction and the complete first chorus.

Introduction and First Chorus: Sections and Style

The fragment we are studying includes three clearly defined sections, which we will refer to as sections 1, 2, and 3, respectively: (1) the opening section, performed by two oboes and two English horns (mm. 1–67); (2) a second instrumental section, initially by the four trombones, later joined by the four horns (mm. 68–104); and (3) the first choral section (mm. 105–161). Each of these three sections has a clear timbral identity (double reeds, brass, and female voices with a mixed ensemble, respectively). The two instrumental sections share the same type of metric/rhythmic activity: they are both written in irregular changing meters in which the basic common unit is the eighth note, and the voices are largely homorhythmic. The choral section, on the other hand, is in $\frac{4}{4}$ meter throughout (which, however, shares the same eighth-note basic value with the previous irregular meters), and features a layered rhythmic texture (the voices move in half notes or longer values, and the instruments move in a continuous stream of eighth notes). Otherwise, the motion from one section to the next is sudden and abrupt, recalling the familiar Stravinskian technique of juxtaposition. Because of the high uniformity within each section (the uniform elements are timbre, rhythm, pitch, dynamics, and attack or articulation), and the general absence of harmonic or linear direction, we can also think of each of these three sections as a "moment" within a "moment form" context.

Contrast between adjacent sections is a key element in *De Staat*'s formal design. In the first place, and as we will see next, each of the three sections in our fragment is based on its own characteristic, specific pitch collection. Sections 1 and 3 are diatonic and relatively consonant (at least within the diatonic collection used in each of them), whereas section 2 is highly chromatic and dissonant. Sections 1 and 3 are scored in the middle-to-high register, and section 2 is scored in the low or middle-to-low registers. Instrumentation and timbre are also elements of contrast, as we have already noted. Within these marked elements of contrast between sections, continuity is provided by the unchanging eighth-note pulse (which remains a constant almost throughout the complete composition) and the unrelenting loud dynamics (also continued, with almost no changes, throughout the complete piece).

Pitch Organization

One of the basic compositional units of *De Staat* is the tetrachord. Several sections in the piece are built on single tetrachords. Other sections, on the other hand, are thoroughly chromatic and result from chromatic collections of pitch classes (including the complete chromatic scale). Pitch organization in ancient Greece was based on tetrachordal units, and Andriessen's preference for tetrachords in *De Staat* has been regarded as a reference to the Greek system.[8] That may be so, although only in a very general sense: Greek tetrachords were always built within the span of a perfect fourth, whereas Andriessen tetrachords are not bound by this constraint. We will now discuss the general pitch organization in each of the three sections we are studying.

Section 1: Mm. 1–67

The opening 67 measures of the piece are built on a single symmetrical tetrachord, B–C–E–F, of the (0156) type. The tetrachord is never transposed, so we always hear the same four pitch classes, [11,0,4,5]. Within this highly static pitch-class content, however, Andriessen achieves a sense of constant motion by creating a very active four-voice polyphony in which contrapuntal motion, involving all four voices almost constantly, never abates, and in which the type of counterpoint changes every few measures. Thus, we can identify the following subsections, determined by the type of counterpoint: (a) mm. 1–4 feature counterpoint by contrary motion with paired voices (two high and two low), with no immediate repetition of pitches; (b) mm. 5–18 include melodic repetition of pitches and are written in free counterpoint; (c) mm. 18–27 feature imitative counterpoint, with all four voices presenting the same motive; the voices are tonally paired, with the two lower voices imitating the upper two at the lower fourth; (d) in mm. 28–41 we hear four successive points of imitation at the unison, separated by rests; (e) mm. 42–59 return to a free contrapuntal texture; and finally (f) mm. 59–67 feature a return to the imitative counterpoint with tonally paired voices, as in mm. 18–27.

The opening four measures of the piece, which do not include immediate repetition of pitches, also feature an interesting harmonic property: in each of the twenty-one attacks in these measures we hear a harmonic (0156) [11,0,4,5] at the same time as we hear chains of melodic (0156) [11,0,4,5] sets in all four voices, as shown in Example 13.7. Despite this harmonic saturation of (0156) sets, we still hear the lines and the strong melodic/contrapuntal motion as the main element in these four measures. Beginning with m. 5, and because of the repetition of pitches, the harmonic combinations range from the complete (0156) set to various trichordal or dyadic subsets of (0156) [11,0,4,5] to occasional unisons.

Section 2: Mm. 68–104

This section illustrates one of the aspects of Andriessen's music that sets it apart from American minimalism: its dissonant chromatic edge. The section begins with the

[8]Andriessen has also pointed out the structural role of number 4 in *De Staat*: there are four of each instrument, and pitch material is often derived from tetrachords. See Trochimczyk, p. 135.

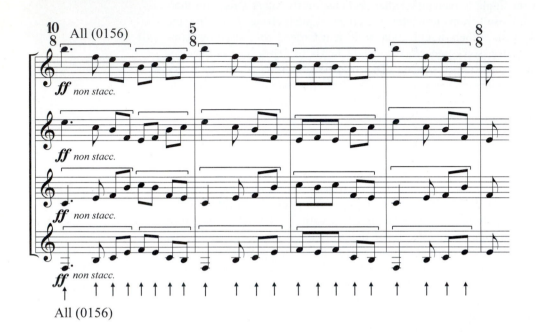

alternation of two harmonic tetrachords, (0167) and (0156), but moves immediately into progressively dissonant counterpoint. The addition of the four horns in m. 87 increases the aggressive, edgy sound of this section: now eight different lines move in homo-rhythmic chromatic counterpoint in loudly amplified dynamics.

Section 3: Mm. 105–161

The third section consists of chorus 1. The words for this chorus are taken from a section of Plato's *Republic,* which explains that to be well understood, people need to sing in a common rhythm, and both mode and rhythm should be in agreement with the text. To convey this message, Andriessen moves back to a diatonic, tetrachordal pitch-class collection, D–E–G♯–A, or (0157) [2,4,8,9]. Four female voices, doubled (with occasional variants) by two violas, perform a haunting, free-flowing melody on the (0157) tetrachord, in long note values, and mostly in unison (with occasional harmonizations by second or, in one single case, by fifth). The rest of the participating instruments perform seven ostinato patterns (labeled A through G in Example 13.8) on either the complete (0157) [2,4,8,9] collection, or on a subset of this collection. Because of the fast tempo, the total harmonic effect of the ostinatos is that we hear a constant background of a harmonic (0157). The complete (0157), however, is not always present, as shown in Example 13.8: in some of the eighth-note attacks we hear harmonic (026) or (015) subsets of (0157).

Example 13.8   The ostinato patterns as heard in m. 106

Conclusions

Our discussion of pitch organization in these three sections confirms that sections 1 and 3 are diatonic, tetrachordal sections (and hence relatively consonant, inasmuch as the resulting harmonic sound is, at most, that of a tetrachord), whereas section 2 is chromatic and highly dissonant.

It is worth mentioning at this point that some published analyses of *De Staat* have focused, among other issues, on aspects of modality and pitch centricity. The assumption for both types of analyses (modal and pitch centered) is that we can determine both mode and pitch center from only a tetrachordal collection. As an exercise, try to do so: what do you think is the mode (thinking in terms of the traditional "church" modes) and the pitch center for section 1? For section 3? (Section 2 is too chromatic for either categorization.) Do not continue reading until you come up with an answer.

You are likely to have experienced the difficulties of trying to determine the "tonic" or "final" for a supposedly full diatonic collection from only four actual pitch classes. It is likely, moreover, that different students will have come up with different interpretations, as have some of the major Andriessen scholars. Thus, in his book cited in footnote 7, Adlington labels section 1 as Lydian on F, and so the tetrachord would be organized as F–B–C–E–(F), while Trochimczyk (also in her book cited in footnote 7) labels it as Phrygian on E (tetrachord E–F–B–C). In a similar discrepancy for section 3, Adlington thinks of it as Mixolydian on E (E–G♯–A–D–[E]), and Trochimczyk as Lydian on D (D–E–G♯–A). This choral section has also been interpreted as Ionian on A (A–D–E–G♯–[A]). What is your reaction to these interpretations? Does Andriessen define clear tonal centers in any way that would warrant this type of modal thinking? A single tetrachord can, of course, be a subset of several different diatonic modal scales, and hence can be interpreted with various modal labels. Do you think this is the best way to hear the tetrachords in *De Staat,* or does it make more sense, musically and analytically, to think of Andriessen's tetrachords as just that, tetrachords, self-sufficient collections of four pitch classes that are not meant to be heard as subsets of implied modal collections?

As a final conclusion, we can review the elements in *De Staat* that set this music apart from American minimalism. Whereas American minimalism tends to be relatively consonant and diatonic, Andriessen's minimalist compositions include sections of chromatic and harshly dissonant harmonies, and display, in general, a tendency to louder dynamics and edgier, more aggressive sound than the compositions by his American counterparts.

ANALYSIS 13.3: PÄRT, *CANTUS* (ANTHOLOGY NO. 38)

The process that led Arvo Pärt (born 1935) to an extreme simplification of means in his music beginning in 1976 is similar to Andriessen's, but instead of adopting simplification as a result of social and cultural concerns, Pärt did so as a result of deep introspection and spirituality. As Paul Hillier, the author of the major study of Pärt's music, has written, "Pärt uses the simplest of means—a single note, a triad, words—and with them creates an intense inner quietness and an inner exaltation."[9] Before reaching this stage as a composer, Pärt, like Andriessen, went through a period of serial and avant-garde experimentation, including the use of extensive collage techniques. Unsatisfied with the

---

[9]Paul Hillier, *Arvo Pärt* (Oxford: Oxford University Press, 1997), p. 1.

♪♪ Example 13.9   Arvo Pärt, *Cantus*, mm. 24–26, first violin parts

M-voice

T-voice

results of this experimentation, Pärt continued searching for a personal voice and, after two separate periods of silence, came up indeed, in 1976, with a unique and highly distinctive style. Pärt's music is often said to be "outside time" or "timeless." Its simplicity is strictly modern and has appealed to a large audience all over the world, and yet some of the main sources of Pärt's are among the oldest Western musical styles: Gregorian and Russian Orthodox chants and Medieval and Renaissance vocal polyphony (particularly Notre Dame organum, Machaut, Ockeghem, Obrecht, and Josquin).

The Tintinnabuli Style

Some of Pärt's best known compositions (such as *Fratres, Cantus, Tabula rasa, Missa sillabica, Cantate Domino,* and *Summa,* all of 1977) are written in a style known as **the tintinnabuli style.** The onomatopoeic word *tintinnabulum* is an ancient Latin term for a small bell. Thus, "tintinnabuli" can be understood as "in the style of tinkling bells." A sounding bell produces a tone rich with partials, which we hear as a cloud of complex resonance ringing out all around us. Pärt's tintinnabuli style achieves a similar effect through the continuous presence of one or more members of a triad (a tonic triad, the one and only triad we hear throughout the whole piece). The two elements of this style are the tonic triad and the corresponding diatonic scale. There is neither chromaticism nor chromatic dissonance. Dissonance is always diatonic and results from linear processes, through which various tones from the diatonic scale are at times combined.

The basic elements of tintinnabuli style are shown in Example 13.9, which reproduces the first violin part for mm. 24–26 of *Cantus*. Hillier uses the terms M-voice and T-voice to refer to the two usual voices that make up a tintinnabuli texture. The **M-voice** is the melodic voice (hence the M), which normally consists of stepwise motion within the diatonic scale proper to the triad for a specific piece. The **T-voice** is the tintinnabuli voice, which sounds the members of the tonic triad. In Example 13.9, the tonic triad is A minor, and the scale is A natural minor. The upper voice is the M-voice (and carries nothing but the natural minor scale), and the lower voice is the T-voice, sounding members of the A minor triad in such a way that the T-voice moves down to the next lowest member of the triad just before a unison with the M-voice can take place (that is, the T-voice keeps moving out of the way of the M-voice).

 Example 13.10   Pärt, *Cantus*, M-voices in mm. 7–16

Cantus in Memory of Benjamin Britten

Pärt's *Cantus* is, in its stark simplicity, a gripping example of how intensely deep and expressive a minimal musical language can be. This is also a piece in which, to paraphrase Reich, the compositional process and the finished, sounding product are identical. The compositional process is as follows:

(1) A bell is sounded (on the pitch A) throughout the piece in groups of three strokes separated by rest.

(2) After the initial three solo bell strokes, five voices enter in canon, from highest to lowest: first violins, second violins, violas, cellos, and basses, respectively. Each of these voices bears the same melodic process: beginning on a high A, each subsequent melodic fragment results from going back to the high A and adding one more pitch each time to a descending A natural minor scale: A/A–G/A–G–F/A–G–F–E, and so on. This process, which defines the five M-voices in *Cantus,* is illustrated in Example 13.10 (in which only M-voices are indicated, with slurs showing each melodic fragment in the descending additive process).

(3) The piece is written in compound time, and the M-voice in the first violins is written following a constant long-short pattern (where long = two shorts). Each of the subsequent M-voices in the canon comes in an octave lower than the previous one, and in note values which are proportionally twice as long as the previous voice's values. In other words, this is a mensuration canon (a type of canon widely used in Medieval and Renaissance music, in which the same melody is presented in either a different meter between *dux* and *comes,* or in proportionally longer or shorter

values). Because each voice presents the melody in augmentation with respect to the previous voice, we hear each voice as being performed at a tempo twice as slow as the previous voice.

(4) Each of the parts of the string orchestra, except for the viola, is divided into two groups and played *divisi.* The top group plays the M-voice we have just described, while the bottom group plays the T-voice. The T-voice consists always of the member of the A-minor triad immediately below the fragment of the A-minor scale sounding at any particular time. As we saw in Example 13.9, the member of the triad in the T-voice changes at the point where both voices would reach a unison. The central instrument, the viola, is the only part that bears only an M-voice and no T-voice.

(5) Eventually all voices, one by one, reach a member of the A-minor triad in the low register, where they stop the melodic process. Beginning in m. 65, where the first violins settle on middle C, the process progressively slows down, until it comes to a full stop on a sustained, low A-minor chord in mm. 103–108.

(6) The work begins *ppp* and follows a single process of gradual dynamic growth, until a *fff* is reached in m. 63 and sustained to the end of the piece.

In summary, we see that a single compositional process, which can be simply formulated, governs the whole piece. What are your observations and conclusions regarding the musical power of such a simple process? Despite its static pitch content, the piece displays a definite forward motion. Why? What elements give this piece its dramatic and expressive intensity? Does the piece fulfill, with such minimal ingredients, its functional purpose as an elegy, and how does it do so?

APPLICATION AND CLASS DISCUSSION

Discuss the aesthetic issues raised by musical minimalism. What is your opinion of the styles we have studied in this chapter, from the point of view of a listener? Simplicity of means is attractive to some listeners, whereas it may also generate negative reactions in others. What would possible arguments be for both positive and negative reactions to minimalism from different listeners? What is your own reaction to this style, and why?

Although the concept of minimalism would seem to imply perceptual ease, is this the case in all the music we have studied in this chapter? Are there perceptual complexities of some kind in this music, and what are they?

Further Listening

The following list provides suggestions for further listening to music by composers studied in this chapter or related to the styles and techniques we have studied (if possible, listen while following the score):

1. Riley, *In C*

2. Reich, *Come Out*

3. Reich, *Drumming*

4. Reich, *Music for 18 Musicians*

5. Glass, *Einstein on the Beach*

6. Andriessen, *De Staat* (complete)

7. Adams, *The Chairman Dances*

8. Pärt, *Fratres*

9. Pärt, *Tabula rasa*

Terms for Review

minimalism	prolongational region
tape loops	the tintinnabuli style
phase shifting	the M-voice
beat-class set	the T-voice
phase-shifting progression	

CHAPTER 13 ASSIGNMENTS

I. Analysis

1. Analyze Reich's *Phase Patterns,* for four electric organs, and write a brief essay explaining your findings. You will find the score and recording for this piece in your music library. The model for your analysis will be the discussion of *Violin Phase* in this chapter. The measure in *Phase Patterns,* however, includes only eight eighth-note beats, in contrast to twelve in *Violin Phase.* Your beat-class calculations will thus have to be in *mod-8* arithmetic. There are only eight integers in this system, from 0 to 7; integer 8 is equivalent to 0, 9 is equivalent to 1, and so on. Consider the bc sets formed by each hand separately, and compare their prime forms. Then investigate the phase-shifting process in the complete piece and determine the progressions and prolongational regions, which you will label following the system we applied to *Violin Phase.* Determine the long-range design for this piece based on the sequence of prolongational regions, and on the design of attack points in each of these regions (here again, consider each hand separately).

2. Study the harmony in the opening section of John Adams's *The Chairman Dances* (mm. 1–91), which you will find in your music library. Listen to the passage several times and identify the different harmonic elements: types of chords, sonorities, or pitch class sets; bass line; and other linear elements that affect and define the harmonic component in this music. How does it all work together? Write a brief essay explaining your findings and provide a harmonic reduction or graph of some kind to accompany your essay.

3. Listen to and study Pärt's *Fratres* or *Tabula rasa.* After you analyze and understand the musical process and the organization of musical materials for your piece of choice, write a brief essay explaining what you have

found. Discuss any aesthetic, perceptual, or performance issues that you may find pertinent to your musical observations.

II. Composition

1. Write a piece in a rhythmically active minimalist style of your choice. You may choose to use one of Reich's phase-shifting pieces as a model, or another one of Reich's later compositions not based on this technique. Or you may choose a style more akin to Andriessen's minimalism as represented in *De Staat*. In any case, be careful in the choice and organization of your pitch materials (make it simple!) and in the planning of your metric and rhythmic processes, which should be as interesting and lively as possible. Moreover, you should devise some large-scale plan for the piece, either as a formal plan, as a plan of prolongational regions, or as a plan of harmonic regions determined by characteristic harmonic or pitch-class collections.

2. Write a piece in a style inspired by Pärt's music. Strive for utmost simplification of means, both in your pitch and temporal structures, although you may or may not choose to use a tintinnabuli style. First choose a basic pitch structure for your piece and a temporal (metric/rhythmic) process that you will follow. Then decide on a general plan for the whole piece, including instrumental and dynamic processes. Let the music and the processes unfold in a quiet and unrushed temporal frame and preserve a strong sense of unity throughout the piece.

Chapter 14

Into the Twenty-First Century

Writing about the present is a particularly challenging task because while we are immersed in the present, we lack the historical perspective provided by distance. Consequently, this chapter will only attempt to provide some notes on what appear to be some of the major trends in present-day composition and on some of the composers that are active and recognized within these trends. Perhaps the most accurate concepts to describe the compositional scene in the early twenty-first century are eclecticism and pluralism. The most contrasting and varied compositional techniques and approaches seem to coexist, and this is perhaps one of the times in the whole history of music when a composer has had the most options (or at least options that are going to be considered "legitimate" by his or her contemporaries) from both the technical and stylistic points of view. Within these options, some trends seem to have emerged, and we will first survey them briefly.

Extensions of Modernist Aesthetics

A first category would be represented by composers who have chosen to continue or extend some of the "modernist" idioms from the twentieth century, such as serialism, aleatoriality and sound mass, or a large variety of post-serial avant-garde techniques developed in the later decades of the twentieth century. One of the leading figures in this category is the influential British composer and teacher Brian Ferneyhough, who has practiced and proposed an aesthetic of "**new complexity**" or "**maximalism,**" characterized by the use of highly complex techniques and textures, and by the frequent intersection of electronic and acoustic techniques. Among composers born after 1950 who would fall into this general category (and who, however, may also appear in some of the other categories) we can cite the Finnish Magnus Lindberg and Kaija Saariaho, the British George Benjamin and Robert Saxton, and the American Tod Machover.

Neo-Romanticism and Neo-Expressionism

A second category is represented by composers who have chosen to do just the opposite. These composers look back to the beginning of the twentieth century or, even farther back to the end of the nineteenth century, to find suitable models more or less anchored in tonality or pitch centricity. In the work of these composers, twentieth-century aesthetics come full circle in a return to the post-Romantic type of chromatic tonality or free atonality that was practiced in the early years of the century (in some cases to a clearly post-Wagnerian or post-Mahlerian aesthetic) .

Within this broad category, we find two broad subcategories. In some cases the music of these composers is clearly neotonal or features some kind of pitch centricity. In the United States, some younger composers have followed the aesthetic line of Aaron Copland, Samuel Barber, Leonard Bernstein, David Diamond, Ned Rorem, or John Corigliano. Their music is neotonal, contrapuntal, with a strong rhythmic profile, and brilliantly orchestrated. Some of the composers who can be included in this group are Christopher Rouse, Richard Danielpour, Aaron Jay Kernis, Jennifer Higdon, and Robert Maggio.

The work of some other composers, however, also establishes a link with the beginning of the twentieth century, but not so much with post-Romantic tonality as with post-Romantic, expressionistic atonality or post-tonality. The work of these composers is highly chromatic and highly motivic, and does not feature clear references to tonal centers, in a way similar to the free atonal music of such composers as Schoenberg and Berg in the early decades of the twentieth century. Composers in this category include the British Oliver Knussen and Thomas Adès, the German Wolfgang Rihm and Manfred Trojahn, the American Augusta Read Thomas, and, here again, the Finnish Kaija Saariaho in some of her works.

Postminimalist and Hybrid Composition

Hybrid composition incorporates influences and techniques from both the Western concert tradition and from either popular music or non-Western music. Influences of pop and rock music are particularly noticeable in some post-minimalist works. The music of Andriessen also seems to have had a lasting impact on some of the younger post-minimalist composers. Important composers influenced by both minimalism and popular music are the Americans Michael Torke and Michael Daugherty and the British Steve Martland. A number of composers around the Bang-on-a-Can Festival in New York, particularly Julia Wolfe, David Lang, and Michael Gordon, also show strong influences from both pop music and Andriessen. The influence of pop and rock, however, is not limited to post-minimalist composers, because it can also be heard in the music of such nonminimalist composers as Adès and Machover.

In the rest of this chapter we will examine fragments of compositions by Augusta Read Thomas, Thomas Adès, and Kaija Saariaho, three composers born after 1950 (the first composers in this category that we have studied in this book), all of whom had established solid reputations by the end of the twentieth century. Their musical output around the turn of the century represents the work of mature composers speaking in distinctive compositional voices.

THE RETURN OF THE MOTIVE

In the first chapters of this book we saw that motives and motivic relationships were an essential component of composition and structural coherence in the early decades of the twentieth century. Although motivic elements have been used by various composers throughout the century, in some of the post-tonal music composed in recent years, motives have fully recovered the prominence they had in the music of composers such as Schoenberg and Webern as one of the central, or in some cases the central, component of pitch organization. This is particularly the case in music that falls into the general category that we have labeled, in our discussion at the beginning of this chapter, as neo-Romantic chromatic atonality or post-tonality. In the following pages we will examine the opening passages of three works by three prominent members of the generation of composers born in the second half of the century, *Spring Song* (1995), by Augusta Read Thomas (born 1964); *Asyla* (1997), by Thomas Adès (born 1971); and *Ariel's Hail* (2000), by Kaija Saariaho (born 1952). All three works have in common a sparse and expressive use of compositional materials, and all three display post-Romantic, post-tonal idioms freely based on the manipulation of intervallic and motivic cells.

ANALYSIS 14.1: THOMAS, *SPRING SONG* (ANTHOLOGY NO. 39)

Augusta Read Thomas's *Spring Song* (1995) is a free-flowing, rhapsodic piece for solo cello. Anthology no. 39 reproduces the opening forty-one measures of the piece, and our analysis will focus on the first fifteen of these. Typically post-Romantic traits in this composition are its chromatic and motivic character, its improvisatory and rhapsodic nature, and its processes of formal growth in *fortspinnung* style. Changing meters and a variety of rhythmic groupings and figures contribute to the improvisatory, flowing character of this music. From a large-scale formal perspective, the piece allows for various interpretations. What is clear is its division into phrases. Phrases grow from previous phrases, and sections are built by addition of phrases, although sectional divisions are not usually clearly defined. The section marked "molto intenso, bell-like" in mm. 33–38 can be interpreted as a refrain or recurring idea because it returns toward the end of the piece, in mm. 78–83. Otherwise, formal relationships are motivic rather than sectional, and motives generate the clearly articulated phrases, which in turn generate the complete composition. Thomas's technique is indeed particularly Schoenbergian in her use of motivic variation as a means of formal growth.

Intervallic and Motivic Analysis by Phrases

We will focus our analysis on the opening six phrases (mm. 1–15), and we will examine the role of interval and motive as they both generate and provide unity to the music. Phrases are marked by various ways of slowing down or stopping the motion, normally by means of a fermata, longer notes, or a ritardando. New phrases may also be marked with indications of expression (such as "delicate and introverted") or by timbral and performance markings ("sul tasto, non vibrato"). Following these markers, we can identify the following six opening phrases: (1) mm. 1–3, (2) mm. 4–5, (3) mm. 6–8, (4) m. 9, (5) mm. 10–13, and (6) mm. 14–15. Despite the brevity of some of these phrases, each of them is a self-contained short formal unit with a clear beginning and

Example 14.1   Augusta Reed Thomas, *Spring Song,* mm. 1–3

a clear end. We will now examine each of these phrases in some detail, following the annotations provided in the accompanying examples.

Phrase 1 (mm. 1–3)

In just three measures, as shown in Example 14.1, phrase 1 establishes some of the essential compositional parameters of the piece. In the first place, we note the prominence of the melodic half step, particularly the very expressive, chromatic descending motion, <−1>. This motion appears four times in the phrase, and a fifth time in ascending form, <+1>. The first three statements of the <−1> motive begin on pitch classes F♯, D♭, and G♯, respectively, which form the (027) [1,6,8] set class.

   The prominence of the <−1> chromatic, dyadic motive suggests the next analytical step, which is to group the semitonal dyad with one of its adjacent pitch classes to form a trichord. This exercise reveals that four of the six resulting trichords are members of the (014) set class, including the opening string of three (014) trichords, and the other two are of the (013) and (012) classes. The three trichords can be generated by linear transformation (of the type we discussed in the section on Ruth Crawford Seeger in Chapter 6) in the network (014)→(013)→(012).

Phrase 2 (mm. 4–5)

Phrase 2, reproduced in Example 14.2, confirms the significance of the <−1> motion (which appears four times) and of the (014) trichord, which also appears four times. Here again, the first three statements of the <−1> motive begin on pitch classes G♯, F♯, C♯, outlining again the same (027) [1,6,8] set class that we saw in mm. 1–2. Two new elements introduced in this phrase are a prominent (016) motive in m. 4 and the tetrachord (0134) made up of two overlapping (014) trichords, which we hear as the closing melodic motion of the phrase, including two <−1> motions (the last of which involves the last two, long notes). In the two opening phrases, we can also note the close motivic relationship between the different set classes we have identified. For instance, the (016) set in phrase 2, G♯–G–D, can be seen as a linear extension of the (014) from phrase 1 (m. 2), which also included the G♯–G dyad, E–G♯–G. The (013) in m. 3, C♯–C–E♭, on the other hand, is also a linear transformation of the (014) C♯–C–E in m. 4, which

Example 14.2   Thomas, *Spring Song,* mm. 4–5

Example 14.3   Thomas, *Spring Song,* mm. 6–13

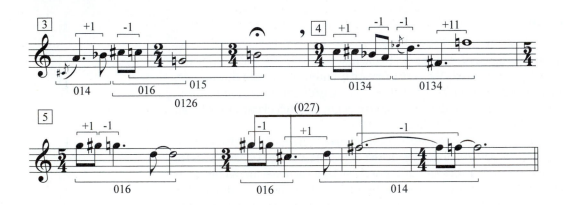

includes the same chromatic dyad C♯–C. Thomas places special emphasis on the particular C♯–C and G♯–G dyads throughout this opening passage.

Phrases 3–5 (mm. 6–13)

Phrases 3–5, as shown in Example 14.3, further feature ten cases of the half-step motive, in either the <−1> or <+1> form. Phrase 4, moreover, consists only of half-step motives and, in a single case, the intervallic inversion of <−1>, that is, <+11>. Two of the half-step motives in phrases 3 and 4 include the dyad C♯–C, and three motives in phrase 5 include the dyad G♯–G. The last three half-step motives in phrase 5 (mm. 11–13) begin on pitch classes G♯, C♯, F♯, representing the third appearance of the (027) [1,6,8] set class in the same function of generating adjacent half-step motivic chains.

The three basic trichords that make up phrase 3 are (014), (016), and (015). The first two of these are already familiar from previous phrases. (015) is a new addition to the trichordal collections in this passage, and it is actually a set that will become very

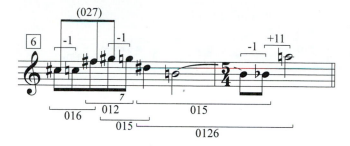

Example 14.4   Thomas, *Spring Song*, mm. 14–15

prominent in the phrases that follow immediately after the passage we are analyzing (phrases 7 and 8). All three trichords are related by linear transformation in the network (014)→(015)→(016). The last four pitch classes of phrase 3 form the tetrachord (0126), which brings together two previously encountered trichords, (012) and (016). Phrase 4, on the other hand, breaks up into two tetrachords of the (0134) class, a set class that we already identified earlier in phrase 2. Phrase 5 consists of three trichords, two of the (016) class, and one of the (014) class.

Phrase 6 (mm. 14–15)

As could be expected, the material in phrase 6 (shown in Example 14.4) does not feature any surprises. There are three instances of the <−1> motive and one of the <+11> motive which, mirroring the closing of phrase 4, here also closes phrase 6. The first two <−1> motives begin on C♯ and G♯, which, together with the intervening F♯, form the already familiar (027) [1,6,8] set class. In this phrase we first hear two overlapping trichords we have heard earlier, (016) and (012), followed by a four-pitch-class motive that combines both of these trichords, (0126). Moreover, we can also observe the presence of two overlapping (015) trichords in m. 14, the set class that was introduced in phrase 3, and which becomes particularly prominent in the following two phrases.

Two Characteristic Motives

Two significant motives appear in several locations and shapes in this opening section. Example 14.5 shows the appearances of the first of these motives, which we will refer to as motive x. Its initial contour, as it appears in the opening motive in m. 1, is <−8, −1>. That is, the motive features a m6 and a m2. Measure 1 includes two more overlapping statements of the same motive, now presented as <−1, +8> and <+8, −1>, respectively. Phrase 3 begins in m. 6 with an inversion of the original contour for motive x, <+8, +1>. Phrase 4 in m. 9 ends with two overlapping statements of motive x, now as <−1, −8> and <−8, +11>. The latter includes the first instance of an inversion of one of the original intervals, <−1> inverted into <+11>. A similar inversion of the other original interval, <−8> inverted into <+4>, takes place in the final appearance of motive x in

Example 14.5   Thomas, *Spring Song*, motive x

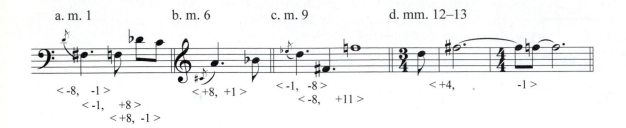

a. m. 1   b. m. 6   c. m. 9   d. mm. 12–13

Example 14.6   Thomas, *Spring Song*, motive y

a. m.2   b. m.4   c. mm.6–7   d. m.10   e. m.11   f. m.14

this section, the closing of phrase 5 in mm. 12–13, where it is presented as <+4, −1>. Note that none of the seven cases of motive x in the passage features the same ordering or sequence of intervals. Finally, you may also observe that the x motives that close both phrases 4 and 5 (mm. 9 and 12–13) are based on the same ordered collection of pitch classes that opens the piece, D–F♯–F.

The second characteristic motive, which we will call motive y, is the (016) motive whose appearances in this passage are shown in Example 14.6. Unlike motive x, motive y shows substantial contour consistency and presents mostly two intervallic shapes, <−1, −6> and its variation <−1, −5>. Only in m. 14 do we find two other variations of the motive, <−1, +6> and a more distantly related <−1, −4> which actually results in a (015) trichord rather than the (016) that makes up the rest of the y motives. A remarkable characteristic of motive y is that each of its seven occurrences include one of two ordered chromatic dyads, G♯–G or C♯–C. Moreover, both of the ordered motives G♯–G–D and G♯–G–C♯ appear twice in the music (in mm. 2 and 11 in the first case, and mm. 4 and 10 in the second case).

Conclusions

Our analysis shows that the compositional focus (as well as the main unifying element) of *Spring Song* is the motive and motivic associations. A central chromatic motive,

<−1> or <+1>, is the element of cohesion for various trichords that include it. Among these, (014) and (016) are the most prominent, but other important trichords are also (012), (013), and (015). All five trichords are related in a network of linear transformations, and various combinations of them generate the tetrachords (0134) and (0126), which appear at various places in the opening section. The particular motives that we have labeled as x and y not only provide further motivic coherence to the passage, but also specific pitch-class references in the form of recurring pitch-class collections.

ANALYSIS 14.2: ADÈS, *ASYLA*, II (ANTHOLOGY NO. 40)

Thomas Adès's four-movement symphony *Asyla* (1997), a powerful and highly expressive work that has contributed strongly to the British composer's world renown, is scored for a large orchestra, which Adès uses in particularly inventive and colorful ways.[1] Anthology no. 40 reproduces the score for the opening 43 measures of the slow second movement. We will limit our discussion to the opening nineteen measures. Much of Adès's music falls within the realm of neo-Romantic, chromatic post-tonality, as is the case with the movement we are examining now. Listen to the complete movement and identify sections, main compositional materials in each of the sections, and section relationships. First focus on the introductory section, mm. 1–10. What is interesting about this section? What is the basic compositional principle that best defines it? Then focus on the main thematic element, the melody in the bass oboe in mm. 11–19. How is this line composed, and how can we analyze it?

The Introduction

After the initial two chords in the trumpets, we hear the introductory section by a group of instruments that Adès is very fond of, the pitched/keyboard percussion instruments (pianos, celesta, cowbells) and the harp. The main compositional process for this section unfolds in the cowbells. Some of the cowbell pitches are doubled or reinforced by the other instruments, and in other cases the other instruments provide supplementary pitch material. Rhythmically, the cowbells are also straightforward, essentially following a pulse of quarter notes, while the other instruments provide elements of rhythmic irregularity that subvert the regular pulse of the cowbells. The result is a superposition of regularity, which we can hear in the pattern that unfolds in the cowbells and which we will define below, and irregularity or unpredictability, which is represented by the other instruments.

A reduction of the cowbell material, shown in Example 14.7, will help us understand the process of regularity. This reduction includes the opening two chords by the trumpets, and, in one case only, a pitch played by the first piano, the A in m. 3, shown

---

[1]Two recent studies of Adès's music that include discussions of the second movement of *Asyla* are John Roeder, "Toward the Analysis of Postmodern Music: Cooperating Continuities in Compositions of Thomas Adès," *Music Analysis,* forthcoming; and Aaron Travers, "Interval Cycles, Their Permutations and Generative Properties in Thomas Adès's *Asyla,*" Ph.D. diss., University of Rochester, 2005.

♪♪ Example 14.7   Thomas Adès, *Asyla,* II, reduction of mm. 1-10

in parentheses in the example. Otherwise, all the remaining pitches can be found in the cowbells. Let us examine the patterning and voice-leading processes in this reduction.

In the first place, we notice a repeated melodic pattern in the top voice of this reduction, a descending line from C to G. This immediately reminds us of a traditional passacaglia or chaconne pattern, the descending tetrachord C–B–A–G, or, in minor, C–B♭–A♭–G, or, in its chromatic variant that brings both of these together, C–B–B♭–A–A♭–G. The line that we hear in the cowbells is itself a variant of the chromatic chaconne pattern, C–B–A♯–A–G. We hear this pattern three times in mm. 1–6, and then a new variant beginning a step higher in mm. 7–10, now as D–C–B–B♭–A. In all these cases, a descending perfect fourth is covered, as is the case in the chaconne tetrachord.

The intervallic constitution of the first three repeated patterns, <−1, −1, −1, −2> immediately establishes the predominance of stepwise motion in the voice leading, and in particular of the descending minor second. The fourth pattern reverses the order of these four intervals to become <−2, −1, −1, −1>. The accompanying voice or voices only confirm the total supremacy of stepwise motion in the passage, with preference for <−1> or <+1> motion, but also with several cases of whole steps and a single case of an intervallic inversion of a whole step, that is, a minor seventh shown as <−10> in m. 6 of the reduction.

The Theme

Several stylistic traits are immediately apparent in the theme first presented by the bass oboe in mm. 11–19: it is motivic, chromatic, sequential, and it is a compound melody (that is, a melody that is made up of two or more lines in different registers). First, let's look at it as a compound melody. A reduction showing the three lines that make up the theme can be seen in Example 14.8. The two-note motive pervading each of the lines is the descending chromatic dyad <−1>, with not a single exception. This motive is one of the reasons why we hear this theme as very expressive (besides the fact that

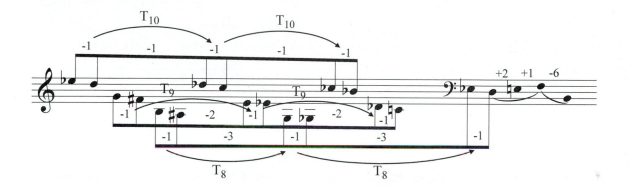

Example 14.8   Adès, *Asyla,* II, reduction of the theme in mm. 11–19 as a compound melody

the actual performance indications for the theme are "*molto cantabile, espr.*"). The expressive and rhetorical power of the descending half step, the "sigh" of Renaissance and Baroque music, has been known by composers for centuries. We will examine the theme from several perspectives that will allow us to discover the astonishing wealth of compositional craft packed into this brief melody.

The Compound Melody

As a compound melody, the theme breaks up into three lines in three different registers. Example 14.8 shows the three lines annotated with an intervallic analysis. In the first place, what kind of theme do you recognize in the upper melody? This is precisely the chromatic passacaglia pattern, now in its complete form, that we encountered in the introduction. This line is fully chromatic: its intervallic contour is thus $<-1, -1, -1, -1, -1>$. The middle line, on the other hand, follows a different constructive principle. While it is still based on the chromatic descending motive, $<-1>$, the motives are now separated by whole steps rather than half steps. The intervallic contour is thus $<-1, -2, -1, -2, -1>$. The lower line follows the same process which has been started by the upper two lines. It is still based on the $<-1>$ motive, but now the motives are separated by descending minor third motions, $<-3>$. The resulting contour is $<-1, -3, -1, -3, -1>$. Each of the three lines is generated by transpositional combination, an operation we learned in Chapter 2 in the context of symmetrical motives in Bartók. In the upper line, the three $<-1>$ motives feature transpositional combination at T_{10}; in the middle voice, the transpositional combination is at T_9, and in the lower voice it is at T_8.

The Sequence

The theme is sequential, and we can think of the first slur in mm. 11–13 as the sequence model; the following two slurs are the sequence fragments. The sequence, however, is not exact, but is rather a modified sequence (that is, the fragments are not exact transpositions of the model). Example 14.9 shows how the sequence works precisely. The

Adès, *Asyla*, II, reduction of the theme in mm. 11–19 as a sequence

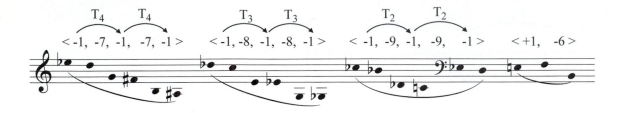

model presents three <−1> motives separated by <−7> gaps. The gap of separation is increased by one semitone in each of the following fragments. Thus, in the second fragment, the <−1> motives are separated by <−8> gaps, and in the third segment by <−9> gaps. The process is thus similar to what we saw in the analysis of the compound melody, where the gap of separation between <−1> motives was also increased by a half step in each of the three lines read from top to bottom. Here again, the <−1> motives in each sequence are related by transpositional combination, at T_4, T_3, and T_2, respectively.

The Collections and Pitch-Class Sets

A particularly interesting aspect of this melody becomes apparent when we consider the various pitch-class collections involved in its composition. First, consider the collections that result from the compound melody as shown in Example 14.8. The upper voice is a fragment of the chromatic scale. The middle voice, on the other hand, is an octatonic fragment. Finally, the lower voice displays a complete hexatonic scale (a scale that we studied in Chapter 2, made up of six pitch classes, and in which there is alternation of half steps and minor thirds). The surprise comes when we look at the scales that result from the sequential fragments in Example 14.9. The first fragment is a complete hexatonic scale, actually the scale with the same pitch classes as the hexatonic scale in the lower line of the compound melody. The second sequential fragment contains the same octatonic collection that we found in the middle line of the compound melody, and the third sequential fragment is built on the same chromatic collection we identified in the upper line of the compound melody. The two levels of hexatonic, octatonic, and chromatic collections are shown in Example 14.10.

The three collections as found in this theme are summarized in Example 14.11. All three fragments are totally symmetrical. The chromatic fragment can be divided into two (012) subsets, and the octatonic and hexatonic fragments can be divided into (013) and (014) subsets, respectively. Here again we see a linear relationship among the trichordal subsets of these collections, (012)→(013)→(014). If we break these collections into <−1> motives, as Adès does in his theme, we identify only five motives among the three collections, which we have labeled as a–e in Example 14.11. These same motives are also identified with the same letters, a–e, on the reduction in Example 14.10.

♪♪♪ Example 14.10   Adès, *Asyla,* II, the collections in the theme

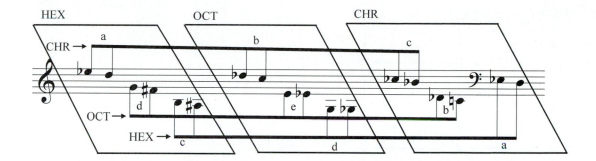

♪♪♪ Example 14.11   The three collections that make up the Adès theme

a. Chromatic

$(012) + (012) = (012345)$

b. Octatonic

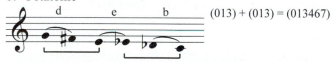

$(013) + (013) = (013467)$

c. Hexatonic

$(014) + (014) = (014589)$

We can summarize the motivic relationships in the theme by means of a 3 x 3 matrix of <−1> motives, as shown in Example 14.12. The letters refer to the <−1> motives we labeled in Examples 14.10 and 14.11. Arrows show the transpositional operations (and the chains of transpositional combinations) that map each motive onto the adjacent motives in the matrix (that is, onto the next motive in the compound melody, shown as the horizontal lines in the matrix, or onto the next motive in the actual melody as heard in the music, shown as the vertical columns in the matrix). We can see that the matrix

A matrix of motives and transpositions for the Adès theme

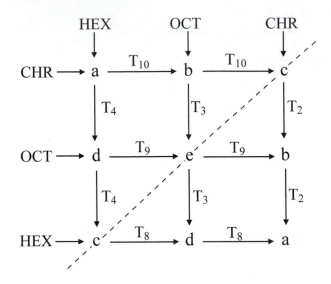

forms a neatly symmetrical network of motives and transpositions. The axis of symmetry is diagonal, as shown on the example by the diagonal dotted line. Motives above and
below the dotted line are arranged symmetrically. Transpositions are, too, although the
symmetrically corresponding transpositions are related by intervallic complementarity; that is, T_4 corresponds with T_8, T_9 with T_3, T_{10} with T_2, and so on.

Conclusions

The fragment of Adès's music that we have analyzed shows some stylistic similarities with the fragment by Augusta Read Thomas. Both compositions are remarkable
in their immediate, expressive eloquence. Both of them rely on the motive and motivic
relationships as a means to achieve this expressive immediacy, and both of them take
advantage of the expressive power of the descending half-step motive, the "sigh" of
old times (which we have already discussed in Chapter 4 of this book, in the context
of Schoenberg's "Angst und Hoffen"). The compositional processes, however, are very
different in each piece. Thomas's processes seem to be mostly rhapsodic and improvisatory in nature, whereas our analysis of the Adès theme shows a carefully planned
motivic structure that brings together, in a symmetrical construct, three also symmetrical pitch-class collections, the chromatic, octatonic, and hexatonic scales, respectively.
Through these materials, Adès connects not only with the expressive world of such
composers as Schoenberg and Berg (particularly through the use of motive and chromaticism), but also with the structural world of a composer like Bartók (through the use
of symmetrical structures and symmetrical scales).

ANALYSIS 14.3: SAARIAHO, *ARIEL'S HAIL* (ANTHOLOGY NO. 41)

Our last analysis will involve the first and only piece in this book composed after the turn of the millennium, in September 2000. In many of her orchestral and ensemble compositions, Kaija Saariaho brings together instrumental and computer music in a way that blends acoustic and electronic sounds in a world of suggestive textural and timbral sonorities. The song that we will study in this chapter, however, is a fully instrumental piece that shows that Saariaho relies on intervals and motives to generate (and provide unity to) a freely growing, rhapsodic discourse which has many common traits with the compositional style of the piece by Augusta Read Thomas that we just studied.

Ariel's Hail (Anthology no. 41) is one of several songs composed by Saariaho on texts by William Shakespeare. In this case, the text uses three fragments from *The Tempest*. In that play, Prospero is the deposed Duke of Milan, stranded on a deserted island with his daughter, Miranda. Ariel is a fiery island spirit who has become Prospero's assistant. The Duke's enemies happen to sail on a boat by the island, and the ship sinks in a storm "performed" by Ariel through Prospero's magic powers. The first stanza in *Ariel's Hail*'s text (from "All hail" to "Ariel, and all his quality . . .") is taken from the scene in which Ariel reports back to his master Prospero after the storm (I.ii). In the second stanza (from "I boarded the King's ship" to "And burn in many places . . ."), Ariel explains how he created havoc on the ship by means of his fire powers (I.ii). The third stanza (from "Then I beat my tabor" to "so I charmed their ears") comes from a scene in which Caliban, Stephano, and Trinculo are plotting to murder Prospero. Ariel spies on them invisibly, and at one point interrupts and confuses them with his music (IV.i).

For our present discussion we will focus on the beginning of the first stanza only (mm. 1–12). Before we do so, study and discuss the complete piece and determine sections, phrases, and relationships among them. Examine and discuss also the relationship between text and form, and the possible instances of text painting.

The Vocal Part

There are three vocal statements in the brief section we are examining (mm. 1–12). This line immediately demonstrates Saariaho's use of intervals and intervallic combinations (pitch-class sets) to compose her music. Saariaho's "favorite intervals" are the minor second and the minor and major thirds (as she told this author in a personal interview). The combination of these intervals (which we will refer to as "Saariaho's signature intervals") creates a number of characteristic pitch-class sets, particularly the trichords (013), (014), (015), and (037), all of which are prominently used in this song. The three vocal statements are shown in Example 14.13, and we can see that each of them can be built by means of two overlapping trichords, (014) and (015) in all cases. The F# in the flute in m. 11, moreover, can also be integrated with the voice to form a (014) with the last two pitch classes of the vocal melody.

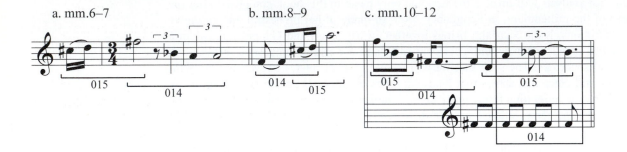

♪♪ Example 14.13   Kaija Saariaho, *Ariel's Hail,* vocal statements, mm. 1–12

The Instrumental Parts

The instrumental parts in the song are written for flute and harp. Let us first examine the harp part. Ariel is a spirit of fire. Nothing represents fire better than a flame. If you look at a flame spot in a fire, you will see that a flame is always similar to itself, yet never exactly the same. Every time the flame flares up it will be higher or lower, larger or smaller than the previous flame. This is exactly what takes place in the harp, in what we can call the flame motive, representing Ariel.

The Flame Motive

In mm. 1–12, the ascending flame motive (which we will refer to as "the flame" in the following commentary) is heard six times in the harp (and a seventh time in m. 12). Each of these motives is similar to but different from each of the other ones, as shown in Example 14.14. The flame motive provides an element of harmonic stability and stasis on the one hand, while on the other it also provides an element of motivic variation. The opening flame in m. 1 is also the smallest one, with only four pitches. The repeated bass pitch, A♯, establishes an area of pitch centricity by pedal which lasts to m 7. After that measure, in mm. 8-10, the bass notes change, but the presence of A♯ (now as a repeated B♭) continues in an inner voice. The four pitch classes of the first flame can be grouped into two equal, overlapping (013) trichords, which add up to a (0134) tetrachord. All these sets are built with Saariaho's "signature intervals," the minor second and the major and minor thirds.

Flames 2 through 5 (mm. 2, 3, 4, and 7, respectively) share the A♯ bass and the same upper tetrachord, a (0156) [1,2,6,7] made up of two equal, overlapping (015) trichords. Here again, both the tetrachord and the trichords result from combinations of Saariaho's signature intervals. Two of these flames, in mm. 3 and 7, contain no elements other than the A♯ (or B♭) bass and the (0156) tetrachord. The initial trichord (including the first three pitch classes) for this flame is (014). The flames in mm. 2 and 7 include each an additional pitch that results in a different initial trichord in each case. The initial trichord in m. 2 is (013), and in m. 4 it is (037), while the added pitch in

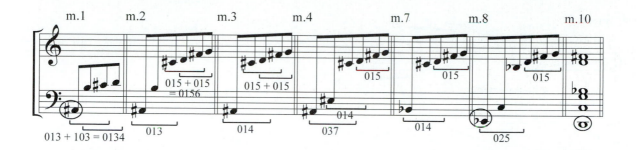

♪♪♪ Example 14.14   Saariaho, *Ariel's Hail*, the flame motive

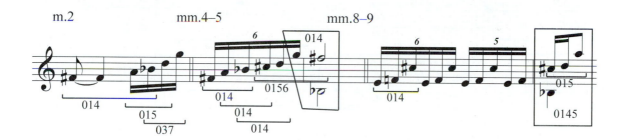

♪♪♪ Example 14.15   Saariaho, *Ariel's Hail*, the flute motives

m. 4 (the E♯) also forms a (014) with the following two pitch classes. Again, these are all trichords that result from Saariaho's signature intervals.

The only flame that departs from the characteristic intervals and from the prevailing trichords in the piece so far is the flame in m. 8, which features an opening (025) trichord (one that includes, for the first time, a major second) followed by the usual (015). The E♭ in the bass, however, takes on a particular significance when we consider the large-scale bass motion from the initial A♯ to the D that closes our section in m. 10. The three bass notes (circled in Example 14.14) are A♯–E♭–D, outlining the familiar (015) set which pervades the vocal melody and the flame motives, but now at the large-scale level.

The Flute Part

The flute part provides a connection between the harp part and the voice. Example 14.15 shows the three main statements of the flute in the section we are studying. All three statements are immediate extensions of flame motives in the harp, and all three have a flame quality themselves. The first one, in m. 2, can be broken up into three overlapping

♪♪ Example 14.16   Saariaho, *Ariel's Hail,* connections between flute and vocal motives

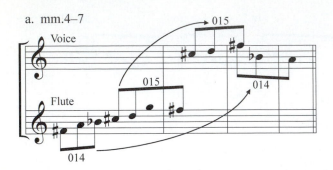

a. mm.4–7

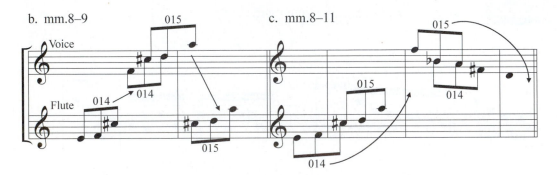

b. mm.8–9   c. mm.8–11

trichords of types we have already encountered in both the voice and the harp, and all three are derived from Saariaho's signature intervals: (014), (015), and (037).

The second flute statement, in mm. 4–5, begins with three overlapping (014) trichords and closes with a (0156) tetrachord, a set class that we had already found as the upper four pitch classes of the harp flame motive. The harp's lonely B♭ in m. 5, moreover, forms a (014) with the last two pitch classes in the flute. Finally, the third statement, in mm. 8–9, begins with a repeated (014) and closes with a (015), which forms a (0145) with the B♭ in the harp. This is a new tetrachord, but one that is not only built on Saariaho's signature intervals, but combines the (014) and (015) trichords.

We should also note that, while the flute part grows from the flame motives in the harp, the vocal part grows out of the flute statements, as shown in Example 14.16. The vocal statement in mm. 5–7 is an elaboration on the same pitches and pitch-class sets that the flute just stated in mm. 4–5 (Example 14.16a). The brief vocal statement in mm. 8–9 again parallels the pitch and pitch-class-set content of the simultaneous flute statement (Example 14.16b). Finally the vocal statement in mm. 10–11 begins with a reversal of both the order of the trichords from the flute statement in mm. 8–9 ([014]–[015] becomes [015]–[014]) and of the basic melodic contour (rapidly ascending at the end of the flute statement, rapidly descending at the beginning of the vocal statement), as shown in Example 14.16c.

Conclusions

Ariel's Hail is the third example in this chapter of a composition built on a limited collection of intervals and on motives that result from those intervals. Saariaho is highly consistent in her use of her "signature intervals" and a limited number of trichords and tetrachords generated by them. These intervals and pitch-class sets provide overriding unity to her song, and relate all voices in an organic whole which, otherwise, is substantially static from the perspective of pitch and harmony. This third example confirms the significance of the trend toward post-tonal, motivic and intervallic composition among some composers at the present turn of the century.

Further Listening

The following list provides suggestions for further listening to music by composers studied in this chapter or related to the styles and techniques we have studied (if possible, listen while following the score):

1. Lindberg, *Kraft* or *Kinetics*
2. Saariaho, *Château de l'âme* or *Du cristal*
3. Kernis, *Colored Field*
4. Higdon, Concerto for Orchestra
5. Knussen, *Where the Wild Things Are*
6. Rihm, *Die Hamletmaschine* or *Oedipus*
7. Penderecki, Violin Concerto no. 2 ("Metamorphosen")
8. Adès, *Asyla*
9. Thomas, *Spirit Musings*
10. Torke, *Run* or *Ash*
11. Martland, *Danceworks*

Terms for Review

new complexity
maximalism
hybrid composition

CHAPTER 14 ASSIGNMENTS

I. Analysis

1. Provide a detailed analysis of Augusta Read Thomas's *Spring Song,* mm. 16–41 (Anthology no. 39), following the analysis of mm. 1–15 that appears in this chapter.

2. Provide a detailed analysis of Saariaho's *Ariel's Hail,* mm. 12–end (Anthology no. 41), following the analysis of mm. 1–12 that appears in this chapter.

3. Write a brief analytical paper on Adès *Asyla,* movement III. Focus on texture, compositional and textural techniques, rhythmic/metric organization, and pitch organization. Explain the stylistic elements that make this movement an example of hybrid composition.

4. Write a brief analytical paper on one of the following songs by Saariaho, all on texts from Shakespeare's *The Tempest*: *Miranda's Lament*, *Caliban's Dream*, or *Prospero's Vision*.

II. Composition

Write a piece in neo-Romantic, post-tonal style for either a solo instrument or a small ensemble (duo, trio) with or without voice. Your models for this piece will be the compositions we have analyzed by Thomas and Saariaho. Your music should be expressive, chromatic, motivic, and use a limited number of intervals and pitch-class sets.

Epilogue

In the Introduction to this book, we compared the history of musical styles and compositional techniques in the twentieth century to a mosaic made up of numerous, sometimes contrasting, stylistic tiles. We explained that at times some composers stood on two or mores tiles at the same time or that they moved among various tiles in the course of their careers. We now have the perspective to look back at what we have studied and verify the validity of such a pluralistic view of the twentieth century. The musical materials we have studied in recent chapters indeed invite us to reflect again on the long-range stylistic developments in the past fifty years and in the twentieth century as a whole. Throughout this book, we have proposed a neutral, nonevaluative (that is, nonjudgmental) approach to the various and contrasting tiles that make up the stylistic mosaic of the twentieth century. In other words, we have treated all the tiles as equally valid, legitimate options for a twentieth-century composer. Some trends have appeared to be more mainstream than others, but in the long range and with the perspective of time and hindsight, some of the trends that originally appeared to be less influential have proven to be lasting and, in our days, are being reevaluated as having had more impact and durability than it had long been assumed they would.

Let us review and summarize the main historical and stylistic paths we have covered in this text. The major compositional trends in the first half of the century, as studied in this book, include, in the first place, the various approaches to *pitch centricity* represented by composers such as Debussy, Stravinsky, Bartók, and Hindemith. We have studied *neoclassicism* as a general approach to form and style that absorbs elements of the musical past, and through them establishes a creative dialogue with that past. We have also explored various musical styles that we could generally label as *modernist*. These styles encompass the music of such American *ultramodern* composers as Ives and Crawford as well as the *atonal music* of the Second Viennese School of composers, Schoenberg, Berg, and Webern. One of the most characteristic compositional methods in twentieth-century post-tonal music is *twelve-tone serialism*, including the various developments and extensions of serialism that took place after World War II. Classical twelve-tone music has been represented in this book by Schoenberg, Berg, Webern, and Dallapiccola, and our study of post-1945 serialism focused on the techniques and music of Stravinsky, Boulez, and Babbitt. *Rhythm, meter,* and *temporality* have been important compositional aspects of twentieth-century music. We have discussed these in a variety of contexts, but very particularly in Chapter 10, with focus on Bartók, Stravinsky, Ives, Messiaen, Carter, and Stockhausen.

If there is no question about the diversity and multiplicity of compositional styles in the first half of the twentieth century, diversity and multiplicity after 1945 become almost overwhelming to the student wanting to find and follow historical and stylistic threads that may illuminate the world of musical composition in the second half of the century. The initial dichotomy between proponents of *rigorous control* (in the form of the various forms of serialism we have studied in Chapter 9) and the proponents of *chance and indeterminacy* (initially, John Cage and the members of the New York School) was resolved in the early 1960s in the form of numerous post-serial styles and techniques that combined elements from both. We have studied some of these procedures (such as *limited aleatory composition, sound masses, textural and spatial composition,* and *net structures*) as they appear in the music of Lutosławski and Ligeti.

A new and further world of musical diversity was open by what we know as *postmodernist* approaches to composition. The dichotomy between conservative and progressive creative impulses (as dubious as it is in itself) fully dissolves in postmodern aesthetic attitudes. The past and the future meet, and the past is integrated into the present in many ways, such as the use of *quotation* and *collage* (as we have studied in the music of Rochberg and Berio) or the reincorporation of *tonal structures* into present-day compositional idioms, particularly in the music of many younger composers whose style could be labeled as *neo-Romantic* or *neo-expressionist.* This brings up the fact that, throughout the twentieth century (and despite the supposedly mainstream role of atonality, serialism, and the wealth of avant-garde, experimental post-serial idioms), there never ceased to exist major composers who continued creating music based on *tonality* or *extensions of tonality* (some of the composers we have mentioned in this context are Copland, Britten, Prokofiev, Shostakovich, Barber, Bernstein, Diamond, and Corigliano). Beginning in the early 1960s, moreover, some composers chose to adopt musical styles based on the extreme *simplification of materials,* which usually also entailed the adoption of more tonal, consonant structures. Although the general term *minimalism* has been used to refer to these styles, we have shown that there is great variety of sound and approaches among musics based on such a general principle as the simplification of compositional materials. Pieces we have discussed in this category include Stockhausen's *Stimmung,* Cage's *4' 33",* and the pieces by Reich, Andriessen, and Pärt we studied in Chapter 13.

There has been, throughout the twentieth century, an interest in the adaptation of electronic and, more recently, digital technologies to support or generate compositional processes. Besides the invention of various electronic instruments in the early decades of the century, two major electronic revolutions took place in the 1950s–60s (the "classical" electroacoustic period) and the 1970s–80s (the age of digital and computer technology). The study of the styles and techniques associated with electronic and computer music falls outside the scope of this book. In Chapter 14, however, we mentioned that in the work of some younger composers, such as Magnus Lindberg, Kaija Saariaho, George Benjamin, Robert Saxton, and Tod Machover, electronic and acoustic music intersect in a world of suggestive textural and timbral sonorities.

The great stylistic and technical variety we find in post-tonal music also requires a corresponding diversity of analytical approaches. Throughout this book we have strived to provide analyses appropriate to the character and type of music being analyzed at each stage. Analyses and analytical techniques have drawn on current scholarship and have followed an eclectic analytical path through the diversity of compositional styles in the twentieth century. In a way, the eclecticism of analytical approaches is dictated by the diversity of the analyzed material. Within this eclecticism, two general approaches can be pointed out. In music based on motives and pitch-class collections, including twelve-tone and serial music, our main tool has been pitch-class set theory. We have used set theory, at one level or another, to understand aspects of pieces by composers as diverse and chronologically distant as Debussy, Stravinsky, Bartók, Crawford, Schoenberg, Webern, Berg, Babbitt, Reich, Andriessen, Thomas, Adès, and Saariaho.

In music that features important structural spatial and registral components, and which functions more in pitch space than in pitch-class space, we have used some type of spatial analysis that accounts for these spatial characteristics. Our analyses of music by Lutosławski and Ligeti fall within this category. Besides these two general approaches, on the other hand, we have also used a variety of contextual analytical techniques, at times of a general type (such our analyses of pitch centricity in Chapters 1 and 2), at other times applicable only to very specific styles (such as the analyses of quotation and collage in Chapter 12), and finally, in some cases, applicable mostly to particularly idiosyncratic individual composers (such as Hindemith, Carter, and Messiaen).

Let us close this Epilogue with some further reflections on the historical study of post-tonal music. The linear conception of progress that has at times been adopted by some historians and composers proposes that only fully original and new art is truly legitimate at a certain historical moment, and that novelty is a sign of progress in the same way as attachment to old styles and forms is a sign of nonprogressive conservatism. Although this aesthetic philosophy validates integral serialism and the avant-garde movements of the 1950s and 1960s, what should we then make of more recent and widespread trends such as quotation and collage, neotonality, minimalism, neo-Romanticism, neo-expressionism, and the like?

As we saw in Chapters 12, 13, and 14, these trends are the norm among many composers in the past three or four decades. Moreover, a great number of younger composers seem to have adopted unabashed neotonal and neo-Romantic idioms. In a way, we are witnessing what the proponents of linear progress could think of as "reverse progress": from integral serialism to quotation and collage to minimalism to neotonality and neo-Romanticism, including a return to early twentieth-century post-tonal styles of motivic composition or even of pitch-centered scalar collections. Does this mean that all of a sudden most composers are backward-looking, "nonprogressive conservatives"?

Or does it mean that the linear-progress philosophy is essentially flawed, and we should instead think of some kind of cyclic or circular model of aesthetic progress as being more appropriate to music and the arts in general? In such a model, the return to old styles and forms, far from being reactionary, would be a type of forward motion and progress. This also leads to a reevaluation (currently in progress in the world of music criticism) of many composers who, through the twentieth century, have been considered too "conservative" to be accepted as mainstream by linear historiography (composers such as Prokofiev, Shostakovich, Britten, Barber, Bernstein, Diamond, Rorem, and many others), but whose music is now revisited, in the light of more recent developments, as being founded on perfectly legitimate twentieth-century aesthetics. The Verdi/Stravinsky maxim to which we have referred several times in the course of this book, "torniamo all'antico e sarà un progresso," seems to have full validity as we begin the twenty-first century. Or, as Sofia Gubaidulina put it, "The contemporary artist is faced with an extremely important task: finding a correlation between intuition and intellectual work. . . . It absolutely does not matter whether it looks new or old. News is good for newspapers . . . but art strives for depth, not for the news!"[1]

---

[1]Vera Lukomsky, "Sofia Gubaidulina: 'My Desire Is Always to Rebel, to Swim against the Stream'," *Perspectives of New Music* 36 (1998): 5–35.

Appendix
The List of Set Classes

The following list shows all set classes containing between three and nine pitch classes (trichords to nonachords). Complementary set classes are listed across from each other (thus, trichords are listed across from nonachords, tetrachords across from octachords, pentachords across from septachords, and so on). In his 1973 book *The Structure of Atonal Music,* Allen Forte assigned a double number to each set class, which we will call the set's Forte name. Forte names appear in the leftmost and rightmost columns in the list. The first integer in a Forte name (as, for instance, in 3–6) refers to the cardinal number of the set class (that is, 3–6 has three pitch classes). The second integer is an order number that indicates where the set appears in the list (3–6 appears in the sixth place in the list of trichords). The second and second-to-last columns are a list of set classes, including all the possible prime forms with a cardinal number of 3 to 9. The third and third-to-last columns show the interval-class vectors for all set classes. Finally, the central column indicates the degrees of transpositional and inversional symmetry. (See Chapter 3 for a detailed explanation of all these concepts.)

TRICHORDS						NONACHORDS
3–1	(012)	[210000]	1, 1	[876663]	(012345678)	9–1
3–2	(013)	[111000]	1, 0	[777663]	(012345679)	9–2
3–3	(014)	[101100]	1, 0	[767763]	(012345689)	9–3
3–4	(015)	[100110]	1, 0	[766773]	(012345789)	9–4
3–5	(016)	[100011]	1, 0	[766674]	(012346789)	9–5
3–6	(024)	[020100]	1, 1	[686763]	(01234568T)	9–6
3–7	(025)	[011010]	1, 0	[677673]	(01234578T)	9–7
3–8	(026)	[010101]	1, 0	[676764]	(01234678T)	9–8
3–9	(027)	[010020]	1, 1	[676683]	(01235678T)	9–9
3–10	(036)	[002001]	1, 1	[668664]	(01234679T)	9–10
3–11	(037)	[001110]	1, 0	[667773]	(01235679T)	9–11
3–12	(048)	[000300]	3, 3	[666963]	(01245689T)	9–12

TETRACHORDS						OCTACHORDS
4–1	(0123)	[321000]	1, 1	[765442]	(01234567)	8–1
4–2	(0124)	[221100]	1, 0	[665542]	(01234568)	8–2
4–4	(0125)	[211110]	1, 0	[655552]	(01234578)	8–4
4–5	(0126)	[210111]	1, 0	[654553]	(01234678)	8–5
4–6	(0127)	[210021]	1, 1	[654463]	(01235678)	8–6

4–3	(0134)	[212100]	1, 1	[656542]	(01234569)	8–3
4–11	(0135)	[121110]	1, 0	[565552]	(01234579)	8–11
4–13	(0136)	[112011]	1, 0	[556453]	(01234679)	8–13
4–Z29	(0137)	[111111]	1, 0	[555553]	(01235679)	8–Z29
4–7	(0145)	[201210]	1, 1	[645652]	(01234589)	8–7
4–Z15	(0146)	[111111]	1, 0	[555553]	(01234689)	8–Z15
4–18	(0147)	[102111]	1, 0	[546553]	(01235689)	8–18
4–19	(0148)	[101310]	1, 0	[545752]	(01245689)	8–19
4–8	(0156)	[200121]	1, 1	[644563]	(01234789)	8–8
4–16	(0157)	[110121]	1, 0	[554563]	(01235789)	8–16
4–20	(0158)	[101220]	1, 1	[545662]	(01245789)	8–20
4–9	(0167)	[200022]	2, 2	[644464]	(01236789)	8–9
4–10	(0235)	[122010]	1, 1	[566452]	(02345679)	8–10
4–12	(0236)	[112101]	1, 0	[556543]	(01345679)	8–12
4–14	(0237)	[111120]	1, 0	[555562]	(01245679)	8–14
4–21	(0246)	[030201]	1, 1	[474643]	(0123468T)	8–21
4–22	(0247)	[021120]	1, 0	[465562]	(0123568T)	8–22
4–24	(0248)	[020301]	1, 1	[464743]	(0124568T)	8–24
4–23	(0257)	[021030]	1, 1	[465472]	(0123578T)	8–23
4–27	(0258)	[012111]	1, 0	[456553]	(0124578T)	8–27
4–25	(0268)	[020202]	2, 2	[464644]	(0124678T)	8–25
4–17	(0347)	[102210]	1, 1	[546652]	(01345689)	8–17
4–26	(0358)	[012120]	1, 1	[456562]	(0134578T)	8–26
4–28	(0369)	[004002]	4, 4	[448444]	(0134679T)	8–28

PENTACHORDS   **SEPTACHORDS**

5–1	(01234)	[432100]	1, 1	[654321]	(0123456)	7–1
5–2	(01235)	[332110]	1, 0	[554331]	(0123457)	7–2
5–4	(01236)	[322111]	1, 0	[544332]	(0123467)	7–4
5–5	(01237)	[321121]	1, 0	[543342]	(0123567)	7–5
5–3	(01245)	[322210]	1, 0	[544431]	(0123458)	7–3
5–9	(01246)	[231211]	1, 0	[453432]	(0123468)	7–9
5–Z36	(01247)	[222121]	1, 0	[444342]	(0123568)	7–Z36
5–13	(01248)	[221311]	1, 0	[443532]	(0124568)	7–13

5–6	(01256)	[311221]	1, 0	[533442]	(0123478)	7–6
5–14	(01257)	[221131]	1, 0	[443352]	(0123578)	7–14
5–Z38	(01258)	[212221]	1, 0	[434442]	(0124578)	7–Z38
5–7	(01267)	[310132]	1, 0	[532353]	(0123678)	7–7
5–15	(01268)	[220222]	1, 1	[442443]	(0124678)	7–15
5–10	(01346)	[223111]	1, 0	[445332]	(0123469)	7–10
5–16	(01347)	[213211]	1, 0	[435432]	(0123569)	7–16
5–Z17	(01348)	[212320]	1, 1	[434541]	(0124569)	7–Z17
5–Z12	(01356)	[222121]	1, 1	[444342]	(0123479)	7–Z12
5–24	(01357)	[131221]	1, 0	[353442]	(0123579)	7–24
5–27	(01358)	[122230]	1, 0	[344451]	(0124579)	7–27
5–19	(01367)	[212122]	1, 0	[434343]	(0123679)	7–19
5–29	(01368)	[122131]	1, 0	[344352]	(0124679)	7–29
5–31	(01369)	[114112]	1, 0	[336333]	(0134679)	7–31
5–Z18	(01457)	[212221]	1, 0	[434442]	(0145679)	7–Z18
5–21	(01458)	[202420]	1, 0	[424641]	(0124589)	7–21
5–30	(01468)	[121321]	1, 0	[343542]	(0124689)	7–30
5–32	(01469)	[113221]	1, 0	[335442]	(0134689)	7–32
5–22	(01478)	[202321]	1, 1	[424542]	(0125689)	7–22
5–20	(01568)	[211231]	1, 0	[433452]	(0125679)	7–20
5–8	(02346)	[232201]	1, 1	[454422]	(0234568)	7–8
5–11	(02347)	[222220]	1, 0	[444441]	(0134568)	7–11
5–23	(02357)	[132130]	1, 0	[354351]	(0234579)	7–23
5–25	(02358)	[123121]	1, 0	[345342]	(0234679)	7–25
5–28	(02368)	[122212]	1, 0	[344433]	(0135679)	7–28
5–26	(02458)	[122311]	1, 0	[344532]	(0134579)	7–26
5–33	(02468)	[040402]	1, 1	[262623]	(012468T)	7–33
5–34	(02469)	[032221]	1, 1	[254442]	(013468T)	7–34
5–35	(02479)	[032140]	1, 1	[254361]	(013568T)	7–35
5–Z37	(03458)	[212320]	1, 1	[434541]	(0134578)	7–Z37

HEXACHORDS

6–1	(012345)	[543210]	1, 1
6–2	(012346)	[443211]	1, 0

6–Z36	(012347)	[433221]	1, 0	(012356)	6–Z3
6–Z37	(012348)	[432321]	1, 1	(012456)	6–Z4
6–9	(012357)	[342231]	1, 0		
6–Z40	(012358)	[333231]	1, 0	(012457)	6–Z11
6–5	(012367)	[422232]	1, 0		
6–Z41	(012368)	[332232]	1, 0	(012467)	6–Z12
6–Z42	(012369)	[324222]	1, 1	(013467)	6–Z13
6–Z38	(012378)	[421242]	1, 1	(012567)	6–Z6
6–15	(012458)	[323421]	1, 0		
6–22	(012468)	[241422]	1, 0		
6–Z46	(012469)	[233331]	1, 0	(013468)	6–Z24
6–Z17	(012478)	[322332]	1, 0	(012568)	6–Z43
6–Z47	(012479)	[233241]	1, 0	(013568)	6–Z25
6–Z44	(012569)	[313431]	1, 0	(013478)	6–Z19
6–18	(012578)	[322242]	1, 0		
6–Z48	(012579)	[232341]	1, 1	(013578)	6–Z26
6–7	(012678)	[420243]	2, 2		
6–Z10	(013457)	[333321]	1, 0	(023458)	6–Z39
6–14	(013458)	[323430]	1, 0		
6–27	(013469)	[225222]	1, 0		
6–Z49	(013479)	[224322]	1, 1	(013569)	6–Z28
6–34	(013579)	[142422]	1, 0		
6–30	(013679)	[224223]	2, 0		
6–Z29	(023679)	[224232]	1, 1	(014679)	6–Z50
6–16	(014568)	[322431]	1, 0		
6–31	(014579)	[223431]	1, 0		
6–20	(014589)	[303630]	3, 3		
6–8	(023457)	[343230]	1, 1		
6–21	(023468)	[242412]	1, 0		
6–Z45	(023469)	[234222]	1, 1	(023568)	6–Z23
6–33	(023579)	[143241]	1, 0		
6–32	(024579)	[143250]	1, 1		
6–35	(02468T)	[060603]	6, 6		

Bibliography

Adlington, Robert. *Louis Andriessen: De Staat.* Burlington, VT: Ashgate, 2004.

Alegant, Brian. "The Seventy-seven Partitions of the Aggregate: Analytical and Theoretical Implications." Ph.D. dissertation, University of Rochester, 1993.

————. "Unveiling Schoenberg's op. 33b." *Music Theory Spectrum* 18/2 (1996), pp. 143–166.

Alphonce, Bo. "The Invariance Matrix." Ph.D. diss., Yale University, 1974

Antokoletz, Elliott. *The Music of Béla Bartók: A Study of Tonality and Progression in Twentieth-Century Music.* Berkeley: University of California Press, 1984.

Babbitt, Milton. "Some Aspects of Twelve-Tone Composition." *Score* 12 (1955), pp. 53–61.

————. "Who Cares if You Listen?" *High Fidelity* 8/2 (1958), pp. 38–40, 126–27.

————. "Twelve-Tone Invariants as Compositional Determinants." *Musical Quarterly* 46 (1960), pp. 246–59.

————. "Past and Present Concepts of the Nature and Limits of Music." *International Musicological Society Congress Report*, pp. 398–403. New York, 1961. Reprinted in *Perspectives on Contemporary Music Theory,* pp. 3–8. Ed. Benjamin Boretz and Edward Cone. New York: W. W. Norton, 1972.

————. "Set Structure as a Compositional Determinant." *Journal of Music Theory* 5 (1961), pp. 72–94.

————. "Twelve-Tone Rhythmic Structure and the Electronic Medium." *Perspectives of New Music* 1/1 (1962), pp. 49–79.

Bailey, Kathryn. *The Twelve-Note Music of Anton Webern.* Cambridge: Cambridge University Press, 1991.

Bass, Richard. "Sets, Scales, and Symmetries: The Pitch-Structural Basis of George Crumb's *Makrokosmos* I and II." *Music Theory Spectrum* 13/1 (1991), pp. 1–20.

Beach, David. "Segmental Invariance and the Twelve-Tone System." *Journal of Music Theory* 20 (1976), pp. 157–84.

————. "Pitch Structure and the Analytic Process in Atonal Music: An Interpretation of the Theory of Sets." *Music Theory Spectrum* 1 (1979), pp. 7–22.

Bernard, Jonathan. "Pitch/Register in the Music of Edgard Varèse." *Music Theory Spectrum* 3 (1981), pp. 1–25.

————. "Inaudible Structures, Audible Music: Ligeti's Problem, and His Solution." *Music Analysis* 6 (1987), pp. 207–36.

————. *The Music of Edgard Varèse.* New Haven, Yale University Press, 1987.

————. "The Evolution of Elliott Carter's Rhythmic Practice." *Perspectives of New Music* 26/2 (1988), pp. 164–203.

————. "The Minimalist Aesthetic in the Plastic Arts and in Music." *Perspectives of New Music* 31 (1993), pp. 86–132.

————. "Problems of Pitch Structure in Elliott Carter's First and Second String Quartets." *Journal of Music Theory* 37 (1993), pp. 231–66.

————. "Voice Leading as a Spatial Function in the Music of Ligeti." *Music Analysis* 13 (1994), pp. 227–53.

————. "Theory, Analysis, and the 'Problem' of Minimal Music." In *Concert Music, Rock, and Jazz since 1945: Essays and Analytical Studies,* pp. 259–84. Edited by Elizabeth West Marvin and Richard Hermann. Rochester: Rochester University Press, 1995.

————, ed. *Elliott Carter: Collected Essays and Lectures, 1937–1995.* Rochester, NY: University of Rochester Press, 1997.

————. "Ligeti's Restoration of Interval and Its Significance for His Later Works." *Music Theory Spectrum* 21/1 (1999), pp. 1–31.

Boss, Jack. "Schoenberg's Op. 22 Radio Talk and Developing Variation in Atonal Music." *Music Theory Spectrum* 14/2 (1992), pp. 125–49.

Boulez, Pierre. "Stravinsky Remains." In *Stocktakings from an Apprenticeship,* pp. 55–110. Translated by Stephen Walsh. Oxford: Clarendon Press, 1991.

Brody, Martin. "'Music for the Masses': Milton Babbitt's Cold War Music Theory." *Musical Quarterly* 77/2 (1993), pp. 161–92.

Buchler, Michael. "Broken and Unbroken Interval Cycles and Their Use in Determining Pitch-Class Set Resemblance." *Perspectives of New Music* 38/2 (2000), pp. 52–87.

Burkhart, Charles. "Debussy Plays *La cathédrale engloutie* and Solves Metrical Mystery." *The Piano Quarterly* (Fall 1968), pp. 14–16.

————. "The Symmetrical Source of Webern's Opus 5, No. 4." *Music Forum* 5 (1980), pp. 317–34.

Burkholder, Peter. *All Made of Tunes.* New Haven: Yale University Press, 1995.

Cage, John. *Silence.* Middletown, CT: Wesleyan University Press, 1961.

————. *A Year from Monday.* Middletown, CT: Wesleyan University Press, 1967.

Carpenter, Patricia. "*Grundgestalt* as Tonal Function." *Music Theory Spectrum* 5 (1983), pp. 15–38.

Carter, Elliott. *Harmony Book.* Edited by Nicholas Hopkins and John F. Link. New York: Carl Fischer, 2002.

Chrisman, Richard. "Describing Structural Aspects of Pitch-Sets Using Successive-Interval Arrays." *Journal of Music Theory* 21/1 (1977), pp. 1–28.

Clendinning, Jane. "The Pattern-Meccanico Compositions of György Ligeti." *Perspectives of New Music* 31 (1993), pp. 192–234.

————. "Structural Factors in the Microcanonic Compositions of György Ligeti." In *Concert Music, Rock, and Jazz since 1945: Essays and Analytical Studies,* pp. 229–56. Edited by Elizabeth West Marvin and Richard Hermann. Rochester: Rochester University Press, 1995.

Cogan, Robert, and Pozzi Escot. *Sonic Design: The Nature of Sound and Music.* Englewood Cliffs, NJ: Prentice-Hall, 1976.

Cohn, Richard. "Inversional Symmetry and Transpositional Combination in Bartók." *Music Theory Spectrum* 10 (1988), pp. 19–42.

————. "Transpositional Combination of Beat-Class Sets in Steve Reich's Phase-Shifting Music." *Perspectives of New Music* 30/2 (1992), pp. 146–77.

Cone, Edward. "Stravinsky: the Progress of a Method." In *Perspectives on Schoenberg and Stravinsky,* pp. 155–64. Edited by Benjamin Boretz and Edward Cone. New York: Norton, 1972.

Dembski, Stephen, and Josep Straus, eds. *Milton Babbitt: Words about Music.* Madison: University of Wisconsin Press, 1987.

Epstein, David. *Beyond Orpheus.* Oxford: Oxford University Press, 1987.

Epstein, Paul. "Pattern Structure and Process in Steve Reich's *Piano Phase.*" *The Musical Quarterly* 72/4 (1986), pp. 494–502.

Forte, Allen. "A Theory of Set-Complexes for Music." *Journal of Music Theory* 8 (1964), pp. 136–83.

————. *The Structure of Atonal Music.* New Haven: Yale University Press, 1973.

————. "Concepts of Linearity in Schoenberg's Atonal Music: A Study of the Opus 15 Song Cycle." *Journal of Music Theory* 36/2 (1992), pp. 285–382.

Graebner, Eric. "An Analysis of Schoenberg's *Klavierstück,* Op. 33a." *Perspectives of New Music* 12 (1973–74), pp. 128–40.

Haimo, Ethan. *Schoenberg's Serial Odyssey.* Oxford: Clarendon Press, 1990.

————. "Atonality, Analysis, and the Intentional Fallacy." *Music Theory Spectrum* 18/2 (1996), pp. 167–99.

Halbreich, Harry. *Olivier Messiaen.* Paris: Fayard/SACEM, 1980.

Hanninen, Dora. "Orientations, Criteria, Segments: A General Theory of Segmentation for Music Analysis." *Journal of Music Theory* 45/2 (2001), pp. 345–434.

Hanson, Howard. *The Harmonic Materials of Twentieth-Century Music.* New York: Appleton-Century-Crofts, 1960.

Hasty, Christopher. "Segmentation and Process in Post-Tonal Music." *Music Theory Spectrum* 3 (1981): 54–73.

Headlam, Dave. *The Music of Alban Berg.* New Haven: Yale University Press, 1996.

Heinemann, Stephen. "Pitch-Class Set Multiplication in Boulez's *Le Marteau sans maître.*" D.M.A. diss., University of Washington, 1993.

————. "Pitch-Class Set Multiplication in Theory and Practice." *Music Theory Spectrum* 20/1 (1998), pp. 72–96.

Hicks, Michael. "Text, Music, and Meaning in the Third Movement of Luciano Berio's *Sinfonia.*" *Perspectives of New Music* 20 (1981–82), pp. 199–224.

————. "The New Quotation: Its Origins and Functions." DMA diss., University of Illinois, 1984.

————. "Interval and Form in Ligeti's *Continuum* and *Coulée.*" *Perspectives of New Music* 31 (1993), pp. 172–90.

Hillier, Paul. *Arvo Pärt.* Oxford: Oxford University Press, 1997.

Hindemith, Paul. *The Craft of Musical Composition.* vol. 1, *Theoretical Part.* Translated by Arthur Mendel. New York: Associated Music, 1942; rev. ed., 1945. vol. 2, *Exercises in Two-Part Writing.* Translated by Otto Ortmann. New York: Associated Music, 1941.

Hook, Julian L. "Rhythm in the Music of Messiaen: An Algebraic Study and an Application in the *Turangalîla Symphony*." *Music Theory Spectrum* 20/1 (1998), pp. 97–120.

Howat, Roy. *Debussy in Proportion*. Cambridge: Cambridge University Press, 1983.

Hush, David. "Asynordinate Twelve-Tone Structures: Milton Babbitt's Composition for Twelve Instruments." *Perspectives of New Music* 21 (1982–83), pp. 152–205.

Hyde, Martha. "The Telltale Sketches: Harmonic Structure in Schoenberg's Twelve-Tone Method." *Musical Quarterly* 66/4 (1980), pp. 560–80.

———. *Schoenberg's Twelve-Tone Harmony*. Ann Arbor, 1982.

———. "Neoclassic and Anachronistic Impulses in Twentieth-Century Music." *Music Theory Spectrum* 18/2 (1996), pp. 200–235.

Isaacson, Eric. "Similarity of Interval-Class Content Between Pitch-Class Sets: The IcVSIM Relation." *Journal of Music Theory* 34 (1990), pp. 1–28.

Johnson, Robert Sherlaw. *Messiaen*. London: Dent, 1989.

Johnson, Timothy. "Harmonic Vocabulary in the Music of John Adams: A Hierarchical Approach." *Journal of Music Theory* 37/1 (1993), pp. 117–56.

Kielian-Gilbert, Marianne. "Relationships of Symmetrical Pitch-Class Sets and Stravinsky's Metaphor of Polarity." *Perspectives of New Music* 21 (1982–83), pp. 209–240.

Koblyakov, Lev. *Pierre Boulez: A World of Harmony*. New York: Harwood Academic Publishers, 1990.

Kramer, Jonathan. *The Time of Music*. New York: Schirmer, 1988.

———. "Beyond Unity: Toward an Understanding of Musical Postmodernism." In *Concert Music, Rock, and Jazz since 1945: Essays and Analytical Studies,* pp. 11–33. Edited by Elizabeth West Marvin and Richard Hermann. Rochester: University of Rochester Press, 1995.

Lambert, Philip . *The Music of Charles Ives*. New Haven: Yale University Press, 1997.

Laugesen, Emily Snyder. "Construing Text as Music in Berio's *Thema (Omaggio a Joyce)* and Stockhausen's *Stimmung*." Ph.D. diss., Columbia University, 2003.

Lendvai, Ernö. *Béla Bartók: An Analysis of His Music*. London: Kahn and Averill, 1971.

———. *The Workshop of Bartók and Kodaly*. Budapest: Edition Musica Budapest, 1983.

Lerdahl, Fred. *Tonal Pitch Space*. Oxford: Oxford University Press, 2001.

Lewin, David. "A Theory of Segmental Association in Twelve-Tone Music." *Perspectives of New Music* 1/1 (1962), pp. 89–116.

———. "A Study of Hexachord Levels in Schoenberg's Violin Fantasy." *Perspectives of New Music* 6/1 (1967), pp. 18–32.

———. "Inversional Balance as an Organizing Force in Schoenberg's Music and Thought." *Perspectives of New Music* 6/2 (1968), pp. 1–21.

———. "A Way into Schoenberg's Opus 15, Number 7." *In Theory Only* 6/1 (1981), pp. 3–24.

———. *Generalized Musical Intervals and Transformations*. New Haven: Yale University Press, 1987.

———. "A Metrical Problem in Webern's Op. 27." *Music Analysis* 12 (1993), pp. 343–54.

Ligeti, György. "Pierre Boulez: Decision and Automatism in *Structure Ia*." *Die Reihe* 4 (1960), pp. 36–62.

Lord, Charles. "An Explication of Some Recent Mathematical Approaches to Music Analysis." Ph.D. diss., Indiana University, 1978.

Losada, Catherine. "A Theoretical Model for the Analysis of Collage in Music Derived from Selected Works by Berio, Zimmermann and Rochberg." Ph.D. diss., City University of New York, 2004.

Lukomsky, Vera. "Sofia Gubaidulina: 'My Desire Is Always to Rebel, to Swim against the Stream'." *Perspectives of New Music* 36 (1998), pp. 5–35.

Maconie, Robin. *The Works of Karlheinz Stockhausen*. Oxford: Clarendon Press, 1990.

Martino, Donald. "The Source Set and Its Aggregate Formations." *Journal of Music Theory* 5/2 (1961), pp. 224–73.

Mead, Andrew. "Pitch Structure in Elliott Carter's *String Quartet No. 3*." *Perspectives of New Music* 22/1 (1983), pp. 31–60.

———. "Large-Scale Strategy in Schoenberg's Twelve-Tone Music." *Perspectives of New Music* 24 (1985), pp. 120–57.

———. "'Tonal' Forms in Arnold Schoenberg's Twelve-Tone Music." *Music Theory Spectrum* 9 (1987), pp. 67–92.

———. "Webern, Tradition, and Composing with Twelve Tones." *Music Theory Spectrum* 15/2 (1993), pp. 172–204.

———. *An Introduction to the Music of Milton Babbitt.* Princeton: Princeton University Press, 1994.

———. "Twelve-Tone Composition and the Music of Elliott Carter." In *Concert Music, Rock, and Jazz since 1945: Essays and Analytical Studies,* pp. 67–102. Edited by Elizabeth West Marvin and Richard Hermann. Rochester, NY: University of Rochester Press, 1995.

Messiaen, Olivier. *The Technique of My Musical Language.* Translated by John Satterfield. Paris: Alphonse Leduc, 1956.

Morgan, Robert. *Anthology of Twentieth-Century Music.* New York: Norton, 1992.

———. "The Modern Age." In *Modern Times: From World War I to the Present,* ed. by Robert Morgan, pp. 1–32. Englewood Cliffs: Prentice Hall, 1993.

Morris, Robert, and Alegant, Brian. "The Even Partitions in Twelve-Tone Music." *Music Theory Spectrum* 10 (1988), pp. 74–101.

Morris, Robert. "A Similarity Index for Pitch-Class Sets." *Perspectives of New Music* 18 (1979–80), pp. 445–60.

———. "Combinatoriality without the Aggregate." *Perspectives of New Music* 21/1–2 (1982–83), pp. 432–86.

———. "Set-Type Saturation among Twelve-Tone Rows." *Perspectives of New Music* 22/1–2 (1983–84), pp. 187–217.

———. *Composition with Pitch-Classes: A Theory of Compositional Design.* New Haven: Yale University Press, 1987.

———. "Generalizing Rotational Arrays." *Journal of Music Theory* 32/1 (1988), pp. 75–132.

———. *Class Notes for Atonal Music Theory.* Hanover, NH: Frog Peak Music, 1991.

Neumeyer, David. *The Music of Paul Hindemith.* New Haven: Yale University Press, 1986.

Newton-de Molina, David, ed. *On Literary Intention.* Edinburgh: University Press, 1976.

Nyman, Michael. *Experimental Music: Cage and Beyond.* New York: Schirmer, 1974.

Osmond-Smith, David. *Playing on Words: A Guide to Luciano Berio's Sinfonia.* London: Royal Musical Association, 1985.

Peles, Stephen, Stephen Dembski, Andrew Mead, and Josep Straus, eds. *The Collected Essays of Milton Babbitt.* Princeton: Princeton University Press, 2003.

Perle, George. "Symmetrical Formations in the String Quartets of Béla Bartók." *Music Review* 16 (1955), pp. 300–312.

———. *Serial Composition and Atonality.* Berkeley and Los Angeles: University of California Press, 1962 (6th ed., 1991).

———. *Twelve-Tone Tonality.* Berkeley: University of California Press, 1977.

———. *The Listening Composer.* Berkeley: University of California Press, 1990.

Potter, Keith. *Four Musical Minimalists.* Cambridge: Cambridge University Press, 2000.

Pritchett, James. *The Music of John Cage.* Cambridge: Cambridge University Press, 1993.

Rae, Charles Bodman. *The Music of Lutosławski.* London: Faber and Faber, 1994.

Rahn, John. *Basic Atonal Theory.* New York: Schirmer, 1980.

Reich, Steve. *Writings about Music.* Halifax: The Press of the Nova Scotia College of Art and Design, 1974.

Robinson, Lisa Brooks. "Mahler and Postmodern Intertextuality." Ph.D. diss., Yale University, 1994.

Rochberg, George. Liner notes to LP "String Quartet no. 3," by the Concord String Quartet. Nonesuch Records, H 71283, 1973.

Roeder, John. "Beat-Class Modulation in Steve Reich's Music." *Music Theory Spectrum* 25/2 (2003), pp. 275–304.

———. "Toward the Analysis of Postmodern Music: Co-operating Continuities in Compositions of Thomas Adès." *Music Analysis,* forthcoming.

Roig-Francolí, Miguel. "Harmonic and Formal Processes in Ligeti's Net-Structure Compositions." *Music Theory Spectrum* 17/2 (1995), pp. 242–67.

———. "A Theory of Pitch-Class-Set Extension in Atonal Music." *College Music Symposium* 41 (2001), pp. 57–90.

———. *Harmony in Context.* New York: McGraw-Hill, 2003.

Schiff, David. *The Music of Elliott Carter.* Ithaca, NY: Cornell University Press, 1998.

Schoenberg, Arnold. "Composition with Twelve Tones." In *Style and Idea,* ed. Leonard Stein. Translated by Leo Black. London: Faber and Faber, 1975.

Schwarz, K. Robert. *Minimalism.* London: Phaidon Press, 1996.

Seeger, Charles. *Tradition and Experiment in the New Music.* In *Studies in Musicology II.* Edited by Ann Pescatello. Berkeley: University of California Press, 1994.

Spies, Claudio. "Some Notes on Stravinsky's Requiem Settings." *Perspectives of New Music* 5/2 (1967), pp. 98–123. Reprinted in *Perspectives on Schoenberg and Stravinsky,* pp. 223–50. Edited by Benjamin Boretz and Edward Cone. Princeton: Princeton University Press, 1968.

Starr, Daniel, and Robert Morris. "A General Theory of Combinatoriality and the Aggregate." *Perspectives of New Music* 16/1 (1977–78), pp. 364–89, and 16/2, pp. 50–84.

Stockhausen, Karlheinz. "Momentform." In *Texte zur elektronischen un instrumentales Musik,* vol. 1. Cologne: DuMont, 1963, pp. 189–210.

Stone, Else, and Kurt Stone, eds. *The Writings of Elliott Carter.* Bloomington: Indiana University Press, 1977.

Straus, Joseph. *Remaking the Past.* Cambridge, MA: Harvard University Press, 1990.

———. *The Music of Ruth Crawford Seeger.* Cambridge: Cambridge University Press, 1995.

———. *Introduction to Post-Tonal Theory.* 3rd ed. Upper Saddle River, NJ: Pearson/Prentice Hall, 2005.

———. *Stravinsky's Late Music.* Cambridge: Cambridge University Press, 2001.

Stravinsky, Igor. *Poetics of Music.* Cambridge, MA: Harvard University Press, 1970.

Stucky, Steven. *Lutosławski and His Music.* Cambridge: Cambridge University Press, 1981.

Taruskin, Richard. *Stravinsky and the Russian Traditions.* 2 vols. Berkeley: University of California Press, 1996.

Travers, Aaron. "Interval Cycles, Their Permutations and Generative Properties in Thomas Adès's *Asyla*." Ph.D. diss., University of Rochester, 2005.

Treitler, Leo. "Harmonic Procedure in the *Fourth Quartet* of Béla Bartók." *Journal of Music Theory* 3 (1959), pp. 292–98.

Trochimczyk, Maja, ed. *The Music of Louis Andriessen.* New York: Routledge, 2002.

Tymoczko, Dmitri. "Stravinsky and the Octatonic: A Reconsideration." *Music Theory Spectrum* 24/1 (2002), pp. 68–102.

van den Toorn, Pieter. *The Music of Igor Stravinsky.* New Haven: Yale University Press, 1983.

———. *Stravinsky and the Rite of Spring: The Beginnings of a Musical Language.* Berkeley: University of California Press, 1987.

———. "Colloquy." *Music Theory Spectrum* 25/1 (2003), pp. 167–202.

Wennerstrom, Mary. *Anthology of Musical Structure and Style.* Englewood Cliffs, NJ: Prentice Hall, 1983.

———. *Anthology of Twentieth-Century Music.* Englewood Cliffs, NJ: Prentice Hall, 1988.

Westergaard, Peter. "Webern and 'Total Organization': An Analysis of the Second Movement of Piano Variations, Op. 27." *Perspectives of New Music,* 1 (1963), pp. 107–20.

———. "Some Problems Raised by the Rhythmic Procedures in Milton Babbitt's Composition for Twelve Instruments." *Perspectives of New Music* 4 (1965), pp. 109–18.

Williams, Kent. *Theories and Analyses of Twentieth-Century Music.* Fort Worth: Harcourt Brace, 1997.

Wimsatt, William, and Monroe Beardsley. "The Intentional Fallacy." *Sewanee Review* 54 (1946), pp. 468–88. Reprinted in William Wimsatt, *The Verbal Icon: Studies in the Meaning of Poetry.* Lexington: University of Kentucky Press, 1954, pp. 3–18.

Wittlich, Gary. "Sets and Ordering Procedures in Twentieth-Century Music." In *Aspects of Twentieth-Century Music,* pp. 388–476. Edited by Gary Wittlich. Englewood Cliffs: Prentice Hall, 1975.

Wuorinen, Charles. *Simple Composition.* New York: Longman, 1979.

Acknowledgment of Sources

The author is grateful to the following scholars whose work has been the point of departure for some of the sections in the specified chapters, and for which each of them has provided his or her kind permission: Marianne Kielian-Gilbert (Chapter 1), Charles Lord (Chapter 4), David Neumeyer (Chapter 5), Peter Burkholder (Chapter 6), Philip Lambert (Chapter 6), David Hush (Chapter 9), Andrew Mead (Chapter 9), Claudio Spies (Chapter 9), Peter Westergaard (Chapter 9), Jonathan Bernard (Chapter 10), Julian Hook (Chapter 10), Michael Hicks (Chapter 12), Catherine Losada (Chapter 12), David Osmond-Smith (Chapter 12), and Richard Cohn (Chapter 13). Specific references to these authors's work can be found in footnotes in each of the chapters, and specific references to examples reprinted from these sources are included in the list that follows.

Example 10.7a STRING QUARTET NO. 4 (Bartók) © Copyright 1929 in the USA by Boosey & Hawkes, Inc. Copyright Renewed. Reprinted by permission.

Example 10.7b © 1914 by Durand & Cie.

Examples 10.18a, 10.19a, and 10.20 STRING QUARTET NO. 1 by Elliott Carter. Copyright © 1961 (Renewed) by Associated Music Publishers, Inc. (BMI) International Copyright Secured. All Rights Reserved. Reprinted by Permission.

Example 10.21 STRING QUARTET NO. 2 by Elliott Carter. Copyright © 1961 (Renewed) by Associated Music Publishers, Inc. (BMI) International Copyright Secured. All Rights Reserved. Reprinted by Permission.

Example 11.2 Stucky LUTOSŁAWSKI AND HIS MUSIC © Cambridge University Press 1981. Reprinted with the permission of Cambridge University Press.

Examples 11.4, 11.5, and 11.6 Ligeti RAMIFICATIONS © 1970 by Schott Musik International. © renewed. All Rights Reserved. Used by permission of European American Music Distributors LLC, sole U.S. and Canadian agent for Schott Musik International.

Example 12.1 Based on Example 3-28, p. 199, of Catherine Losada, "A Theoretical Model for the Analysis of Collage in Music Derived from Selected Works by Berio, Zimmermann and Rochberg" (Ph.D. dissertation, City University of New York, 2004). Reprinted with author's permission.

Example 12.2 Based on Example 3-23, p. 192, of Catherine Losada, "A Theoretical Model for the Analysis of Collage in Music Derived from Selected Works by Berio, Zimmermann and Rochberg" (Ph.D. dissertation, City University of New York, 2004). Reprinted with author's permission.

Example 12.4 "Text, Music, and Meaning in Berio's *Sinfonia,* 3rd Movement" by Michael Hicks. *Perspectives of New Music* 20 (Fall-Winter 1981/Spring-Summer 1982): 200. Reprinted with author's permission. Berio SINFONIA © 1969 by Universal Edition (London) Ltd., London. © renewed. All Rights Reserved. Used by permission of European American Music Distributors LLC, U.S. and Canadian agent for Universal Edition (London) Ltd., London.

Examples 12.5 and 12.6 Berio SINFONIA © 1969 by Universal Edition (London) Ltd., London. © renewed. All Rights Reserved. Used by permission of European American Music Distributors LLC, U.S. and Canadian agent for Universal Edition (London) Ltd., London.

Example 12.7 Based on example 4-13, p. 222, of Catherine Losada, "A Theoretical Model for the Analysis of Collage in Music Derived from Selected Works by Berio, Zimmermann and Rochberg" (Ph.D. dissertation, City University of New York, 2004). Reprinted with author's permission. Berio SINFONIA © 1969 by Universal Edition (London) Ltd., London. © renewed. All Rights Reserved. Used by permission of European American Music Distributors LLC, U.S. and Canadian agent for Universal Edition (London) Ltd., London.

Example 12.8 Based on Example 4-24, p. 231, of Catherine Losada, "A Theoretical Model for the Analysis of Collage in Music Derived from Selected Works by Berio, Zimmermann and Rochberg" (Ph.D. dissertation, City University of New York, 2004). Reprinted with author's permission. Berio SINFONIA © 1969 by Universal Edition (London) Ltd., London. © renewed. All Rights Reserved. Used by permission of European American Music Distributors LLC, U.S. and Canadian agent for Universal Edition (London) Ltd., London.

Example 13.3 "Transpositional Combination of Beat-Class Sets in Steve Reich's Phase-Shifting Music" by Richard Cohn. *Perspectives of New Music* 30, no. 2 (Summer 1992): 150–151. Reprinted with author's permission.

Example 13.6 Reich VIOLIN PHASE © 1969 by Universal Edition (London) Ltd. London. © renewed. Used by permission of European American Music Distributors LLC, U.S. and Canadian agent for Universal Corporation, sole U.S. agent for Universal Edition (London) Ltd., London.

Examples 13.7 and 13.8 DE STAAT (Andriessen) © Copyright 1994 by Boosey & Hawkes Music Publishers Ltd. Reprinted by permission of Boosey & Hawkes, Inc.

Examples 13.9 and 13.10 Pärt CANTUS IN MEMORY OF BENJAMIN BRITTEN © 1981 by Universal Edition A.G., Wien. All Rights Reserved. Used by permission of European American Music Distributors LLC, U.S. and Canadian agent for Universal Edition A.G., Wien.

Examples 14.1, 14.2, 14.3, and 14.4 SPRING SONG by Augusta Read Thomas. Copyright © 1995 by G. Schirmer, Inc. (ASCAP) International copyright secured. All Rights Reserved. Reprinted by permission.

Musical Example Index

Subject Index

Page numbers in **bold** indicate important terms; page numbers in *italics* indicate figures and examples.